The Cambridge Companion to John Donne

The Cambridge Companion to John Donne – the first comprehensive guide to his works to be published – introduces students (undergraduate and graduate) to the range, brilliance, and complexity of John Donne. Sixteen new essays, written by an international array of leading scholars and critics, cover Donne's poetry (erotic, satirical, devotional) and his prose (including his sermons and occasional letters). Providing readings of his texts and also fully situating them in the historical and cultural context of early modern England, these essays offer the most up-to-date scholarship and introduce students to the current thinking and debates about Donne, while providing tools for students to read Donne with greater understanding and enjoyment. Special features include a chronology; a short biography; chapters on political and religious contexts; a chapter on the experience of reading his lyrics; a meditation on Donne by the contemporary novelist A. S. Byatt; and an extensive bibliography of editions and criticism.

THE CAMBRIDGE
COMPANION TO
JOHN DONNE

EDITED BY
ACHSAH GUIBBORY
Barnard College, Columbia University

CAMBRIDGE UNIVERSITY PRESS
Cambridge, New York, Melbourne, Madrid, Cape Town, Singapore, São Paulo

CAMBRIDGE UNIVERSITY PRESS
The Edinburgh Building, Cambridge CB2 2RU, UK
Published in the United States of America by Cambridge University Press, New York

www.cambridge.org
Information on this title: www.cambridge.org/9780521540032

First published 2006

Printed in the United Kingdom at the University Press, Cambridge

A catalogue record for this book is available from the British Library

ISBN-13 978-0-521-83237-3 hardback
ISBN-10 0-521-83237-3 hardback
ISBN-13 978-0-521-54003-2 paperback
ISBN-10 0-521-54003-8 paperback

CONTENTS

LIST OF ILLUSTRATIONS

CONTRIBUTORS

ILONA BELL, *Williams College*

A. S. BYATT, *London, UK*

TOM CAIN, *Newcastle-upon-Tyne University*

ACHSAH GUIBBORY, *Barnard College, Columbia University*

ANDREW HADFIELD, *Sussex University*

DAYTON HASKIN, *Boston College*

JUDITH SCHERER HERZ, *Concordia University*

ARNOLD HUNT, *The British Library*

LYNNE MAGNUSSON, *University of Toronto*

ARTHUR F. MAROTTI, *Wayne State University*

PETER McCULLOUGH, *Lincoln College, Oxford University*

ANNABEL PATTERSON, *Yale University*

TED-LARRY PEBWORTH, *University of Michigan-Dearborn (emeritus)*

JONATHAN F. S. POST, *UCLA*

L. E. SEMLER, *University of Sydney*

ALISON SHELL, *Durham University*

RAMIE TARGOFF, *Brandeis University*

HELEN WILCOX, *University of Groningen*

PREFACE

It is the right time for a Cambridge Companion to Donne, for important new work on Donne is being done on both sides of the Atlantic, indeed in countries around the world, and volumes of the ambitious Variorum edition of the poetry are appearing. Even if these things were not the case, we would still need a Companion, for Donne matters to students as much as ever. He may have lived four hundred years ago, but he seems so contemporary, for he explores issues that absorb us and that undergraduates are eager to talk about: love, sex, the problems of intimacy, spiritual longing, the challenges of faith, and the prospect of death and what, if anything, comes after. He seeks truth, while questioning authority, refusing to take things – even God – on trust. We watch Donne search for stability, fulfillment, and permanence in an age of religious and political conflict, a world rapidly changing with the emergence of new sciences and technologies. The world Donne inhabited was, of course, different from ours, and yet there are striking points of contact.

So Donne continues to speak to readers who are, often, seduced by his passionate wit from the first encounter. Students respond intensely to Donne's poetry but they also need help learning "how" to read Donne. He presents a special set of challenges and problems, but, as Coleridge suggested, once we learn how to read Donne, we know how to read poetry. This volume of new essays, each by a scholar with a special expertise and take on Donne, will, I hope, provide necessary tools. Offering new perspectives, these essays assimilate and add to the rich tradition of Donne criticism, to which we are all indebted. They also incorporate contributions from other disciplines (e.g, linguistics, or history) that can illuminate and contextualize Donne's writing. When we historicize Donne, we find his writing opens a window onto the past, revealing the complex interrelations among religion, politics, love, and gender that existed in early modern England. But our primary concern is, always, better to understand Donne's texts.

The following chapters cover the full range of Donne's writing, while bringing multiple contexts to bear on it. The early chapters discuss Donne's biography (Jonathan Post), the unique problems presented by Donne's often unstable poetic texts (Ted-Larry Pebworth), and various contexts for Donne's writings: his relation to literary predecessors and contemporaries (Andrew Hadfield); the social context and nature of his writing (Arthur Marotti); the religious world Donne inhabited (Alison Shell and Arnold Hunt); and the political world of early modern England (Tom Cain). The chapters by Cain and Shell/Hunt have different focuses and arguments, but both examine the close interrelation between religion and politics in this period, and thus should be read together. Although this first set of chapters emphasizes context, most of them also discuss Donne's literary "texts" in some detail, embodying our belief that text and context are interwoven and interdependent. The second group of chapters focuses more intensely on Donne's poetry and prose, beginning with Judith Herz's chapter on the experience of reading Donne's poetry. Subsequent chapters explore Donne's modes of writing: satirical (Annabel Patterson), erotic (Guibbory), devotional (Helen Wilcox), and the sermons (Peter McCullough). Three specific aspects of Donne's writing then require further attention: Donne's distinctive use of language (Lynne Magnusson), the issue of gender and the role of women in his poetry (Ilona Bell), and Donne's obsession with death (Ramie Targoff). Having traveled from his life to his death, we learn from Dayton Haskin about Donne's afterlife apparent in later editions and Donne's reception, and in the creative "reinvention" of his writing by later artists. The concluding chapter is by a novelist who has herself reinvented Donne in her own work. A. S. Byatt, whose intelligence and wit are a match for Donne, draws on her experience as a reader and writer – and the insights of neuroscience – to discuss Donne's "feeling thought," a concept made famous by T. S. Eliot but now given a new significance. This chapter offering the perspective of a contemporary writer is an important and unique feature of this Companion, exemplifying how (and why) Donne matters, not just to academic scholars or in the classroom but to practicing creative writers. Finally, Liam Semler has compiled a select bibliography of works that incorporates the authors' suggestions for further reading and introduces students to the rich resources of scholarship on Donne.

Each chapter is written to stand on its own, but they are interconnected, and even more powerful as a whole. Some clearly intersect – mine on "erotic writing" and Bell's on "gender matters," for example, or those by Cain and Shell/Hunt on Donne's political and religious worlds. Marotti and Magnusson define different social dimensions of Donne's writing. Magnusson and Herz both focus on Donne's language, although one could say that virtually all of the chapters attend to language. Although generic concerns appear in several chapters (most notably Marotti's, Patterson's, and McCullough's), the volume is organized, not by genre, but according to topics that allow the authors the freedom to discuss a broader, more interesting selection of Donne's writings, and that allow different patterns to emerge. Structuring the Companion in this way means that the *Songs and Sonets*, for example, and the sermons are treated in more than one chapter, allowing readers to experience different perspectives on Donne's texts. So, for example, while the *Satires* are the focus of Patterson's essay, they also figure importantly in Hadfield's. While McCullough focuses on Donne's sermons, Targoff also concludes with a close reading of a Donne sermon, in this case the famous "Deaths Duell" sermon. Like most things, Donne's writing is best approached through multiple perspectives, but these chapters also give a sense of the debates about Donne, who, like Proteus, resists being tied down and provokes us repeatedly to reconsider the brilliance of his writing and insight.

My thanks go to all of the authors, who have made extraordinary contributions; to my students of Donne over the years (both at the University of Illinois and more recently at Barnard College), who continue to surprise me; to my indispensable colleagues and long-term friends in the John Donne Society, who have shaped my thinking about Donne (especially Dennis Flynn, Dayton Haskin, Tom Hester, Judith Herz, and Jeanne Shami); to Dayton Haskin and Jonathan Post for their especially helpful advice on this volume; and to Sarah Stanton at Cambridge University Press, who first asked me to consider doing it.

ABBREVIATIONS

Bald   Bald, R. C., *John Donne: A Life*, Oxford: Oxford University
            Press, 1970
Carey   Carey, John, *John Donne: Life, Mind and Art*, London, Faber
            and Faber; New York: Oxford University Press, 1981
ELR   *English Literary Renaissance*
Flynn   Flynn, Dennis, *John Donne and the Ancient Catholic Nobility*,
            Bloomington: Indiana University Press, 1995
Gosse   Edmund Gosse (ed.), *The Life and Letters of John Donne*, 2 vols.,
            London: 1899; rpt Gloucester, MA: Peter Smith, 1959
JDJ   *John Donne Journal*
JEGP   *Journal of English and Germanic Philology*
OED   Oxford English Dictionary, 2nd edn.
SEL   *Studies in English Literature*
Walton   Walton, Izaak, "The Life of Dr. John Donne," in *The Lives
            of John Donne, Sir Henry Wotton, Richard Hooker,
            George Herbert and Robert Sanderson*, ed. and intro. by
            George Saintsbury, London: Oxford University Press,
            1927; rpt. 1950

The following editions of Donne have been used (and cited by abbreviated
titles as listed), unless otherwise noted in individual essays. Original spelling
is retained in quotations but u/v and i/j are modernized.

Biathanatos   Ernest W. Sullivan, II (ed.) *Biathanatos*, Newark:
                 University of Delaware Press, 1984
Devotions   John Sparrow (ed.) with bibliographical note by
                 Geoffrey Keynes, *Devotions upon Emergent
                 Occasions*, Cambridge: Cambridge University Press,
                 1923

Essays in Divinity	Evelyn M. Simpson (ed.), *Essays in Divinity*, Oxford: Clarendon, 1952
Letters	*Letters to Severall Persons of Honour* (1651), facsimile reprint by M. Thomas Hester (ed.), New York, Scholars' Facsimiles and Reprints, 1977
Poems	Herbert J. C. Grierson (ed.) *The Poems of John Donne*, 2 vols., volume I (The Text of the Poems, with Appendixes), London: Oxford University Press, 1912; rpt. 1968
Pseudo-Martyr	Anthony Raspa (ed.), *Pseudo-Martyr*, Montreal: McGill-Queen's University Press, 1993
Sermons	Potter, George R. and Evelyn M. Simpson (eds.), *Sermons*, 10 vols., Berkeley and Los Angeles: University of California Press, 1953–62

CHRONOLOGY

1534	Henry VIII breaks with Rome; Act of Supremacy declares him head of Church of England
1535	Sir Thomas More executed for refusing to accept Henry as head of English church
1543	Copernicus *De Revolutionibus Orbium Coelestium*, with revolutionary hypothesis of sun (not earth) as center Vesalius's *De humani corporis fabrica libri septem*, his new anatomy based on dissection
1547	Henry VIII dies; Edward VI becomes king
1553	Edward VI dies; Mary I becomes queen
1554	England officially "Catholic" again; "Marian" (Protestant) exiles flee to Geneva
1559	Elizabeth I crowned Queen in January; Act of Supremacy requires Oath of Allegiance; Act of Uniformity requires attendance in Church of England and use of Book of Common Prayer (England once again a "reformed" nation)
1563	First edition of John Foxe's anti-Catholic *Acts and Monuments (Book of Martyrs)*
1564	William Shakespeare born
1570	Queen Elizabeth I excommunicated by Papal Bull
1572	John Donne born
1576	Father, John, dies; mother remarries
1580	Jesuit "mission" in England commences; Parliament begins to pass series of acts making practice of Catholicism synonymous with treason
1581	Jesuit priest Edmund Campion executed (December); others to follow
1584	Donne matriculates at Hart Hall, Oxford University
1585	Donne perhaps traveling abroad? Or at University?
1587	Donne at Cambridge? Or traveling abroad?

1586	Death of Sir Philip Sidney
1587–88	Christopher Marlowe's *Tamburlaine the Great, Part I* performed (published 1590)
1588	The Spanish Armada defeated; England rescued from "Catholic threat"
1590	Spenser's *The Faerie Queene*, Books I–III published
1591	Sidney's *Astrophil and Stella* published
1592–95	Donne at Lincoln's Inn; writes (most of?) the elegies
1594	Donne's brother Henry dies, imprisoned for harboring a priest
1594–96	Shakespeare's *Romeo and Juliet*
1596	Second edition of *The Faerie Queene*, including Books IV–VI
1596	Donne in Essex's (Robert Devereux) expedition to Cadiz
1597	Donne in expedition to Azores Islands – writes "The Storme," "The Calme"?
1597 or	Donne becomes secretary to Sir Thomas Egerton
1598	Writes the satires?
1599	June 1599, Bishops' Ban (by John Whitgift, Archbishop of Canterbury, and Richard Bancroft, Bishop of London) on printing satires; recall and public burning of some
1600	William Gilbert's *De Magnete, Magneticisque Corporibus, et de Magna Magnete Tellure* ("On the Magnet, Magnetic Bodies, and the Great Magnet, the Earth")
1600–01	Shakespeare's *Hamlet*
1601	Execution of Essex, after his failed rebellion
	Donne briefly member of Parliament; secretly marries Anne More (December), niece of employer (Egerton) and daughter of Sir George More
1602	Sir George More has Donne briefly committed to jail (February) when marriage is revealed
1603	Death of Queen Elizabeth; James VI of Scotland comes to English throne as James I
1604	Christopher Marlowe's *The Tragical History of Dr. Faustus* first published
1605	November 5, [Roman Catholic] Gunpowder Plot to blow up Parliament and King is discovered
	Francis Bacon publishes *The Advancement of Learning* calling for new science
1605–06	Shakespeare's *King Lear*
1606	Donne moves with family to Mitcham
	Ben Jonson's *Volpone* performed (published 1607)
	James I charters The Virginia Company

1607	Jamestown (Virginia) founded
1608	Donne writes *Biathanatos*
	John Milton born
1609	Donne writes many of the Holy Sonnets?
	William Shakespeare's *Sonnets* published
1610	Galileo's *Siderius Nuncius* ("Starry Messenger")
	Donne's *Pseudo-Martyr* published, arguing Roman Catholics can take Oath of Allegiance to king
	Donne receives honorary MA from Oxford University
	Elizabeth Drury, fifteen-year-old daughter of Donne's patrons, Sir Robert and Lady Drury, dies
1611	*The First Anniversary* ("The Anatomie of the World") published
	Donne travels to France with Sir Robert Drury
	Ignatius his Conclave (Conclave Ignatii)
	The King James Bible (Authorized Version) published
	Aemelia Lanyer's *Salve Deus Rex Judaeorum* published
	Shakespeare's *The Tempest*
1612	"Of the Progress of the Soule" published in *The First and Second Anniversaries*
	Donne and family move to Drury Lane
1614	Donne serves as member of Parliament
1615	Donne ordained as priest in the Church of England in January; appointed a royal chaplain to James I
1616	October, Donne appointed Reader in Divinity at Lincoln's Inn (Inns of Court)
	Ben Jonson's *Workes* published (folio)
	Shakespeare dies
1617	August 15 – Anne More Donne dies (aged 33) after giving birth to stillborn child
	Donne writes holy sonnet, "Since she whom I lovd"
1618	beginning of the Thirty Years War over religion in Europe
1618–19	Synod of Dort confronts challenge of Arminius, and reaffirms Calvinism
1619	Donne travels with Viscount Doncaster's diplomatic mission to Germany; preaches at the Hague and at Heidelberg
	Donne writes "A Hymne to Christ, at the authors last going into Germany"
1620	Francis Bacon's *Great Instauration*
	The *Mayflower* ship lands in Massachusetts; Plymouth Colony founded

1621 First edition of Robert Burton's *Anatomy of Melancholy*
 November – Donne becomes Dean of St. Paul's Cathedral
 Lady Mary Wroth's "The Countess of Montgomery's *Urania*"
 and *Pamphilia to Amphilanthus* published

1622 James I's Directions to Preachers; Donne preaches at Paul's
 Cross in its support
 Donne made honorary member of the Virginia Company

1623 *Mr. William Shakespeares Comedies, Histories and Tragedies*
 (folio)
 December – Donne severely ill

1624 *Devotions upon Emergent Occasions* (republished in 1634,
 1638)
 Donne appointed to St. Dunstan's West

1625 James I dies; Charles I becomes king

1626 Death of Launcelot Andrewes

1627 Donne preaches at marriage of the daughter of the Earl of
 Bridgewater

1628 William Laud appointed Bishop of London
 William Harvey publishes his discovery of the circulation of
 blood

1629 Charles I dissolves Parliament, beginning his eleven-year
 "personal rule"

1631 February 25, Donne preaches last sermon, Death's Duell at
 the king's court;
 March 31, Donne dies; buried April 3, St. Paul's

1632 *Deaths Duell* published (republished 1633)

1633 William Laud becomes Archbishop of Canterbury
 Poems by J. D. (first edition of Donne's poetry)
 Juvenalia: Or Certaine Paradoxes and Problems published
 George Herbert's *The Temple* published

1634 Milton's *Mask* (otherwise known as "Comus") performed for
 Earl of Bridgewater

1635 Second edition of Donne's *Poems*, with engraving of Donne
 by William Marshall

1640 Donne's *LXXX Sermons*, published by Donne's son,
 dedicated to Charles I – Izaak Walton's "Life of Donne
 published" with the sermons
 Parliament meets for first time since 1629; Roots and
 Branches Petition to Parliament to reform the church from
 Laud's "popish" abuses

1641   *Of Reformation*, John Milton's first tract arguing for reform
        of the English church
1642   English Civil War breaks out
        Isaac Newton born
1643   Parliament abolishes episcopacy
1645   Parliament replaces Book of Common Prayer with Directory
        of Public Worship
1644   Laud tried by Parliament as traitor for attempting to bring in
        popery and to "return" England to Rome
1645   Laud executed (January)
        John Milton's *Poems* published, with engraving of the author
        by William Marshall
1646   *Biathanatos* published for first time (by Donne's son)
1649   January 30, Charles I executed for "treason"
        Donne's *Fifty Sermons*, published by son
        Descartes publishes *A Discourse of a method*
1651   Donne's *Letters to Severall Persons of Honour*, published by
        his son
        Donne's *Essays in Divinity* published
        Thomas Hobbes, *Leviathan*
1652   Donne's *Paradoxes, Problems, Essays, Characters* published
1653   Oliver Cromwell becomes Lord Protector of England
1660   Restoration of monarchy; Charles II assumes throne
        Donne's *XXVI Sermons* published
1662   Act of Uniformity reestablishes the national Church
        of England
1667   Milton's *Paradise Lost* (first edition)
1669   Donne's *Poems* (finally including elegies omitted from earlier
        editions)

I

JONATHAN F. S. POST

Donne's life: a sketch

"The first poet in the world in some things," as Jonson said of Donne,[1] was also the first poet in English whose life was regarded as both sufficiently extraordinary and usefully emblematic to be made into a biography. It was not a writer's life in the modern sense, in which materials are excavated and analyzed in order to illuminate the specific circumstances that went into the creation of the art. Of this kind of literary biography, the early modern period is lacking, but a celebrated "life," nonetheless, was written by the first of English biographers, the pious Izaak Walton, initially for the post-humous edition of Donne's *Sermons* (1640).

Walton was a generation younger than his subject, and at times as much given to fiction as fact but, thanks to his work (constructed from notes gathered by Donne's friend, Henry Wotton), and to the emendations and additions it has received at the hands of modern scholars, Donne's life, if disputable in the particular, remains, in the aggregate, more vividly imagin-able than that of almost any other writer in early modern England.[2] Although gaps in the record exist, often where we most want illumination – of the *Songs and Sonets*, for instance – a thumbnail sketch of Donne might see his life falling into four phases. The first extends from his birth in 1572 to about 1591, when, after studying at home and university and traveling abroad, Donne resettled in London in search of a career. Although our knowledge of Donne's activities and whereabouts for this early period is least reliable, the current thinking continues to underscore Donne's precarious status as a Catholic "aristocrat." His namesake father was a prosperous but short-lived ironmonger (he would die when the poet-preacher was only four), descended from the Dwns of Kidwelly, Wales. Their own aristocratic circumstance is made visually explicit in the "donor" triptych of the family painted by Hans Memling ("Virgin and Child," *c.* 1475, now in the National Gallery in London). More significantly, Donne's eventually thrice-married mother, Elizabeth, was descended from Sir Thomas More and the wide circle of Catholic sympathizers associated with the martyred Lord Chancellor. More had been executed in 1534 for refusing to subscribe to the Act of Supremacy declaring Henry VIII to be the true spiritual head of the Church of England. That Donne identified deeply with this family history of persecution is made clear from an often-quoted remark of his from the "Advertisement to the Reader" to *Pseudo-Martyr* (1610): "as I am a Christian, I have beene ever kept awake in a meditation of Martyrdome, by being derived from such a stocke and race, as, I believe, no family (which is not of farre larger extent, and greater branches,) hath endured and suffered more in their persons and fortunes, for obeying the Teachers of Romane Doctrine, then it hath done" (p. 8).

"As I am a Christian" – but in the 1580s, the decade of the defeat of the Spanish Armada, Donne was also a Catholic living under a Protestant queen. As such, he was educated at home by tutors, probably Catholic priests, and perhaps his learned Jesuit uncle Jasper Heywood, whose literary accomplishments included translating three of Seneca's ten tragedies in the early 1560s. Much later again, this time in a preface to *Biathanatos*, his unpublished pamphlet on suicide, thought to be written around 1607–08, Donne would speak about his early schooling with an aura of mystery and intrigue savored by his biographers: "I had my first breeding, and conversation with Men of a suppressed and afflicted Religion, accustomed to the despite of death, and hungry of an imagin'd Martyrdome" (p. 29). Just possibly, the famous "metaphysical shudder" was born amid this "breeding and conversation."

One further consequence of Donne's Catholicism involved his early matriculation at Oxford (with his younger brother, Henry) at age twelve. The records give Donne's age as eleven, probably in order to avoid the requirement of having to subscribe to the Act of Supremacy and the Thirty-Nine Articles, imposed on all students at age sixteen by a 1581 Oxford Matriculation Statute. For reasons of conscience, Walton tells us, Donne did not stay for the degree, whereupon he would have had to subscribe to the Oath. But whether he went to Cambridge, as both Walton and Bald suggest, or whether he left Oxford much earlier, as Dennis Flynn has recently argued, and set out for Paris in the company of other noble Catholics, and then began a tour of the continent that included participating in the siege of Antwerp, remains a matter of considerable debate, much enabled by the paucity of factual information relating to these early years (Flynn, pp. 134–46, 170–72; Bald, pp. 46–52).

Two related points about Donne's time at university are worth making. First, notwithstanding Donne's evident brilliance – Walton reports the contemporary remark "*that this age had brought forth another* Picus Mirandula; *of whom Story says, That he was rather born, than made wise by study*" (p. 23) – schooling was less important than the social connections it enabled. Second, while at Oxford, Donne developed a habit of making lifelong friends with people as notably different from one another as Henry Wotton, future ambassador to Venice and Provost of Eton College, and Richard Martin, who would emerge in Parliament under James VI and I as a leading spokesman for the opposition party against royal absolutism (Bald, p. 43).[3] The latter point bears emphasizing, not just because Donne's epistles in verse and prose constitute a significant part of his writing, but because the centrifugal pull of diverse friendships, which would soon include aristocrats like Henry Percy, fellow amateur poets and budding connoisseurs of art, like Christopher Brooke, and court hopefuls like the generous spendthrift Sir Henry Goodyer, helped to offset the centripetal pull of a family often bent on exile and martyrdom.

A second phase, beginning in 1591 and continuing into 1602, might be said to coincide with the final anxious years of Elizabeth's rule when matters of succession, mixed with patriotic fervor, became especially prominent. It is marked, at one temporal extreme, by our first look at Donne, aged eighteen, in the (lost) miniature, probably by Nicholas Hilliard, that underlies the engraving produced by William Marshall for the 1635 publication of Donne's *Poems*, and, at the other, by his clandestine marriage to Anne More in December, 1601, which soon led to their financially-imposed exile from London shortly thereafter. On the basis of the engraving, one should not conclude too much about how Donne actually looked (figure 1). Nor should one put too much interpretive weight on either the translation Walton provided for the motto *Antes muerto que mudado* ("Sooner dead than changed"), which the hagiographically minded biographer rendered as "*How much shall I be chang'd, / Before I am chang'd*" (Walton, p. 79), or the accompanying poem he produced for the occasion, which sets the "golden Age" of Donne's elder years against the "dross" of his youth. But the engraving does indicate a truculent Donne, more soldier than scholar, broad shouldered, hand on sword, sporting a cruciform earring, the dangling icon of his residual Catholicism: an emerging someone about to make a mark in an emerging city.

The London Donne re-entered was itself undergoing rapid change and expansion. From the accession of Henry VIII in 1509 to the restoration of Charles II in 1660, the population increased ten-fold in number: from about 50,000 people to half a million.[4] Parish steeples might remain the city's most visually conspicuous connection to its medieval past, but the streets were becoming as crowded as those of ancient Rome, a point Donne vividly captures in the first, and probably earliest of his satires (when the bookish recluse is lured out of his study to observe London's seamy underside) and then further develops in the remarkable, nightmarishly congested fourth satire.

This was for youth, Strength, Mirth, and wit that Time
Most count their golden Age; but t'was not thine.
Thine was thy later yeares, so much refind
From youths Drosse, Mirth, & wit; as thy pure mind
Thought (like the Angels) nothing but the Praise
Of thy Creator, in those last, best Dayes.
    Witnes this Booke, (thy Embleme) which begins
With Love; but endes, with Sighes, & Teares for sins.

Will: Marshall. sculpsit.

IZ: WA:

Figure 1 Donne in 1591; from an engraving by William Marshall, prefixed to *Poems*, 1635.

Nor could it be said that London, and by extension England, was any longer an island entire of itself. During Elizabeth's reign, the nation began to utilize the navigational technologies associated with exploration and to compete against Portugal and Spain for new world booty. By 1580, Francis Drake had girdled the globe, as Magellan had done a half-century earlier. A few years later, in 1583, Humphrey Gilbert, accompanied by Walter Raleigh, laid claim to Newfoundland – "O my America! my new-found-land," as Donne would eagerly exclaim about the female body in his most sexually charged elegy beginning "Come, Madam, come" – and shortly thereafter Ralegh sought to establish colonies in both South America (Guiana) and Roanoke Island, off the North Carolina coast. The post-Gutenburg explosion of print, moreover, allowed readers to stay current with these events, whether through the burgeoning travel literature of the day or the ever-increasing production of sophisticated maps by continental cartographers like Gerard Mercator and Abraham Ortelius. The great sixteenth-century Antwerp publisher, Christopher Plantin, in fact, chose a compass as his insignia, and by the 1660s, the Dutch painter Johannes Vermeer had rendered, with exquisite concentration, not just "The Geographer," compass in hand, deep in thought, but his near twin, "The Astronomer" – the latter reminding us of the astronomical discoveries associated with Copernicus, Kepler, and Galileo. Mapmindedness, writes a recent historian of cartography, had become a contemporary phenomenon.[5]

Donne, at whatever stage, was pre-eminently worldly in his thinking. Compasses would have as much a place in his poetry as the Straits of Magellan. Dante, not Spenser, was part of his upbringing; Durer as well as Hilliard were at his finger tips. But the London he re-entered in the 1590s – to return to the immediate – was still a small world, geographically and socially. Although few buildings from Donne's time survive, most of the places associated with his name are within easy walking distance of one another. From Bread Street, where he was born, to Lincoln's Inn, where he studied law and later preached, takes little more than fifteen minutes. Even less time is necessary to walk from the Inns of Court to York House, at the bottom of Drury Lane, in which he would serve as Egerton's secretary; and from here to St. Clement Danes Church, where his wife, Anne (More) Donne would be buried in 1617, requires only about five minutes, and about the same again to St. Dunstan's West, one of several parish churches that Donne would hold. And from St. Dunstan's to St. Paul's, where Donne would be installed as Dean in 1621, is another ten minutes. Lining the Thames River near Drury Lane, as well, were the great houses belonging to Essex (Robert Devereux) and Somerset (Sir Robert Ker) – two of his patrons – and, of course, on the other side of the river, in Southwark, were brothels, bear gardens, and the large out-door amphitheatres, including, as of 1599, the Globe. What separated people was not so much distance as class – a rigid social hierarchy, narrow at the top, and presided over by the monarch, attended by court favorites – and, of course, religious difference. When in disgrace Donne eventually found housing in Mitcham, a suburb of London, in the early 1600s, he sounded, at times, as if he might well be living in the Antipodes.

The 1590s were, however, remarkably full for Donne: a decade given to poetry, entertainment, theological inquiry, family stress, military adventure, and career advancement. Having come into his inheritance of about 750 pounds from the early death of his father, he was reported by his Oxford acquaintance, Sir Richard Baker, to be living, at this point, at the "*Innes of Court*, not dissolute, but very neat; a great visiter of Ladies, a great frequenter of Playes, a great writer of conceited Verses" (Bald, p. 72). Conceited verses, in conjunction with visiting ladies, sounds more appropriate to the amatory lyrics in the *Songs and Sonets* and some of the *Elegies* than to the *Satires*, with their harsh judgments of the times. Experimenting with politically edgy satire and the Ovidian erotic poem – and its potentially pornographic matter – was in vogue at the Inns of Court in the waning days of Elizabeth's reign and in step with "a new and aggressively sexualized form of distinctly English literature ... emerging into definition in the 1590s,"[6] an emergence that would be perceived by the authorities as politically disruptive and lead to works being banned at the end of the decade. (Not being printed, Donne's poems escaped the pyre, which consumed books by Thomas Nashe, John Marston, and John Davies.) As for his being "a great frequenter of Playes," the best record of his visits to the theater – his writings are bereft of references to specific plays, although not incidents – is the utter originality of his lyrics conceived as dramatic monologues.

A second portrait of Donne, thought to date from the middle of the decade, speaks to the process of refinement he was undergoing in the 1590s as Inns-of-Court man-about-town – and to his habitual fascination with his own changing identity. In the "Lothian" portrait, as it is called, Donne now appears in the suave posture of a melancholy lover, indicated in the crossed arms and wide-brimmed hat, the portions of the picture most in shadow (figure 2). No longer apparent are traces of books and a quill, visible when the portrait was discovered in 1959, and an appropriately subtle indicator of Donne's authorial activities at this stage. Most striking, of course, are the illuminated features in the picture: first the elongated fingers, then the piercing eyes and sensuous mouth, as they draw a mannerist attention to the sitter's elegant sexuality confirmed on a more explicitly irreverent level in the Latin motto, transposed from the third collect for Evensong, and arching

Figure 2 Donne in the pose of a Melancholy Lover.

over Donne's head like a rainbow: "*Illumina tenebr[as] nostras Domina*" – "lighten our darkness, Lady."[7] We might even imagine the absorption of the earlier cruciform earring into the image of the lover's crossed arms.[8]

Donne would later be haunted by recollections of his amatory exploits during these years, but the unsettled subject of religion – and persecution – was also never far from his thoughts. Sharply telescoping the chronology during his time at the Inns of Court, Walton reports that Donne did "presently lay aside all study of the Law ... and [began] seriously to survey, and consider the Body of Divinity as it was then controverted betwixt the *Reformed* and the *Roman* Church" (p. 25). But Walton omits mentioning the event that perhaps prompted this urgent inquiry, in favor of underscoring the deliberative nature of Donne's quest for the true church, including his extended observations on the writings of Cardinal Bellarmine. In early 1594, Donne's brother, Henry, died from the plague in prison, where he had been committed for harboring a Yorkshire priest, William Harrington, in his chambers in May 1593. Henry's death saved him from witnessing the grisly scene of Harrington "drawne from Newgate to Tyborne; and there hanged, cut downe alive, struggled with the hang-man, but was bowelled, and quartered" (Bald, p. 58).

Donne is silent on the matter of Henry's death, but at issue here in the reporting is a biographical conundrum centering on the problem of evaluating Donne's theological leanings. When did Donne "convert" to Anglicanism? And at what psychological cost, to borrow the darker terminology put into use by John Carey, who prefers to characterize Donne's "conversion" as his "apostasy" from Catholicism? And here one is concerned not just with determining dates involving matters of outward conformity – Donne could not have been in Egerton's service by the end of the decade if he was not, in some sense, subscribing to the Church of England – but with assessing the inward consequences accompanying such a shift in belief, a shift that Walton, for one, saw occupying Donne's mind well into James's reign. In the absence of personal testimony from Donne during these years, much can only be hypothesized about his state of mind in the 1590s. But most scholars agree that one of the keys to understanding Donne's habits of thought can be found in "Satyre III," his strenuous and brilliantly skeptical inquiry into "true religion," often assumed to have been written in the mid-to-late 1590s.

As for Donne's military adventures to Cadiz and the Azores, from June 1596 to September 1597, we are on firmer footing with regard to dates. We might also observe, à propos the two portraits, that while the sword still remained within Donne's reach, the pen produced the more lasting results. Donne's participation in these separate attacks against Spain, led by Essex, is a well-documented, small, but fascinating chapter in his life, and can only be touched on here.[9] We do not know precisely how and in what capacity he came to be part of these expeditions, which, militarily speaking, were small fires in the much larger pan-European conflagration between Catholics and Protestants. But they put Donne in some exciting company (Sir Walter Ralegh, for one), perhaps secured a connection, begun at the Inns of Court, with Thomas Egerton, the son of his future employer, who would die a hero's death in Ireland in 1599 (Donne would bear the sword at his funeral), and they indicate as well his attachment to England's anti-Spanish policy, whatever his precise theological leanings at the moment.

But patriotism is not the pronounced theme in the poetry dealing with these adventures. The point is the more surprising – and interesting – if one recalls the jingoism frequently associated with the theaters in the 1590s, in which characters like the Mariner from *Edward III* stand and deliver set pieces describing English valor, even in defeat.[10] Donne's epigrams from these ventures are more like brief snapshots capturing the ironic mix of violence and pathos of battle ("A burnt ship," "Sir John Wingefield") – the kind of thing a modern poet like Wilfred Owen might write; and the most ambitious of his attempts at scene painting, the pair of *fin-de-siècle* verse epistles to his Inns of Court friend Christopher Brooke, "The Storme" and "The Calme," speak as much to Donne's divided and restless state of mind at this point in his career as they do of nature's disabling effects on the ship and its crew.

Back on land by October 1597, Donne was in Egerton's employment within a year. The route to preferment often has been charted from the Inns of Court, through a circle of friends, to the position of Egerton's secretary. But the most interesting event is not Donne's manner of arrival, or even his daily activities as Egerton's factotum that enabled his "whistle-blowing" fifth satire,[11] but the means of his sudden departure from York house: eloping with Egerton's sixteen-year-old niece, Anne More (no relation to Sir Thomas More), sometime in December 1601, and thereby earning both his father-in-law's and his employer's wrath in one fell swoop. Sir George More had the twenty-nine-year-old Donne and his friends, Christopher and Samuel Brooke, thrown in jail. He also attempted, unsuccessfully, to have the marriage annulled. (Then, as now, civil ceremonies were legally binding.) The episode is fully documented in a series of letters Donne wrote to both Sir George and his employer, in one suggesting to the bride's father that it was in his and therefore his daughter's, and of course Donne's, best interest for Sir George to look kindly upon an event that had been "irremediably done."[12]

What is remarkable is the apparent impulsiveness of Donne's actions, and the inability of later critics to supply a satisfactory explanation other than the obvious romantic one. Over-reaching might be seen to have played a part but for the devotion Donne always showed his wife, in letters to friends, and in both the highly personal sonnet he wrote on the occasion of her death in 1617 and the plaque he raised to her memory in St. Clement Danes church. Of course, we know about Anne Donne only from John Donne's point of view. Like many other women of the times, she left no spoken or written record of her thoughts, but Walton does describe her as having been "curiously and plentifully educated" (p. 31). It sounds as if she could have followed her husband's thinking – and understood his poetry too, as readers have often felt.[13] "So much company, therefore, as I am, she shall not want," Donne wrote to her brother in 1614, three years before Anne would die at age thirty-three after giving birth to their twelfth child, "and we had not one another at so cheap a rate as that we should ever be so weary of one another" (Oliver, p. 76).

Donne was eventually forgiven by both his father-in-law and his employer, but Egerton's sense of office would not permit Donne to be reinstated. Egerton was among the few Elizabethan officials apparently above reproach, which was one of the reasons why he was chosen Lord Keeper – that, and the part the former recusant played in the 1580s prosecuting important Catholics like the Jesuit Edmund Campion and Elizabeth's half-sister, Mary Queen of Scots. Whatever his personal feelings for Donne, Egerton was not about to relent on an employment matter that had sparked so much scandal in the small world of London. The punning phrase "*John Donne – Anne Donne – Undone*" began immediately to circulate, in variant form, and, as the century wore on, it became a well-known jest, reported even among "The Royal Apothegms of King Charles" (1669), where its elevated currency probably prompted Walton finally to include the quip in his 1675 edition of Donne's life.[14]

With wife in hand, children on the way, and no visible means of income, Donne began a long, frustrating search for employment that would last until January 23, 1615, when he would be ordained deacon and priest. There are no portraits of him in this third phase. But an increasing number of letters survive, and these depict, among other things, the highly awkward position of dependency in which Donne now found himself as he tried, again and again, to climb the slippery slope of preferment. Here is one sentence from a (1608?) letter to James Hay, whose own successful career was launched when he came south from Scotland with the King and was thereupon appointed a gentleman of the bedchamber: "I have been told that when your Lordship did me that extreme favour of presenting my name, his Majesty remembered me by the worst part of my history, which was my disorderly proceedings several years since in my nonage" (Oliver, p. 41). To help him sustain his family, Donne occasionally did receive favors from friends and patrons – most notably Sir Henry Goodyer, Magdalen Herbert, and Lucy Harrington, Countess of Bedford. But the letter to Hay, who would become another lifelong friend, suggests how hard it was, given the king's disposition, for Donne ever to pry open the door to courtly preferment.

During these years of exile – their first child would be called, appropriately enough, "Constance" – the Donne family moved often: initially to Pyrford, near Loseley House, the More family estate in Surrey, until 1606, when they moved to a two-story cottage in Mitcham and remained there until 1611. Then, thanks largely to the help he received from Sir Robert Drury, and after a brief stop in the Isle of Wight, the family settled in a house on Drury Lane and remained there until taking possession of the Deanery of St. Paul's in 1621. Initially, Donne split his time between his growing family and going abroad in search of employment: sometimes to London, where he kept lodging in the Strand and enjoyed the conviviality of the Mermaid Tavern; and yet even here he could hardly have escaped for long the sense of his life as spectacle for common observation. "Newes here is none at all," wrote John Chamberlain to Dudley Carleton on February 14, 1609, "but that John Dun seekes to be preferred to be secretarie of [the] Virginia [company]" (Bald, p. 162). Donne also journeyed twice to the continent, from 1605 to early 1606, to Paris and perhaps Venice, and then again to France as part of the large Drury entourage from 1611 to 1612.

As is often the case with Donne, the powers of camaraderie are balanced against, or, more often now in conflict with, the forces of family. The tension is sometimes concentrated in a single letter, as in this frequently quoted one to Goodyer:

> I write not to you out of my poor library, where to cast mine eye upon good authors kindles or refreshes sometimes meditations not unfit to communicate to near friends, nor from the highway, where I am contracted and inverted into myself, which are my two ordinary forges of letters to you, but I write from the fireside in my parlour and in the noise of three gamesome children and by the side of her whom, because I have transplanted into a wretched fortune, I must labour to disguise that from her by all such honest devices as giving her my company and discourse. Therefore I steal from her all the time which I give this letter and it is therefore that I take so short a list [run-up] and gallop so fast over it. I have not been out of my house since I received your packet.
>
> (Oliver, p. 33)

The Mitcham years were filled with restlessness of a different kind than what animated Donne in the 1590s. Amid the raw vapors rising from the vault below his study, he probably wrote many of his holy sonnets, the most intimate and troubled of the devotional poems, and also his treatise on suicide, *Biathanatos*. As we discover, too, from a letter written to that pillar of Protestantism, Magdalen Herbert, around 1607, Donne was composing what has come to be known as the "La Corona" sequence of devotional sonnets; and, again, in even greater detail in a letter to Goodyer from 1608 that sheds considerable light on his attempts to navigate between the Roman and the Reformed Church, Donne outlines some of his motives for composing "for [his] lesser chapels, which are my friends," the poem called "The Litanie" (Oliver, p. 38).

In order to enhance his chances for secular preferment, Donne also turned, for the first time, to the world of print and propaganda. (To this point, reflecting an aristocratic bias against publication, only one of his lyrics, "The Expiration," had appeared in print, in Ferrabosco's 1609 *Book of Ayres*.) In the immediate aftermath of the Gunpowder Plot (1605), the king had issued his Oath of Allegiance (1606) requiring all citizens to swear obedience to England's temporal ruler. *Pseudo-Martyr* (1610), dedicated to James, was Donne's attempt to convince English Catholics that it was possible to do so without betraying their faith. This was soon followed by *Conclave Ignati* (1611; English version same year), a quick outgrowth of the scathing satire against Jesuits that had concluded *Pseudo-Martyr*.[15] Still, neither work helped Donne gain preferment. In fact, although *Pseudo-Martyr* did lead to an honorary MA from Oxford in 1610, ironically, as the story goes, it only seemed to confirm in James's mind Donne's suitability for church, not state, employment.

Donne's other venture into print in this period met with more embarrassment than success, of even an ironic kind. The incident remains of particular interest, though, in part because modern criticism has found much value in the two extended verse elegies collectively known as *The First* and *Second Anniversaries* that Donne wrote to commemorate the death in December 1610 of fifteen-year-old Elizabeth Drury, the daughter of his patrons, Sir Robert and Lady Drury. The first, "An Anatomie of the World," Donne saw into print in 1611 before setting out for France with Drury. The sequel, "Of the Progresse of the Soule," he wrote while abroad; the two were then published together, with some other poems, in 1612.[16] But their appearance, separate or together, raised eyebrows among the patron-conscious literati because of the hyperbolic praise Donne bestowed on the young Elizabeth. Jonson was reported to have said "that Donne's *Anniversary* was profane and full of blasphemies," and "that he told Mr. Donne, if it had been written of the Virgin Mary it had been something; to which [Donne] answered that he described the idea of a woman, and not as she was."[17]

Donne was stung by the adverse reception his venture into publication got. In two letters written in quick succession from abroad concerning the matter he noted, "I hear from England of many censures of my book of Mistress Drury." Licking his wounds, he spoke with regret about "descend[ing] to print anything in verse," continued the high-minded line of defense Jonson had attributed to him, and revealed, as well, further annoyance over the very real possibility that some "ladies" might think he was insincere in his praise (Oliver, pp. 62–63).

That Donne should be so touchy on this issue points in a number of directions: certainly to the highly stratified, status-conscious society he was forced to navigate, not always successfully (and sincerely); and, just possibly to lingering concerns about his Catholic heritage, which, at one level, *Pseudo-Martyr* sought to address. And yet, Donne was not so offended that he could afford to withdraw *The Second Anniversary* from publication in 1612 when it was still possible to do so. Nor did he altogether swear off publishing his verse. Two years later, in a letter to Goodyer dated December 20, 1614, he speaks in a hushed voice – "so softly I am loath to hear myself – and so softly that, if that good Lady [Bedford] were in the room with you and this letter, she might not hear" – of the necessity "of printing my poems and addressing them to my Lord Chamberlain [Robert Ker, the Earl of Somerset] . . . . for I must do this as a valediction to the world before I take orders" (Oliver, pp. 79–80).

Donne's quest for temporal preferment ended in January 1615, without his ever following through on his valedictory publishing pledge. As is the case with Hamlet's indecisions, Donne's delay at fulfilling a responsibility that others found highly suitable to him has invited many explanations. For the high-church Walton, the forty-two-year-old Donne required time for spiritual growth. "Jack Donne" needed time to become "John Donne," which, in Augustinian fashion, entailed coming to terms with the "many strifes within himself concerning the strictness of life" (Walton, p. 46) that find acute expression in one of the few, clearly datable (and great) poems from the period leading up to his ordination, "Goodfriday, 1613. Riding Westward." For the more skeptical Bald, the ministry was the only option left for Donne after so many failed attempts to win secular employment. (As late as March 1614, an episode Walton omits, Donne wrote Somerset asking for the ambassadorship to Venice.) Donne's true conversion to the church begins, for Bald, only with the death of his wife (p. 328). For the still more skeptical Carey, Donne's decision to enter the ministry is simply a further extension of the ambition that drove him to seek worldly preferment in the first place.

As with Donne's other "conversion," from Catholicism to Protestantism, the evidence admits conflicting views. One might briefly note, as a way of signaling the range of possibilities, that the new seal Donne chose to symbolize the change in his life – the device of Christ crucified to an anchor used "on the letter written on the day of his ordination to Sir Edward Herbert" (Bald, p. 305) – was followed the next year by the stylish portrait of him in ruff done by Isaac Oliver in 1616 (figure 3). And both of these representations, tending in opposite directions, were followed by a third, more complicated one in verse in 1617: that of a grieving husband arguing, ingeniously, that a tenderly jealous God has taken away his wife in order to assure that "the World, Fleshe, yea Devill" will not put divinity out of the speaker's thoughts ("Since she whom I lov'd," 14). Nonetheless, by 1620, Donne's appearance in yet

Figure 3 Donne in 1616; from a miniature by Isaac Oliver.

another picture wearing the dress of a Roman orator, but looking monastic, suggests, visually at least, that worldly and spiritual identities were beginning to converge (figure 4).[18]

The last phase, Donne's years in the church, can be summarized more briefly, if only because, to quote Walton, those activities "which had been occasionally diffused, were all concentred in Divinity."[19] Except for one sojourn abroad in 1619, Donne remained in or around London until his death in 1631. At court, Somerset was out, George Villiers, elevated to Duke of Buckingham in 1623, in. But Donne's friendships were wider than those of a single court faction, just as his theology – and his church – were born of convictions broader than what might be attributed to either Germany or Rome.

Figure 4 Donne in 1620, as shown in the portrait in the Deanery of St. Paul's Cathedral.

Donne's clerical career began auspiciously when he was appointed royal Chaplain to the king. Then, if the chronology is right, it took an odd turn when he failed to be awarded a Doctor of Divinity by Cambridge (which James had promised), but was rumored, instead, to have been granted the Deanery of Canterbury, which was not true but, according to the gossipy Chamberlain, created envy among his contemporaries. His career soon got back on track with the receipt of several benefices. One, the rectory of Sevenoaks, was a sinecure from his old employer Egerton, and it was in conjunction with a visit in July 1617 that the remarkable Anne Clifford, then wife to the third Earl of Dorset, Richard Sackville, noted in her *Diary* hearing Donne preach. (His poems and sermons would be among the books later depicted in her triptych portrait by Jan van Belcamp known as the "Great Picture of Lady Anne Clifford.") But Donne's most important early appointment was, without doubt, as Reader in Divinity at Lincoln's Inn on October 24, 1616. Here, among some old academic acquaintances and in familiar haunts not far from his house in Drury Lane, Donne first assumed regular preaching duties – fifty sermons in his first year – and began to hone the public rhetorical skills that would soon lead to his becoming one of London's most eloquent and prominent sermonizers – the "Golden Chrysostome" of eulogistic record.[20]

As a measure of his success with this most favored of Jacobean literary forms, to say nothing of ongoing personal connections, Donne was invited to preach in a variety of different settings, each with its own cliental and specific ecclesiological concerns: at court, both at Whitehall and Denmark House, Queen Anne's residence; and at Paul's Cross, with its mixed, open-air audience and opportunities to preach on controversial topics. And, of course, Donne preached frequently at both St. Paul's, after he was appointed Dean in 1621, and nearby St. Dunstan's West, a living held by the Earl of Dorset, to which Donne was appointed in 1624, and where Walton, then a linen draper, was a parishioner.

Donne's one sojourn abroad after his ordination was as chaplain in the service of Viscount Doncaster (the same James Hay). The venture turned out to be a futile, costly, diplomatic mission to head off the conflict between a resurgent Hapsburg empire and resistant Protestant states that would lead to the Thirty Years War. The embassy's journey took Donne through Heidelberg, Germany, to Bohemia – modern-day Czechoslovakia – then north to the Netherlands where, among other cities visited, he delivered a sermon at the Hague and received a medal honoring the Synod of Dort, which he later bequeathed to Henry King. Still, the most memorable impression Donne left of this excursion was in the first of three great valedictory hymns he wrote after taking orders: "A Hymne to Christ, at the Authors last going into Germany."

Donne took his ministerial duties seriously, at one point vowing indignantly in a late letter (against rumors of his affecting ease in his sickness), "that I might die in the pulpit; if not that, yet that I might take my death in the pulpit, that is, die the sooner by occasion of my former labours" (Oliver, p. 117). More debatable is how much Donne felt bound as a preacher by the political favors he received. A sermon itself is occasional, and often requires, as scholars have shown, a full reading of the historical context if one is to catch the political drift. Sermons were not subject to censorship, but a sermonizer who offended the king could spend the night – or more – in the Tower. One of Donne's most controversial acts involved his being invited (that is, required) to preach at Paul's Cross on behalf of James's *Directions to Preachers*, which the king had published in an attempt to restrain the barrage of criticism directed from London pulpits against official policy favoring Spain in the immediate aftermath of the defeat of the Elector Palatine in 1620. Donne seems to have negotiated James's absolutist politics here well enough to cause serious debate among current scholars as to his leanings.[21] A few years later, under Charles I, Donne would himself become anxious when the king signaled suspicions about a sermon he had preached.

Donne's later years were marked by periods of extremely poor health. Given the presence of the plague that raged through London in 1625, sickness itself was hardly unusual, but in Donne, illness often brought with it remarkable bursts of creative inspiration, especially when the sickness was his own. As one critic has recently put the matter, when Donne "felt most gravely threatened he also felt compelled to produce his most defiantly lively writing."[22] The year 1623 was one of those charged valedictory moments. Suddenly struck down by what is now called "relapsing fever" in early December of that year, Donne used the intervals of recovery and lucidity to pen, with near super-human speed and concentration, the series of prose meditations tracing the effects of his sickness titled *Devotions upon Emergent Occasions*. By January 9, the work was already registered with the Stationers' Company for publication, the speed perhaps owing, in part, to the presence of some enterprising Fleet Street printers among Donne's St. Dunstan's congregation. Although the focus here is characteristically on himself, as it is in the "companion" work, the "Hymne to God My God, in my sicknesse," Donne had no qualms, as a divine, about publishing this emblematic portrait of his sufferings, much as, some years later, with death approaching, he would choose to leave not one but two images of himself to posterity in the statue carved by Nicholas Stone and in the famous sermon, "Death's Duell, " preached at Whitehall "Before King Charles I (February 25, 1631)."

Before we arrive at Donne's saintly end, though, a few more worldly concerns bear mentioning. In conjunction with describing the great grief Donne felt over the death of his wife, Walton reported that Donne "gave voluntary assurance" to his remaining children "never to bring them under the subjection of a step-mother" (p. 51). The little we know of the seven Donne children then still alive has been compactly summarized in Bald's biography (pp. 547–56). The oldest son, John, followed haltingly in his father's clerical and literary footsteps, seeing into print much of his father's work, including the *Letters to Severall Persons of Honour* (1651). The next son, George, assumed his father's active star. He became a soldier, and at the time of Donne's death, he was a Spanish captive languishing in prison in Cadiz. But the most intriguing saga for literature students involves the oldest child, Constance. In one of the more remarkable family alliances – the ever-watchful Chamberlain called it "the strangest match" – Donne's twenty-year-old daughter married the recently widowed Edward Alleyn, "the old player,"[23] in early December 1623, just as Donne was succumbing to relapsing fever. No doubt the marriage was arranged. The 57-year old Alleyn was wealthy, and agreed to a settlement of 1500 pounds payable to Constance at his death. The match, in turn, added another touch to Alleyn's ongoing bid for respectability as the founder of Dulwich College – the dignity of a knighthood would elude him. But for reasons apparently having to do with a loan Donne promised Alleyn, the two men fell out in 1625, at which point, the aging actor and now Master of the King's Bears, who had made his fortune on the wrong side of the Thames, accused the Dean of St. Paul's, now on the right side of the river, of reneging on his promise and using words "more 'fitting you 30 years ago when you might be question[ed] for them then now under so reverent a calling as you are'" (Bald, pp. 464–65). Alleyn was to die within the year, and Constance would remarry, but the strange fracas points, by way of the pulpit, to the never-quite-forgotten stigma of Donne's raucous youth.

The other matter of more than anecdotal interest involves Donne's will, and here I mean only to point to the accumulated nature of particular gifts that distinguishes it from his own father's will executed some sixty years earlier (Bald, pp. 560–67). The son was not as wealthy as his father, which is hardly surprising. But the possessions he did have, he gave with great care to named individuals. This was especially true for the many pictures Donne somehow acquired during his life. Except for a picture of James and "that Picture of myne which is taken in Shaddowes" (the Lothian Portrait), all are of religious subjects. As was customary with inventories from this period, the paintings in the will are identified by location rather than artist.[24] As such, they invite us to imagine, in some detail, the interior of the Deanery as a reflection of its occupant's taste and interest.

To select just a few: in the parlor were two pictures of a more formal sort, the historian Paolo Sarpi of Venice, and Fulgentius, bishop of Ruspa in North Africa (507–27 CE). In the little dining room was a picture of "The blessed Virgin Marye," its Catholic subject matter and placement reminding us that Donne's durable Catholic mother was part of his household until two months before his own death. In his study, too, was a second portrait of the Virgin (with Joseph), to be given to "my ancient frend Doctor Brooke Master of Trinitie Colledge in Cambridge," in company with "the picture of layinge Christe in his Toombe," left to the Earl of Kent. Four large pictures of the "fowre great prophettes" were to remain in the hall. A "Picture of Adam and Eve," hanging in the "greate Chamber," was to be bequeathed to the Earl of Dorset, and "in my Chamber" is "the Picture of Marie Magdalene"

Figure 5 Donne, from the effigy by Nicholas Stone in St. Paul's Cathedral.

for my "kynde Frend Mr. George Garrard." The subject matter and location of that last picture is especially provocative (the converted "Jack" looking at the converted Mary.) But the whole arrangement, and the manner in which the gifts are disposed, speak to a sophisticated awareness of religious and social inclusiveness, artful to the close.

Donne died on March 31, 1631. Most biographers rightly give way to Walton's account of Donne's last sermon – "when, to the amazement of some beholders he appeared in the Pulpit, many of them thought he presented himself not to preach mortification by a living voice: but, mortality by a decayed body and a dying face" (p. 75) – and, with a few emendations,[25] to the detailed attention given to the minister's somber preparations for death, including having his picture drawn with eyes shut, standing on an urn, somehow wrapped in a winding sheet, "with so much of the sheet turned aside as might shew his lean, pale, and death-like face, which was purposely turned toward the East, from whence he expected the second coming of his and our Saviour Jesus" (p. 78). Having retired from "his beloved study" to his "bed chamber," Donne apparently meditated on this emaciated image in his closing hours – in the same room that also contained the picture of Mary Magdalene. As for its afterlife, the sketch served not only for the Droeshout engraving of Donne soon to appear on the frontispiece to *Death's Duell* (1632) but as the model for the marble statue carved by Stone and his workers, still in St. Paul's (figure 5). By the finest of ironies, the erection of the statue, anonymously paid for at the time, was later revealed to be by Donne's physician, Simeon Fox, youngest son of John Fox(e) author of the fiercely Protestant *Book of Martyrs*, scourge of Catholics, and whom Donne had satirized in the curious work of his known as *The Courtier's Library*.[26] One wonders whether the son still felt too much of the father's heat to declare openly the part he was playing in creating the new idol of St. Paul's.

NOTES

1 Ian Donaldson (ed.), *Ben Jonson* (Oxford: Oxford University Press, 1985), p. 597.
2 The principal biographical sources underlying this essay are Walton's *Life*; Carey, *Donne*; Flynn, *Donne and the Ancient Catholic Nobility*; and Bald, *Donne*, with additional comments from Barry Spurr, "The John Donne Papers of Wesley Milgate," *JDJ* 15 (1996), 189–201.
3 For further information on Martin and Wotton, respectively see Tom Cain, "Donne and the Prince D'Amour," *JDJ* 14 (1995), 83–111, and, in the same issue, Dennis Flynn, "Donne, Henry Wotton, and the Earl of Essex," 185–218.
4 Lawrence Manley (ed.), *London in the Age of Shakespeare: An Anthology* (University Park: Pennsylvania State University Press, 1986), p. 1.
5 P. D. A. Harvey, *Maps in Tudor England* (Chicago: University of Chicago Press, 1993), p. 15. I owe this point to my student Kevin Sher.

6 Lynda E. Boose, "The 1599 Bishops' Ban, Elizabethan Pornography, and the Sexualization of the Jacobean Stage," in Richard Burt and John Michael Archer (eds.), *Enclosure Acts: Sexuality, Property, and Culture in Early Modern England* (Ithaca: Cornell University Press, 1994), p. 192.

7 My comments are indebted to Annabel Patterson, "Donne in Shadows: Pictures and Politics," *JDJ* 16 (1997), 1–35, esp. 9–11; see also Appendix E in Helen Gardner (ed.), *The Elegies and The Songs and Sonnets* (Oxford: Clarendon Press, 1965). A more esoteric reading of the painting's symbolism can be found in Kate Gartner Frost, "The Lothian Portrait: A Prolegomenon," *JDJ* 15 (1996), 95–125.

8 For the symbolism of Donne's crossed-arms posture see Ann Hurley, "More Foolery from More?: John Donne's Lothian Portrait as a Clue to his Politics," in Ann Hurley and Kate Greenspan (eds.), *So Rich a Tapestry: The Sister Arts and Cultural Studies* (Lewisburg: Bucknell University Press, 1995), pp. 72–87.

9 See Bald, ch. 5, and Flynn, "Donne, Henry Wotton, and the Earl of Essex," 185–218.

10 Giorgio Melchiori (ed.), *Edward III* (Cambridge: Cambridge University Press, 1998), III.i.141–84; see the accompanying note about the speech possibly influencing Donne's "The Storme" and "The Calme."

11 "Whistleblowing" is Dennis Flynn's word in "Donne's Most Daring *Satyre*: 'richly For service paid, authorized'," *JDJ* 20 (2001), 107–20, at 108.

12 P. M. Oliver (ed.), *John Donne: Selected Letters* (New York: Routledge, 2002), pp. 9–16, at p. 9. In the absence of a definitive single edition of Donne's letters, and because Oliver includes letters not published in the 1651 *Letters*, I quote from Oliver's text.

13 The lure of Anne Donne is well represented by the essays in M. Thomas Hester (ed.), *John Donne's "desire of more": The Subject of Anne More Donne in His Poetry* (Newark: University of Delaware Press, 1996).

14 See Ernest W. Sullivan, II, "Donne's Epithalamium for Anne," in Hester (ed.), *Donne's "desire of more,"* pp. 35–38.

15 For a history of the publication circumstances, in part correcting Walton's account, see T. S. Healy, SJ (ed.), *John Donne: Ignatius his Conclave* (Oxford: Clarendon Press, 1969), pp. xi–xxix.

16 For the compositional history of the *Anniversaries* see W. Milgate (ed.), *The Epithalamions, Anniversaries, and Epicedes* (Oxford: Clarendon Press, 1978), pp. xxix–xxxiv.

17 Donaldson (ed.), *Ben Jonson*, p. 596.

18 For responses to this portrait see Paul Sellin, *So Doth, So Is Religion: John Donne and Diplomatic Contexts in the Reformed Netherlands, 1619–1620* (Columbia: University of Missouri Press, 1988), p. 200, notes 58 and 59.

19 Walton, p. 48.

20 R[ichard].B[usby], "In Memory of Doctor Donne," in Grierson (ed.), *Poems*, vol. I, p. 386.

21 See Jeanne Shami, "'The Stars in their Order Fought Against Sisera': John Donne and the Pulpit Crisis of 1622," *JDJ* 14 (1995), 1–58.

22 Andrew Motion, intro. to *John Donne: Devotions upon Emergent Occasions* and *Death's Duel* (New York: Random House, 1999), p. xii.

23 Chamberlain's comments can be found in Aileen Reid and Robert Maniura (ed.), *Edward Alleyn: Elizabethan Actor, Jacobean Gentleman* (London: Dulwich

Picture Gallery, 1994), p. 29. I have drawn on essays in this volume by S. P. Cerasano, Susan Foister, and J. R. Piggot for further information on Alleyn.

24 Susan Foister, "Paintings and Other Works of Art in Sixteenth-Century English Inventories," *The Burlington Magazine* 123 (1981), 273–82.

25 For a history of corrections made to Walton's account, see Richard S. Peterson, "New Evidence on Donne's Monument: 1," *JDJ* 20 (2001), 1–51.

26 Bald, p. 533. See also Donne, *The Courtier's Library, or Catalogus librorum*, edited and translated by Evelyn Mary Simpson (London: Nonesuch Press, 1930), p. 44, and Donne's satirical entry as translated: "*The Art of copying out within the compass of a Penny all the truthful statements made to that end by John Foxe, by Peter Bales.*"

2

TED-LARRY PEBWORTH

The text of Donne's writings

The most important fact to keep in mind when considering the texts of John Donne's writings is that Donne preferred manuscript circulation to print publication for both his prose and his poetry, and that preference has significant consequences for the study of his texts. Although printing was introduced into England in 1475, it did not immediately triumph over scribal publication. Indeed, for more than two hundred years after the introduction of printed books intended for mass circulation, many writers continued to publish primarily via manuscript copies of their works sent to selected audiences. Moreover, during the early modern period, manuscript publication was not a peripheral phenomenon or an inferior form of transmission, but was important in the commerce of disseminating texts and was considered by many – including John Donne – to be superior to print. His choice of manuscript publication makes a crucial difference in the way a reader should view Donne's texts.

Unlike his friend and almost exact contemporary Ben Jonson, who collected and oversaw the printing of his *Workes* (1616), John Donne scorned print publication and avoided it as much as possible. Nearly all of the few works of his that were printed in his lifetime were committed to the press at the urging of friends or in obedience to the king or a noble patron, and of those few that were printed several were issued anonymously. Donne considered the offering of his poetry and prose to the masses under his name a violation of his dignity and gravity as a gentleman and found the idea of being considered a professional writer offensive. As he wrote to his friend Henry Goodyer in 1609, Donne sought to pursue "a graver course, then of a Poet, into which (that I may also keep my dignity) I would not seem to relapse" (*Letters*, p. 103).

As a consequence, aside from three brief commendatory poems and the elegy on the death of Prince Henry, included in the books of others, the only authorized printings of Donne's poems during his lifetime are the two *Anniversaries* on the death of Elizabeth Drury, with their accompanying "Funerall Elegie," which appeared successively in 1611 and 1612, probably at the instigation of Elizabeth's father Sir Robert Drury, Donne's patron at the time.[1] It is telling that even with these poems, Donne avoided acknowledging his authorship on the title pages; and in a letter to George Gerrard (or Garrard) dated April 14, 1612, he lamented their printing as a lapse in gentlemanly conduct, characterizing his decision to allow print publication as a kind of fall from grace: "Of my Anniversaries, the fault that I acknowledge in my self, is to have descended to print anything in verse, which though it have excuse even in our times, by men who professe, and practice much gravitie; yet I confesse I wonder how I declined to it, and do not pardon my self" (*Letters*, p. 238).

Two years later, when he was pressured by the Earl of Somerset (Sir Robert Ker), then one of his patrons, to print a collection of his poems before entering Holy Orders, Donne expressed the fear that such a general publication might offend another, long-time patron, the Countess of Bedford, and he vowed his determination to restrict the proposed book's distribution. Writing on December 20, 1614 to Goodyer, who had introduced him to the countess and who frequently acted as their go-between, Donne remarked,

> One thing more I must tell you; but so softly, that I am loath to hear my self: and so softly, that if that good Lady were in the room, with you and this Letter, she might not hear. I am brought to a necessity of printing my Poems, and addressing them to my L[ord] Chamberlain. This I mean to do forthwith; not for much publique view, but at mine own cost, a few Copies.   (*Letters*, pp. 196–97)

Although a collection of his poetry seemed fated to be set in type, Donne clearly intended to treat the distribution of its copies as one would that of manuscripts, not offering them in large numbers for sale to the commonalty, but giving them in limited numbers to members of an intimate coterie of friends, patrons, and prospective patrons. Apparently Donne somehow managed to avoid printing his poems altogether, for no publication from 1615 is known. During the rest of his life, his poetry continued to exist and circulate almost exclusively in manuscript.

Donne's attitude toward the print publication of his poetry is reflected in the fate of many of his prose pieces as well. Considering how many inches of library shelf space his prose now occupies, it is telling to realize that Donne allowed the printing of only nine prose works during his lifetime, and six of those were individual sermons, three of which were printed by royal command. Moreover, of those nine printed works, he acknowledged authorship on the title pages of only seven: *Devotions upon Emergent Occasions* (1624) and the six sermons (published separately and in various small collections between 1622 and 1627). The two early printed prose works were issued anonymously, *Pseudo-Martyr* in 1610 and *Ignatius his Conclave* in both Latin and English editions in 1611, though Donne's authorship of them was known by some of their readers at the time of their respective publications. All the rest of his prose works – *Paradoxes and Problems, Biathanatos, Essays in Divinity*, and a large body of letters and sermons – remained in manuscript throughout Donne's lifetime and were circulated, if at all, only in that medium and then only to a restricted few of his trusted friends and patrons.[2]

There were several reasons why Donne preferred manuscript rather than print publication for most of his works. First, there was the fear – mentioned earlier – of being known as a professional writer, or apparently even worse, a professional poet. Donne was ever mindful of his position among the gentry and the *gravitas* that he thought was expected of him in that position; and he did not want the opprobrium of being classed with popular versifiers in print, such as John Taylor the Water Poet, who were often the objects of ridicule in higher social circles.

It was, of course, fashionable for gentlemen of Donne's day to write verse, but only as a pleasant avocation, and to circulate it in manuscript to a selected audience. Indeed, such a practice often served as a kind of resumé sent to prospective employers. Young men at the universities and the Inns of Court were able to showcase their cleverness and intellectual acumen in that fashion, thereby recommending themselves for employment as secretaries to powerful magnates and important members of the royal court. But they ran the risk of annoying those prospective employers if they "descended to print" any of their writings, as Donne phrased it in his letter to Gerrard quoted earlier.

Second, in Donne's case there was the fact that several of his works – primarily though not exclusively early pieces – might be found objectionable on moral, political, or theological grounds by current or prospective patrons, up to and including the monarch himself. His elegies, some of which are explicit in their sexuality, his satires, some of which are politically questionable, and his sportive prose paradoxes, some of which are socially and morally outrageous, are cases in point.

Donne clearly recognized the possible danger in publishing these incautious works to a general audience, as is evidenced by a letter that he sent to his friend Henry Wotton in 1600. In that letter, he enclosed – apparently at Wotton's insistence – copies of some of his paradoxes, providing them, he protests, "Only in obedience." After dismissing the enclosed compositions as "nothings" that were "made rather to deceave tyme then her daughth[e]r truth," Donne implores Wotton to promise him, "upon the religion of your frendship that no coppy shalbee taken for any respect of these or any other compositions sent to you." He expresses his anxiety about the circulation of his work in terms of fear and shame, telling Wotton that "to my satyrs there belong some feare and to some elegies and these [i.e., the enclosed paradoxes] perhaps some shame."[3]

If Donne considered the print publication – indeed, any wide circulation – of his satires, elegies, and paradoxes potentially dangerous to his reputation and his prospects of employment, he certainly regarded the print publication of his treatise on suicide, *Biathanatos*, and to a lesser extent his *Essays in Divinity*, as unthinkable. To anyone contemplating a career in the Established Church, the liberal tolerance expressed in the latter was not apt to curry favour with either the staunchly anti-Roman Catholic George Abbot, then Archbishop of Canterbury, or King James. "[S]o Synagogue and Church is the same thing," Donne writes in Book II of the *Essays*, "and of the Church, *Roman* and *Reformed*, and all other distinctions of place, Discipline, or Person, but one Church, journeying to one *Heirusalem*, and directed by one guide, Christ Jesus" (*Essays in Divinity*, p. 51).

Even more theologically and morally suspect was Donne's *Biathanatos*, the treatise that has as its "Paradoxe, or Thesis, that *Selfe-homicide* is not so Naturally Sinne, that it may never be otherwise" (*Biathanatos* [1647], title-page). That Donne was frightened of what its print publication might to do his reputation, even after his death, is clear from a letter he wrote to accompany a manuscript copy of the treatise that he sent for safe keeping to Sir Robert Ker in 1619, just before accompanying Viscount Doncaster on a diplomatic mission to Germany. "It was written by me many years since," he explains,

> and because it is upon a misinterpretable subject, I have always gone so near suppressing it, as that it is onely not burnt: no hand hath passed upon it to copy it, nor many eyes to read it: onely to some particular friends in both Universities, then when I writ it, I did communicate it: And I remember, I had this answer, That certainly, there was a false thread in it, but not easily found: Keep it, I pray, with the same jealousie; let any that your discretion admits to the sight of it, know the date of it; and that it is a Book written by *Jack Donne*, and not by D[octor] *Donne*: Reserve it for me, if I live, and if I die, I only forbid it the Presse, and the Fire: publish it not, but yet burn it not; and between those, do what you will with it. (*Letters*, pp. 21–22)

Even as the mature Donne seeks to distance himself from *Biathanatos* by referring to it as a composition of the youthful, indiscreet Jack Donne, he nevertheless wishes to preserve the treatise. But because he fears that it might well be misinterpreted by ordinary readers if it were printed for general distribution, he resolves to restrict its readership by circulating it only in manuscript.

In addition to its preserving his status as an amateur gentleman author and guarding his reputation from censorious general readers, Donne also valued manuscript publication for aesthetic reasons, for its social cachet, and for the enjoyment he obviously found in personally circulating his works to specific friends and patrons.

He records his aesthetic preference for manuscripts over printed books in a Latin verse letter to one Dr. Andrews, a medical doctor otherwise unidentified. Englished by H. W. Garrod, the poem reads in part:

> What the printing-presses bring to birth with inky travail we take as it comes;
> but what is written out by hand is in greater reverence.
>
> ...
>
> A book which, if it has been baptised merely in the blood of the printing-press,
> goes to shelves resigned to moth and dust;
> let it but come to us written by the pen, and it is received with reverence and
> wings its way to the high-perched cases which shrine the ancient Fathers.
>
> (1–2, 5–8)[4]

Donne's remarks to Dr. Andrews express the social cachet of possessing manuscript rather than printed copies of works. One of the chief attractions of manuscripts lay in their personal, human quality. Unlike printed books machine-generated in hundreds of virtually identical copies, each manuscript book was individually crafted, and no two were exactly alike. In addition, each was considerably more expensive to produce than a printed volume of comparable size. As a consequence, handwritten books were thought by many to be more prestigious than printed ones. As Peter Beal observes, "The reader who got hold of an expensive handwritten text felt in some measure that he was privy to coveted and restricted access to the work in question; he was an 'insider,' part of some unclearly defined coterie, or privileged network, of select readers of that kind of literature."[5]

Finally, as is evidenced by many of his surviving letters, Donne enjoyed sending his works in manuscript to selected friends and receiving their reactions to them. Such acts were obviously a major component in his "religion" of friendship, as expressed in the letter to Wotton quoted earlier. Over the years, there were multiple, often overlapping coteries to whom Donne sent selected works in both prose and poetry; and the membership of each was fluid, some members dropping out and others joining as time passed and as the nature of Donne's works changed. First, there was the coterie of friends dating from his years at Oxford and at the Inns of Court, his service with the Earl of Essex, and his employment with Lord Keeper Egerton. Its members were mostly young men like Donne himself with whom he was on intimate terms. Second, there was also a circle of poets and lovers of poetry who were probably Donne's acquaintances rather than his close friends. Then, after his career prospects were dashed by his imprudent marriage, Donne entered the patronage culture of his age with some urgency and developed a circle of patrons and prospective patrons among the gentry and the aristocracy to whom he sent selected works to curry favor and monetary rewards.[6]

From the surviving artifactual evidence, it is clear that many of these original recipients of his manuscript poetry and prose either made additional copies themselves or had copies made by scribes of various levels of competency for further distribution to their friends and acquaintances, and so continued – and complicated – their textual transmission.

If Donne had himself kept copies of all of his poetry and prose, in most or all of their successive revisions, and if, after his death, those authorial copies had been supplied to the printers preparing the posthumous publications of his works, we as readers could rest assured that, with the exception of the imposition of printing house styling in punctuation, italicization, and spelling, the earliest printings of them represent fairly accurately what Donne actually wrote. In fact, while he must have preserved either autograph copies or personally corrected scribal copies of some of his prose works, notably *Biathanatos*, *Essays in Divinity*, eighty or more sermons, and many letters, unfortunately few of them have survived, and the extent of the tampering done to the texts of those lost manuscripts either by Donne's son as editor or by their early printers cannot easily be identified.

With his poetry, the situation is even more complicated. At the time of his death, Donne apparently had in his possession no complete collection of his poetry and, aside from Latin verses inscribed in two printed books, a copy of his Latin epitaph for his wife, and the copy of a verse epistle that he sent to Lady Carey, no poetical manuscripts in his own hand survive. What do survive, in addition to dozens of copies of individual poems and many small collections, are some thirty major collections of his poetry in manuscript (though none containing the complete canon), transcribed by or for collectors of his verse at various removes from his now lost autograph copies and in several different and textually differing lines of transmission.

Unfortunately, when the first collection of Donne's poems was printed in 1633, two years after his death, the compiler and printer had at their disposal textually corrupted manuscript collections on which to base that first printing. The second edition of Donne's *Poems* (1635) draws upon additional manuscript sources, from different lines of transmission, augmenting and altering the texts printed in 1633; and the final seventeenth-century edition (1669) reflects both the use of still other manuscript collections and editorial alterations made on no manuscript authority as it further augments the canon and modernizes spelling. Clearly, then, transmission primarily through manuscripts has complicated the editorial task of discovering and restoring what Donne actually wrote.

A major feature of manuscript transmission is its lack of stability in canon, attribution, and text. For an author, the fluidity of manuscript has both advantages and disadvantages, both allowing and diminishing authorial control. On the one hand, manuscript transmission allows an author ongoing control of a work. He or she can, for example, tailor individual copies of the same piece to suit changing circumstances and specific recipients. He or she can add to, subtract from, and rearrange canon as often as desired. Even after a work has begun to circulate, a manuscript author can feel free to revise the text at will, experiencing none of the inhibition that a print author may feel toward changing a work once it has been set into type and distributed in hundreds of identical copies.

On the other hand, however, manuscript transmission allows for none of the overall, permanent control that an author can find in print. In manuscript, even multiple copies of the same work personally prepared by the author can and nearly always do differ in details; and once a work leaves the physical possession of its author, it is open to virtually infinite non-authorial variation at the hands of selective, inattentive, or officious copyists.

A copyist may, for example, omit or change attribution, omit or rearrange individual pieces within a composite work, or augment one author's work with pieces drawn from another – all of these actions affecting canon. In addition, a copyist inevitably tampers with the text being transmitted. If the original being copied is unclear or ambiguous, the copyist may misread and consequently mistranscribe words or punctuation marks. If the scribe does not understand the meaning of a difficult passage, he or she may rewrite it to make the meaning immediately evident, a practice termed "trivialization" by textual editors. If the scribe disapproves of what an author has written – on moral, theological, political, or any other grounds – he or she may silently alter the text to conform to his or her own sense of propriety. And if the copyist considers himself or herself to be a competent author as well as a transmitter, he or she may decide to "improve" the text's wording, punctuation, or meter. Or a copyist may, simply through haste or carelessness, make any number of mistakes in transcription. Over all these deliberate or inadvertent changes in attribution, canon, ordering, and text, the author has absolutely no control. As a consequence, there is in scribal transmission little of the sense of a definitively established canon and text that one can experience in the medium of print publication.

Scribal tampering is discoverable throughout Donne's canon, in both prose and poetry. Apparently, his contemporaries who collected poetry and prose and wrote them into their personal manuscript anthologies often vied with each other for works by well-known public figures. Especially after he became Doctor Donne and Dean of St. Paul's, some of those collectors attached Donne's name to all manner of anonymously circulated prose and poetry to enhance the prestige of their miscellanies, especially, in Donne's case, if those works might be considered beneath the dignity of such an august churchman. Many of those spurious attributions are easily exposed, but some cannot be so confidently dismissed.

For example, Donne's authorship of the bitingly satirical "Julia" and the sardonic "Tale of a Citizen and his Wife" are still the subject of debate. Both were first printed in the second edition of Donne's *Poems* (1635) but are included in only a very few of the thirty surviving large manuscript collections of his poetry ("Julia" in four and the complete "Citizen" in three), making the bibliographical evidence for Donne's composition of them inconclusive. As a consequence, depending on which modern edition of Donne's poetry one consults, these two poems may be included as either canonical or of doubtful authorship, or they may be excluded entirely.

The same problem exists with several of the brief prose works attributed to Donne in manuscript collections and in the posthumous *Paradoxes, Problems, Essayes, Characters, Written by Dr Donne Dean of Pauls* (1652), a volume prepared for the press by Donne's son. In her edition of Donne's *Paradoxes and Problems* (1980), Helen Peters labels as "dubia" two of the twelve paradoxes, the two characters, and the essay attributed to Donne in the 1652 collection. In addition, she increases the canon with two problems surviving only in manuscript copies, and she prints two versions each of three of the problems. Not everyone, however, will agree with her editorial decisions.[7]

Another problem inherent in manuscript transmission concerns the contents and arrangement of a composite work. Nowhere can that difficulty be more strikingly illustrated than in the textual fate of Donne's *Holy Sonnets*. All but one of the large manuscript collections that contain the *Holy Sonnets* present them in a sequence of twelve poems, but they do so in two distinct forms. These two manuscript sequences have eight sonnets in common, but each has four not present in the other, and their ordering differs. To further complicate their textual history, the editor of the 1633 *Poems*, using one strand of the manuscript transmission, printed one of these twelve-poem sequences, whereas the editor of the 1635 edition consulted another strand, and finding four different poems in its sequence of *Holy Sonnets*, inserted them at different points among the twelve printed in 1633, thereby creating a sixteen-poem sequence.

This augmented 1635 sequence of the *Holy Sonnets* was reprinted in all of the subsequent seventeenth-century editions of Donne's poetry, and its contents and ordering were followed by most of Donne's editors during the nineteenth and twentieth centuries. The early manuscript transmission, however, points toward authorial revision. After its initial circulation in a twelve-poem sequence (which has yet to be printed as such),[8] Donne revised the *Holy Sonnets* by discarding four of the poems in the original twelve, replacing them with four new poems, and reordering the whole (creating the sequence printed in 1633). The 1635 sequence of sixteen sonnets never existed as such prior to that date, four years after Donne's death.

Instances of verbal variants abound in the early manuscript and printed sources of Donne's poetry, and it is often difficult to decide which are scribal corruptions and which may be authorial revisions. Moreover, in making those decisions, one cannot rely solely on the number of early witnesses for each reading. A case in point occurs in copies of one of Donne's most popular holy sonnets, the one beginning "At the round earths imagin'd corners." In the catalogue of agencies that cause death (6–7), the seventeenth-century editions of Donne's *Poems* and all of the surviving early manuscripts save one read the second agent as "death" itself, creating the awkward repetition that death causes death: "All whom warre, death, age, agues, tyrannies / Despaire, law, chance, hath slaine" (*Poems* [1633], p. 34). Only in the Westmoreland manuscript, written in the hand of Donne's friend Rowland Woodward and the surviving artifact closest to an autograph copy of the poem, does one find the reading "dearth" (for "death") in line 6.[9] Very early in the poem's manuscript transmission, a scribe must have either misread "dearth" as "death" or experienced an eye-skip to "deaths" in line 8 and, as a consequence, created a corruption of the text that was repeated throughout the rest of the poem's early transmission, first in manuscript and subsequently in print. Even though they each used an early printed source of this sonnet as their copy-text, all of Donne's twentieth-century editors accepted the Westmoreland manuscript's "dearth" as the authorial reading and emended their reading texts accordingly.

A verbal variant of a different kind – one that significantly affects our interpretation of the poem – occurs in the early artifacts of one of Donne's most popular elegies, the one beginning "Come, Madame, come" and commonly headed "To his Mistress going to bed." This seduction poem is obviously one of the poems to which Donne was alluding when he warned Wotton that to "some" of his elegies there belonged "some shame." Indeed, the poem was considered so scandalous by the licenser of the 1633 *Poems* that he "excepted" (i.e., rejected) it for publication in that volume, and it was not printed among Donne's poems until the edition of 1669. In urging his mistress to undress and come to bed, the speaker argues that, in doing so, "There is no penance, much lesse innocence" or "There is no penance due to innocence" (46). This is a significant variant, for its wording is a major determining factor in the reader's attitude toward the sexual act that one expects to follow. The sardonic former statement – there is no penance for, and certainly no innocence in, what we are about to do – supports the idea that the woman spoken to is either a bawd or a married woman being urged to commit adultery. The variant statement – what we are about to do is innocent and therefore requires no penance – supports the idea that the speaker is coaxing his new bride into the nuptial bed. If they are married, their sexual union is indeed innocent, necessitating no penance.

Approximately one-third of the early manuscripts (including the authoritative Westmoreland manuscript) have the former reading of the line, while two-thirds (and the printing in the 1669 *Poems*) have some form of the latter. Most of Donne's twentieth-century editors have followed the 1669 text, printing "due to" in line 46. A few, however, have accepted the "much less" version of the line as Donne's original wording and have seen the "due to" version as an attempt – either by choice or through necessity – to make the poem more acceptable by suggesting that the couple are married. It is instructive to note that although their texts have never been printed in full in an edition of Donne's poetry, seventeen of the early scribal copies of the elegy that have the "due to" reading in line 46 transfer lines 31 and 32 – "To enter in these bonds is to be free, / Then where my hand is sett, my seale shalbee" – to stand just before line 46, strengthening the idea that the couple are joined in the bonds of matrimony. It is also of interest that the copy of the elegy in the Bridgewater manuscript – which reads "due to" in line 46 but does not move lines 31–32 – has this note written in the margin, keyed to the phrase "enter in these bonds": "why may not a man write his owne Epithalamion if he can doe it so modestly."[10]

Verbal variants that are likely or possibly authorial in origin are to be found throughout the early artifacts of Donne's poetry. Three examples can show something of their nature. In "A Lecture upon the Shadow," for instance, the speaker remarks that a love that must be diligently hidden from others either "hath not attaind the *least* degree" or "hath not attain'd the *high'st* degree" (12, emphasis supplied), depending on which manuscript source one consults. Such a variant reflects a major difference in emphasis. "The good-morrow" has two different conclusions in the textual sources. Copies in the 1633 *Poems* and in several of the manuscripts read the final couplet "If our two loves be one, or, thou and I / Love so alike, that none doe slacken, none can die" (lines 20–21). Copies in other manuscripts and in the 1635–69 *Poems*, however, read the concluding couplet "If our two loves be one, both thou and I / Love just alike in all, none of these loves can die." Finally, Donne's famous "Hymne to God the Father" exists in three distinct versions in the early sources. In two of those versions, the poem is addressed to Christ, not God, and concludes "And hauing donne that, thou has donne / I *haue* no more" (17–18, emphasis supplied), whereas the version addressed to God reads the final line "I *feare* no more." The most striking difference in text occasioned by the change in the poem's addressee occurs in lines 15 and 16, however. In the two versions addressed to Christ, those lines read "Sweare by thy selfe that, at my death, thy [*or* this] *Sunne* / Shall shine as *it* shines now and heretofore" (emphasis supplied). The version addressed to God allows a more explicit statement of the ubiquitous Son/Sun pun: "But sweare by thy selfe, that at my death thy *sonne* / Shall shine as *he* shines now, and heretofore."[11]

The modern reader, accustomed to the relative fixity of print publication, must be willing to accept a different attitude toward text when reading Donne. When there are successively different texts of a work of an author who writes for print publication, the reader assumes that the author is striving toward an ideal statement of his or her conception, a "final" text intended to replace and indeed to cancel those that preceded it. With a coterie writer, such as Donne, who published almost exclusively in manuscript, however, different authorial texts may not inevitably represent the progress toward an "ideal" text (though of course in some cases they may). Instead, they may reflect different concepts of a work written at different times under different circumstances, and all may have been considered by their author to be of more or less equal value. As Harold Love declares, "Versions produced in this way do not so much replace as augment each other."[12] Modern readers then must readjust their thinking about what constitutes a "work," not invariably conceiving of it as a single text (and successive revisions of it therefore as merely strivings toward that ultimate text), but instead conceiving of a "work" as a *series* of authorial texts in which changes have been made either simply for the sake of change or as ongoing adaptations to the expectations of specific readers.

Reading the texts of a manuscript writer such as Donne, then, demands attention to the variant readings found in the early manuscript copies. Many of those variants may be scribal blunders, trivializations, or "improvements"; fortunately, a knowledge of the kind of changes that seventeenth-century scribes made as they copied texts can aid in identifying most of them as nonauthorial corruptions. But in other cases, variants in text may very well represent different conceptualizations of a work entertained at different times by the author. Not everyone will agree on the extent or the exact nature of authorial revision represented in works circulated in manuscript, but the careful reader should always be sensitive to the fluidity of those texts and hesitant to accept any single text as "the" text.

NOTES

1 For bibliographical information on the publications issued during Donne's lifetime, see Geoffrey Keynes, *A Bibliography of Dr. John Donne Dean of Saint Paul's*, 4th edn. (Oxford: Clarendon Press, 1973), passim. For the individual poems and poem fragments published during his lifetime, see Ernest W. Sullivan, II, *The Influence of John Donne: His Uncollected Seventeenth-Century Printed Verse* (Columbia: University of Missouri Press, 1993), pp. 55–96.

2 For the extant early manuscripts of Donne's poetry and prose, see Peter Beal (comp.), *Index of Literary Manuscripts*, vol. 1, 1450–1625 (London: Mansell, 1980), pt. 1, pp. 243–564, 566–68.

3 Leicestershire Record Office MS DG7/Lit.2 (Burley MS), ff. 308v–309.

4 H. W. Garrod, "The Latin Poem Addressed by Donne to Dr. Andrews," *RES* 21 (1945), 40.

5 Peter Beal, *In Praise of Scribes: Manuscripts and Their Makers in Seventeenth-Century England* (Oxford: Clarendon Press, 1998), p. 19.

6 See, e.g., Ted-Larry Pebworth, "The Early Audiences of Donne's Poetic Performances," *JDJ* 15 (1996), 127–39.

7 Helen Peters (ed.), Textual Introduction, *Paradoxes and Problems* (Oxford: Clarendon Press, 1980), pp. l–xcvii.

8 This initial twelve-poem sequence will be printed as such in the *Holy Sonnets* volume of Gary A. Stringer (gen. ed.), *The Variorum Edition of the Poetry of John Donne* (Bloomington: Indiana University Press, in press).

9 New York Public Library, Berg Collection, Westmoreland MS, f. [34]v.

10 Huntington Library MS EL 6893 (Bridgewater MS), f. 106v.

11 For the three versions of the hymn, see Ted-Larry Pebworth, "The Editor, the Critic, and the Multiple Texts of Donne's 'Hymne to God the Father,'" *South Central Review* 4.2 (Summer 1987), 16–34. See also Pebworth, "Manuscript Poems and Print Assumptions: Donne and His Modern Editors," *JDJ* 3.1 (1984), 1–21.

12 Harold Love, *Scribal Publication in Seventeenth-Century England* (Oxford: Clarendon Press, 1993), p. 53.

3

ARTHUR F. MAROTTI

The social context and nature of Donne's writing: occasional verse and letters

John Donne preferred known readers for his writing and, at least initially, controlled its dissemination in the manuscript medium.[1] Almost all of his poetry and a great deal of his prose were composed for restricted audiences in a series of social environments in which he functioned through his secular and ecclesiastical careers. These included the Inns of Court and London in the 1590s; the late-Elizabethan court and government during his service as a secretary to the Lord Keeper, Sir Thomas Egerton, from 1598 to 1602; the early Jacobean social circle surrounding his patroness Lucy, Countess of Bedford; the single-sex environment of politically active men associated with the meetings at the Mitre and Mermaid taverns;[2] and the socially mixed environment of the Jacobean and Caroline courts. He circulated his work in manuscript both as single items and as groups of texts. For example, he sent individual verse epistles to friends and patronesses. He enclosed prose paradoxes or problems in some of his letters; in others sermons.[3] He let his close friend Ben Jonson forward his five satires to the Countess of Bedford, and he himself gave some of his holy sonnets, along with a complimentary poem, to the Earl of Dorset. He allowed such friends as Henry Goodyer and Sir Robert Ker to see large collections of his poetry.[4] Although Donne regularly showed his writing to individuals within the social circles to which he belonged, in the processes of manuscript transmission his poems only really reached a wider audience in the 1620s, eagerly received by students at both universities and by others compiling manuscript anthologies of verse.[5]

In his letters Donne often enjoined his friends not to allow copies of what he sent them to be made. When he sent some of his work to Sir Henry Wotton, he asked that Wotton accept the restrictions he wanted on its circulation:

> Only in obedience I send you some of my paradoxes ... Yet Sir though I know
> their low price, except I receive by your next letter an assurance upon the

religion of your friendship that no coppy shalbee taken for any respect of these or any other my compositions sent to you, I shall sinn against my conscience if I send you any more ... I meane to acquaint you with all myne [writings]: and to my satyrs there belongs some feare and to some elegies, and these perhaps, shame. Against both which affections although I be tough enough, yet I have a ridling disposition to bee ashamed of feare and afraid of shame. Therefore I am desirous to hyde them with out any over reconing of them or their maker. But they are not worth thus much words in theyre disprayse.[6]

Donne's final stance is one of aristocratic *sprezzatura*, but, as an ambitious government servant hoping for further preferment, he was genuinely afraid that his youthful recreational writing would embarrass him by getting out to a wider audience. Ben Jonson said of the later Donne that "since he was made Doctor [he] repenteth highlie and seeketh to destroy all his poems."[7]

The more democratic readership of printed literature was not one Donne desired for most of his work. Donne was well aware of the "stigma of print,"[8] which applied more clearly to imaginative writing, particularly poetry, than to non-fictional prose. In defense of the Jacobean Oath of Allegiance, Donne published *Pseudo-Martyr* (1610) and *Ignatius his Conclave* (1611). In publishing sermons and *Devotions upon Emergent Occasions* (1623), Donne assumed public authority through the medium of print. But, at least in that portion of his career before he became an ecclesiastical spokesperson for Church and monarch, he was a private author functioning within the world of script.

I focus in this chapter on the verse epistles and prose letters, texts that stretch chronologically throughout Donne's adult life. These works are rooted in his deeply held beliefs about interpersonal communication and about the social functions of writing, even as they engage in intense forms of self-scrutiny. From them we can develop a sense of the social networks in which Donne and his work were enmeshed and of the social and political contexts of his writing. When discussing the verse epistles, I distinguish between poems addressed to social equals or friends and poems written to social superiors, usually patronesses. In the first case, the rhetorical decorum is that of the humanist familiar letter. In the second, Donne renegotiated the terms of the rhetoric of complement[9] to turn the occasion of addressing a socially superior person into one in which he could assume a moral and cultural authority and an independence that, strictly speaking, clashed with the subservient stance he adopted.

The verse epistle was one of the new poetic forms Donne attempted in the 1590s. After entering Lincoln's Inn, Donne found himself, at the age of twenty, in an intellectually and culturally rich environment with access to both the pleasures and the opportunities of London and the court. Here he composed verse letters to male friends, cultivating his own role as poet and attempting to stimulate communal verse composition. One of the best surviving manuscripts of Donne's work, the Westmoreland manuscript,[10] was written in the hand of Rowland Woodward, to whom he addressed several of these poems and whose younger brother was the recipient of several others. It preserves a set of early verse epistles to male friends in a larger collection of Donne's writing grouped by genre. Collectively, these verse epistles define a group of young men with whom Donne felt he shared intellectual, poetic, and sociopolitical aspirations.

During the sonnet craze of the 1590s, Donne, like William Shakespeare and Richard Barnfield, used the form to celebrate affectionate friendship between men. One critic has argued that these poems are homoerotic.[11] In his lyric poetry, Donne avoided the sonnet form for expressing heterosexual desire – though in two of these early epistolary sonnets he refers, with Petrarchan language, to a woman whom he calls "the Saint of his Affection" ("To Mr C. B." ["Thy friend, whom thy deserts"], 3), distinguishing heterosexual love from friendship. In "To Mr I. L." ("Blest are your North parts"), Donne refers to his beloved's staying with his friend. But Donne also used Petrarchan language in his poems to men, for example in the four epistles to Thomas Woodward.

The verse letters to Thomas Woodward, Rowland Woodward, Everard Guilpin, Henry Wotton, Beaupré Bell, Christopher Brooke, Samuel Brooke, and the yet-unidentifed "I. L." have some features in common. Several appeal to a shared interest in writing poetry. Donne addresses an encomiastic epistle to Thomas Woodward ("To Mr T. W." ["All haile sweet Poet"], 1) whose verse, he says, is superior to his. In another epistle he adopts the same humble stance ("To Mr T. W." ["Hast thee harsh verse"], 1). He addressed a short (six-couplet) poem to Rowland Woodward that assumes a shared devotion to "the Muse" ("To Mr R. W." ["Muse not that by thy Mind"], 8) and requests a poem in return. Another epistle to the same friend ("Kindly I envy thy songs perfection") suggests that the verse exchange between friends actually took place. In "To Mr E[verard] G[uilpin]" ("Even as lame things"), he calls Highgate "that Parnassus, where thou art" (4). Donne advises Samuel Brooke to "wisely take / Fresh water at the Heliconian spring" ("To Mr S. B." ["O Thou which to search out the secret parts"], 7–8) for he sees in this friend "bright sparkes of Poetry" (12). He refers to the "Muse" of another friend ("To Mr I. L." ["Of that short Roll of friends"], 13). In "To B[eaupré] B[ell]" ("Is not thy sacred hunger of science"), he refers to mutual verse composition.

The two famous verse letters to Donne's Lincoln's Inn friend Christopher Brooke, "The Storme" and "The Calme," written on the occasion of Donne's serving as a gentleman-volunteer on an ill-fated expedition to intercept the

Spanish treasure fleet in the Azores, belong to a period of transition from the Inns environment to that of court employment. In these self-critical, reflective epistles, Donne treats his friend as an alter ego ("Thou which art I" ["The Storme," 1]), as someone able to read between the lines of the poems to appreciate the depth of his personal disillusionment and his critical attitudes toward the world of social and political ambition. It is not surprising that these two pieces came to be circulated with Donne's *Satires.*

The verse letter "To Mr Rowland Woodward" ("Like one who'in her third widowhood") was probably written after Donne entered the employment of Sir Thomas Egerton. It can be grouped, along with "The Storme" and "The Calme," with a series of more mature verse letters to male friends in which Donne reflects on moral issues and comments on the political world in which he became involved. Here Donne complains about his ceasing to write poetry ("So'affects my muse now, a chast fallownesse" [3]), but he also expresses the serious man of business's rejection of two kinds of verse he had already composed: "love-song weeds, and Satyrique thornes" (5). Although, like other Inns of Court poets, Donne had tried to adapt to his contemporary world such ancient forms as the Ovidian love elegy, the formal verse satire, and the epigram, the socially iconoclastic content of such verse obviously worried him later. Active, virtuous engagement in the world, in the context of the contemporary prejudice against poetry as the "idle toys" of young men, demands a rejection of both amorous lyrics and satires. In the epistle to Woodward, he admits to an ongoing attraction to "Poetrie" (7), but he adopts a Christian stoic stance: "There is no Vertue, but Religion" (16); "Seeke wee then our selves in our selves" (19). The verse letter, with its moral, philosophical, and religious subject matter, is portrayed as a superior form.

At the end of the Elizabethan and the beginning of the Jacobean era, Donne wrote four verse epistles to Henry Wotton reflecting on his politically active friend's moral functioning in the public world. In all the verse (and prose) epistles to men, Donne treats friendship as the enabling condition for deep communication. The first of the poems to Wotton begins "Sir, more then kisses, letters mingle Soules." This poem is part of a game of competitive versifying in which a group of young men connected to the Earl of Essex engaged around 1598, a time when both Donne and Wotton were becoming active in Court circles. Donne uses the occasion to comment on the three environments in which he was involved ("Countries, Courts, Towns" [8]). He is worried about the corrupting process in which a "Utopian youth" is "growne old Italian" (46). In telling Wotton "dwell" "in thy selfe" (47) and purge the bad rather than use "[a] dramme of Countries dulnesse" (61) to correct "Courts hot ambitions" (60), Donne adopts the stance of the moral advisor – which he then renounces by stating "I advise not you, I rather doe / Say o'er those lessons, which I learn'd of you" (63–64). He ends the poem by complimenting Wotton for surviving European travels and keeping intact till his return "that faith" (68) he had when he left England. In the context of a friendship that may have begun at Hart Hall, Oxford, Donne is free to speak frankly to Wotton without worrying about giving offense. Of course, the ludic nature of the competitive versifying turns some of Donne's moral posturing into high comedy.

In the second epistle to Wotton ("Here's no more newes, then virtue"), dated July 20, 1598 in the Westmoreland manuscript, Donne says "I haunt Court, or Towne" (6), taking a cynical view of the public world of politics: "Suspitious boldnesse to this place belongs" (16). He treats courtiers' behavior as the actions of "mimicke antiques" (22), concluding the poem with the salutation "*At Court*; though *From Court*, were the better stile" (27). Donne also wrote a verse epistle to Wotton while the latter was serving with the Earl of Essex in the late 1590s on the ill-fated Irish expedition, "H. W.*in Hiber. belligeranti*," a poem that places their friendship above the advancement Wotton pursued in following his patron/employer to the wars. A final verse epistle to Wotton was written several years later, "To Sir H. W., at his going Ambassador to Venice." Both Wotton's and Donne's fortunes had altered by this time – Wotton having survived the fall of Essex, was given an important diplomatic post, and Donne, after Sir Thomas Egerton fired him at the urging of the father of the woman with whom he had eloped, had lost his court employment. Married for over two years, with a growing family and poor prospects for new employment, Donne both congratulates his friend and refers to his own disastrous circumstances.

Donne's closest friend in the early Jacobean era was Sir Henry Goodyer. Only one verse letter to him survives, but we have a large number of prose letters from Donne to Goodyer in which the poet shared some of his deepest thoughts and feelings. In the poetic epistle to Goodyer ("Who makes the Past"), written at a time the addressee seems to have been in some self-created financial difficulties, Donne aggressively adopts the role of advisor-friend. The other verse letter involving Goodyer is "A Letter written by Sir H. G. and J. D. *alternis vicibus*," a twelve-stanza complimentary verse epistle collaboratively written at Goodyer's Polesworth estate and sent to two women of station.

Donne shared a friendship with Sir Edward Herbert, George Herbert's brother and the son of a woman to whom Donne was close for many years, Magdalen Herbert, Lady Danvers. This relationship produced not only competitive versifying, but also a verse letter sent to Herbert when he was in military service in France, "To Sir Edward Herbert, at Julyers."

Deliberately appealing to Herbert's philosophical interests, this poem finally compliments its addressee as a model of virtue in action.

Donne's surviving prose letters, the vast majority of which were written to men, register a high degree of self-consciousness about the genre. In fact, they delineate a theory of epistolary communication that applies to much of Donne's other writing. Especially in writing to such close friends as Goodyer and George Garrard, Donne allowed himself to reflect metacommunicatively on the epistolary medium in order to define the artifact he was creating and his desired relationship with his addressees. The letter, for Donne, most closely approached his dream of perfect communication: "this writing of letters ... is a kind of extasie, and a departure and secession and suspension of the soul, which doth then communicate it self to two bodies" (*Letters*, p. 11).

Donne was aware that the letter was an open genre, allowing the writer to engage in various activities, including meditation, theological and philosophical speculation, moral persuasion or homiletic exhortation, petitioning, historical narration, and the relaying of news. However, he often characterizes the contents of his letters as "nothing." He made his relationship to his closest friends the central subject of his missives. In one letter to Goodyer he says:

> I Send not my Letters as tribute, nor interest, nor recompense, nor for commerce, nor as testimonials of my love, nor provokers of yours, nor to justifie my custome of writing, nor for a vent and utterance of my meditations; for my Letters are either above or under all such offices ... onely I am sure that I desire that you might have in your hands Letters of mine of all kinds, as conveyances and deliverers of me to you ...   (*Letters*, pp. 109–10)

Donne puts the emphasis not on what is said but on how his letters sustain friendship, which he calls a "second religion" (*Letters*, p. 85). In a letter to Goodyer, he says "I have placed my love wisely where I need communicate nothing" (*Letters*, p. 115).

"Nothing" is one of Donne's favorite words. In times of illness, depression or poor career prospects, he refers to himself as "nothing." When bothered about his lack of employment, Donne wrote Goodyer:

> ... to be no part of any body, is to be nothing. At most, the greatest persons, are but great wens, and excrescences; men of wit and delightfull conversation, but as moales for ornament, except they be so incorporated into the body of the world, that they contribute something to the sustentation of the whole. This I made account that I begun early, when I understood the study of our laws: but was diverted by the worst voluptuousness, which is an Hydroptique immoderate desire of humane learning and languages: beautifull ornaments to great

fortunes; but mine needed an occupation, and a course which I thought I entred well into … And there I stumbled too, yet I would try again: for to this hour I am nothing, or so little, that I am scarce subject and argument good enough for one of mine own letters: yet I fear, that doth not ever proceed from a good root, that I am so well content to be lesse, that is dead.   (*Letters*, pp. 51–52)

Reading such a letter, we should not be surprised that its author penned a long treatise on suicide.

Unlike most contemporary correspondence, Donne's letters are surprisingly short on "news."[12] In one letter to Goodyer he says what he writes is "so empty of any relations, as that they oppresse not your meditations, nor discourse, nor memory" (*Letters*, p. 120). Donne had an aversion to relaying news. He teases Goodyer in one letter: "I would write you newes; but your love to me, may make you apt to over-beleeve news for my sake. And truly all things that are upon the stage of the world now, are full of such uncertainties, as may justly make any man loth to passe a conjecture upon them …" (*Letters*, p. 199). This does not, however, keep him from occasionally relaying insider gossip and commenting on current events.[13] Generally speaking, however, there is dearth of topical allusions, gossip, and ephemeral detail in Donne's epistolary writing.

Occasionally Donne allowed himself to write about personal matters. For example, in a 1607 letter to Goodyer written the night his wife delivered one of their many children, he confessed: "It is … the saddest lucubration and nights passage that ever I had. For it exercised those hours, which, with extreme danger of her, whom I should hardly have abstained from recompensing for her company in this world, with accompanying her out of it, encreased my poor family with a son" (*Letters*, p. 147). He sometimes discussed his own and his family's illnesses, as well as his own bouts of depression.[14] He alludes in another letter to Goodyer to the domestic scene in which he writes one missive:

> I write not to you out of my poor Library … But I write from the fire side in my Parler, and in the noise of three gamesome children; and by the side of her, whom because I have transplanted into a wretched fortune, I must labour to disguise that from her by all such honest devices as giving her my company, and discourse, therefore I steal from her, all the time which I give this Letter, and it is therefore that I take so short a list, and gallop so fast over it, I have not been out of my house since I received your pacquet.   (*Letters*, pp. 137–38)

This sort of social positioning of writing in a realistic setting resembles that of the later epistolary novel.

Often Donne characterized the contents of his letters as his "meditations" (*Letters*, p. 78). Not surprisingly, Donne's letters contain some of his most uninhibited ecumenical and skeptical thoughts on religion.[15] In one of the early letters to this friend, Donne expressed confidence in his correspondent's receptivity to deep speculations: "my meditations are neither too wide nor too deep for you, except onely that my way of expressing them may be extended beyond your patience and pardon" (Letters, p. 19). Sometimes he regarded himself as engaging in a stronger form of didacticism and making his letters virtual homilies or sermons.[16]

We find some of Donne's most reflective and philosophical pieces of writing not only in his prose letters, but also in his verse epistles. In the encomiastic context of patronage poetry, Donne demonstrates the same intellectual intensity we find in many of the letters to male friends. These complimentary verse letters are still among the least studied of Donne's poems. Put off by encomiastic hyperboles and by the social decorum of the hierarchical relationships many of them foreground, modern readers have generally found little to admire in these works. In response to the challenge of formulating a satisfactory critical approach to these poems, some scholars have connected their encomiastic rhetoric with the social relationships the poems mediated, revealing some of the interesting stresses and frictions that enlivened these texts for both the author and his readers.

Donne addressed eight encomiastic verse epistles to Lucy, Countess of Bedford, the patroness to whom he was introduced by Goodyer and with whom he had an ongoing relationship of clientage for many years (particularly in the period from 1607 to his ordination in 1615).[17] Lady of the Bedchamber and closest friend of Queen Anne, she was a Jacobean power-broker to whom Donne looked for help in repairing his ruined career prospects in the years following his marriage. In forming a social relationship with her, Donne entered the social circle of her friends and clients, including Goodyer, Garrard, and Sir Thomas Roe, as well as Cecilia Bulstrode, Jane Meautis, and Lady Markham. Donne used Goodyer as an intermediary, sending him poems and letters to be delivered to the Countess and arranging it so that she would see some of the letters he wrote to his friend.

Donne praised Lady Bedford for her virtues, beauty, and learning, elevating her above the social context of the Jacobean court to treat her as a symbol of transcendent values. Although his decision to write verse epistles to her and to other upper-class women required him to adopt a deferential stance, Donne subverted these conditions and asserted his own intellectual and moral authority. Often patently pushing his encomiastic language over the top, he incorporated sharp commentary and intellectual complexities in his poems, taking a critical view of the corrupt world in which his addressees and his acts of praise were situated. He characteristically put himself as a rational thinker at the center of the poems and constructed complex metaphors and arguments, subjecting his reader to his intellectual, moral, and literary authority. Donne constructed in his encomiastic verse letters contradictory portrayals of the self and the social establishment, defining the self as simultaneously autonomous and socially dependent, on the one hand, and the person praised as inherently good and as worthy only because of social contingencies.[18]

In his first poem to the Countess, "Reason is our Soules left hand," Donne signals his awareness of the ability of his addressee to benefit him socially, politically, and economically, but he also comes across as a strong-minded person unwilling to abase himself totally in order to flatter the great. Though inflating his rhetoric of praise, calling Lady Bedford "The first good Angell, since the worlds frame stood / That ever did in womans shape appeare" (31–32), he alludes to the morally perilous court in praising her "learning and religion, / And virtue" (25–26) as protection against "what can be done or said" (28). He introduces an ethical perspective that puts in question her ability to remain untainted by her surroundings – even as he sustains rhetorically the polite gestures of compliment.

In "You have refin'd mee," when Donne calls the court "not vertues clime" (7), he insists on the Countess's transcendent virtue, as well as her religion and beauty, but he asserts that she needs someone like him to interpret her good qualities ("darke texts need notes" [11]), just as in another epistle ("Honour is so sublime perfection"), he argues (subversively) that prominent persons need those below them to attribute "honor" to them before they can possess it.[19] He employs witty religious metaphors to express his response to Lady Bedford's "vertuous Soule" (32), but then admits that his assertions about her "Tast of Poetique rage, or flattery" (63). In the last stanza of the piece he characterizes the whole poem as "busie praise" (67). The effect is double – both encomiastic and critical.

The 1609 verse epistle, "You that are she," was probably meant as an introduction to a funeral elegy for Lady Bedford's cousin, Lady Markham, who died in May of that year.[20] In this piece Donne portrays the Countess as the repository of her deceased friend's virtues. He uses some of the poetic figures he later develops fully in his *Anniversaries*, but here Donne is uncharacteristically self-effacing, except insofar as he flaunts witty metaphors that require his continual explication. Offering both sympathy and instruction, Donne assumes a confidently superior role in the poem, despite his deferential offer of praise to its addressee.

"T'Have written then" begins by apologizing for not responding to a letter written by Lady Bedford.[21] Donne admits that, in not writing, he might be revealing his resistance to dependency: "I seem'd to shunne beholdingnesse" (6). In characterizing himself as a sanctioned encomiastic poet who "hath sought vertues in corners" (19), he reveals a misogyny lying beneath the surface of his idealization of this noblewoman: "corner," as in Othello's fear that he might "keep a corner in the thing I love / For others' uses" (*Othello*, III.iii.272–73), was a term for the female genitalia.[22] Donne's hyperbolic praise of Lady Bedford's virtue, which allegedly "ransomes one sex, and one Court preserves" (26), is not really developed in the poem, which veers off in another direction to reflect satirically on human moral corruption. After winding through a complicated set of private reflections, Donne stops this part of the poem abruptly with the statement "But I must end this letter" (71) and brings together the realistic and encomiastic points of view in arguing that "Even in you, vertues best paradise, / Vertue hath some, but wise degrees of vice" (75–76). His explanation is a convoluted one (75–82, 87–90). The poem concludes with a gesture of renewed praise that is logically inconsistent with some of what Donne has said. It is as though he can neither locate his acts of praise and the person he praises in the real world, nor separate them from it. But, then, much of the poem has been instruction and advice, along with unsparing moral analysis. One might conclude from it all that the "virtuous" lady being complimented did not really measure up to the praise offered her and the poet offering the praise was more than a little uncomfortable with the gesture.

"To the Countess of Bedford. On New-yeares day" similarly converts the occasion of complement into one of advice-giving. Donne imagines Lady Bedford a model of behavior for those to whom in the future the poet can "show ... What you were" (11–12) in "verse built of your just praise" (21), but then he disqualifies himself for the task and urges her to "turne to God" (33) for instruction in how to become a moral exemplar, though he himself articulates what it is she should do. He returns to the problem of the Countess's immersion in a morally corrupt court, claiming now that it is neither good nor bad in itself, but in large part "[i]ndifferent" (43). In allowing for "some vaine disport, / On this side sinne" (44–45), he characterizes Lady Bedford's participation in courtly recreations and business as morally acceptable, portraying her as someone with the "discreet warinesse" (57) needed as a tool for survival in an environment of vicious competition. He thus attempts to reconcile his awareness of the real behavior (and questionable reputation) of Lady Bedford with the wish to idealize her, but the strains are evident.

Probably on the occasion of his leaving the country for his trip to France with a new patron, Sir Robert Drury, Donne wrote an awkwardly valedictory poem, "Epitaph on Himself To the Countess of Bedford." Imagining himself dying, he offers "this last funerall Scrowle" (4), a poem that makes Donne's self-destructive abandonment of his patroness into another occasion of moral instruction. It is as though he were self-consciously breaking his habit of using encomiastic verse to sustain his relationship with Lady Bedford. The one other verse epistle he subsequently wrote to her, "To the Countesse of Bedford *Begun in France but never perfected*," is an abortive attempt. In this piece, which reiterates his "thankfullnesse" for her "favours" (5), he apologizes for giving to others the praise he had reserved for her (11–13).

Although Donne had earlier told Goodyer, in response to a suggestion that he write an encomiastic piece for another noblewoman, that he had reserved "all the thoughts of womens worthiness" (*Letters*, p. 104) for Lady Bedford, he did compose verse letters for the Countess of Huntington, Magdalen Herbert, Sir Robert Rich's two sisters (Lady Carey and Mrs. Essex Rich), and the Countess of Salisbury. The two poems to the Countess of Huntington are the most interesting, since they draw upon a history of personal interaction and, in them, Donne allows himself to engage in sophisticated teasing.[23] In the first ("That unripe side of earth"), written to the Countess when she was seventeen, Donne combines intellectual and linguistic convolutions, conventional complement, comic indecorum, and surprising frankness as he highlights the problems he has defining the sort of "love" proper to encomiastic verse. In the second epistle to the Countess of Huntington ("Man to Gods image"), Donne's easy social familiarity with the addressee made it possible for him to write a more affectionate, playful poem than was possible for other social superiors. He could even indulge in a facetious rehearsal of misogynistic tropes, inauspiciously preparing for his acts of praise by suggesting negative things about women before treating the Countess as an incarnation of a virtue manifested in her roles as wife and mother. Aware of the "flatteries" (49) typically found in all encomiastic verse, he denies that this is what he is crafting in this epistle, insisting that she deserves the good things he is saying about her.

"To Mrs M.H.," addresses the topic of the remarriage of Magdalen Herbert, with whom Donne enjoyed a friendship until her death in 1627.[24] Earlier he had sent her his set of religious sonnets, *La Corona*, along with a prefatory letter and sonnet.[25] In this verse epistle, which testifies to a comfortable degree of social familiarity, Donne comically refers to his own position as one person among many "noble ambitious wits" (35) gathered in her "Cabinet" (34). Donne finally turns his envy of her husband-to-be, the (younger) Lord Danvers, into a compliment: "so much I doe love her choyce, that I / Would faine love him that shall be lov'd of her" (51–52).

The two remaining verse epistles to noblewomen ("A Letter to the Lady Carey, and Mrs Essex Rich" and "To the Countesse of Salisbury") are weak performances in which the psychological and social strains are evident.

Donne abandons his desperate search for patronage – that is, until he renews it in the pursuit of ecclesiastical preferment. The verse letters are at their worst when Donne's relationship with a patroness was tenuous or deteriorating, and at their best when, as in the early pieces to Lady Bedford, they are occasions for the kind of virtuoso intellectual moves Donne makes on a grand scale in the two *Anniversaries*.

Donne wrote those long poems while a client of Sir Robert Drury, using the occasion of praising Drury's deceased fifteen-year-old daughter to engage in an extended philosophical, satirical, religious meditation on the self and the world. He took those meditative and didactic features of his encomiastic verse and inflated them into (alternately) heroic and mock-heroic grandeur. Freed from the context of a live relationship with an actual woman, he was free to let his imagination soar. Ben Jonson joked about the inappropriateness of heaping such inflated praise on an adolescent girl: "if it had been of ye Virgin Marie, it had been something."[26] Donne regretted publishing the poems and tried to respond to the envious pique of patronesses offended at what he had done:

> Of my Anniversaries, the fault that I acknowledge in my self, is to have descended to print any thing in verse ... my purpose was to say as well as I could: for since I never saw the Gentlewoman, I cannot be understood to have bound my self to have spoken just truths, but I would not be thought to have gone about to praise her, or any other in rime; except I took such a person, as might be capable of all that I could say. If any of those Ladies think that Mistris *Drewry* was not so, let that Lady make her self fit for all those praises in the book, and they shall be hers.
>
> (*Letters*, p. 239)

Here he admits that *all* his encomiastic verse is fictional, not dependent on the actual moral condition of the person praised. Writing was its own excuse for being, and the act of seeking or sustaining patronage legitimated exaggeration, if not outright lying. The *Anniversaries* make clear what is implicit in Donne's other encomiastic verse, that such writing was used by him to do what he did in all his poetry and prose: to engage in self-conscious, philosophically and religiously reflective, critical examinations of the self and the world in a style of language and complex thinking he found most congenial. The desired audiences for such pieces either had or had to have attributed to them the intellectual and cultural sophistication needed to appreciate such work.

NOTES

1 In this essay, I use material from my book, *John Donne, Coterie Poet* (Madison and London: University of Wisconsin Press, 1986), especially pp. 34–37 and 192–232.

2 See Bald, *Donne*, pp. 187–95; I. A. Shapiro, "The 'Mermaid Club'," *Modern Language Review* 45 (1950), 6–17, 58–63.

3 See Donne, *Letters to Severall Persons of Honour (1651)* – hereafter *Letters* – pp. 87–88, 99, 108, and *A Collection of Letters Made by Sr Tobie Mathews Kt.* (1660) – hereafter *Collection of Letters* – pp. 298–99, 304–5 (printed in Gosse, vol. II, p. 233).

4 See *Letters*, pp. 196–97, 22.

5 See Alan MacColl, "The Circulation of Donne's Poems in Manuscript," in A. J. Smith (ed.), *John Donne: Essays in Celebration* (London: Methuen, 1972), pp. 28–46.

6 This letter appears in the Burley Manuscript (Leicestershire Record Office, DG7 Lit2), a commonplace book of Sir Henry Wotton. I cite it from John Donne, *Selected Prose*, chosen by Evelyn Simpson, ed. Helen Gardner and Timothy Healy (Oxford: Clarendon Press, 1967), p. 111.

7 "Conversations with William Drummond of Hawthornden," cited in A. J. Smith (ed.), *John Donne: The Critical Heritage* (London and Boston: Routledge and Kegan Paul, 1975), p. 69.

8 See J. W. Saunders, "The Stigma of Print: A Note on the Social Bases of Tudor Poetry," *Essays in Criticism* 1 (1951), 139–64.

9 "Complement" was the language of courtesy and respect used for polite address to a social superior. See *OED*, meanings 8 and 9.

10 New York Public Library, Berg Collection.

11 George Klawitter, *The Enigmatic Narrator: The Voicing of Same-Sex Love in the Poetry of John Donne* (New York: Peter Lang, 1994), pp. 1–26.

12 See John Carey, "John Donne's Newsless Letters," *Essays and Studies* 34 (1981), 45–65.

13 See, for example, *Letters*, pp. 120–34, 187–90.

14 See, for example, *Letters*, pp. 43–45, 49–52, 59, 70–72, 152–53, 168, 174–75, 241–43, 249, 273, 316–18. See also his long consolatory letter to his mother on the occasion of his sister's death (*Collection of Letters*, pp. 323–27; Gosse, vol. II, pp. 88–90).

15 See, for example, *Letters*, p. 29.

16 See *Letters*, p. 99; *Collection of Letters*, pp. 306–07.

17 See Bald, pp. 170–77, and Margaret Maurer, "The Real Presence of Lucy Russell, Countess of Bedford, and the Terms of John Donne's 'Honour is so sublime perfection'," *ELH* 47 (1980), 205–34.

18 See David Aers and Gunther Kress, " 'Darke Texts Need Notes': Versions of Self in Donne's Verse Epistles," *Literature and History* 8 (Autumn 1978), 138–58.

19 For an interpretation of this poem, see Maurer, "The Real Presence," and Marotti, pp. 227–29.

20 See Wesley Milgate (ed.), *The Satires, Epigrams and Verse Letters* (Oxford: Clarendon Press, 1967), p. 260.

21 Probably many letters to Lady Bedford have not survived. Donne refers to a voluminous correspondence between them (*Collection of Letters*, 110; Gosse, vol. I, p. 234).

22 See Eric Partridge, *Shakespeare's Bawdy*, rev. edn. (New York: Dutton, 1969), p. 86.

23 See Bald, pp. 110–11, 179–80; Milgate, pp. 242–43; and John Yoklavich, "Donne and the Countess of Huntington," *Philological Quarterly* 43 (1964), 283–88.

24 See Bald, pp. 118–19, 180–84, 495–96, and Helen Gardner (ed.), *The Elegies and Songs and Sonnets* (Oxford: Clarendon Press, 1965), pp. 251–55.

25 See the letter in Simpson, *Selected Prose*, pp. 124–25. Four letters to Mrs. Herbert are printed from Sir Isaac Walton's *Lives* in Gosse, vol. 1, pp. 164–67.

26 "Conversations with Drummond," in Smith, *Critical Heritage*, p. 69.

4

ANDREW HADFIELD

Literary contexts: predecessors and contemporaries

In his search for poetic inspiration, Donne seems to have paid close attention to two distinct, albeit inter-related, bodies of poetry: the work produced in the years after the end of the Roman republic and the establishment of the empire, and the poetry written by his immediate contemporaries in London. In doing so he styles himself as a metropolitan poet, making a link between the greatest city of the ancient world on the cusp of its expansion and assumption of world domination, and a similar situation in contemporary England. Donne had direct experience of English maritime power, sailing on the Cadiz voyage under Essex and Raleigh (June–August 1596), and the "Islands" voyage to the Azores (July–October 1597), during which he wrote "The Storme" and "The Calme." He later applied for the position of secretary of the Virginia Company (1609), and, had he been successful, would probably have sailed with Sir Thomas Gates in June of that year and suffered shipwreck on the Bermudas, an event that helped inspire Shakespeare to write *The Tempest*.

Donne was, of course, hardly alone in demonstrating enthusiasm for such poets as Ovid, Catullus, Martial, and Juvenal, or in trying to adapt and imitate their writings. Christopher Marlowe translated Ovid's *Elegies*, the first book of Lucan's epic poem of the Roman civil war between Caesar and Pompey, the *Pharsalia*, and also wrote the Ovidian epyllion, *Hero and Leander*; William Shakespeare's *Venus and Adonis* is a similar Ovidian work and he chose to narrate the foundation of the Roman republic in *The Rape of Lucrece*; when Ben Jonson collected together his poems in his ground-breaking folio edition of his *Workes* in 1616, he included a complete book of epigrams in imitation of Martial, and a number of poems in *The Forest* and *The Underwood* were adaptations and imitations of Catullus's lyrics; and so many poets published aggressive satires in the style of Juvenal in the 1590s that they were eventually banned in 1599. Donne's work emerges as part of the creative ferment of late Elizabethan England, which had as one of its principal co-ordinates the poetry of Julio-Claudian Rome, a busy city at the heart of the world, with its cultural magnificence, prominent citizens leading important lives, erotic and political intrigue, and endemic corruption. In his poetry, Donne represents his own life in terms that resemble those of his Roman forebears.

Donne's classicism strikingly contrasts to that of Ben Jonson, who is generally labelled the most classical of English Renaissance poets. Jonson attempts to forge a plain and clear style in his work which will survive as long after his death as that of the poets of Augustan Rome. He makes every effort to write about types and situations that have a universal relevance beyond the moment of their inception. When Jonson writes on the death of his first daughter, he adapts Martial's lament for the death of his slave girl, Erotion, ending his poem with the couplet, "This grave partakes the fleshy birth; / Which cover lightly, gentle earth." Martial concludes his with the lines, "Lie lightly on her, turf and dew: / She put so little weight on you" (Book 5, epigram 39).[1] The sincerity of the elegy exists in the attempt to construct a funeral monument in verse that future generations will be able to read. When Jonson writes on sex he again adapts Roman poetry, as in the song "To Celia" in *Volpone*, which has as its literary predecessor, Catullus's poem to Lesbia. Where Catullus has "We should live, my Lesbia, and love / And value all the talk of stricter / Old men at a single penny" (5, lines 1–3), Jonson translates/adapts, "Come, my Celia, let us prove, / While we may, the sports of love; / Time will not be ours for ever; / He at length our good will sever."[2] The theme is the familiar one of *carpe diem*, the need to act quickly before time rushes away. The language is designed to offset this need for sudden action (and, given the speaker, Volpone, the moral is clear enough).

Donne pursues a different route, attempting to capture the immediacy of Ovid's poems of frantic lust, or Juvenal's patrician scorn for the dirt and squalor of the city. When Donne uses a theme familiar from Latin poetry, he emphasizes its urgent significance as a motif spoken by a lover in the heat of the moment, designed for short-term gain in the speaker's life, but undoubtedly having rather longer-term significance in the life of the reader. "The Flea," for example, belongs to an extensive genre of poems in which the lover describes an animal that is able to explore his beloved's body to which he is denied access, such as Catullus's famous poem about his mistress's sparrow, which ends with the lament, "Would I could play with you as she does / And lighten the spirit's gloomy cares!" (2, lines 9–10). But the most obvious precursor is a medieval poem attributed to Ovid, which inspired a number of lyrics written throughout Europe about fleas which could reach parts the would-be lovers were not allowed to touch. Donne's poem opens with a stanza of energetic argument resulting from immediate physical desire:

> Marke but this flea, and marke in this,
> How little that which thou deny'st me is;
> It sucked me first, and now sucks thee,
> And in this flea, our two bloods mingled bee;
> Thou know'st that this cannot be said
> A sinne, nor shame, nor losse of maidenhead,
> Yet this enjoyes before it wooe,
> And pamper'd swells with one blood made of two,
> And this, alas, is more then wee would doe.   (1–9)

It has been argued that Donne plays on the confusion of the letters 'f' and 's' in early modern texts in line 3, relating the natural action of the flea to the natural action that the man would like to perform with the woman. Even if this reading is mistaken, the stanza is replete with sexual references. There is extensive play on the mingling of blood, the exchange of bodily fluids, as well as the speaker's hint that his aroused state must be obvious to the lady: "pamper'd swells with one blood made of two" clearly does not refer simply to the flea after its meal. We understand that the speaker's desire for sexual contact is such that he finds it difficult to be delayed in his designs, hence the urgency of his words.

The dramatic representation of desire recalls the tone and style of the first book of Ovid's erotic *Elegies*, especially the fourth elegy, which describes the torment of the lover on learning that his mistress is attending the same dinner party with her husband, the fifth elegy, which recounts a splendid afternoon in the company of Corinna, or the sixth elegy, which describes the attempts of the lover to sneak past the guards into his mistress's house at night. The sixth elegy, with its refrain, "tempora noctis eunt. execute poste seram," translated by Marlowe as "Night goes away, I pray thee ope the door," has a similar air of desperate erotic tension and the comic excess that lust generates. The lover addresses the porter:

> Why enviest me? this hostile den unbar,
> See how the gates with my tears water'd are.
> When thou stood'st naked, ready to be beat,
> For thee I did try thy mistress fair entreat …
> With stiff oak propp'd the gate doth still appear.
> Such rampir'd gates besieged cities aid,
> In midst of peace why art of arms afraid?[3]   (17–20, 28–30)

The frustrated lover, like Donne's speaker, sees images of sex in everything – the reminder of the porter's transgression, the door, and the contrast between the soft arts of peace and the dangerous arts of war developed by Marlowe elsewhere in *Tamburlaine the Great, part two*.[4] The lover later accuses the porter of failing to answer because he has his mistress with him. Both Donne and Ovid are acutely aware that lust often makes those suffering from its effects appear ridiculous to those immune to its immediate impact.

The same might also be said of Donne's notorious erotic elegy beginning "Come, Madam, come" (often titled "Going to Bed") which is replete with Ovidian sexual energy and tension, as the lover demands that his mistress undress for him, and describes the process, real or imagined, for the reader. Ovid is keenly interested in women's bodies in his poetry, and recounts an undressing in the fifth elegy:

> I grabbed the dress; it didn't hide much,
> but she fought to keep it,
>
> only half-heartedly though.
> Victory was easy, a self-betrayal.
>
> There she stood, faultless beauty
> in front of me, naked.
>
> Shoulders and arms challenging eyes and fingers.
> Nipples firmly demanding attention.
>
> Breasts in high relief above the smooth belly.
> Long and slender waist. Thighs of a girl.
>
> (Book I, Elegy 5, 13–22)

Corinna's denuding bears little comparison to Donne's lengthy, lecherous description of his mistress undressing, as the poet extends the familiar form of the blazon as far as he can. Whereas Corinna's clothes are off after a token struggle, Donne's lover luxuriates in the act of the woman stripping, making use of the tried and tested comparison between the arts of love and the arts of war, implicit in Ovid's erotic writings:

> The foe oft-times having the foe in sight,
> Is tir'd with standing though he never fight.
> Off with that girdle, like heaven's Zone glittering,
> But a far fairer world incompassing.
> Unpin that spangled breastplate which you wear,
> That th'eyes of busie fooles may be stopt there.
> Unlace yourself, for that harmonious chyme
> Tells me from you, that now it is bed time.
> Off with that happy busk, which I envie,
> That still can be, and still can stand so nigh. (3–12)

Donne is deliberately overgoing Ovid in the force, extent, and daring of his erotic poetry, responding to requests, such as that made in Sir Philip Sidney's

An Apologie for Poetrie, that English writers try to rival the cultural achievements of the ancients. Donne's poem, which was censored in the early editions of his poetry and not printed until after the Restoration, makes Ovid seem rather tame in comparison. Indeed, if Donne is responding directly to a specific literary work it is likely to have been Marlowe's *Hero and Leander*, which was published posthumously in 1598. Marlowe's poem contains two physical descriptions of the lovers. Whereas Hero is quite deliberately described in terms of her clothes, Leander is seen in explicitly fleshy and sexual terms: "Even as delicious meat is to the taste, / So was his neck in touching, and surpass'd / The white of Pelops' shoulder" (Sestiad 1, 63–65). Both Marlowe's and Donne's blazons constitute a confidence in the range and abilities of English poets to better their classical forebears at their own literary games.

Donne reminds readers of the imperial importance of London in the elegy, providing the poem with an explicitly political sub-text:

> Licence my roaving hands, and let them go
> Before, behind, between, above, below.
> O my America! my new-found-land,
> My kingdome, safeliest when with one man man'd,
> My mine of precious stones, my empery,
> How blessed am I in this discovering thee! (25–30)

The lover casts himself as the imperial ruler; the lady becomes his conquered territory. Critics have rightly read these lines in terms of Donne's interest in the exploration of the New World, especially the exploits of Raleigh in the 1590s. But these lines should also be related to Donne's interest in imperial Rome, for they carry the suggestion that the triumphs of the English under Elizabeth and James will overgo those of their forbears.

Donne's *Satires* have a similar relationship to Juvenal as many of his erotic poems have to Ovid. Juvenal is a model writer, to be treated with immense respect; and to be bettered if possible. Juvenal's satires are an acknowledgement of the triumph of Rome as the world's first city. He rails against vice that he believes cannot be removed, only avoided, unlike his illustrious predecessor, Horace, who wrote his satires as a means to correct bad behavior. Juvenal has no real desire to leave Rome behind and seek a more temperate life in the provinces. When he opens the second satire with the wish that he might escape "Northward beyond the Lapps to the world's end, the frozen / Polar ice-cap," because he has been forced to listen to "Highflown moral discourse from that clique in Rome who affect / Ancestral peasant virtues as a front for their lechery," we know that he is only indulging in rhetorical excess. Rome is only bad because it has triumphed and so contains all forms of life: the satirist and the object of his satire live side by side in a symbiotic relationship.[5]

Juvenal's first satire has the unfortunate poet forced to listen to a dreadful poetry reading, and wishing that he could exact his revenge on the talentless bore who is droning away in front of the audience:

> Must I *always* be stuck in the audience at these poetry readings,
> Never on the platform myself, taking it out on Cordus
> For the times he's bored me to death with ranting speeches
> From that *Thesiad* of his? Is X to get off scot-free
> After inflicting his farces on me, or Y his elegies? Is there
> No recompense for whole days wasted on prolix
> Versions of *Telephus*?   (1–7)

Juvenal's instinct is to retreat into a private world away from the awfulness of life lived in public spaces. Donne's first satire has a similar opening, as his speaker desires to be left alone with his books, and to escape from the superficial courtier who insists on shadowing him. Donne makes it clear where his priorities should lie:

> Away thou fondling motley humourist,
> Leave mee, and in this standing woodden chest,
> Consorted with these few bookes, let me lye
> In prison, and here be coffin'd, when I dye;
> Here are Gods conduits, grave Divines; and here
> Nature's Secretary, the Philosopher[.]   ("Satyre i," 1–6)

Nevertheless, he consents to tour the bustling life of the city with the courtier, who greets "Every fine silken painted foole we meet" (72). On their journey they encounter numerous fools, avoiding grave and sensible figures. Each time the courtier speaks Donne replies with a withering insult, culminating in the final meeting with a "many-coloured Peacock" (92). The courtier admires the fashionable clothes he wears and then imitates his stoop because he thinks it is part of a new style imported from France or Italy. As Donne warns him, he is right, but only because it is a symptom of the pox. Spying his love in a window, the young man leaves Donne, "Violently ravish'd to his lechery" (108). The lady in question is clearly a woman of easy virtue, and the "motley humorist" finds himself no longer in control of the social situation:

> Many were there, he could command no more;
> Hee quarrell'd, fought, bled; and turn'd out of doore
>   Directly came to mee hanging the head,
>   And constantly a while must keepe his bed.   (109–12)

The courtier ends up having to retreat from society in spite of his desires, an ironic mirroring of the poet's stated wishes at the start of the satire. In fact, he avoids having to be away from the buzz of city life for longer by luck rather than design, the beating he receives saving him from a dose of the pox.

The courtier may be an alter-ego of the poet, suggesting that the city is both a curse (because of its vice) and a cure (because the poet has something to write about). The moralist and the social butterfly are really one and the same. The satire may, in addition, ironically comment on Donne's representation of himself in his erotic verse, the beating or the pox being seen as a just reward for the sexual exploits narrated elsewhere. The books are vital for the poet, but the satire cannot be written if the poet is not a part of the city, hence the need for him to participate in, but also to be distanced from, its life. Donne's *Satires* make the case that vice has always been a part of human nature and cannot simply be dismissed or avoided. "Satyre III" describes mankind's ongoing search for true religion and the apparently impossible task of sorting out the grain from the chaff. The speaker expresses the fear that new developments in religious observance are no more than "fashions" (line 57), as superficial in their way as the whims of courtly behaviour. Truth, he informs us, is hard to reach: "On a huge hill, / Cragged, and steep, Truth stands, and hee that will / Reach her, about must, and about must goe; / And what that hills suddenness resists, win so" (79–82). Truth is almost impossible to understand, but, like London, it cannot be avoided if one wants to write. Donne's sense of his duty as a poet in the satires is Juvenalian – although, of course, his concern with contemporary religious issues marks the distance that mankind has travelled from classical Rome. Juvenal's penultimate satire indulged in a rare digression about mankind's innate foolishness: "Mankind was on the decline while Homer / Still lived; and today the earth breeds a race of degenerate / Weaklings, who stir high heaven to laughter and loathing" (78–80). Donne is able to qualify Juvenal's pessimism with his religious faith: "So perish Soules, which more chuse mens unjust / Power from God claym'd, then God himselfe to trust" ("Satyre III," 109–10). However, the representation of urban man in both sets of satires is similar as Donne translates what he can of the literary culture of early imperial Rome to late Elizabethan England.

Donne's reaction to the culture of Petrarchan verse that had come to dominate English poetry in the 1580s and 1590s is equally complex but more ambivalent. Petrarchan poetry was by no means a monolithic entity; neither did much of it owe anything other than the most superficial of debts to the work of Francesco Petrarca. Nevertheless, the dominant trends can be defined.

Petrarch was probably the most influential poet in Renaissance Europe through the dissemination of his massive collection of lyrics in Italian, *The Canzoniere*, and, to a lesser extent, the *Trionfi*, written in the second half of the fourteenth century. These poems describe the effects of the poet meeting an unobtainable, beautiful woman, Laura, to whom he remained dedicated even though she married another man and then died. Petrarch credited Laura's beauty with leading him to a spiritual awareness and an eventual appreciation of the majesty of God's grace. Petrarch's poetry is characterized by its Christian Neoplatonism, the belief that earthly goods are an inferior copy of the ideal forms that God has established in heaven. Love on earth is to be treasured but it provides only the most fleeting glimpse of the rich rewards that can be enjoyed in the afterlife.

One of Petrarch's most celebrated lyrics describes how the poet had a wonderful vision of a deer:

> A Doe of purest white upon the grass
> wearing two horns of gold appeared to me
> between two streams beneath a laurel's shade
> at sunrise in that season not yet ripe.
>
> The sight of her was so sweetly austere
> that I left all my work to follow her,
> just like a miser who in search of treasure
> with pleasure makes his effort bitterless.
> "No one touch me," around her lovely neck
> was written out in diamonds and in topaz,
> "It pleased my Caesar to create me free."
>
> The sun by now had climbed the sky midway,
> my eyes were tired but not full from looking
> when I fell into water, and she vanished.[6]

The doe is Laura, who is dead and appears before Petrarch to lead him away from his sinful earthly life to a spiritual one. The imagery of the octave marks her out as intensely desirable, the woman as the hunted deer being a common image in European love poetry (in English, the pun is often on hart/heart hunting). The sestet, however, reveals that she is unobtainable because she is promised to a higher lord, Caesar, who stands for God. The poet is still blinded by his earthly passion, not yet realizing the religious dimension of his love, and needing further guidance from the lady to bring him to true enlightenment. His fall into water associates him with the earthly elements below the moon, unready for the ascent to heaven.

Petrarch's work pervades European poetry throughout the fifteenth and sixteenth centuries. Writers adapted his Neoplatonism, often in rather less strictly religious forms; wrote elaborate sonnets about remote ladies who had enormous power over their lives; and made use of Petrarch's characteristic antitheses, the most frequently imitated example being, "I freeze in fire and burn in ice." Petrarch was introduced as a significant model for English poets to imitate by Sir Thomas Wyatt and Henry Howard, Earl of Surrey, both poets at the court of Henry VIII. Wyatt adapted Petrarch's *Canzoniere* 190 as the sonnet, "Whoso list to hunt," retaining the central conceit of the lover hopelessly pursuing a deer who informs him that she has been claimed by Caesar, but transforming the poem into a narrative about an earthly lover who is prevented from having his mistress by a more powerful man (undoubtedly the king himself). This poem, along with other poems by Wyatt and Surrey, and other writers, was published in the first printed verse miscellany in English, Richard Tottel's *Songes and Sonettes* (1557). The title clearly had an influence on the title of Donne's erotic poems, when they were published as *Songs and Sonets* in the first collected edition of his verse in 1635, though whether Donne had a hand in the name, and whether there was any ironic implication in it, is a matter for speculation.

Donne reacts against prevailing Petrarchan conventions in his work, representing women at times as equals, at others as despicable creatures (although perhaps no more contemptible than the men he represents in the *Satires*), not perfect and distant beauties who can ennoble their men; he pushes antitheses to absurd limits, notably in the comparison between the lovers and a pair of compasses in "A Valediction: forbidding mourning"; and he rejects the jog trot iambic pentameter and conspicuously poetic diction of much Italianate English verse in favour of harsher rhythms and more collo-quial speech-forms. However, it would be a mistake to imagine that Donne simply burst onto the poetic scene and transformed everything in one fell swoop. The vogue for Petrarchan poetry was often inherently shrouded in irony. Sir Philip Sidney, whose long sonnet sequence, *Astrophil and Stella*, had started the fashion for such literary works, made use of Petrarch in both admiring and sardonic ways. In sonnet 15 Astrophil argues that poets look-ing for inspiration should turn away from earlier poetry and simply use the example of Stella. He refers to "poore *Petrarch's* long deceased woes" (7), as if his work were now dated and old-fashioned, a reference that reminds the reader that Sidney's sequence is anything but ignorant of previous poetry, and that many of the poems are intensely Petrarchan in nature.[7] Simultaneously, it alerts us to the fact that Sidney has grand poetic ambitions – as Donne was to have later – knowing the value of Petrarch's work, but also wishing to advance English poetry beyond it through his own efforts. Sidney, like Donne later, indulges in elaborate conceits that push the stock character-istics of Petrarchan poetry as far as they will go. Sonnet 9 opens with the ornate line, "Queene *Vertue's* court, which some call Stella's face" (1), an apparently Petrarchan, Neoplatonic description, linking the poet's object of desire with spiritual ennoblement. The poem is an elaborate description of Stella's face. Her visage is "Alabaster pure" (3); her hair is a golden roof; her mouth, a door of "Red Porphir, which lock of pearl makes sure" (6); her cheeks are porches made of red and white marble; and her eyes of black touchstone. This magnificent edifice leaves the poet helplessly in her thrall, a sign perhaps of his naiveté, and the fact that he is constructing an ideal woman without any relation to the real one he is representing. Later on in the sequence, when Stella does actually get to speak, she rejects his advances (fourth song, ninth song). Astrophil demonstrates that the Neoplatonic ideal of love is unworkable in a witty, anti-Petrarchan sonnet that takes apart the platitudinous and reductive philosophy practiced in Petrarch's name:

> Who will in fairest book of Nature know
> How Vertue may best lodg'd in beautie be,
> Let him but learne of *Love* to reade in thee,
> *Stella*, those faire lines which true goodnesse show.
> There shall he find all vices' overthrow,
> Not by rude force, but sweetest soveraigntie
> Of reason, from whose light those night-birds flie,
> That inward sunne in thine eyes shineth so:
> And not content to be Perfection's heire
> Thy selfe, doest strive all minds that way to move,
> Who marke in thee what is in thee most faire,
> So while thy beautie drawes the heart to love,
> As fast thy Vertue bends that love to good:
> "But ah," Desire still cries, "give me some food."   (sonnet 71)

The last line spectacularly undercuts the previous thirteen, introducing a note of bathos into Astrophil's attempt to persuade the reader that Stella will lead him to spiritual enlightenment, as Laura did for Petrarch. Astrophil is too base a lover to imitate the Italian master. His journey takes him back down to earth and his god is that of the flesh not the soul. The book of Nature tells him that he cannot escape the tyranny of the flesh, an irony given that he is reading it in the hope of learning the opposite lesson. The poem is also, of course, an acknowledgment that a poetic tradition does not necessarily describe reality, a truth that we are then invited to apply to Sidney's sequence.

Donne's reaction to Petrarchan tradition was rather more savage than Sidney's, partly, one suspects, because he was writing nearly two decades later, by which time such poets as Sir John Davies had already characterized the Petrarchan lover as "a patiente burden-bearing Asse" in his manuscript collection, *Gullinge Sonnets*.[8] There were other reasons too. Many of

Donne's lyrics seem to be written for or about his wife, probably in the wake of Edmund Spenser's sonnet sequence, the *Amoretti* (1595), written about his courtship of his second wife, Elizabeth Boyle, which helped revise the convention of the distant and disdainful lady of the Petrarchan poem. Furthermore, as Achsah Guibbory has persuasively argued, many of the more obviously misogynistic poems, which cast women in the power of men, are undoubtedly "the product of, and a reaction to, the historical situation of England's rule by a woman."[9] The second edition of Donne's poems in 1635 began with "The Flea" and "The good-morrow," two love poems possibly written for his wife, but they were followed and balanced by two assaults on women's characters, "Song" ("Goe, and catche a falling starre") and "Womans constancy," sending a clear warning to the reader not to expect standard Petrarchan fare. The "Song," which may be designed to stand as a pointed contrast to the romantic lyrics collected in a volume such as Thomas Campion's *A Book of Airs* (1601), is a light, scornful piece, listing a series of impossible tasks before daring the reader to find a constant woman:

> If thou beest borne to strange sights,
>   Things invisible to see,
> Ride ten thousand daies and nights,
>   Till age snow white hairs on thee,
> Thou, when thou retorn'st, wilt tell mee
> All strange wonders that befell thee,
>   And swear
>   No where
> Lives a woman true, and fair. (10–18)

The poem bears a striking resemblance to the task that the old woman sets for the rapist knight in Chaucer's *The Wife of Bath's Tale*, which Donne could have read in a number of editions published in the late sixteenth century, and which had such a crucial influence on the development of late sixteenth-century English poetry. Whereas Chaucer's protagonist eventually realized that women wanted the power to choose, earning himself the reward of a lovely, faithful wife in the process, Donne's speaker has no idea where his quest will end, his cynical voice suspecting that even the appearance of fidelity will offer no hope of resolution:

> Though at the next doore wee might meet,
>   Though shee were true, when you met her,
> And last, till you write your letter,
>   Yet shee
>   Will bee
> False, ere I come, to two, or three. (22–27)

The last line injects a note of humour into the poem, reminding the reader not to take it all too seriously – and, in the process, perhaps undermining our initial sense that this is a lyric written just for the eyes of men. The speaker's assertion that the woman will prove false once he has visited two or three more constructs an image of both sexes playing the field and complaining about each other's lack of constancy. A similar representation of sexuality appears in the next poem in the volume, "Womans constancy," which opens with the striking couplet: "Now thou hast lov'd me one whole day, / Tomorrow when thou leav'st, what wilt thou say?" The accusation might be read in the light of the fickle and myopic speaker of the previous poem (although it is unlikely that Donne ordered the poems himself).

Such poems are not simply light, scornful works that expose the ridiculous and outdated traditions of poetry that had taken hold of literary culture in England in the late sixteenth century. They are also ways of searching for certainty and security in an uncertain, chaotic world: evidence, perhaps, that Donne was troubled by the difficult political circumstances under which he lived, and saw his marriage as a unique example of "Woman's constancy" in an inconstant world. The figures in much of his poetry, in contrast, are often represented as restless, dissatisfied, and superficial people with no depth or substance, whatever the complexities of the arguments they are capable of spinning. Donne's best poetry is adept at relating the superficial to the profound, connecting the demotic and the philosophical.

This skilful combination of tone and substance is particularly evident in "The Extasie," one of the longer poems in *Songs and Sonets*, and one which has been recognized as "one of Donne's great poems."[10] However, it has all too often been read as if it were a solemn, philosophical argument, existing among a number of somewhat more disposable lyrics, rather than a poem of the same order, demanding to be read in terms of the same poetic traditions.[11] The title refers to a divine experience when the fortunate individual is transported to a higher plane in order to learn wisdom not normally granted to human beings because it is inaccessible through reason and sensory perception. The opening stanza is at odds with the expectations the title raises:

> Where, like a pillow on a bed,
> A pregnant banke swel'd up, to rest
> The violets reclining head,
> Sat we two, one anothers best. (1–4)

These lines lead the reader to expect that the poem will develop as a pastoral lyric. The lovers are situated in a beautiful, isolated retreat, the familiar *locus amoenus* ("pleasant place") of romance. Hence, after reading the first stanza, we should be aware that all is not quite as it seems, especially if we see any significance in the adjective, "pregnant," which, of course, could simply be a description of the rounded bank. It also, however, reminds us of a state the woman will undoubtedly experience if their romance continues, or one of them may have already experienced if the couple in question are John and Anne Donne.

Pastoral is among the most complex of literary forms. As many Renaissance literary critics noted, the superficial simplicity invariably hid an allegorical message that was at odds with the surface material.[12] Donne rarely employed pastoral forms, his verse being set in London when it had a setting at all, so his use of a pastoral opening here is all the more noteworthy, one designed to emphasize that "The Extasie" should not be taken exactly as it first appears. The bizarre imagery of the next lines, with its complex mixture of quasi-scientific language and images of erotic rapture, bears out such suspicions:

> Our hands were firmly cimented
> > With a fast balme, which thence did spring,
> Our eye-beames twisted, and did thred
> > Our eyes, upon one double string[.]　　　　　(5–8)

The lovers are experiencing a strange encounter which does not obey the normal rules of physical reality. Donne provides an elaborate description of the pure refinement of the couple's love that allows them to go beyond the constraints of their bodies:

> Our soules, (which to advance their state,
> > Were gone out,) hung 'twixt her, and mee.
> And whil'st our soules negotiate there,
> > Wee like sepulchral statues lay;
> All day, the same our postures were,
> > And wee said nothing, all the day.
> If any, so by love refin'd,
> > That he soules language understood,
> And by good love were growen all minde,
> > Within convenient distance stood,
> He (though he knew not which soule spake
> > Because both meant, both spake the same)
> Might thence a new concoction take,
> > And part farre purer than he came.　　　　　(15–28)

The lovers are united and become one through their perfect union. They do not even need to speak, so advanced is their state of love that their souls can communicate, making the organs of speech redundant. There is a similar moment in Milton's *Paradise Lost*, Book VIII, when Adam asks Raphael whether angels have sexual intercourse in heaven. Raphael appears embarrassed, and answers "with a smile that glowed / Celestial rosy red, love's proper hue" (618–19) that the love of angels goes beyond the physical earthly love that men and women can experience:

> Whatever pure thou in the body enjoy'st
> (And pure thou wert created) we enjoy
> In eminence, and obstacle find none
> Of membrane, joint, or limb, exclusive bars:
> Easier than air with air, if spirits embrace,
> Total they mix, union of pure with pure
> Desiring; nor need restrained conveyance need
> As flesh to mix with flesh, or soul with soul.[13]   (VIII, 622–29)

It is quite possible that Donne's poem is a source of Milton's passage. Milton undoubtedly read Donne's poems and probably heard him preach at St. Paul's Cathedral when he was a child.[14] Raphael explains to Adam that he simply will not be able to understand how angels behave and that the best Raphael can provide him with is an approximation of the higher state that exists nearer God. Donne has his speaker imagine a hypothetical observer, extensively refined by his own experience of love, able to understand their behavior because he has ceased to be human and has become "all mind." This observer will learn from their example.

The argument of "The Extasie" is therefore cumulative in its depiction of relative states of awareness. The lovers are so far beyond ordinary mortals that their union will only make sense to a pure being who has himself gone beyond the human. The ecstasy they experience moves them up beyond ordinary creation and towards the realm of the angels. Donne is making use of the popularization of Neoplatonism in the sixteenth century, inspired by thinkers such as Pico della Mirandola and Marsilio Ficino, as well as Petrarch.[15] The lovers will reach a higher plane through the perfection of their mutual love, taking them beyond ordinary human experience and up towards the divine love of the angels, as celebrated in poems such as Edmund Spenser's *Four Hymns*.

Just as Donne appears to be celebrating the achievement of his lovers in creating a "new soule" (45), the poem is dramatically transformed. The speaker changes tack and asks why, if their love is so pure and beyond reproach, they neglect their bodies. After all, "They are ours, though they are not wee, We are / The intelligences, they the sphaere" (51–52). They cannot be reduced to their bodies because they have gone beyond them to a higher plane, but, just as God takes notice of the lower spheres of creation, so they should make some use of what they have. Their souls will still interact even if the bodies start off the process of intermingling. It may seem demeaning for them to descend to such depths, but it is their sorry duty to have to do so:

> To'our bodies turne wee then, that so
> Weake men on love reveal'd may looke;
> Loves mysteries in soules do grow,
> But yet the body is his booke.   (69–72)

These next to the last four lines of the poem shows how far "The Extasie" is simultaneously enveloped in irony, and a serious work of erotic literature. The use of the adjective "pregnant" in the second line reminds us that love simply cannot be as ethereal as the speaker claims in the first half of the poem, as we realize towards the end. The transformation we witness bears a strong resemblance to that in Sidney's sonnet cited above, a reminder that however men dress up the language of love, whatever Petrarchan conceits and formulae they use, the reality of earthly love cannot be ignored. Donne acknowledges this reality when he compares the body to a book. The language of love has already been written and he is using and exposing it in this poem: indeed, in the whole collection.

Although Donne's poems can appear as cynical and dismissive reflections on the nature of love, this would be a superficial reaction to them. Donne makes use of a series of precursors, styles, types, and literary examples, often treating the material at his command in a sardonic or ironic way. It does not follow that he refuses to take the literature of love seriously. On the contrary, *Songs and Sonets* is often an extremely serious volume, putting all previous love poetry in its place and suggesting that the earthly love of John and Anne Donne was one of the few constants in a chaotic and changeable world.

NOTES

1 Ben Jonson, *Poems*, ed. Ian Donaldson (Oxford: Oxford University Press, 1975); Martial, *The Epigrams*, trans. James Michie (Harmondsworth: Penguin, 1978, rpt. of 1973).
2 *The Poems of Catullus*, trans. Guy Lee (Oxford: Oxford University Press, 1990).
3 Christopher Marlowe, *Ovid's Elegies*, Book I, Elegy VI, in Millar Maclure (ed.) *The Poems* (London: Methuen, 1968), lines 17–20, 28–30; Ovid, *Amores*, trans. Guy Lee (London: John Murray, 1968).
4 Act IV, scene i.
5 Juvenal, *The Sixteen Satires*, trans. Peter Green (Harmondsworth: Penguin, 1967), p. 75.
6 Petrarch, *Selections from The Canzoniere and Other Works*, trans. Mark Musa (Oxford: Oxford University Press, 1985), *Canzoniere* 190.

7 Sir Philip Sidney, *Astrophil and Stella*, in Maurice Evans (ed.), *Elizabethan Sonnets* (London: Dent, 1977), pp. 2–61.

8 Sir John Davies, "Gullinge Sonnets" (*c.* 1594), in Evans (ed.), *Elizabethan Sonnets*, pp. 179–83, at p. 180.

9 Achsah Guibbory, "'Oh Let Mee Not Serve So': The Politics of Love in Donne's *Elegies*," *ELH* 57 (1990), 811–33.

10 Wilbur Sanders, *John Donne's Poetry* (Cambridge: Cambridge University Press, 1971), p. 99.

11 See, for example, Carey, *Donne*, pp. 252–55.

12 See Brian Vickers (ed.), *English Renaissance Literary Criticism* (Oxford: Clarendon Press, 1999), pp. 179–89, passim.

13 John Milton, *Paradise Lost*, ed. Alastair Fowler (Harlow: Longman, 1968), Book VIII, lines 618–19, 622–29.

14 Barbara Lewalski, *The Life of John Milton* (Oxford: Blackwell, 2000), p. 6.

15 See Ernst Cassirer, Paul Oskar Kristeller, and John Herman Randall, Jr. (eds.), *The Renaissance Philosophy of Man* (Chicago: University of Chicago Press, 1948).

5

ALISON SHELL AND ARNOLD HUNT

Donne's religious world

To say that Donne's religious world was, overwhelmingly, a Christian world may seem to be stating the obvious. But it is true not just in the simple, practical sense that the Christian religion was established by law, but also in the less obvious sense that it was hard for most people in the early modern period to think outside a Christian paradigm. In a letter to his friend Sir Henry Goodyer, Donne wrote simply that "Religion is Christianity." By contemporary standards, this was a boldly inclusive definition of religion: one that embraced the whole of Christianity, Catholic and Protestant alike. Donne was at pains to stress that he had "never fettered nor imprisoned the word Religion" by confining it to any single Christian confession or "immuring it in a *Rome*, or a *Wittenberg*, or a *Geneva*; they are all virtual beams of one Sun ... connaturall pieces of one circle" (*Letters*, p. 29). Yet, by modern standards, it may strike us as a narrowly exclusive definition. For Donne, as for his contemporaries, Christianity held an absolute monopoly of religious truth; it was not merely part of religion, but the whole.

In early modern England, there were few visible reminders of the existence of other religions. The Jews had been expelled from England in 1290 and were not readmitted until 1655, and even then not officially. There was a small community of Spanish and Portuguese Jews in London, but they practiced their religion in secret; few outsiders were aware of their presence, and the verdict of one modern historian is that "as far as anyone knew, there were no Jews in England" at this time.[1] By the early seventeenth century, as England began to establish diplomatic and commercial relations with the countries of the eastern Mediterranean, the first Muslims began to appear in London. The 1633 edition of Stow's *Survey of London* contains an account of the funeral ceremonies performed by the Persian ambassador and his entourage for "one *Coya Shawsware*, a Persian Merchant" who died in 1626 and was buried near the churchyard of St. Botolph's Bishopsgate, just outside the city walls.[2] But it is significant, and symbolic, that most of our knowledge of the Muslim presence in London comes from occasional entries in the Bishop of London's official registers giving orders for the Muslim servants of English merchants to receive Christian baptism: their Muslim identity officially acknowledged for the first time just as it was about to be extinguished.[3]

Donne's theological education, and his experience of foreign travel, left him unusually well-informed about non-Christian religions. He had an excellent knowledge of Hebrew, and was able to cite Talmudic commentaries on the Old Testament; he may not have known any Arabic, but had evidently read parts of the Koran in a Latin translation. He even appears to have visited a synagogue – perhaps in Holland, while on his Continental tour with Sir Robert Drury in 1612 – and later turned this experience to good use in one of his sermons, where he gives an eyewitness account of the Jewish custom of offering prayers for the dead.[4] Yet despite his interest in other religions and cultures, his observations on Judaism and Islam are securely rooted in an assumption of religious superiority. In the *Essays in Divinity* he remarks that it is to the advantage of the Christian churches to make the Talmud and the Koran widely available, since these works are so far inferior to the Bible – and, in the case of the Koran, "so obnoxious and self-accusing" – that they refute themselves (p. 8).

What of atheism? It has been argued that "there was plenty of scope in sixteenth- and seventeenth-century England for a wide degree of religious heterodoxy," ranging from mild skepticism to outright unbelief.[5] There were certainly some, perhaps many individuals who expressed doubts about the authority of the scriptures, the extent of God's providential intervention in the world, or the immortality of the soul. Donne was familiar with these skeptical ideas: in the *Essays in Divinity*, he discusses some of the main arguments against the authority of the Bible (for example, apparent errors in numbering and chronology) and some of the main objections to miracles (for example, why the power of working miracles seems to have lapsed). One of the prayers included in the *Essays* describes how the weapons of reason and intellect can be turned against religion, and could be read as an admission that Donne himself had passed through a skeptical phase before returning to Christian orthodoxy: "Thou hast set up many candlesticks, and kindled many lamps in mee; but I have either blown them out, or carried them to guide me in by and forbidden ways ... I have arm'd my self with thy weapons against thee" (p. 97). In one letter, Donne remarks, "that religion is certainly best, which is reasonablest" (p. 43), anticipating one of the major intellectual projects of the later seventeenth century, the attempt to justify religion in rational terms.

Many sixteenth- and seventeenth-century writers were convinced that atheism was on the increase. As Michael Hunter has suggested, the fear of atheism arose from the new situation brought about by the Protestant Reformation: the fracturing of Christian unity, and the consequent aware- ness of "alternatives in religious outlook between which, for the first time, people had to choose."[6] But it is significant that early modern writers tended to use the term "atheism" to refer to the denial of Christian orthodoxy (in particular, the denial of Christ's divinity) rather than to the denial of God's existence. Indeed, there is a good case to be made that "atheism" in the strictly materialist sense – that is, a rejection of any divine or supernatural agency in the universe – was literally unthinkable before the scientific revo- lution of the seventeenth and eighteenth centuries.

When called upon to describe his religious position, Donne generally preferred to do so with the single word "Christian" – as in *Pseudo-Martyr*, where he characterizes himself as one who "dares not call his Religion by some newer name than *Christian*" (p. 14). But in his will, written in December 1630, three months before his death, he chose to define himself in more detail, not merely as a Christian but as a member of the established Church of England. "I give my good and gracious God an intire Sacrifice of Body and Soule with my most humble thankes for that assurance which his blessed Spirit ymprintes in me nowe of the Salvation of the one and the Resurrection of the other, And for that constant and cheerfull resolution which the same Spiritte establishes in me to live and dye in the Religion nowe professed in the Churche of England" (printed in Bald, p. 563). That Donne should have felt it necessary to express his orthodoxy in this way tells us a lot about the religious culture of early modern England; for this was a culture in which confessional allegiance was an integral part of religious identity. It was not enough for Donne to affirm his belief in the articles of the Christian creed; he also had to declare his conformity to the authority of the English Church.

These confessional labels – "Catholic," "Protestant," "Church of England" – are indispensable for any understanding of Donne's religious world. But they can also be deeply misleading insofar as they confer an illusion of stability on a religious landscape that was, in fact, constantly shifting; where the limits of orthodoxy were continually being tested, debated, and redefined, and where Catholic and Protestant doctrines were not always as sharply opposed as religious polemicists sought to make them appear. As Michael Questier has remarked, it would be a mistake "to see the English Reformation just as a struggle between two tightly consolidated blocs, Roman and Protestant, facing each other across a deserted religious no-man's-land" (see also chapter 6, p. 85).[7] There was frequent traffic between the two sides: a fact which Donne, as a convert from Catholicism, knew only too well. In short, this was a culture in which religious identities could never be taken for granted. Donne's contemporaries do not seem to have doubted his loyalty to his adopted church, and his status as one of the iconic figures of seventeenth-century Anglicanism was assured by his inclusion in Izaak Walton's *Lives* (1670) alongside George Herbert and Richard Hooker. But in recent times his religious opinions have come under close scrutiny from critics who are less certain of his wholehearted commitment to the Church of England. John Carey finds Donne's sermons uncomfortably ambiguous in their attitude to Catholicism, his other theological writings wildly exaggerated in their anti-Catholic polemic, and his poems "remarkably clear and full" in their acknowledgement of Catholic ideas, "the work of a man who has renounced a religion to some manifestations of which he is still, at a profound level, attached."[8] Donne himself admitted in the preface to *Pseudo-Martyr* that his conversion from Catholicism to Protestantism had not been an easy one, and that he had "a longer work to doe than many other men" in overcoming "certaine impressions of the Romane religion" (p. 13). If we follow Carey's reading of the poems and sermons, it seems that Donne may have remained more Catholic than he cared to admit.

Against John Carey we may set Helen Gardner, who was anxious to acquit Donne of "sustained intellectual dishonesty" in becoming a member of the Church of England while remaining, at heart, a Catholic. "His devotional temper is Catholic," she wrote, "but his devotion is a 'rectified devotion'; his theological position is Protestant." Yet even Gardner found it hard to explain Donne's ordination as a clergyman of the Church of England, for, as she noted, "Donne never speaks as if he felt any direct inward call to the ministry" – though she hastened to add that "he can hardly be reproached for this."[9] Many commentators have argued that it was only because Donne failed in his hopes of secular employment that he made the decision to seek an alternative career in the Church. R. C. Bald wrote in his biography of Donne that it was not until after the death of his wife in 1617 that he began to take a serious interest in spiritual matters (Bald, pp. 302, 328). Even if we see his conversion as motivated by genuine conviction, not merely expediency, the image may still persist of Donne as a man who allowed his head to govern his heart, and who argued himself into the Church of England for intellectual rather than emotional reasons.

And even supposing that Donne gradually matured into a deeper attachment to his adopted church, there is still room for doubt about where he should be placed on the spectrum of religious opinion. Later generations of Anglicans liked to portray the Church of England as a haven of moderation and compromise, mediating between the extremes of Catholicism and Protestantism. But few observers in the early seventeenth century would have regarded the Church of England as anything other than a Protestant church, closely allied with the Calvinist or "Reformed" churches of France, Holland, and Switzerland. Not only were its leading divines ferociously anti-Catholic, they also upheld a strict Calvinist doctrine of double predestination – in which every human being was divinely predestined to heaven or hell, regardless of their own actions – and saw this as one of the central tenets of Christian orthodoxy. Not surprisingly, many critics have found it hard to believe that Donne could cheerfully have subscribed to such a narrow and intolerant version of Christianity – particularly in the light of "Satyre III," which pokes fun at Catholics and Calvinists alike, and refuses to be pinned down to any single form of confessional allegiance. It is not enough, then, to say that Donne was a Christian. We have to determine what sort of a Christian he was, and to assess the nature of the journey he undertook from Catholicism to conformity. But this essay is not a contribution to the argument over the emotional authenticity of his conversion: rather, it traces Donne's developing views on ecclesiology, the Christian religion as outwardly expressed in the Church.

Donne as Catholic

During the whole of Donne's lifetime, England was officially a Protestant nation. But a significant minority of its inhabitants remained Catholic: how many will never be known, though contemporary anti-Catholic commentators believed undercover popery was rife in England. They would not have been surprised by the recent scholarly desire to play up the importance of "church-papists," those who attended Church of England services while also engaging in Catholic worship or retaining Catholic sympathies. Church-papists are by definition hard to pin down, most detectable on an individual basis where enough evidence survives to illustrate inconsistency. In the early modern era as at other times, an individual's religion could be a fluctuating entity, with emotional pressures or theologically motivated curiosity over-riding the need to give a systematic justification for one's belief and practice. Though Catholic apologists complained in print that church-papistry denoted spiritual weakness, it can also be seen as a sign of Catholicism's continued hold on popular sympathy.[10] But for Catholic leaders exhorting their flocks, recusant Catholics remained the ideal: individuals who refused to attend services, and were fined for their pains. Recusants were more conspicuous to contemporaries and, because their non-attendance was monitored, they are more recoverable to the historian. In theory, the cost of conscience in Elizabethan England was staggering; fines were set at 12d per day in 1559, and increased to £20 per month in 1581.[11] Though fines could be reduced and were often unsystematically collected, they suggest why Catholicism became to some degree a gentlemanly and aristocratic preserve.[12]

Many Elizabethan and some Jacobean Catholics were persecuted, and the martyrs of this persecution rivet the attention so much that it is easy to forget the activities of the Catholics who escaped, or who enjoyed some level of toleration, or who were never noticed in the first place. Since it was only Catholic priests whose activities were treasonable, the authorities were more interested in hunting down priests than Catholic laymen, and lay Catholics at different periods or in different parts of the country would have had very discrepant experiences. Freedom of worship could almost exist in areas such as the north-west of England, where Catholicism remained strong and enjoyed plenty of support from the local aristocracy, or in London, where the embassy chapels catering to foreign Catholics could also facilitate the worship of native Londoners. At court, crypto-Catholic noblemen like Henry Howard, Earl of Northampton, could play an important part in government and diplomacy, and towards the end of Donne's life, the Catholic presence at court was enhanced through the presence of Charles I's queen, Henrietta Maria.[13] Though one needed to be a member of the Church of England to take one's university degree, Donne's *alma mater*, Hart Hall in Oxford, was well known as a place where Catholics could at least benefit from a university environment.[14] Another way to evade the worst consequences of recusancy would have been for a family to combine Catholic witness with temporizing, to avoid the forfeiture of estates. Since under common law a husband was not liable for his wife's debts, a conforming husband married to a recusant wife could minimize depredations to an estate while still keeping the faith in the family. More generally, women had enormous importance in maintaining post-Reformation English Catholicism, as managers of households and as educators of the young.[15]

All this should be borne in mind when looking at Donne's early life. Donne's mother, Elizabeth Heywood, belonged to one of the best-known Catholic families in England, connected by marriage to many others: the Ropers, the Rastells, and most illustriously the descendants of Sir Thomas More, Henry VIII's Lord Chancellor who was executed for opposing England's break with Rome (see Flynn, *John Donne*). Donne's parents appear to have been lifelong Catholics and his brother, Henry Donne, was imprisoned for harboring a Catholic priest and died in jail. This inheritance was literary as well as religious, and Donne could count a number of witty Catholics among his ancestors and relations: not only Sir Thomas More, but John Heywood, the poet and playwright who acted as jester at the court of Mary I, and went into a self-imposed religious exile on the continent within a few years of Elizabeth I's coming to the throne.[16] The Jesuit Jasper

Heywood, John Heywood's son and Donne's uncle, is best-known in a literary context for his translations from Seneca, the ancient Roman playwright and moralist whose writing had an enormous influence on English Renaissance literature, encapsulating stoical ideals of behavior which have been seen as speaking to the condition of English Catholics (cf. chapter 6, pp. 85–86).[17]

In *Pseudo-Martyr*, a distinctly anti-stoical work which argues that brave suffering is not praiseworthy in itself, Donne tells the reader that his pre-occupation with martyrdom stems from his ancestry: "I have beene ever kept awake in a meditation of Martyrdome, by being derived from such a stocke and race, as, I beleeve, no family, (which is not of farre larger extent, and greater branches,) hath endured and suffered more in their persons and fortunes, for obeying the Teachers of Romane Doctrine" (p. 8). Generations of critics have seen Donne's preoccupation with discontinuity in belief as an agonistic reaction to his family inheritance. Donne's satirical epic "*Metempsychosis*: The Progresse of the Soule," written early in his career, is cryptic and incomplete but obliquely admits to this conflict. Though displaying "lingering Catholic affiliations," (Carey, p. 134), it is structured around a satiric inversion of the "argument from antiquity" (one of the strongest weapons in the Catholic church's polemical armoury), which maintained that no other church could illustrate an unbroken line of descent from the Apostles. Heresy, not orthodoxy, provides the element of continuity in Donne's narrative. The poem's title refers to the Greek philosopher Pythagoras's belief in the transmigration of souls. As Donne explains in his preface, the soul of heresy "to whom *Luther*, and *Mahomet* were / Prisons of flesh" (66–67) was first embodied in the apple eaten by Eve, and has jour-neyed onward through time through the bodies of a mandrake, a sparrow, three fish, a whale, a mouse, a wolf, a bitch, an ape, and Themech – Cain's sister and wife – with hints of a more contemporary incarnation. But the speaker of "*Metempsychosis*" is too skeptical to be straightforwardly Catholic or even obediently Christian, firing off questions inspired by the fall of man which were to reverberate through heterodox discourse long after Donne's time: "Would God (disputes the curious Rebell) make / A law, and would not have it kept? Or can / His creatures will, crosse his? Of every man / For one, will God (and be just) vengeance take?" (103–06). Though the speaker then restrains himself, "Arguing is heretiques game" (118), a poem dedicated to showing how heretics can argue from tradition temporarily inveigles the reader into making common cause with heresy. Here as else-where, Menippean satire, the genre in which Donne is writing, can be a privileged space for philosophical experimentation.[18]

It is another classical precedent, the formal verse satire associated with the ancient Roman poets Horace and Juvenal, that inspires Donne's most famous inquiry into the effect of religious pluralism and controversy on the individual. Like "*Metempsychosis*," "Satyre III" dates from Donne's early life and employs a frequently skeptical approach to contemporary religious difficulties. Its speaker's injunction, "doubt wisely; in strange way / To stand inquiring right, is not to stray" (77–78), has a prophetically agnostic ring to it, but the poem goes on to explain that this mental liberty is only provisional. Truth stands on a "huge hill, / Cragged, and steep," and "hee that will / Reach her, about must, and about must goe" (79–81). Religious inquiry is conceived as something strenuous and personal. The individual is discouraged from allowing other, fallible human beings to make up his mind for him – "wilt thou let thy Soule be tyed / To mans lawes, by which she shall not be tryed / At the last day?' (93–95) – and the law of the land is seen as something that must not be submitted to without good reason: "That thou mayest rightly power obey, her bounds know" (100).

If "Satyre III" has one overriding theme, it is that where religion is concerned, an individual's secular obligations have strictly defined limits, whether in the public domain or at a private, familial level. The poem is predicated on the question of which religious denomination to choose, but the speaker exhorts his addressee: "unmoved thou / Of force must one, and forc'd but one allow; / And the right; aske thy father which is shee, / Let him aske his ..." (69–72). This last line is a pivotal moment in the satire; like "*Metempsychosis*," "Satyre III" explores the topic of religious continuity, here by linking notions of familial authority to those of Church tradition. Both Catholics and Protestants acknowledged that Christians had a duty to sustain apostolic tradition; Catholics saw that tradition as visible and continuously testified to in the Church as well as in scripture, while Protestants, contending that Catholic corruptions nullified this argument, advocated a return to New Testament precedent. In "The Litanie," probably written some time after "Satyre III," Donne again addresses the fallibility of his ancestors by focusing on the flaws of the Church Fathers: theological writers whose works were regarded as authoritative by Catholics and endorsed to different degrees by the Protestant churches, but never regarded as on a level with scripture or above human error.[19] The poem mimicks one liturgical function of Catholic litanies, to give a list of saints and ask for their prayers. But it asks the "sacred Academe above / of Doctors" to "pray for us there / That what they have misdone / Or mis-said, wee to that may not adhere" (109–10, 113–15). The terms "patristics" and "Church Fathers" indicate how the notion of family inheritance has always given metaphorical shape to views on Church tradition. For Donne, filial respect is praiseworthy, but one can only abide by paternal authority if one's forefathers are right.

In his acknowledgment of the familial dimension to authority and Church tradition, Donne is invoking an impersonal and widely shared train of thought, not simply talking about his own circumstances. But it is hardly surprising that poems like "Satyre III" and "The Litanie" have been read as semi-autobiographical. One must never automatically identify Donne with the speakers of his verse; nevertheless, it is hard to believe that any author, let alone one with Donne's religious inheritance, would not have thought of his own family when writing lines like those quoted above. But in Donne's work, hints at personal revelation are all the more thrilling because they are indirect and never fully followed up, which is why attempts at autobiographical exegesis are invariably difficult to sustain. Like the first coterie readers of Donne's poetry, we are likely to apply our knowledge of his life to "Satyre III"; yet the poem is an outward-looking composition, largely written in the second person and posing a series of ethical challenges to its audience. One sees greater reflexivity in a poem like "The Litanie," where the speaker invites psychobiographical analysis at one moment and takes up a spokes-manlike stance the next, alternating between the first-person singular and the first-person plural as if glancing confessional insights are constantly being called to account by the liturgical framework. Most reflexive of all is the way in which, having posed such a pointed critique of Church tradition, the speaker foresees the opposite danger, and warns against too much religious individualism in his request that the Apostles may "pray still, and be heard, that I goe / Th'old broad way in applying; O decline / Mee, when my comment would make thy word mine" (79–81). Certainly, the ideals of inclusivity and shared meaning led naturally on from Donne's preoccupation with Church tradition, and informed his Protestant writing.

Donne as Protestant

Donne declared in 1610 that his decision to join the Church of England had not been a sudden or precipitate one, but was the result of a long period of study in which he "survayed and digested the whole body of Divinity, controverted between ours and the Romane Church" (*Pseudo-Martyr*, p. 13). We do not know precisely when he converted from Catholicism to Protestantism, but we have three prose works – all written in the period 1608–14, between his conversion and his ordination – which shed some light on his reasons for doing so. The first is *A Catholike Appeale for Protestants* (1609), a massive work of anti-Catholic controversy by Donne's patron Thomas Morton, dean of Gloucester and later bishop of Durham. Though published under Morton's name, this was a collaborative work written by "a certaine number of Divines" with Morton as general editor; we know from one of Donne's surviving letters that he was reading the manuscript of the *Catholike Appeale* in March 1608, eighteen months before publication, and it is possible that Morton was employing him as a research assistant to gather material for the book (Bald, pp. 210–12; see also chapter 6, p. 91). The second is Donne's own *Pseudo-Martyr* (1610), written in defence of the new legal restrictions imposed on Catholics in the aftermath of the Gunpowder Plot; and the third is his *Essays in Divinity*, later described by his son as "the voluntary sacrifices of severall hours, when he had many debates betwixt God and himself, whether he were worthy, and competently learned to enter into Holy Orders" (p. 4).

One common theme running through all these works is a fascination with names and naming. "Names," writes Donne in the *Essays in Divinity*, "are either to avoid confusion, and distinguish particulars ... Or else, names are to instruct us, and express natures and essences. This *Adam* was able to do." At the beginning of the world, when Adam "named every thing by [its] most eminent and virtuall property," there was a perfect congruence between names and things. But now, the close connection between names and things has been severed. The unstable meaning of words has created new forms of ambiguity, a point Donne illustrates with a list of words, such as "anathema" and "heresy," which have changed their meaning over time and been applied to "other significations, than their nature enclined to" (pp. 23, 45).

In the *Catholike Appeale* and *Pseudo-Martyr*, this interest in names is turned to polemical advantage, in trying to detach certain words from their generally accepted Catholic interpretation and reclaim them for Protestant use. The *Catholike Appeale* grapples with the word "catholic" itself, arguing that the Church of England upholds the doctrine of Christ and the apostles in all its original purity and is therefore, properly speaking, a part of the Catholic Church. *Pseudo-Martyr*, as its title suggests, tackles the word "martyr," and argues that the Roman Catholic priests who have given their lives for their religion are counterfeit martyrs because they died for an unjust cause.[20] Both works thus share a common style of argument, in claiming to be reattaching words to their true meanings, and also invoke a common rhetoric of inclusivity, in claiming to be rescuing words like "catholic" and "martyr" from the narrow and divisive meanings imposed on them by the Church of Rome.[21] In *Pseudo-Martyr*, Donne does not quarrel with the principle of giving one's life as a martyr for the Catholic faith, but argues that the Roman Church has smuggled its own false doctrines into its definition of the term Catholic. "To offer our lives for defence of the Catholique faith hath ever been a religious custome, but to cal every pretence of the Pope, Catholique faith, and to bleede to death for it, is a sicknesse and a medicine, which the Primitive Church never understoode" (p. 19).

To depict oneself as generously inclusive, and one's opponent as narrowly exclusive, was of course a very effective polemical strategy; but for Donne, it was also a matter of personal conviction. In a crucial passage in the *Essays*, he defends his membership in the Church of England but makes it clear that he regards the Church of Rome as part of the "universal, Christian, Catholick Church." He approaches the subject, in characteristically indirect fashion, via a discussion of names and their meanings. Many of the characters in the Old Testament, he points out, are denoted by more than one name: "Esau" and "Edom," for example, are one and the same person. Why should God have permitted this apparent ambiguity in the Holy Scriptures? Perhaps, Donne suggests, it was to teach us "that an unity and consonance in things not essentiall, is not so necessarily requisite as is imagined" (pp. 48–49). If one man can have several different names, surely the Church can adopt different forms of worship and government while still remaining one in Christ; and surely it is possible for the Protestant churches to reject the false doctrines of the Roman Church while remaining in fundamental unity with her.

In making these remarks, Donne was joining in an ongoing debate among English Protestant writers on whether the Church of Rome could be regarded as a true church, and, if so, in what sense. By the early seventeenth century, most writers had come round to the view that the Roman Church was a true church "in some sense" (*secundum quid*), in that she still retained a foundation of true faith, though with a superstructure of false doctrine on top of it.[22] This apparent concession served a number of useful purposes. In particular, it enabled Protestants to exonerate themselves from the charge of novelty. As they saw it, they had not built new churches on entirely new foundations; rather, they had pulled down the tottering superstructure of the Roman Church in order to build something stronger on the old foundations. In Donne's words, it was right that the Protestant churches, "keeping still the foundation and corner stone Christ Jesus, should piously abandon the spacious and specious super-edifications which the Church of Rome had built thereupon" (*Essays*, p. 49). This made it possible to present the Reformation in more positive terms, as a process of creative reconstruction rather than wanton destruction.

This metaphor of the church as building was a commonplace of Jacobean religious polemic, but different writers used it in different ways and drew sharply differing conclusions from it. Some argued that the Church of Rome was a building whose foundation could not bear its weight – that is, a church whose errors were so great, and so severe, that they shattered the foundation of true faith on which they were built. Donne explicitly rejected this argument, declaring that the foundation was "not destroyed" but merely "hid and obscured." And what of the building itself? Many writers argued that the Roman Church was permeated with idolatry to the point where, like a building riddled with woodworm or dry rot, the whole structure was inherently unsound. Again, Donne firmly rejected this argument, describing Roman Catholic doctrines as being "of so dangerous a construction, and appearance, and misapplyableness, that to tender consciences they seem'd Idolatrous, and are certainly scandalous and very slippery, and declinable into Idolatry" (*Essays*, p. 49).[23] Donne is choosing his words with great care here. He acknowledges that the doctrines of the Roman Church may seem like idolatry, and may tend towards idolatry, but he is careful not to say that they are idolatrous in themselves: a significantly more moderate stance than that of many of his contemporaries.

Other writers, though, were thinking along much the same lines as Donne, and had come to realize that by stressing the fundamental unity of the Catholic and Protestant churches, it was possible to take much of the heat out of religious controversy. An important passage in the *Catholike Appeale* points out that the Roman Church maintains the fundamental articles of faith – the unity of the Godhead, the three persons of the Trinity, the divinity of Christ, and "the power of his death and resurrection, by which we have remission of sins, and after death life everlasting" – and argues that it is quite possible for Roman Catholics to be saved as long as they do not deny any of these articles, do not reject any further truths that may be opened to them, and do not place too much confidence in their own merits rather than the mercy and forgiveness of Christ.[24] There is no evidence to suggest that Donne wrote this particular passage, but as probably one of the team of scholars involved in writing the book, he would have read it, and on the basis of his other writings it seems safe to say that he would have approved of it. It suggests that from the very beginning of his career in the Church of England, Donne was part of a group of divines who were trying to adopt a more moderate and irenic approach towards the Church of Rome.

One of these divines was John Overall, who at that time was Dean of St. Paul's, the post that Donne was later to occupy. Although the *Catholike Appeale* was published under Morton's name, it was later claimed that Overall "revised and amended" the work, and "in truth was the chief author of it."[25] As Regius Professor of Divinity at Cambridge in the 1590s, Overall had been one of the first English divines to challenge the commonly received view that the Pope was the Antichrist. But his moderation was not limited to his attitude to Roman Catholicism; he was also a leading opponent of the hard-line Calvinist position on predestination, and it is possible he influenced Donne in this respect as well. In "Satyre III," Donne poked fun at those who took the Calvinist church of Geneva as their sole model of true religion: "Crants to such brave loves will not be enthralled, / But loves her only, who at Geneva is called / Religion ..." (49–51). But in joining the Church of England, he was coming into a church that was closely allied with that of Geneva – more closely, perhaps, than he would have liked. The Church of England was widely assumed to be doctrinally identical to the Protestant Reformed churches of the Continent, differing only in its system of church government; and many English clergy subscribed to a strict Calvinist doctrine of double predestination in which every human being was divinely predestined to heaven or hell, regardless of their own actions. Did Donne share these views – or did he, like Overall, find himself at odds with the prevailing Calvinist orthodoxy?

By the early seventeenth century, two main theories of predestination had emerged within the English Church: one rigidly determinist, the other more moderate. The first – commonly known as "supralapsarianism," or, more informally, as "high Calvinism" – held that God's decree of predestination must logically have preceded his decree to permit the fall of Adam, and was therefore completely irrespective of human sinfulness. Defenders of this position liked to quote the words of St. Paul, in the Epistle to the Romans, to show that God had absolute power over his creation: "Shall the thing formed say to him that formed it, Why hast thou made me thus? Hath not the potter power over the clay, of the same lump to make one vessel unto honour, and another unto dishonour?" (9:20–21). The great advantage of supralapsarianism was that it affirmed and safeguarded the absolute sovereignty of God; but the corresponding disadvantage was that, in doing so, it made God appear to be an arbitrary tyrant, who had created some human beings merely in order to damn them, and consigned them to hell without any regard to their sins. The result was that this theory – having at one stage been the dominant school of thought within Reformed theology, with the backing of Calvin's successor Theodore Beza and his leading English disciple William Perkins – rapidly fell from favor after 1600 as its pastoral disadvantages became obvious.

The second theory – known as "infralapsarianism" – tried to solve these problems by reversing the order of the decrees, so that God's decree of predestination came after, not before, his decree to permit the fall of Adam. In other words, predestination was no longer irrespective of human sinfulness. Those who were saved, were saved *in spite of* their sins, as an act of divine mercy; those who were damned, were damned *because of* their sins, as an act of divine justice. This theory became increasingly popular in the early seventeenth century as a moderate alternative to the high Calvinist position; and Donne seems to lend it his support in the *Essays in Divinity*, where he writes that "out of a corrupt lumpe" God "selects and purifies a few." The idea that God's predestination is applied to mankind in a state of sinfulness – a "corrupt lumpe" or *massa perditionis* – is the hallmark of the infralapsarian position. Yet Donne accompanies this with a warning against enquiring too closely into the workings of God's predestination. "Who asks a charitable man that gives him an almes, where he got it, or why he gave it?" We should simply be grateful to God for his abundant generosity (p. 87).

Donne was notably reluctant to discuss the doctrine of predestination; and when he dealt with the topic in his sermons, he nearly always did so negatively, by way of an attack on the high Calvinist position. Preaching at Lincoln's Inn in 1619, he criticized certain unnamed "men" who "speak of decrees of reprobation, decrees of condemnation, before decrees of creation," while in a Paul's Cross sermon ten years later he denounced "men that will abridge, and contract the large mercies of God in Christ, and elude, and frustrate, in a great part, the generall promises of God" (*Sermons*, vol. II, no. 11, p. 246; vol. IX, no. 4, p. 119). These remarks are consistent with a view of Donne as a moderate infralapsarian, uncomfortable with the high Calvinist emphasis on reprobation and the accompanying doctrine of "limited atonement," which held that Christ had died for the elect alone, not for the whole world. But they could also be read as a sign that Donne had allied himself with Overall and other English divines who rejected the Reformed doctrine of predestination. These divines – usually referred to as Arminians, after the Dutch theologian Jacobus Arminius – adopted an alternative view of predestination as a response to human faith. According to this theory, God foresaw that some individuals would have faith in Christ, while others would not; accordingly, he elected the former and rejected the latter. This had the great advantage of making God appear just and reasonable, but it horrified many Protestant theologians by its emphasis on human free will, which seemed to undermine the sovereignty of God. If Donne held this view, then he would, by contemporary standards, have been on the extreme liberal wing of Reformed theology, and arguably outside the Reformed mainstream altogether – but if so, his desire to make inclusiveness a priority, and avoid multiplying controversial issues, might well have worked against positive advocacy of an Arminian position.

Conclusion

Donne's emotionally charged interest in finding common ground between the denominations comes out, perhaps, most strongly of all in his letters and verse. In an extraordinary and self-revealing passage in a letter to his friend

Sir Henry Goodyer, he declares that men cannot easily be made to change their settled habits and customs in religion:

> As some bodies are as wholesomly nourished as ours, with Akornes, and endure nakednesse, both which would be dangerous to us, if we for them should leave our former habits, though theirs were the Primitive diet and custome: so are many souls well fed with such formes, and dressings of Religion, as would distemper and misbecome us ... You shall seldome see a Coyne, upon which the stamp were removed, though to imprint it better, but it looks awry and squint. And so, for the most part, do mindes which have received divers impressions. (*Letters*, pp. 101–02)

Here, Donne seems at first glance to be endorsing the attitude he mocks in "Satyre III" through the depiction of Graccus, who "thinkes that so / As women do in divers countries goe / In divers habits, yet are still one kinde, / So doth, so is Religion" (65–68). But Graccus is a religious indifferentist, whereas Donne does not minimize the significance of the differences between confessions; his liberal attitude arises from being acutely conscious of the shaping power of environment and upbringing. "Once a Catholic, always a Catholic" could be the implication of the letter, and Donne even goes on to compare the "Roman" and the "Reformed" religion in markedly balanced terms which seem to imply that his own temperamental preference would be for Catholic spirituality without some of the doctrines: the Roman religion "seems to exhale, and refine our wills from earthly Drugs, and Lees, more than the Reformed, and so seems to bring us nearer heaven" (p. 102). Most strikingly intimate of all is the comment: "And when you descend to satisfie all men in your own religion, or to excuse others to al; you prostitute your self and your understanding, though not a prey, yet a mark, and a hope, and a subject, for every sophister in Religion to work on" (p. 103).

This feeling that one cannot justify one's religion to everyone, and perhaps should not even try, reveals the other side of Donne's search for common ground between the denominations. Sexualized metaphors for religious activity, as here, pervade Donne's writing throughout his life, though they are more often used to denote the Church as a potential or actual partner. It is a critical commonplace that Donne insistently links religion and woman – often with the effect of ironizing religion and denigrating women, thus picking up on the double-edgedness implicit in St. Paul's original description of the Church as the spouse of Christ. In this marriage, Christ remains the unerring point of reference, but since the Church is only the aggregate of believing mankind, she can be portrayed as a foolish wanderer, a glorious unspotted bride, or anything in between. The ecclesiastical fissures of the Reformation inspired polemicists of all denominations to coin comparisons between false churches and undesirable women, and churches identified as false could be seen as possessing attributes of the Whore of Babylon from the Book of Revelation – an accusation most commonly levelled by Protestants against the Catholic Church.

Donne's religious verse and his verse about religion employ polemical female personifications of the Church. "Satyre III" presents various satirical characters whose imprudence in courtship reflects their religious delusions: the Calvinist Crantz and the religious relativist Graccus; Mirreus, the Catholic, searching for a mistress last seen a thousand years ago; Graius, a member of the Church of England who, like a ward of court wishing to avoid financial penalties, takes a wife simply because his guardian proffers her; and the over-prudent skeptic Phrygius who, "knowing some women whores, dares marry none" (64). The satire is tilted more towards the characters than the churches, and the possibility that one might choose the right mistress for the wrong reason is left open. All the same, the poem does not explicitly endorse any of these potential relationships and looks forward to a later verse, Donne's holy sonnet "Show me deare Christ, thy spouse, so bright and cleare."

This sonnet is built around the woman/church metaphor, and the open questions in the first half of the poem present Catholicism and Protestantism in what appear to be an even balance. The speaker asks if Christ's spouse is the Catholic Church, "richly painted" "on the other shore," or the one which "rob'd and tore / Laments and mournes in Germany and here" (2–4) (cf. chapter 6, p. 87). We are presented with two alternatives, which may or may not exclude each other: the true Church either "dwells ... with us," in the Church of England, or seekers after truth have to journey further afield, working towards her "like adventuring knights" (9). Finally, Donne's speaker asks Christ, "Betray kind husband thy spouse to our sights, / And let myne amorous soul court thy mild Dove / Who is most trew, and pleasing to thee, then / When she'is embrac'd and open to most men" (11–14). This plea takes its bearings from the standard reversals of sacred parody, whereby sexual language or behavior is subsumed to a religious end. But the wording is unusually stark, and the postulation unusually risky; the Church as Christ's prostituted spouse, and – even more – Christ himself as complaisant cuckold, is a disorienting image with which to conclude. Though the need for inclusiveness is the whole point of the poem, and there is no reason to doubt the sincerity of Donne's wish for it, the deliberate coarseness of his metaphor maximizes a sense of danger. In place of "Satyre III's" apprehension that religious choice may lead to damnation, we are left with the image of religious inclusiveness as sexual indiscriminacy. Perhaps no English poet has ever been so conscious of the dark side of religion.

NOTES

1 David S. Katz, *The Jews in the History of England 1485–1850* (Oxford: Clarendon, 1994), p. 109. Cf. James Shapiro, *Shakespeare and the Jews* (New York: Columbia University Press, 1996), pp. 62–76.
2 John Stow, *Survey of London* (1633), p. 780.
3 Nabil Matar, *Islam in Britain 1558–1685* (Cambridge: Cambridge University Press, 1998).
4 Bald, *Donne*, p. 262.
5 Keith Thomas, *Religion and the Decline of Magic* (1971; rpt. Harmondsworth: Penguin, 1973), p. 198.
6 Michael Hunter, "The Problem of 'Atheism' in Early Modern England," *Transactions of the Royal Historical Society*, 5th ser., 35 (1985), 135–57 (quotation 154).
7 Michael Questier, *Conversion, Politics and Religion in England, 1580–1625* (Cambridge: Cambridge University Press, 1996), p. 9.
8 Carey, *Donne*, p. 37.
9 Helen Gardner (ed.), *The Divine Poems* (Oxford: Clarendon Press, 1952), p. 131.
10 Alexandra Walsham, *Church Papists* (London: Boydell / Royal Historical Society, 1993), ch. 2.
11 Michael A. Mullett, *Catholics in Britain and Ireland, 1558–1829* (Basingstoke: Macmillan, 1998), p. 15.
12 John Bossy, *The English Catholic Community, 1570–1850* (London: Darton, Longman and Todd, 1975). Marie B. Rowlands (ed.), *Catholics of Parish and Town, 1558–1778* (London: Catholic Record Society, 1999), discusses Catholics from the lower orders.
13 Linda Levy Peck, *Northampton* (London: George Allen and Unwin, 1982); Erica Veevers, *Images of Love and Religion* (Cambridge: Cambridge University Press, 1989).
14 Flynn, *Donne and The Ancient Catholic Nobility*, pp. 131–32.
15 Marie B. Rowlands, "Recusant Women, 1560–1640," in Mary Prior (ed.), *Women in English Society, 1500–1800* (London: Methuen, 1985), pp. 149–80.
16 For Heywood's life, see Dictionary of National Biography (DNB).
17 See J. H. M. Salmon, "Seneca and Tacitus in Jacobean England," in Linda Levy Peck (ed.), *The Mental World of the Jacobean Court* (Cambridge: Cambridge University Press, 1991), ch. 10.
18 See Alison Shell, "Multiple Religious Conversion and the Menippean Self: the Case of Richard Carpenter," in Arthur F. Marotti (ed.), *Catholicism and Anti-Catholicism in Seventeenth-Century Texts* (Basingstoke: Macmillan, 1999), pp. 154–97.
19 Gardner, p. 81, dates "The Litanie" to the autumn of 1608.
20 This argument was commonly used in the Reformation. See Brad Gregory, *Salvation at Stake* (Cambridge, Mass.: Harvard University Press, 1999), ch. 8.
21 Jeanne Shami, "Labels, Controversy, and the Language of Inclusion in Donne's sermons," in David Colclough (ed.), *John Donne's Professional Lives* (Cambridge: D. S. Brewer, 2003), pp. 135–57.
22 On the "true church" debate, see Anthony Milton, *Catholic and Reformed* (Cambridge: Cambridge University Press, 1995), and "The Church of England, Rome and the True Church: the Demise of a Jacobean Consensus," in Kenneth

Fincham (ed.), *The Early Stuart Church, 1603–1642* (Basingstoke: Macmillan, 1993).
23 See Milton, *Catholic and Reformed*, pp. 176–87, on "fundamentals and additions."
24 Thomas Morton (?), *A Catholike Appeale* (1609), pp. 443–46.
25 Note by John Cosin in his copy of the book, quoted in Milton, *Catholic and Reformed*, p. 233 n. 26.

6

TOM CAIN

Donne's political world

Scholars have disagreed over Donne's political attitudes for some years now, some representing him as a committed (or just a cynical) monarchist, others as an early modern liberal, subtly critical of the claims to "absolute" power made by the Stuart kings. The first group cite explicit absolutist statements and the implications of monarchic figures in his poetry. They emphasize his apparent ambition and his cultivation of powerful courtiers. Some make this case with regret for what they judge to be Donne's opportunism; others see him as coerced by the dominant discourse of power. Those who qualify this view read the monarchic imagery of the love poems not as endorsing absolutism but as asserting the lovers' autonomy. Against his explicit endorsements of monarchic rule they set the levelling implications of his emphasis on a common humanity, and on mankind's equality before God, discovering between the lines of his later work a continuation of the disparagement of monarchy found in the *Satires*. They note Donne remained on good terms with "oppositionist" friends, and was not the only person in England who changed his religious allegiance in the second half of the sixteenth century: so did many thousands of others. They infer a lack of ambition from his impolitic marriage, and from hints that he was subsequently reluctant to re-enter the political world.

In fact Donne is much less of a time-server than some have averred, less of a subtle dissident than others would like him to have been. Criticism of the monarchy is found at the beginning and the end of his political life, but the conflict between integrity, proto-liberalism, and an acceptance of Jacobean absolutism is more apparent than real, and is largely a result of applying anachronistic political values to the period. Even David Norbrook's influential essay on Donne's politics, which warns against anachronistic analysis, finds in the growth of absolutist theory of the 1600s "a shift to the right," a nineteenth-century concept.[1] Donne's political views developed before the Civil Wars initiated British party politics; lines of division were unclear. Parliament had not yet become a center of opposition, and though James I theorized about the divine origins of his power, he ruled largely within established laws. "Absolutism" meaning autonomous monarchy was accepted by virtually the whole political nation, including those who opposed the extension of royal prerogative powers (powers not subject to any parliamentary or legal restriction). Disagreements over the prerogative were seen as containable, and appeared less threatening than a Roman Catholic church reinvigorated since the mid-sixteenth-century Council of Trent. Politics was in this and other respects inseparable from religion, and it is to contemporary Christianity that we must turn to make sense of Donne's politics.

Donne's insistence that it is "our first Originary, naturall, and Congenite obedience, to obey the Prince" (Pseudo-Martyr, p. 134) sounds like servile conformity to modern readers. But obedience was then, as the Homily against Disobedience put it, "the very root of all virtues."[2] The founding myths of Christianity were about the disastrous consequences of disobedience. The first to challenge God's authority was the archangel Lucifer, cast out from Heaven with his fellow rebels. Their fall was followed by that of Man, whose fatal act of disobedience could only be redeemed by a compensatory act of filial obedience by Christ. Consequently Donne associates rebellion with Satanic "Treasons, and Seditions" (Sermons, vol. IV, no. 9, p. 245), and praises Elizabeth Drury because "she crucified / Every first motion of rebellious pride" (Second Anniversary, 365–66).

For Donne, God as king and father presided over a patriarchal structure which was by definition hierarchic. The imperfect post-lapsarian hierarchies of earth were conceived in its image. Donne sees this order under threat in the First Anniversary (1611) where, like Shakespeare in Troilus and Cressida (1.iii.75–137), he equates its demise with a descent into chaos:

> Prince, Subject, Father, Sonne, are things forgot,
> For every man alone thinkes he hath got
> To be a Phoenix, and that then can bee
> None of that kinde, of which he is, but hee.   (215–18)

That God favored a hierarchic structure over a democratic one predicated a political structure in which the king held power from God, with those at other levels having their assigned political parts. As subjects, all owed obedience to the king, but each owed deference to those above them in "degree," and what Donne called charity to those below, from the king to the poorest subject. The fundamental social embodiment of this hierarchic system was the family, the constitutional one the combination of king, lords and commons in parliament.

A less obvious but important corollary was the system of patronage (from the same root as patriarchy) through which monarchic power functioned. Donne has been much criticized because, looking for a job, he cultivated such favorites as the Earl of Somerset, later to be convicted of complicity in the murder of his and Donne's friend, Thomas Overbury. Donne knew nothing of this at the time, and the wide awareness that favoritism could present political problems did not undermine general acceptance that powerful patrons had a legitimate role as conduits of that royal favor which godlike "is defus'd o'r all, / From which all Fortunes, Names, and Natures fall" (Epithalamion at the Marriage of the Earl of Somerset: "Ecclogue," 23–24). Thus when Donne acknowledges that there is nothing Somerset can call his own "more absolutely and entirely" than himself, what seems now "abject dependence"[3] is for Donne the appropriate acknowledgement of his obligation to "a person whom God had made so great an instrument of his providence."[4]

This is one kind of contextualization. We also need to see Donne's politics in the light of events which had shaped his England. Over the forty years before his birth the country had lurched from traditional Roman Catholicism to a Catholicism which denied Papal hegemony, to a moderate Protestantism, succeeded by thoroughgoing Calvinism, and back to Roman Catholicism until, in 1559, Elizabeth restored a moderate Protestant Church of England which retained such Papist institutions as Bishops. As this overview suggests, during Donne's formative years the nation could not simply be divided into opposing Catholic and Protestant camps (cf. chapter 5, p. 67). Belief spread over a spectrum in which only those at the extreme ends were in militant opposition to each other and to the compulsory Church of England. Extreme policies – the burning of heretics, the destruction of images – were indeed divisive, but there were strong elements of continuity: the church hierarchy, the clergymen's vestments, rituals still recognizable in Cranmer's translations, and the uninterrupted presence of many parish priests. When Henry VIII broke with Rome over Papal authority in 1533–34, few were moved to place the Italian Pope above the English King; indeed, the orthodox Catholic Philip II of Spain was soon to declare war on the Papacy over the same issue. The most famous of those who did defend Papal supremacy was Donne's great-great uncle, Sir Thomas More. Donne admired More, "a man of the most tender and delicate conscience that the world saw since St. Augustine" (*Biathanatos*, p. 62). Six decades after More's execution, however, Donne, like the majority of his compatriots, if with more difficulty than most, came to reconcile loyalty to the old Catholic faith with the Anglican church which he still saw as "Catholic."

Only a small minority of English Catholics supported the militant doctrines of the Council of Trent, which encouraged them to depose their heretical monarch. The majority adhered to an older Catholicism in which national loyalties were at least as strong as those to Rome. Elizabeth had been anointed by a Catholic bishop in a Catholic coronation, so that, illegitimate heretic or not, she still commanded their loyalty. There is evidence that Donne's immediate family belonged to this loyalist group. When his brother Henry died in prison in 1593 for harboring a Catholic secular priest (one living "in the world" and not belonging to a religious order), it was believed Jesuits, fierce proponents of Counter-Reformation militancy, had betrayed him. The secular priests, unlike the Jesuits, asserted their loyalty in all but their religion. Donne's uncle Jasper Heywood, though himself a Jesuit, was a loyalist and opposed his order's policy. Henry's betrayal and death is a probable determinant for John's move away from Roman Catholicism, a motive more than strong enough to counter the construct of ambitious but tortured "apostate" (a religious turncoat) offered by John Carey.[5] Later, Donne criticized the Counter-Reformation church for turning "opinions" into "articles of faith" (*Sermons*, vol. X, no. 7, p. 174). The new Catholicism was a "younger religion"; Protestant Anglicanism, whatever its imperfections, seemed closer to the church of his forefathers. Do not, he warned a congregation, adopt "the slavery, and bondage of *mens traditions*; you that are in possession of the ancient Religion, of Christ, and his Apostles" (*Sermons*, vol. VI, no. 4, p. 98). In a letter of April 1627, which gives the most succinct summary of his politics, he was even able to claim "My tenets are always, for the preservation of the Religion I was born in, and the peace of the State, and the rectifying of the Conscience; in these I shall walke" (*Letters*, pp. 306–07).

This linking of peace with religion is typical of Donne. The Jesuit appeal to violence was a major factor in the opposition of men like him to post-Tridentine Catholicism. Between 1588, when the Spanish Armada sought to depose the heretic Elizabeth, and 1610, when Donne published *Pseudo-Martyr*, Catholic justification of the assassination of heretical rulers was blamed for the murders of two kings of France, and the attempted murder of James I along with his principal heirs and the entire membership of both houses of parliament in the Gunpowder Plot of 1605.

Although Donne's political attitudes changed over his adult life, certain constants emerge, this commitment to peace being one. With it goes a reiterated desire to avoid disputation: "I would at last contentious men would leave wrangling, and people to whom those things belonged not, leave blowing of coales" he said in 1626 (*Sermons*, vol. VII, no. 4, pp. 121–22). With it too goes an emphasis on the unifying essentials of Christianity (cf. chapter 5, pp. 75–76), which leads him to see the various churches, whatever their differences as "still one Corporation" (*Letters*, p. 164). This tolerance caused him and his friend Richard Martyn to be called "libertines in religion,"[6] but it was a cornerstone of Donne's politics, reinforcing another constant, his passionate belief in the unity of humanity:

The *Church* is *Catholike, universall,* so are all her *Actions; All* that she does, belongs to *all* ... All *mankinde* is of one *Author,* and is one *volume.*
(*Devotions,* Meditation 17, p. 97)

This belief extended to the Native Americans, often categorized as sub-human by Donne's contemporaries, but to Donne "neighbours," for

a man is thy Neighbor, by his Humanity, not by his Divinity; by his Nature, not by his Religion: a Virginian is thy Neighbor, as well as a Londoner; and all men are in every good man's Diocess, and Parish.   (*Sermons,* vol. IV, no. 3, p. 110)

Closely related to this is his belief in charity, "because we doe stand in need of one another ... When a poore wretch beggs *of* thee, and thou givest, thou dost but justice, it is his" (*Sermons,* vol. II, no. 10, p. 214).

A literary-political principle which Donne always applied and which complicates assessment of his politics was that of decorum, the framing of his discourse to fit the form, audience and occasion.[7] The early satires and elegies circulated during the 1590s among friends from the Inns of Court, the London law schools which provided a sophisticated audience which could be trusted with a kind of discourse that could not and should not be published more widely. Much later, in the holy sonnet beginning "Show me deare Christ," Donne agonized to a similarly restricted audience (the poem only survives in one manuscript) over the fate of Protestantism during the Thirty Years War, questioning God's purpose (cf. chapter 5, p. 80); but these doubts could not be shared with the congregation to whom he preached "to establish and settle them, that suspect Gods power, or Gods purpose, to succour those, who in forraine parts, grone under heavie pressures" (*Sermons,* vol. IV, no. 7, p. 183). What now seem hypocritical distinctions of audience and intent were another consequence of that hierarchical society to which Donne and even his most outspoken friends were committed.

The *Satires* do, however, testify to Donne's serious disillusionment with the last decade of Elizabeth's reign. Like many contemporaries, especially those with a Catholic background, he looked forward to the coming of the intellectual and supposedly more tolerant James. During the later 1590s Donne had attached himself to the Earl of Essex, who then offered hopes of reform and religious toleration, going as a gentleman volunteer on Essex's expeditions to Cadiz and the Azores in 1596–97. After Essex's fall Donne reflected on the earl's impetuosity; but he diagnosed the "ague" which afflicted court and state as deriving from Elizabeth herself, a disease curable only by her death: "thus it must be," he told Wotton, "till we get above the moone whose motions as some have ingeniously [av]erred do make us variable."[8] Elizabeth was commonly identified with the moon goddess Cynthia.

Donne is usually more cautious than this, and in another letter worries that there is "some danger" in his *Satires*, a reminder that fear limits even his most restricted discourse. When his brother was arrested, Donne himself apparently came under surveillance: "here I'have beene, / By staying in London, too much overseene" ("To Mr. E. G.," 5–6), and the *Satires* often invoke the dark late-Elizabethan world of informers. Donne feared slander and gossip throughout his life. In "Satyre IV" his *persona* fears he is "Becomming Traytor" simply through listening:

> ... mee thought I saw
> One of our Giant Statutes ope his jaw
> To sucke me in; for hearing him.   (131–33)

Such fears make the criticism of kings in "Satyre II" all the more significant. There the lawyer Coscus lies to every suitor "Like a Kings favorite, yea like a King" (69–70), and the narrator remarks, "Bastardy abounds not in Kings titles, nor / Symonie and Sodomy in Churchmens lives, / As these things do in him" (74–76). These are startlingly gratuitous similes. The characterization of kingly power in "Satyre III" is less reckless, in that it grows directly from the argument for religious integrity:

> ... men do not stand
> In so ill case here, that God hath with his hand
> Sign'd Kings blanck-charters to kill whom they hate,
> Nor are they Vicars, but hangmen to Fate.   (89–92)

The final line offers a definition of kingship which neither Elizabeth nor James could have accepted, for both believed that the monarch was God's vicar on earth.

Though the Queen could not be satirized, her frowns and smiles in "Satyre IV" make her subtly complicit in the corrupt transactions of her court:

> ... He knowes
> When the Queene frown'd, or smil'd, and he knowes what
> A subtle States-man may gather of that;
> He knowes who loves; whom; and who by poyson
> Hasts to an Offices reversion.   (98–102)

In "Satyre V" her exoneration from such corruption is complicated by a comparison that insidiously suggests she is its source:

> Greatest and fairest Empresse, know you this?
> Alas, no more then Thames calme head doth know
> Whose meades her armes drowne, or whose corne o'rflow ... (28–30)

A passage in Thomas More's *Utopia* which Donne later marked suggests he was aware of the hostile implications: "from the prince, as from a never failing spring, flows a stream of all that is good or evil over the whole nation."[9]

Another early poem, the elegy "Variety" uses political vocabulary to lament a lost sexual liberty:

> The golden laws of nature are repeald,
> Which our first Fathers in such reverence held;
> Our liberty's revers'd, our Charter's gone,
> And we're made servants to opinion ...
> Onely some few strong in themselves and free,
> Retain the seeds of antient liberty.   (48–51, 62–63)[10]

The appeal to "first Fathers" and a lost "Charter" invokes a version of English history which Edward Coke and others were soon to promote, in which the freedoms of Saxon England were regained after the Norman conquest, notably in the great "Charter," Magna Carta. Those who "retain the seeds of ancient liberty" are reminiscent too of Romans like Cato who died defending the republic against the autocratic ambition of Julius Caesar.

The subversive implications of this elegy are hedged about with facetiousness. So are similar ones in the prose *Problems* composed around 1608–10. *Problem 1* again blames "opinion" for the loss of liberty. Courtiers are often atheists, Donne proposes, "because they see that Opinion, and neede of one another, and feare, makes the degrees [i.e., different ranks] of Servants Lords and Kings" (*Paradoxes and Problems*, p. 23). This contrasts with the more orthodox statement that "God hath placed his Creatures in divers rankes, and in divers conditions" (*Sermons*, vol. VII, no. 17, p. 417). *Problem 10* wonders at the power of eloquence, which can "perswade people to take a yoake of Soveraignty and then beg and make lawes to tye them faster, and then give monny to the Invention, repayr and strengthen it" (p. 33). The genre of the "Problem" encouraged such contentious opinions, and the audience envisaged for these writings was again a limited one; but, as with the elegy "Variety," it is significant that Donne was drawn to sentiments so different from those he defended soon after in *Pseudo-Martyr*. They remain the most subversive of his comments on monarchy in the Jacobean period.

Despite his low opinion of the late-Elizabethan state, Donne's aim in the 1590s was for a career in its service. His mentor Thomas Morton referred later to Donne's "expectation of a state employment" and his "education and abilities" (Bald, p. 205). Trained in the law, Donne was fluent in Latin,

French, Spanish, and Italian. He had, he wrote, "begun early" to equip himself for a career

> when I understood the study of our laws: but was diverted by the worst voluptuousnes, which is an Hydroptique immoderate desire of humane learning and languages: beautifull ornaments to great fortunes; but mine needed an occupation, and a course which I thought I entred well into, when I submitted my self to such a service, as I thought might [have] imployed those poor advantages, which I had. (*Letters*, p. 51)

Donne's "advantages" made him a strong candidate for "state employment," and he made a promising start by becoming in late 1597 or 1598 a secretary to the Lord Keeper Egerton, head of the English legal system and a senior Privy Councillor. The appointment brought Donne close to the center of political power, and when through Egerton's influence he became an MP in 1601 he must have believed it was another important step. Donne is not recorded as contributing to any debate in Parliament, his role presumably being to represent Egerton's interests. Whatever circumspection he showed in the House of Commons, however, he signally failed to apply to his emotional life. Before this Parliament was dissolved he married Anne More, against the wishes of her influential father, a fellow MP. The repercussions were such that after a subsequent decade of unemployment he was to tell Goodyer that "I dyed at a blow then when my courses were diverted" (*Letters*, p. 122). Briefly imprisoned, sacked by Egerton, his wife's dowry withheld, his own inheritance largely spent, Donne's short political career came to an end.

The recklessness of the marriage suggests Donne was not as ambitious as most biographers assume. His reaction to exile from the world of power was in part to question his desire for advancement, even as he continued, in a desultory way, to look for it. His book-motto, which translates "Rachel I have served and not Leah," refers to a conflict between the contemplative and active lives in which Rachel stands for contemplative withdrawal. *Utopia* had explored the same issue, and much in Donne's poetry depends on his role as a liminal figure, exploiting the contrasts between the solitary poet and the populated worlds of London, the court, even, in the holy sonnet beginning "At the round earths imagin'd corners," the entire human race, past and present. The man who wrote there "But let them sleepe, Lord, and mee mourne a space" (9) may not have been fitted to climb high "because something in him just wasn't interested."[11] He may also have believed that Robert Cecil, the most powerful figure in the country after the monarch, opposed him. He had probably satirized Cecil in the cryptic "*Metempsychosis:* The Progresse of the Soule" (1601); certainly he played no part in public life until Cecil's power declined in 1610. But these years saw the arrival, in 1603, of a new monarch, who was to direct Donne's career towards the church, and with whom he shared many values. His reign marked a period in which Donne could subscribe to the ruler's principles without compromising his own.

Like Donne, James I was an irenic man who looked for a resolution of doctrinal differences, and the re-uniting of Christendom. Like Donne, he believed that kingly power was divinely sanctioned, but should be used only for the good of his subjects. Like Donne, he mistrusted both the Counter-Reformation Catholic Church and the Calvinists who had humiliated him as king of Scotland. Both groups – especially now the Catholics – held that his right to rule was based on an implicit contract with his subjects, and that if he broke it he could be deposed. Thomas Hobbes was later to develop the idea of the contract in ways which rejected such conditional terms; Donne, as much concerned with *"Peaceable* and *religious* Tranquility"* as Hobbes, anticipated him in his most explicit statement of political theory, *Pseudo-Martyr*, the first published (and probably the least read) of his works. Nowhere is the interpenetration of religion and politics which shaped Donne's life more clear than in the central argument of *Pseudo-Martyr*: that English Catholics could and should subscribe to the Oath of Allegiance to the king demanded after the Gunpowder Plot. The refusal of a similar demand in 1534 had led to Thomas More's execution. Donne now believed such a choice would be a pseudo-martyrdom.

Donne's whole life was a preparation for the argument of *Pseudo-Martyr*, but he had been working directly towards it for some years, helping Thomas Morton write his polemical defences of Anglicanism (see chapter 5, p. 74). Research for Morton paved the way for a book which combines impressive knowledge of canon law with broad mockery of Catholic superstition (Donne was writing his satire on the Jesuits, *Ignatius his Conclave*, at about the same time). At the core of *Pseudo-Martyr* is Donne's account of the origins of monarchic power.

Fatherhood, beginning in 1602–03, may have reinforced his belief in the patriarchal system. Though the commitment is already evident in "Satyre III," where truth is sought through the patriarchal line (71–72), the two earliest portraits of Donne show a clean-shaven challenger of the established order, the later ones a bearded and sober patriarch (see figures in chapter 1). The wider context had also changed with Elizabeth's death and the Gunpowder Plot, and the patriarchal authority over church and state that James represented now seemed the best defence against religious violence of the kind seen in France. Whereas Elizabeth had been an unmarried "virgin" queen, the accession of a king with a family made patriarchal theories more topical, especially as James had already written much about the good king's authority. Other prominent writers moved in the 1600s to defend the kingly power, influenced by such European theorists as Justus Lipsius and Jean Bodin. Monarchy was, Sir Walter Raleigh wrote, "the best Regiment [form of government] . . . which resembleth the Soveraigne Government of God himselfe."¹² This resemblance implied just government, although, like Donne, Raleigh had experienced monarchy's potential arbitrariness, and was at pains, like him, to distinguish it from tyranny.

To establish the king's independence of Papal authority, and justify the Oath of Allegiance, Donne developed his own version of a political theory just then gaining currency.¹³ He denies that kings' power derives "*Immediately* from God" (*Pseudo-Martyr*, p. 131), but also denies that it derives conditionally from the people. Rather than having transferred their individual powers to a ruler, mankind has been "imprinted" – hard-wired – by God with the desire to be subject to a sovereign power:

> God hath *Immediately* imprinted in mans Nature and Reason, to be subject to a power immediately infus'd from him; and … hee hath enlightned our Nature and Reason, to digest and prepare such a forme, as may bee aptest to doe those things, for which that *Power* is infus'd; which are, to conserve us in *Peace* and in *Religion*.   (p. 131)

Only after the community has instituted a form of sovereign authority (a single monarch is usually "aptest," but an assembly is a possibility) does God infuse that authority with power. Because this power comes "immediately from [God] himselfe" (p. 131), it is unconditional:

> For God inanimates every State with one power, as every man with one soule: when therefore people concurre in the desire of such a *King*, they cannot contract, nor limitte his power: no more then parents can condition with God, or preclude or withdraw any facultie from that Soule, which God hath infused into the body, which they prepared, and presented to him.   (p. 133)

It follows that obedience is also unconditional; it is in fact part of the same divine pre-programming:

> for *power* and *subjection* are so *Relative*, as since the King commaunds in all things conducing to our *Peaceable* and *Religious* being, wee must obey in all those. This therefore is our first Originary, naturall, and Congenite [i.e. innate] obedience, *to obey the Prince*: This belongs to us as we are *men*; and is no more changed in us, by being *Christians*, then our *Humanity* is changed.   (p. 134)

Certain inescapable consequences follow. One is the obligation (traditional in much Protestant theory) to suffer bad kings without resisting, since their power, too, was infused by God:

> for thou who gavest *Augustus* the *Empire*, gavest it to *Nero* too … Though *Kings* deface in themselves thy first *image*, in their own *soule*, thou givest no man leave to deface thy second *Image*, imprinted indelibly in their *Power*.
>   (*Devotions*, Expostulation 8, p. 44)

Another consequence is the justification of *arcana imperii*, secret political acts not scrutinized by Parliament. Since his power derives from God, the king can use it outside of the law for the public good (*salus populi*):

> For it is impossible, that any Prince should proceede in all causes and occurrences, by a downright Execution of his Lawes ... And therefore these disguisings, and averting of others from discerning them, are so necessarie, that though ... they seeme to be within the compasse of deceite and falshood, yet the end, which is, maintenance of lawfull Authoritie, for the publike good, justifies them.
>
> (*Pseudo-Martyr*, p. 57)

This position, still the defence of modern intelligence services, though without the divine sanction, separated Donne from friends like Richard Martyn and Christopher Brooke, for whom it represented a threat to the rule of law. This may be why Donne's rhetoric suggests an uneasiness that is found again when he directs the lawyers of Lincoln's Inn away from the slippery Roman principle, "The pleasure of the Prince is above all Law," towards the unchangeable law of charity (*Sermons*, vol. III, no. 7, p. 185).

Donne's purpose in *Pseudo-Martyr*, however, was to emphasize the autonomy of the king in relation to the Papacy; this makes him emphasize the king's "absolute" power, but his purpose was not to threaten the rule of law or the rights of Parliament. He later described Parliament as "*the hive* of the Kingdome, from whence all her *honey* comes; that house where *Justice* her self is conceived, in their preparing of *Laws*, and inanimated, and quickned and borne by the Royall Assent, there given" (*Sermons*, vol. IV, no. 9, p. 246.) His broad sense of the relationship between the law and the prerogative is expressed in the following conceit:

> now the Gospell growes a Tyran, and wee will not be under a tyrannous government; If hee will govern by his Law, that hee be content with our coming to Church every Sunday, and our receiving every Easter, wee will live under his Law; but if he come to exercise his Prerogative, and presse us to extraordinary duties, in watching all our particular actions, and calling our selves to an account, for words and thoughts, then Christ and his Gospell become a scandal.
>
> (*Sermons*, vol. III, no. 7, p. 181)

The conceit depends on the shared assumption that such intrusive action by earthly kings would indeed be a scandal. Donne always stresses the distance between a tyrant and a monarch in terms of law. Thus, sins are tyrannical, set "above us, as *Lords*, and *Tyrans*, that came in by conquest, and so put what Laws they list upon us" (*Sermons*, vol. II, no, 3, p. 118), whereas God is a king who rules by just laws:

Let us be glad that [the kingdom of God] ... is *but* a kingdome, and *no more*, not a *Tyranny*; That we come not to a *God* that *will damme* us, because he *will* damme us, but a God that proposes *Conditions*, and enables us to performe those conditions.   (*Sermons*, vol. III, no. 4, p. 125)

It is against this normal rule within the law that the occasional use of prerogative powers is justified. Such uses must not "exceede their true endes (which are just authority, and the publique good) or their lawfull waies to those ends, which should ever be within the compasse of vertue, and religion" (*Pseudo-Martyr*, p. 57). For Donne, the king's *raison d'être* was to deliver peace, social and religious order, "the publique good." When Donne reaffirmed this later, meditating on the heart as the king of organs during his illness of 1623, he emphasized the selfish origins of the originally free man's acquiescence in the bargain; agreement comes

from the very *first dictates of Nature*; which is, in the first place, to have care of our own *Preservation*, to look first to ourselves ... And this is the reward of the pains of *Kings*; sometimes they neede the power of law, to be obey'd; and when they seeme to be obey'd *voluntarily*, they who doe it, doe it for their owne sakes. O how little a thing is all the *greatnes of man*, and through how false glasses doth he make shift to *multiply it*, and *magnifie* it to himself?
(*Devotions*, Meditation 11, pp. 61–62)

Donne was always willing to remind kings in this way of the limits of their greatness. When the royal physicians attend him Donne meditates that kings are as subject to sickness as "their lowest subject ... Are they *gods*? He that called them so, cannot flatter. They are *Gods*, but *sicke gods*" (Meditation 8, p. 42).

Above all, earthly greatness is diminished in the perspective of eternity. Donne saw human history as a providential process from the Creation, through the Fall and the Crucifixion, to the Second Coming of Christ. Like many contemporaries he believed the Last Judgment was not far away. He meditates often on the end of history, and the subsequent reunion with God; and while the prospect of judgment is desperately frightening, the fact that kings and their favorites will simply join the queue makes it a comprehensively levelling process:

he that hath no *grave*, but a *dung-hill*, hee that hath no more *earth*, but that which he carries, but that which hee is, hee that hath not that *earth*, which hee is, but even in that, is anothers slave, hath as much proportion to *God*, as if all *Davids worthies*, and all the *worlds Monarchs*, and all *imaginations Gyants*, were kneaded and incorporated into one, and as though that one were the survivor of all the sonnes of men, to whom *God* had given the world.
(*Devotions*, Expostulation 2, p. 7)

This powerful figurative realization of an orthodox Christian view humbles kings as effectively as would a more direct assault. The *Devotions* were, nevertheless, dedicated to Prince Charles, an indication that such reminders of royal mortality do not mean Donne abandoned the monarchist theories of *Pseudo-Martyr*. Indeed another passage in *Devotions* offers one of his most Shakespearian endorsements of the hierarchic state whose heart is the king. The infection of his body – "fumes" – is analogous to rumor in the state, much as seditious gossip is an infection in "Satyre IV":

> infectious fumes, are, in a State, *infectious rumors*, detracting and dishonour-able *Calumnies*, *Libels*. The *Heart* in that *body* is the *King*; and the *Braine*, his *Councell*; and the whole *Magistracie*, that ties all together, is the *Sinewes*, which proceed from thence; and the *life* of all is *Honour*, and just *respect*, and due *reverence*; and therefore, when these *vapors*, these venomous *rumors*, are directed against these *Noble parts*, the whole body suffers.
>
> (*Devotions*, Meditation 12, pp. 69–70)

Honor, respect, and reverence are key terms in Donne's patriarchal politics, but his dislike of divisive, seditious gossip derives also from his irenicism. Christ's power to reconcile made him Donne's ideal king (*Sermons*, vol. II, no. 8, pp. 186–87) and he did not need the injunction in James's *Directions to Preachers* to avoid "bitter invectives and undecent rayleing speeches against the persons of either Papists or Puritanes."[14] His public defence of these *Directions*, commanded by James, has made some readers uneasy over what they see as Donne's capitulation to authoritarianism.[15] The "discreet" way Donne tackles his sensitive task is typical. He concentrates first on Paul's precept that "all things be done decently and in order." James's *Directions* are conducive to order, but it is Paul's authority that counts most. The importance of preaching and reassurance about God's providence, needed in the wake of Protestant defeats in Europe, are followed by Donne's defence of the *Directions*, and further reassurance that James (who had just released imprisoned Catholics in pursuance of the negotiations to marry Prince Charles to the Spanish Infanta) remained a defender of Protestantism. Donne was probably sincere in saying he was "not willing only, but glad to have my part" in defending the *Directions*, ministering as they did to the "*God of peace*, of unitie, and concord" (*Sermons*, vol. IV, no. 7, pp. 201–02).

Any scruples he had were probably over the ineffectiveness of James's policies. Not only did he most likely write "Show me dear Christ" at around this time, but long letters to Sir Thomas Roe (Gosse, vol. II, p. 175) and Goodyer (*Letters*, pp. 154–59) show his concerns. Such discussion of foreign affairs (not to be shared with congregations) is significantly frequent in

Donne's letters, and testifies to another constant in his politics. Like his Inns of Court contemporary Edwin Sandys, whose ecumenical *Europae Speculum* (1605) has much in common with Donne, he probably met Paolo Sarpi, another opponent of the Papacy, in Venice in 1604–05, and remained in touch with him and other like-minded European intellectuals.[16] Donne's languages and knowledge of European politics led to a journey to Northern Europe in 1611–12 with Sir Robert Drury, when Donne anatomized the French court for Goodyer with the kind of incisiveness that one wishes he had felt able to apply to the English one (*Letters*, pp. 120–27). In 1619 he accompanied the Viscount Doncaster on an embassy to Germany and the Netherlands to mediate in the looming wars of religion. Though ordained by then, Donne acted as secretary to the embassy for some six months, a diplomat as well as a chaplain.[17] This engagement with foreign affairs helps explain Donne's presence from at least 1616 to 1623 on a list of eleven recipients of a cipher for decoding letters from abroad. George Abbot, the Archbishop of Canterbury, is also on the list (Bald, pp. 569–70). Donne was probably involved in gathering and interpreting intelligence connected with the Protestant cause on the Continent.

This is one piece of evidence that Donne was closer to the Calvinist Archbishop Abbot than has usually been thought. In the 1620s, Abbot was under political pressure from the "anti-Calvinist" Arminians in the English church, who emphasized free will (rather than predestination), the universality of grace, and the importance of sacraments over preaching (see chapter 5, p. 78). Abbot had both theological differences with the Arminians, over the availability of grace to all and the relative importance of preaching and the sacraments, and political differences over the extent of the king's "absolute" power. Donne agreed with the Arminians over universal grace, but not over preaching, and, it seems, not over their exaltation of regal power. It is thus significant that he told Goodyer that he had "been some times with" Abbot in 1621, during the weeks following Abbot's accidental shooting of a gamekeeper (*Letters*, p. 158).[18] That the Archbishop had killed a man gave his enemies an opportunity to convene a commission of inquiry. Donne's visits show him going out of his way to show solidarity with Abbot when he was at his weakest. In his sermon to the Virginia Company in November 1622, before Abbot had been pardoned by the king, Donne was emphatically closer to him than the Arminians in his insistence on preaching the gospel "to all men" (*Sermons*, vol. IV, no. 10, p. 280).

When James died in 1625 there was a short period when Charles favored Donne's brand of Anglicanism. He asked Donne to preach on his first appearance as King, rather than the more senior Arminian Bishop Neile, whose task it should have been.[19] This was the high point of Donne's influence. As William Laud gained ascendancy over Charles, Donne's status waned, and in 1627 he was accused of sympathy with the discredited Abbot after a court sermon to which "exceptions" were taken and "displeasure kindled." Donne had preached obedience and warned against seditious "whispering," and "came very near looking for thanks" (*Letters*, pp. 305–06), but half his sermon had been about preaching by which "Orthodoxall and fundamentall truths, are established against clamorous and vociferant innovation" (*Sermons*, vol. VII, no. 16, p. 396). Laud probably believed he and his allies were the "clamorous" innovators, and he may have been right.

To Donne the downgrading of preaching would have been both divisive and an attack on a fundamental duty, and after consternation at the royal anger, though he avoided the issue in Court sermons, he returned to it pointedly at St. Paul's, again seeming to target Laud:

> let no man, though an *Angell* of the Church, though an *Archangell* of the Church, *Bishop* or *Archbishop*, refuse to heare a man of inferiour place, or inferiour parts to himself; neither let any man be discouraged by the fewnesse or meannesse of his Hearers: For, as the Apostle saith, ... *Entertain strangers, for thereby some have entertained Angels unawares*, so, preach to all, and that seat that thou thinkest empty, may have *Angels* in it.
>
> (*Sermons*, vol. VIII, no. 12, p. 272)

Donne's relation to the Arminian group has been complicated by his agreement with their insistence that salvation was available to all; but in this continued emphasis on preaching, which the Arminians regarded with increasing suspicion, and in his wariness of a rapprochement with Rome, he remained aligned with moderate Calvinists like Joseph Hall, Morton, and Abbot.[20] Above all, the Arminians around Laud were politically identified with an absolutism that went much further than Donne's in its downgrading of traditional parliamentary and legal rights.

Powerful evidence that Donne was growing alarmed by the Arminians' almost mystic advocacy of the king's absolute power, following a series of contentious legal judgments that supported the king, is found in the marginal annotations Donne made in his copy of *Utopia*, sometime around 1628–29.[21] Though brief, they deserve attention as the most private and unguarded form of his discourse that survives. In them he is critical of Charles's contentious use of extra-parliamentary methods of raising revenue, such as the controversial ship-money tax, which was widely regarded as illegal, and of those who maintain that the king can do no wrong. He annotates a passage in which More discussed counsellors' dubious schemes to "heap up treasure" for a king with the words (in Latin) "All these things have happened in our time." Against a passage on how judges may be bent to favor the royal prerogative he wrote "ship-monie"; and against "a king, however much he wishes, can do nothing wrong; for all that all men possess is his, as are they themselves, and so much is a man's own as the king's generosity doth not take away from him" he made the terse note "criers up of the Kings prerogative." In the late 1620s, these "criers up" can only be the Arminian divines clustered around Laud and Charles. Donne did not keep these views private. Preaching at court in 1629 at the height of parliamentary controversy about what many regarded as the king's abuse of the preroga-tive, he made his point more discreetly, but clearly. God, he said, ruled by law: He "hath laid a holy necessity upon himself to judge according to that law" (*Sermons*, vol. VIII, no. 15, p. 350).[22] The implication was that the king did not. During the last years of his life, Donne had returned to the critical stance towards the monarchy that he had held in the 1590s.

NOTES

1 "The Monarchy of Wit and the Republic of Letters: Donne's Politics," in Elizabeth G. Harvey and Katherine Eisaman Maus (eds.), *Soliciting Interpretation: Literary Theory and Seventeenth-Century English Poetry* (Chicago: University of Chicago Press, 1990), pp. 5, 17.

2 *An Homily against Disobedience and Wylful Rebellion*, in David Wooten (ed.), *Divine Right and Democracy: An Anthology of Political Writing in Stuart England* (Harmondsworth: Penguin, 1986), pp. 94–98, at 94.

3 Carey, *Donne*, p. 86.

4 Gosse, vol. II, pp. 23, 41.

5 Carey, *Donne*, passim. For the circumstances of Henry's death, see Tom Cain, "Elegy and Autobiography: "The Bracelet" and the Death of Henry Donne," *JDJ* 22 (2003), 1–26.

6 *A True Historical Relation of the Conversion of Sir Tobie Matthew*, ed. A. H. Mathew (London: Burns and Oates, 1904), p. 86; cf. Bald, *Donne*, p. 188.

7 This is related to the "discretion" which Jeanne Shami locates as a central char-acteristic of the sermons; "Donne on Discretion," *ELH* 47 (1980), 48–66.

8 Evelyn M. Simpson, *A Study of the Prose Works of John Donne* (Oxford: Clarendon Press, 1948), p. 308. Simpson prints the Burley Letters in chapter 12.

9 Marked with a line in the Latin version in his copy of More's *Lucubrationes* (1563), now in University of San Francisco library; see John B. Gleason, "Dr. Donne in the Courts of Kings: a Glimpse from Marginalia," *JEGP* 69 (1970), 599–612. Passages from *Utopia* are from the translation by G. C. Richards (Oxford, 1923).

10 Excluded from the canon by Helen Gardner, but reinstated in the *Variorum* as *Elegy 17*.

11 Barbara Everett, "Donne and Secrecy," *Essays in Criticism* 51 (2001), 51–67, at 61.

12 *The Prince, or, Maxims of State* (London, 1642), p. 4.

13 For a description of the rise of "designation theory," see J. P. Somerville, *Politics and Ideology in England, 1603–1640* (London: Longman, 1986), pp. 22–27. For a detailed study of *Pseudo-Martyr*, see Somerville, "John Donne the Controversialist: The Poet as Political Thinker," in David Colclough (ed.), *John Donne's Professional Lives* (Cambridge: D. S. Brewer, 2003), pp. 73–95.

14 Neil Rhodes, Jennifer Richards, and Joseph Marshall (eds.), *King James VI and I: Selected Writings* (Aldershot: Ashgate, 2003), p. 383.

15 The fullest analysis of the sermon is by Jeanne Shami, "'The Stars in their Order Fought Against Sisera': John Donne and the Pulpit Crisis of 1622," *JDJ* 14 (1995), 1–58.

16 See Dennis Flynn, "Donne's Politics, 'Desperate Ambition,' and Meeting Paolo Sarpi in Venice," *JEGP* 99 (2000), 334–55.

17 See Paul R. Sellin, *'So Doth, So is Religion': John Donne and Diplomatic Contexts in the Reformed Netherlands, 1619–1620* (Columbia: University of Missouri Press, 1988), p. 10.

18 The significance of the letter has been missed because the text is corrupted, printing "since by accident" for "since his accident." Abbot referred to the event as "my unhappy accident." For underestimation of Donne's connections with Abbot, see Shami, "'The Stars in their Order Fought Against Sisera'," 8–9.

19 Peter E. McCullough, "Donne as Preacher at Court: 'Precarious Inthronization'," in *John Donne's Professional Lives*, pp. 187–88.

20 For the debate on Donne's Arminianism, see Achsah Guibbory, "Donne's Religion: Montagu, Arminianism and Donne's Sermons, 1624–30," *ELR* 31 (2001), 412–39, and Jeanne Shami, "Labels, Controversy, and the Language of Inclusion in Donne's sermons," in *John Donne's Professional Lives*, pp. 135–57.

21 See Gleason, "Dr. Donne in the Courts of Kings," pp. 600–02.

22 Paul W. Harland, "Donne's Political Intervention in the Parliament of 1629," *JDJ* 11 (1992), 21–37.

7

JUDITH SCHERER HERZ

Reading and rereading Donne's poetry

Reporter to Bob Dylan: "What are your songs about?" Dylan: "Some of my songs are about four minutes, some are about five, and some, believe it or not, are about 11 or 12."[1] "Pedantique wretch," he might have called the reporter had he been channeling Donne, "for Godsake hold your tongue." For there is a similar defiance, a snarkiness, a catch-me-if-you-can in many Donne utterances, both in those that come down on the side of love, of desire made holy, of making the lovers' "little roome, an every where," and in those that flippantly dismiss such possibilities. He may feel himself "two fooles . . . / For loving, and for saying so / In whining poetry," but he persists and dares the reader to determine just what "draw[ing his] paines / through Rimes vexation" is all "about." ("Vexation" is an interesting word for both writer and reader). "The triple Foole" from which these lines come is hardly a complex poem, but its playful self-consciousness strikes a note that one will hear in a number of Donne poems, both the serious and the silly. Can grief be real and its expression truthful if "he tames it, that fetters it in verse?"

Verse is certainly offered as recourse in "The Canonization," once the prudent, practical friend is told to hold his tongue and is sent back to his worldly occupations while the lovers are left to build their pretty rooms. Whatever else that poem does (and it does a great deal as it opens out into a very specific world of courts, coins, courtiers, and the whims of kings, as well as into the development of literary theory in the twentieth century), it makes an emphatic claim for poetry. It tries out ways of saying "I" and "we" as it looks for a language for that newly forming subjectivity. It discards the ready-made Petrarchan discourse of tears and tempests, it tries out the alchemical, it seems to settle for the religious (they are to be saints of love, after all), but the transcendent and the worldly jostle oddly in the last stanza as the poem folds into itself, addresses itself from within and yet seeks a source outside itself, above itself, as confirmation of its claims: "Beg from above / A patterne of your love."

Where is the reader in all of this? What is s/he doing in order to navigate between stanzas, to gain access to the text? After all, nearly every one of

Donne's poems, and "The Canonization" more than most, has trailing after it more interpretive crumbs than Hansel and Gretel ever dropped. This is not the space to lay claim to any one of them, to *a* reading, but rather to lay out some of the pleasures (baffled, baffling, vexing as some may be) involved in the process of meaning making, in probing the preposition "about." There are readers who want to hold it all together, to argue that everything fits, and there are those for whom the center does not hold as stanza and figure flare out and fly apart, and there are, of course, those who use the inside of the poem as access to its outside, to John Donne, a figure in and of his world. However, if one reads *for* the problems and not for their myriad possible solutions, both inside and outside are enriched, the pleasure of the reading only increased. Dylan's remark has further relevance, too, for Donne's poems are about and, as well, are instances of duration; four minutes or five, they extend in space, in time, in and through language, in the body, in the book, and in the immense trajectory of their never quite fulfilled desires. Their language always *almost* means.

"How astonishing it is that language can almost mean / and frightening that it does not quite. Love we say / God we say ..."[2] Thus the contemporary American poet Jack Gilbert in his "The Forgotten Dialect of the Heart," a poem about loss, an elegy for his wife, and a meditation on language, on words as objects, as things. Both the title and the quoted line have a wonderful aptness for Donne, both for his subject matter and for his relation to language. Love and God are his persistent subjects; the slippery fit between sign and referent, the elusive "almost" of fixing meaning, provide their condition and, often, their subject, too. Donne is certainly a dialectician of the heart (half) remembering its language but also making it up as he goes along, not so much by making up words (as Shakespeare did) but by changing the look, the sound, the voices of poetry. For any poet, the language of poetry is always already written (this is Sidney's problem in *Astrophil and Stella* as he stumbles over "other men's feet," trying to find his own), but far more than Sidney, indeed far more than any writer before him with the possible exception of Shakespeare, Donne set out *avant la lettre* to follow the Ezra Pound dictum, to make it new.

Donne tries out language, testing it, punning it, as if he can't believe that words have singular meaning, as if language were a "protective fiction"[3] that might mean what it says, but just might not (and who is to tell what it is saying?). However, there are powerful readings that argue that Donne indeed does mean what he says. William Empson's is probably the best, especially his 1957 *Kenyon Review* article, "Donne the Spaceman": Donne "believes what he says in the poems."[4] There he argues for the seriousness of Donne's belief in separate planets in such poems as "The good-morrow," and hence his belief in more than one Christ, a belief, Empson acknowledges regretfully, that Donne later abandoned (p. 130). John Crowe Ransom's comment on accepting the piece for the journal underlines the seriousness: "I don't think [Donne] could be magnificent without the burden of thought which you attribute to him."[5] Donne certainly thinks in poetry, but where I hesitate is in making that thinking add up to a coherent set of beliefs even within poems, to say nothing of the whole corpus. For Donne, I would argue, the poem comes first. Once it is underway, its requirements, what language and figure demand, quite literally pay the piper and call the tune.

To a degree, Empson did acknowledge the difficulty in fixing meaning. "Donne's mind is rather hard to make sense of, because it is so invincibly balanced, or simply legal; it cannot help seeing all the alternatives as if in a chess-game" (p. 111). Often the poems do proceed as if they were briefs – logical and forensic. Some obviously mock that legal training, that way of thinking, as when he has his woman speaker in "Womans constancy" recite a catalogue of excuses and evasions in the language of contracts and oaths, which he will presumably offer when he leaves after having "lov'd ... one whole day." Of course, in the jokey finish of that poem, she is no better than he, "for by tomorrow, I may think so too." There is something of this playful casuistry in other poems too, "Breake of day," for example, which is also in a woman's voice. Even in some poems that make serious claims for a love that will endure beyond that single day, those alternatives that Empson speaks of make their presence felt. The summing up of "The good-morrow" hinges on a destabilizing "if," the grandiose predictions of "The Anniversarie" are qualified by the admission that "this is the second of our raigne," and the speaker in "The Sunne Rising" knows only too well that the sun is a "pedantique wretch" and no amount of cajoling on his part will alter the terms of the contract. (There is a nice pun on contract in line 26 with the legal sense shadowing the meaning of "to compact": "Thou sunne art halfe as happy'as wee, / In that the world's contracted thus".) The world he would shut out remains the poem's underlying preoccupation.

Sometimes the balance isn't quite so fine. There are poems that mock the self, others, less engagingly, that mock the lover who refuses him, the woman who can never be read, never be true, and some both the he and she in a paroxysm of disgust. "Loves Alchymie" is the best example of the latter; it's a virtuoso performance of sound and sense, the words "like hammer blows" – *dig, get, tell, told*, to borrow the poet X. J. Kennedy's description of language in "Batter my heart."[6] It reprises Shakespeare's Sonnet 129, "The expense of spirit," but more maliciously. And yet as it employs the alchemical vocabulary that in "The Canonization" promises transcendence, but, here, the deceptive and the illusory, one hears a desire not so readily debased. To be sure, the poem's concluding couplet, no matter how you punctuate it, is nasty, rude and crude ("*Mummy*, possest"), and that voice sounds through the poem. However, the close of the first stanza speaks the lovers' dream in reality's (and possibly the poet's) despite:

> And as no chymique yet th'Elixar got,
> But glorifies his pregnant pot,
> If by the way to him befall
> Some odoriferous thing, or medicinall,
> So, lovers dreame a rich and long delight,
> But get a winter-seeming summers night.　　　(7–12)

Because the poem is clearly misogynous, one often doesn't attend to the skill of the lines, to the handling of meter and rhythm, to the placing of the words, indeed to the words themselves as skilfully deployed objects. It is probably best read as a dramatic monologue, for it is theatrical, not lyric; one might call it "The Lusts of Iago" or, possibly, of Edmund. It has the ring of speech, each line seeming to find its own necessary shape, the getting and spending momentarily halted by those two unexpected words, *odoriferous* and *medicinall*, which require a drawing out of sound, an activation of the senses, a pause before entry into the next line's temporary dream. It is only momentary, however; in the following stanza scorn is the dominant note, the finer claims of loving minds, which are so often sounded in his other poems, flatly dismissed.

Still one knows what one is reading in that poem. There are others, though, where our reading depends almost entirely on the assumptions we bring to the text. Is "The Flea," for example, a nicer Loves Alchymie, a seduction poem of a lady who does not have *that* much honor to lose, the last line a bit of a sneer? Or is it a serious seduction poem addressing the woman he will soon wed "though parents grudge," and, since they love each other, honor is not the issue? Is his argument, thus, a reiteration of something already understood, even if not entirely believed, by the flea-killing beloved? Here I take no sides, but emphasize instead the poem's virtuosity and skill. It is both a lawyer's brief and a vividly imagined little play. It takes a conventional topos – lots of poets imagined themselves as fleas in bed with their ladies – but restages it, the flea now bed and church, the lovers "cloysterd" within, the death of the flea an act of sacrilege. There are dizzying shifts in scale, a sense of time passing ("about" two minutes, Mr. Dylan), the faintly audible sound of another voice (a little like "Womans constancy"), lots of action (looking, denying, sucking, swelling, grudging, killing, triumphing, arguing), and an entirely enigmatic ending: "Just so much honor, when thou yeeld'st to mee, / Will wast, as this flea's death tooke life from thee." Like the best of Donne, it makes one listen and look closely; whether it is flippant or serious or both is in some sense beside the point. Donne seems more interested in finding out what he could do with the flea than what the flea could do for him. The figure is often more important than what it illustrates. It is precisely this quality that the often-invoked word, wit, identifies.

"Wit" and its figure the "metaphysical conceit," that is the unexpected, indeed the unlikely, metaphor, the comparison just this side of catachresis, are terms that occur in all discussions of Donne's style. "Wit focuses an interest in the rendering of our ambiguous state when sensation and idea interfuse in the language itself, opening an absolute consequence in the momentary encounter, and registering the shock of metaphysical predicaments in the play of the sense," in A. J. Smith's description.[7] The term "metaphysical," referring both to abstruse subject matter and the stylistic disturbances accompanying it, was early on applied to Donne's poetry, and for the most part disapprovingly. Drummond of Hawthornden talked of poets who use "metaphysical ideas and scholastic quiddities" in their verse; Dryden complained that Donne "affects the metaphysics ... and perplexes the mind of the fair sex with nice speculations of philosophy"; and Samuel Johnson in his *Life of Cowley* described "a race of writers who may be termed the metaphysical poets" in whose poetry "the most heterogeneous ideas are yoked by violence together."[8] What are apparently jettisoned are standard notions of decorum, of the appropriate, the fitting. The flea leaps from the lovers' bed into the heart of religious mystery, or the body of the lover becomes a love token at the end of time. And we believe these claims for they are so well argued, so precisely made. Metaphysical poetry argues; it is complex and intellectual, and it depends on surprise (but in Donne's case, a surprise that the poem often makes true). Dexterity, inventiveness, the pleasure of and in the word, and the fusion, often exorbitant, of the carnal and the spiritual, of body and soul: these are certainly the essential ingredients of metaphysical wit.

And the reader takes pleasure in these words as they beget new words, which often split away from their usual associations, begging the question: how does one read a given poem? For example, even more than "The Flea," "The Dissolution" is a poem that does not disclose itself. Is it an elegy, the death in the opening line real and lamented, or is it sexual death? It certainly seems real enough for the first four, possibly eight lines, but then what does he mean by "my fire doth with my fuell grow?" Or, reverting again to Shakespeare's "expense of spirit" sonnet, what is he saying in "this death, hath with my store /My use encreas'd"? Complicating this are the echoes that readers carry from other Donne poems, from the two *Anniversaries* for example. The refrain "shee is dead" in the first, "An Anatomie of the

World," signals both an individual death and the decay of the word, but these are the very words of this poem's opening. The "rustie peece discharg'd" as metaphor for the soul released from the body in the second, "Of the Progresse of the Soule," is here figured as "my soule more earnestly releas'd, /will outstrip hers; as bullets flown before / A later bullet may o'rtake, the pouder being more." More? Is that possibly a pun on his wife's name? Could this be a poem on her death? It doesn't feel like it, but it's nearly impossible to tell. Do we hear sorrow or the erotic, sincerity or cynicism? Is there grief or the performance of grief or no grief at all? The rhyme scheme and line scansion might suggest grief, for they are markedly disordered, the first eight lines rhyming *abcd/bacd*, the next several spinning into couplets with the appearance of something like a quatrain, *eeffe*, then some more couplets and a concluding *jkkj*. The line lengths are also unpredictable as are the line rhythms. Such observations offer a way into meaning making, but they are hardly definitive. Imagining grief or desire could produce the same results. Because Donne's poems are so finely balanced, so aware of the alternatives to any of their assertions, their simultaneity of reference doubled by the simultaneity of the reader's response, they baffle provocatively and usefully any attempt to fix their meanings, directing our attention to the words, their figuration, shape, and patterns, often more than to the ideas.

The words are surprising, often not the words expected. They have, in Jonathan Post's nice phrase, "the newness of tart particularity."[9] There are things in Donne's words, John Carey observes; "words are packed into his poems like boulders."[10] This recalls William Carlos Williams's claim in "Patterson" that there are "no ideas but in things," a line with particular resonance for Donne: *Suns, spheres, mines, clymes, rags, time, school boys, prentices, princes* and *states* in one, or *doctors, Goths, vandals, gyants, witches, massacres, pictures, dampes* in another; *rafters, tiles, houses, muscles, sinews, veins* in yet another. Indeed nearly every poem offers a list of such possibilities inherent in the stubbornly concrete. It is as if the idea begins to form after the words have been given their head, allowed to run free, invite in their friends, make the poem. Once an argument begins to take shape, it is examined closely, put under pressure, sometimes discarded, sometimes triumphantly reasserted, the intellect engaged along with the emotions.

His words are strong, they have punch. Donne is a master of the monosyllable, the small word that holds the line taut ("like gold to ayery thinnesse beate" in "A Valediction: forbidding mourning"; *beat*, not the lighter 'spun'), but that carries the line along in the rhythms of speech, which often sustain a normal iambic scansion ("Twere wholesomer for mee, that winter *did* / Benight the glory of this place." "Twicknam garden"). Donne's scansion has always been a topic of debate following from Ben Jonson's remark that Donne "for not keeping of accent deserved hanging."[11] Yet as John Hollander, working with the principle of contrastive stress, has demonstrated, Donne's poetry is often more regular than it at first seems,[12] especially when one makes the distinction between the line and the syntactic unit. Still, metrical innovation is an important part of Donne's accomplishment as a poet. Noting the disturbed rhythms, the stress displaced from its expected pattern, the "variable cadences to evoke emotional states," C. A. Patrides suggested, in his edition of the poems, that "Donne's 'rough cadence' taught generations of poets [he referred specifically to Pope and Browning] to look with their ears."[13] "Particularity" resides both in sound and image, in rhythm and figure; one must hear and see simultaneously. Despite a critical tradition beginning in the early twentieth century in the essays of Rupert Brooke, Herbert Read, and T. S. Eliot that Donne does not visualize, his poetry is amazingly full of things seen. Not only does Donne look at things, but he requires intent observation from his readers.

But the question remains: we observe closely, but what do we see and hear? Often one has the sense that a poem is pointing to something inaudible or invisible except to a few, to a specific audience, to a coterie, to an unnamed person. Could the addressee in "The Flea" be Anne More? Is she behind the scene in "The Curse," too, as Ilona Bell argues?[14] As well, a poem's controlling idea – the stance it takes to its putative subject – is often hard to identify, especially when it seems abruptly to turn about, to contradict itself, to undo its opening claims. "The Funerall" comes to mind, and so does "Aire and Angels," a poem that would have had a simpler critical history without its final three lines, which seem to deny its earlier assertions and radically change its voice. It is now aphoristic and dismissive ("Just such disparitie / As is twixt Aire and Angells purite / 'Twixt women's love, and mens will ever bee") where it had earlier seemed to adore and desire. It is possible that the adoration, if that's the right word, was from the start tinged with something else. It is hard to know since there seems to be so insistent an undertone of punning in the text (this is said with the *caveat* that readers may find more puns than poets put there, but once heard, once released, the puns become part of the experience of the poem). And just what is this final "disparitie," especially since an angelic gender switch seems to have occurred – she is the angel at the start, he at the end? Some would have it mean mutuality, admittedly within a masculine hierarchy; others hear insolence and rudeness. There are few poems that have invited so many and such conflicting readings as this one, but that is part of the pleasure it offers.[15] "Aire and Angels" is "intolerant of doctrinaire interpretations," cautioned Patrides in his footnote to the poem. One reads, as I have been arguing, *for* the problems, not for their solutions. This poem has more than most.

Indeed it is often the endings that complicate interpretation as we have seen with both "Loves Alchymie" and "The Flea." In talking of "Song: Goe, and catche a falling starre," the Canadian poets Doug Beardsley and Al Purdy, in their conversations about and poems to Donne, note, in Purdy's words, how extraordinary it is that "he's so right at the outset, [that] you wonder how he can be so wrong at the end."[16] Christopher Ricks has observed a similar process: "the better the best things in Donne's poem, the more he is driven to rend it with his ending."[17] Speaking less as a prosecutor, Arnold Stein observed, in part thinking of the last lines of "Aire and Angels" but also of endings that merely workmanlike do their job, "there are improvised endings that do not matter and ones that continue speaking in the reader's mind."[18] The ending to "Aire and Angels" somehow manages to do both.

However, it is not just some endings that continue to speak in the reader's mind. One of the great pleasures in reading Donne is coming upon a line that lifts you out of the poem, out of yourself, either for the surprise of its language or for the heart stopping humanity and exactness of its thought. The first stanza of "The Sunne Rising" has both. Using the traditional aubade or morning song in which the lovers lament the encroaching day, Donne's speaker calls out in exasperation, addressing the sun as he never had been addressed before: "Busie old foole, unruly Sunne," he is called. Part of the irony of the exclamation is that the sun is all too "ruly," as the fourth line acknowledges when he is called a "sawcy pedantique wretch," "sawcy" for peering into their privacy, but, worse, a pedant, keeping school, chiding school boys and driving all the clock run, rule run business of the world. Well, says the speaker, busy yourself with "kings" and "prentices," "court-huntsmen" and "countrey ants," just so long as you leave us alone, because

> Love, all alike, no season knows, nor clime,
> Nor houres, dayes, moneths, which are the rags of time.   (9–10)

Those two lines, especially the latter, bring that opening noisy stanza to a stunning silent close. It is the unexpected word "rags" that gives the line its charge, diminishing the sun's power more completely than the bravado and bluster of the opening, indeed than the subsequent stanzas and their games with kings, princes, states and the spice trade. By the close of the poem, the sun, which entered with or without the lovers' leave, is now domesticated, invited to spend all his time in their chamber, since, after all, they are the whole world. Stanzas two and three are a beautifully imagined riff on many of Donne's favorite themes and words, but it is the first stanza that makes it an astounding poem and that stanza's last line that pays for all.

The opening lines of "Loves growth" offer another example:

> I scarce believe my love to be so pure
> As I had thought it was,
> Because it doth endure
> Vicissitude, and season, as the grasse.   (1–4)

The opening three lines are quiet and meditative, surprise in the voice but not in the language: *love, pure, endure*. But "endure" does not complete the thought, but moves surprisingly to the striking *vicissitude*, its *s*'s sliding into *season*, and *as* (which takes the stress) and then *grass*. Insofar as it reverses the many biblical allusions of flesh as grass where the comparison points to death, to the withering of the grass, Donne's use is surprising. For grass in this line endures vicissitude. It is the figure of his love, not entirely pure, but vital, springing back to life, fuller than before. Yet the traditional allusion sounds as well; that one word carries both pathos and triumph.

Imagining death, its intimations, its approaches, its touch on the body, the glimmerings it offers of heaven, these are constants in Donne's poetry. There are lines in the two *Anniversary* poems that move from the poems' avowed aim of praise of Elizabeth Drury to reveal Donne's imagination straining at the limits of its subject:

> Think then, my soule, that death is but a Groome,
> Which brings a Taper to the outward roome,
> Whence thou spiest first a little glimmering light,
> And after brings it nearer to thy sight:
> For such approaches doth heaven make in death.

This figure of light next merges with a figure of music (a repeated motif in Donne's contemplation of death) and then, like *grass*, like *rags*, another comparison emerges, which, like the previous example, is startling in its simplicity, in its evocation of the ordinary:

> Thinke thee laid on thy death-bed, loose and slack;
> And thinke that, but unbinding of a packe,
> To take one precious thing, thy soule from thence.

Other comparisons follow. The images rapidly succeed one another as if there is always one more, and, in fact, there is.

These last examples come from *The Second Anniversary* (85–89, 93–95) which, taken together with the first, can be read as a single long poem. Indeed one way to read Donne is to move through all of the poems as if *Songs and Sonets* were itself a Long Poem carried not so much by a narrative thread as by an ongoing exploration of self in language. An objection to this, that there is no evidence that Donne ever designed anything called 'Songs and Sonets,' and that the order of the poems varies in different manuscripts and in the 1633 and 1635 editions, in a sense only confirms this point. One poem after another tries out a series of poses, cycling and recycling its vocabulary, all spoken by a voice that is instantly recognizable, "irremediably Donne," Jonathan Post calls it, yet which speaks in multiple voices, tones, and registers and performs many selves, all vying to be the single self.

"Speaks" is the operative word here. John Hollander places Donne within the tradition of "the lyric of insistent talk, rather than the lyric of written flow" (p. 46). It talks high, it talks low, with "masculine persuasive force" as Donne claims in "Elegie: On his Mistris" ("By our first strange ..."), and sometimes with a bit of a sneer, a merely fashionable cleverness. At other times, however, it speaks with a calm, almost gossipy intimacy, although learned and allusive, too, as in the opening stanza of "A Valediction: of the book," or gently, quietly as in "Sweetest love, I do not goe." There is, of course, also the Donne of excess, of extreme statement. Often very pleased with himself, he makes ever more outrageous assertions, as if mere hyperbole were too modest; the poems become acts of "poetic self ravishment" in Post's phrase (p. 3), but not accidentally so. The aim seems to have been to outrage, to astonish (himself, too), as if to say "you didn't think all this could be in one poem, did you?" The American poet Patrick Donnelly gets at something important in Donne's poetry in his assertion that "cockiness and gratitude, whimsy and psalm, head and heart ... inhabit the same poetic space."[19]

The reader is always aware of someone behind the words, although it is often hard to see him. He is always yet never himself, always desiring to be more, even if more is the absolute zero of nothingness. It's this quality that makes me suspicious of the grief in "A nocturnall upon S. Lucies day," for example (although I'm in a minority here). But issues of sincerity may be beside the point. One notes that the "she" whose death is lamented is given no space at all, while the speaker declaims his variations on the theme of nothingnesse. It is he who is "every dead thing," he who is now "the first nothing grown." There is nothing more nothing than he – asserted almost with pride. Yet there seems to be a reality on the other side of the poem, as well: "oft a flood have we two wept ... oft did we grow / To be two Chaosses, ... and often absences / Withdrew our soules, and made us carcasses" (22–27), earlier absences now foreshadowing this final absence. Beyond the showmanship, the witty deployment of figures of this nothing (making it many things!), a deep melancholy pervades the text, although whether it is an ego loss or an ego affirmation is hard to tell. Yearning and pyrotechnics, grief and its performance, self and absence of self: it's not clear that we need to distinguish among them.

Saying farewell is one of Donne's repeated gestures, to the beloved, to life itself. But each of these valedictions (the four poems so named, but also others that perform that gesture) becomes another way of saying "I am here." *Don't forget me* he insists to his mistresses and, more urgently, to God, even in the paradoxical counter statement to that imperative in the holy sonnet "If poysonous minerals": "that thou remember them, some claime as debt, / I thinke it mercy, if thou wilt forget." What remains? What sign can one give of the persistence of the self, of soul and body? When is goodbye not goodbye at all? In "A Valediction: of my name, in the window," he finds ways to leave evidence behind. His name engraved on the window's glass keeps him there as a ragged bony presence, a "ruinous anatomie," awaiting his return to "recompact his scattered body," and as permanent talisman to prevent any future lover from supplanting him. The engraved name also functions there as a death's head, a reminder of "Lovers mortalitie," but it is in the two poems, "The Funerall" and "The Relique," where that traditional emblem makes its most original appearance, especially in its merging of themes of mortality and love.

In the first it is "that subtile wreath of haire, which crowns my arm," in the second "a bracelet of bright haire about the bone." It is a stunning figure, a death's head made from a love token and made to carry multiple, indeed, contradictory meanings. It is presented as requiring, yet resisting, interpretation. In "The Funerall," those preparing him for burial are told not inquire too closely, for the "wreath of haire" points to something too mysterious, too private to disclose. But for all the extravagant claims of the opening, the poem turns abruptly about at its mid point. A note of cynicism, of mocking bravado, replaces wonder. He no longer knows why she had given it to him. However, he concludes, if he can't have her after all, then, at least, he can take some of her with him to his grave. "The Relique" on the other hand moves in precisely the reverse direction. It starts with the commonplace of a woman's faithlessness, but then it opens into wonder and miracle. Before that, however, it offers what may be the most startling figure in all of Donne's poems. The "bracelet of bright haire" is to serve the lovers as an identifying sign, so that at judgment day, here wonderfully called "that last busie day," the lovers will recognize each other and at that very last moment, when all those bodies are rushing from their graves, these two will "make a little stay." That phrase more than any other carries the intensely corporeal nature of Donne's understanding of the soul's business, his awareness of time's onrushing, of lovers' mortality, and the poignancy of the lovers' touch.

"Touch," for Donne, "is the model of all the senses," Elaine Scarry argues. He "insists on the obligation to touch the human body, whether acutely alive or newly dead."[20] For Donne's is a poetry of the body, however much he attempts to discover strategies of transcendence. This is central to John Carey's argument in his chapter on Donne and the body where he focuses on the little read but quite wonderful "*Metempsychosis*: The Progress of the Soule" (very different from *The Second Anniversary* that, confusingly, has the same name) and "Donne's bid to haul our bodies into his descriptive activities" (p. 156) as he "steps up the physicality of his words" (p. 151), asserting, as Scarry phrases it, "a broader continuity between language and the material realm it seeks to represent" (p. 76). Donne's speakers are often anatomists, who offer their own bodies to be anatomized. In "The Dampe," doctors cut up his body and survey its parts; in "The Funerall," his body is seen from within, held together by the sinewy threads descending from his brain. One of his favorite words is *carcass*, his own, his lover's, even the world's carcass, its rotting body, the subject of *The First Anniversary*. The *Devotions upon Emergent Occasions* also offer an anatomy lesson in their close tracking of his still living body as it moves through sickness, towards death and tentatively back to health. In the late hymns to God, written, most likely, just at the point when, after this illness, he finds himself back in his body, he offers similar anatomizings. The metaphysical yearning to get beyond the body, for transubstantiation, for becoming other, for becoming the lover, is a powerful drive in Donne's poetry, but at least as important, indeed possibly more so, is the sense of the physical in the metaphysical, the here and now of the body. It is a poetry that takes the pulse, that searches the heart as organ as much as abstraction.

Passion may be the best word to get at the various and to a certain degree contradictory claims I have been making. Does Donne believe what he so often passionately asserts? Absolutely at the moment of its articulation, one feels, although not necessarily beyond the poem's last words. That "believing" might derive from emotions as various as joy, desire, despair, disgust, or, simply, pleasure at the sound of his own voice, his own cleverness. The poems are flooded with feeling; they are mercurial, wildly inventive. Thus the question may better be phrased: does the poem mean what it says? Here, too, I think the answer is yes, in spite of internal contradictions, shifts in voice, refusal to make itself add up, to become the organic whole claimed as the mark of success by nineteenth-century Romantic poets and twentieth-century New Critics. Another way of asking this question is: does the reader believe the poem? The answer, at once yes and no, is a function of the reader's role as both actor and audience, as both inside and outside the text. Positioned as spectator at some exciting game, the reader wonders how, indeed whether, the writer is going to pull it off, get it all together, keep those balls, those flashing figures, spinning from hand to hand without dropping them. At the same time, the reader is inside the poem as the lines are getting made, anticipating them, working them out, making his/her own meanings. Applying Helen Vendler's terms to Donne, one can say that the voice of the lyric is the reader's voice.[21]

There must be a reader, one who is also an actor, also a speaker (read these poems aloud! give them voice; they will be easier to enter that way, since their rhythms are often those of speech). Reading, according to Timothy Bahti, "is [a] co-constitutive activity," an activity that the reader, directed by the text, must complete.[22] But this is a process that once completed is not ended, neither by poem nor reader, for lyric poems "by their end ... have inverted the end into its opposite, a non-end ... [T]hey have inverted the attempts at interpretation into discoveries of where reading has to rebegin, never end ... readings [become] rebeginnings or not-yet-readings" (p. 13). Although Bahti does not discuss Donne (he regrets this in his Introduction), his argument returns us at the end to endings and most particularly to the endings of Donne's poems. They require us to rebegin, both those poems where endings do not seem particularly troubling and those that send us, off balance, back to the start, wondering how we got from there to here and back again, and those where the endings flummox us entirely.

But flummoxed or not we are always engaged (or nearly always; there are trivial poems, too, just as there are trivial sonnets in the 154 of Shakespeare). The world opened by Donne's poems, all of them, the *Songs and Sonets*, the *Holy Sonnets*, the *Anniversaries* and other funeral poems, the *Satires*, *Elegies*, verse letters, the so many poems not even touched on here, is amazingly full both in its material density and specificity, and in its longings, human and divine. It is hard to be indifferent to Donne. As many have noted, he makes one feel part of humanity, and not only because of the assertion, "I am involved in mankind," in that much repeated "no man is an island" passage in Devotion 17. It is, more crucially, because Donne satisfies and speaks to and about so many aspects of our humanity, our emotions, our intellect, our appetites and aspirations, both the high and the low, certainly more than just those aspects of ourselves that we fondly suppose to be our nobler qualities.

NOTES

1 Cited by David Plotz, "Why he's still with us," *Slate*, posted March 8, 1998.
2 Jack Gilbert, *The Great Fires: Poems 1982–92* (New York, 1994), p. 5.
3 Tilottama Rajan, "'Nothing Sooner Broke': Donne's *Songs and Sonets* as Self-Consuming Artifact," *ELH* 49 (1982), 817. Rajan argues that the "self-consciousness of the *Songs and Sonets* is precisely the product of a doubt as to whether language – as human intervention rather than divine dictation – can constitute the truth" (805).

4 William Empson, in John Haffenden (ed.), *Essays on Renaissance Literature*, vol. 1: *Donne and the New Philosophy* (Cambridge: Cambridge University Press, 1993), p. 88.
5 Quoted by Haffenden, *Essays on Renaissance Literature*, p. 59.
6 "X. J. Kennedy's Poetry Month Pick," 4/16/04. *Poetry Daily*. www.poetry.com. During poetry month, April 2004, a different poet chose and discussed a poem each day. Of the 29 choices taken from all times and places, four were Donne poems! As I've shown elsewhere, Donne's poetry continues as an ongoing provocation and stimulation to poets, novelists, painters. "Under the Sign of Donne," *Criticism* 43 (2001), 29–58.
7 A. J. Smith, *Metaphysical Wit* (Cambridge: Cambridge University Press, 1991), p. xi.
8 William Drummond of Hawthornden, "A letter on the True Nature of Poetry" (n.d.), in R. MacDonald (ed.), *Poems and Prose* (Edinburgh: Scottish Academic Press, 1976), p. 192; John Dryden, "A Discourse Concerning the Original and Progress of Satire" (1693), in J. Kinsley (ed.), *The Poems of John Dryden* (Oxford: Oxford University Press, 1958), p. 604; Samuel Johnson, "The Life of Cowley," in G. B. Hill (ed.), *The Lives of the English Poets*, vol. 1 (1905), p. 18.
9 Jonathan F. S. Post, *English Lyric Poetry: The Early Seventeenth Century* (London: Routledge, 1999); see chapter 1, "Irremediably Donne," p. 6.
10 Carey, *Donne*, p. 117.
11 "Conversations with William Drummond of Hawthornden," in C. H. Herford and Percy Simpson (ed.), *Ben Jonson*, vol. 1 (Oxford: Clarendon Press, 1925), p. 133. Jonson's comment is also included in A. J. Smith (ed.), *John Donne: The Critical Heritage* (London and Boston: Routledge, 1975), p. 69.
12 See John Hollander, *Vision and Resonance: Two Senses of Poetic Form* (New Haven: Yale University Press, 1985). In the chapter, "Donne and the Limits of Lyric," he shows how contrastive stress (stress falling on those words that stand in an important syntactic relation to each other) "engage fundamental grammatical relationships" (p. 55).
13 C. A. Patrides, *John Donne: the Complete English Poems* (1985; rpt. London: J. M. Dent, 1994), p. xxxi.
14 Ilona Bell, "'If It Be a Shee': The Riddle of Donne's 'Curse'," in M. Thomas Hester (ed.), *John Donne's 'desire of more': The subject of Anne More Donne in His Poetry* (Newark: University of Delaware Press, 1996), pp. 106–39, and "Courting Anne More," *JDJ* 19 (2000), 59–86. See also Theresa M. DiPasquale, "Receiving a Sexual Sacrament: 'The Flea' as Profane Eucharist," in Raymond-Jean Frontain and Frances M. Malpezzi (eds.), *John Donne's Religious Imagination* (Conway, AR: UCA Press, 1995), pp. 81–95.
15 The *John Donne Journal* devoted an entire issue to the poem (vol. 9.1, 1990); included there is a survey of critical responses from 1912–89. As editor of that issue, Achsah Guibbory remarked, "Perhaps it is because, no matter how well we historicize the poem as the product of a culture and society different than our own, it still speaks to something important in our experience" ("Editor's Preface").
16 Doug Beardsley and Al Purdy, *The Man Who Outlived Himself* (British Columbia: Harbour Publishing, 2000), p. 33.
17 Christopher Ricks, "Donne After Love," in Elaine Scarry (ed.) *Literature and the Body* (Baltimore: The Johns Hopkins University Press, 1988), p. 39.

18 Arnold Stein, "Interpretation: 'Aire and Angels,'" *JDJ* 9.1 (1990), 72.
19 "Patrick Donnelly's Poetry Month Pick," 4/19/04, "The Sun Rising," *Poetry Daily*. www.poetry.com.
20 Elaine Scarry, "Donne: 'But yet the body is his booke'," in Scarry (ed.) *Literature and the Body*, p. 88. Two books provide important contexts for this point, although Donne makes only an incidental appearance: Elizabeth Harvey (ed.), *Sensible flesh: On Touch in Early Modern Culture* (Philadelphia: University of Pennsylvania Press, 2003); David Hillman and Carla Mazzio (eds.), *The Body in Parts: Fantasies of Corporeality in Early Modern Europe* (New York and London: Routledge, 1997).
21 Helen Vendler, "'Tintern Abbey': Two Assaults," *Bucknell Review: Wordsworth in Context*, Pauline Fletcher and John Murphy (eds.) (Lewisburg, PA: Bucknell University Press, 1992), p. 184.
22 Timothy Bahti, *Ends of the Lyric: Direction and Consequence in Western Poetry*. (Baltimore: The Johns Hopkins University Press, 1996), p. 10.

8

ANNABEL PATTERSON

Satirical writing: Donne in shadows

What is satire? Always a difficult question to answer, the nature of satire perplexes people with an urge to pin things down. Satire might be called a stance, an attitude, which indicates from the start that one isn't always in that state of mind, but assumes it from time to time. It tends to be an attitude of the young and clever. An attitude to what? To what the young and clever person sees around him, that is to say, society, the behavior of others. The satirist is the polar opposite of the lyricist, especially one who writes devotional lyrics, in a private engagement with the absolute. Satire is a public engagement with the times; a critical engagement; sometimes a hostile and contemptuous one. It is a stance that can take a number of different literary forms – a play, a novel, an epigram. When we say "*a* satire," however, we mean a "formal verse satire," that is to say, a poem modeled to some degree on the Roman satirists, Horace, Juvenal, and Persius.

One might say that John Donne was all his life a repressed satirist. When he was a young man he had a brief period of intense satirical experimentation, in the context of exchanging poems with other young satirists, especially his friend Everard Guilpin. But even then he was conscious of the fact that satire was not a respectable mode of writing, and might get him into serious trouble. Perhaps in the year 1600, and if so while about twenty-seven years old, he wrote to his friend Sir Henry Wotton:

> Only in obedience I send you some of my paradoxes ... they are but swaggerers: quiet enough if you resist them ... yet Sir though I know there low price[,] except I receve by your next letter an assurance upon the religion of your friendship that no coppy shal bee taken for any respect of these or any other my compositions sent to you, I shall sinn against my conscience if I send you any more. I speake that in playness which becomes (methinkes) our honestyes; and therefore call not this a distrustfull but a free spirit: I meane to acquaint you with all myne: and to my satyrs there belongs some feare and to some elegies and these perhaps, shame. Against both which affections although I be tough

enough, yet I have a ridling disposition to bee ashamed of feare and afrayd of
shame. Therefore I am desirous to hide them . . .[1]

The letter is pure Donne in its self-analysis of the "ridling disposition" which
both enjoys satire and fears its consequences. Donne's letter teeters between
openness and concealment, between the free spirit of the young intellectual
and the distrustfulness inculcated by late Elizabethan law and society. "In
obedience" he sends his friend the poems. But he demands the limited kind of
confidentiality that we now associate with the terms "scribal publication" or
"coterie writing." That is to say, the satires (and the elegies) are not to be
shown to anybody outside a close circle of friends. And for good reason. On
June 4, 1599, perhaps just a year before this letter was written, the so-called
Bishops' Order prohibited, among other things, the publication of formal
verse satire, and ordered a series of book burnings. Joseph Hall's
Virgidemiarum, John Marston's *The Scourge of Villanie*, Everard Guilpin's
Skialethia, Thomas Middleton's *Microcynicon* ("Snarling Satires"), all of
which had created or followed a new fashion of rewriting Roman satire,
were called in, and most of them that could be found were burned, though
Hall's satires, much milder than the rest, were reprieved.[2]

The letter is also pure Donne in that it reveals how consistently he thought
in the conventional terms of genre. He has written paradoxes, satires, and
elegies, that is, erotic poems on the model of Ovid's *Amores*, which are only
called elegies because Ovid wrote them in the elegiac couplet, hexameters
followed by a "limping" or foot-short pentameter. When Donne's poems
circulated in manuscript among his friends, they did so in generic groupings,
with these titles. When they were eventually published after his death, the
groupings survived the hazards of posthumous publishing.

Thus for Donne, at this stage of his life, although we might readily detect
satirical intent in most of the paradoxes and the elegies, the "satyrs" so called,
of whose circulation he was actually afraid, are exclusively the group of five
poems we now call "the *Satires*," and which reprocess Roman satire in terms
of contemporary London, its follies and vices. Of the three groups of youthful (law-school) efforts, paradoxes, satires, and elegies, it is the satires that
would be the most dangerous if they circulated outside the circle of friends,
and his authorship of them were known.

Joseph Hall declared in his *Virgidemiarum*, which translates as a "scourge
made of a bundle of twigs," that he was the first English satirist. This was in
the year 1597. Most likely, the first English satirist was in fact John Donne,
whose satires, circulating in manuscript a few years earlier, may well have
inspired the new fashion. Wesley Milgate points out that on the title-page of
one of the manuscripts of Donne's satires (H 51) is written "Jhon Dunne his

Satires Anno Domini 1593."[3] The date is confirmed by topical references within the first satire. If Hall were competing with Donne by claiming the precedence of print, Guilpin, whose *Skialethia* was published early in 1598, admitted a debt by blatant imitation of the opening lines of Donne's first satire. (Milgate, p. 117). But we know these two were earlier corresponding on the subject of satire from Donne's verse letter to his friend, "To Mr. E. G.," which is a cover letter for some "slimy rimes" he transmits, and complains that there is nothing going on in London for a satirist to work with: "Nothing whereat to laugh my spleen espies / But bearbaitings or Law exercise," (pp. 208–09). Thomas Fulton, who has most effectively resituated Donne's satires in their coterie context, suggests that the verse letter is a response to Guilpin's own first satire, which highlights the term "spleen" (as derived from Persius's first satire).[4]

Donne's second satire has been dated 1594, by virtue of its apparent response to the publication of the anonymous sonnet sequence, *Zepheria*, whose author must have been a lawyer, judging from his diction. This increases the implication of coterie writing among the Inns of Court men, with satire absorbing literary criticism into its idea of social surveillance. When John Marston publicly entered the contest, late in the day, with the appearance of the *Scourge of Villanie* in September 1598, he insisted on his Juvenalian credentials, not least by giving his second satire the title *Difficile est satyram non scribere* (It is difficult *not* to write satire) from Juvenal's opening satire. Like Hall, Marston also constantly reverts to the poetaster theme that Donne had reintroduced in his second satire.

But it did not take Donne long to outgrow or exceed his classical models, and to move beyond literary criticism or the superficial scorn of superficial people. In the middle of his series there appears the remarkable third satire, sometimes entitled "Of Religion," in which he tackles the most crucial issue of the Elizabethan era, and one which had no classical Roman correlative: how to choose a religion in an age when the different factions of Christianity were divided against each other. I believe that "Satyre III" was written in response to the trial and execution in 1595 of Robert Southwell, the Jesuit priest and poet, an event that would tend to focus the attention of a brilliant young man with literary talents born into a Roman Catholic family. If so, this would explain Donne's opening moves, his realization that the seriousness of his topic demanded a new tone of voice. Despite Thomas Fulton's important advice, that we should not separate out "Satyre III" from its satirical coterie context, there is nothing like it in the work of Hall, Guilpin, or Marston. Though examples of religious hypocrisy may appear – Hall makes mock of the traffic in benefices (II.5) and devotes an entire satire to anti-Catholic insult (IV.7), and Marston occasionally slips in an attack on extreme

Puritanism (IV, Reactio), none of Donne's competitors make the dangerous decision to focus on the issue of personal religious choice and its relation to the laws of the land.

"Satyre IV" is dated by Milgate rather tightly in the period between March and July 1597, when Donne embarked on the Islands expedition. The satire was recognized at the time as an attack upon the Elizabethan court, for which read the Elizabethan regime. In it, Donne has progressed from the relatively cheerful account of sartorial excess in the first satire, and the relatively limited attack on legal corruption in the second satire, to a Dantesque vision of the Elizabethan court as hell, a hell supported by a legal system that was itself not so much corrupt as tyrannical. It corresponds to the "rotten state" that Donne mentions in "The Calme" (39), the second half of his commentary on the Islands expedition, the "rotten state" that, like Hamlet's Denmark, alienates the intellectual and sends him on a dangerous sea-voyage.

"Satyre V," however, seems to have been written explicitly for Sir Thomas Egerton, the queen's new Lord Keeper, whose secretary Donne became in late 1597. It too, even more explicitly, is focused on the law, as a system for whose integrity Egerton is now responsible. But the move to direct address to Egerton ("You Sir" [31]) and behind him to the queen ("Greatest and fairest Empresse" [28]) means, in effect, that the fifth satire is a move *away* from satire, towards the genre of advice to princes. It is as though the descent into hell had persuaded Donne that the only way up, the only practical exit, was to abandon the stance of the satirist, alienated and intimidated, and to replace it with the modest proposal of reform from within. That Donne's inclusion within the system was both marginal and, as we know from hindsight, fragile, gives the poem a certain extraneous pathos beyond that which it deliberately invokes. After his disastrous marriage to Egerton's niece, and his being both fired and imprisoned to punish him for this impertinence, the move to accommodation would be more urgent, though not complete until the reign of James I, and the writing of *Pseudo-Martyr* in 1610.

Drummond of Hawthornden, who seemed to know a good deal about Donne's satires by way of Ben Jonson, implied that their numerical order was also the order of composition. Though written at different moments over a five- or six-year period, they retroactively create a master narrative: a story of increasing social knowledge and analytic power, of increasing disillusionment, followed by compromise. There is no such narrative in the satires of any of his contemporaries. One can rearrange the satires of Hall or Guilpin or Marston with no loss (or gain) of coherence. In fact, the more one returns to Donne's satires after having attempted to read the satires of Hall, Guilpin, and especially Marston, whose hysterical overstatement makes it impossible to concentrate on what his target might be, the more they rise above the group project of being satirical in late Elizabethan London. They are simply better, more interesting. Alvin Kernan, in the first major study of the group, asserted that "No author of Elizabethan satire had a clear idea of what was basically wrong with his society."[5] J. B. Leishman complained that the Elizabethan satirists differ from their Roman predecessors in the "absence of a clear outline and plan, a tendency to pile detail upon detail and to present us with just one damned thing after another."[6] Lawrence Manley, who cites these verdicts in order to disagree with them, nevertheless praises "the improvisational structure of verse satire – its preference for metonymy over metaphor," as "an analytic instrument strikingly appropriate to the represented superficiality of the social types most often condemned."[7] But Donne cannot be covered by these generalizations, whether deprecatory or approving. Each of his satires has a clarity of structure, sometimes a narrative of its own, that holds together the seemingly disparate rebukes or cameo appearances. There are far fewer bad characters, far fewer fictional, pseudo-classical names in his satires than in Hall or Marston, and by the fourth and fifth satires this gambit of style has (with the exception of one Glorius) completely disappeared. But most importantly, there is a growing sense, as we move through the series, that the problems in law, in government, and in enforced religious orthodoxy all somehow entail each other. These, for Donne, are the problems that should engage the satirist; not monopolies, which nearly produced a crisis in the 1597 Parliament; not bad harvests; not the enormous costs of the military campaign in Europe, the facts that modern historians see as putting strain on the Elizabethan regime in the later 1590s. It is not surprising that law, government, and religion should be Donne's issues. What is surprising is the way he manages to suggest that everything corrupt is interconnected. This feat of synthetic imagination is accomplished not by metonymy but by metaphor.

We will now fill out *this* generalization by looking more closely at the first three satires, noting in particular how Donne signals their differences from each other by his opening definitions of tone. How different this is from Marston's banal "Now grim Reproofe, swel in my rough-hev'd rime," (Satire 3:1) or his claim to alternate between "serious jest, and jesting seriousnes" (Proem, Book 3).[8] In the first satire, a loose imitation of Horace (I.ix), a genial tolerance is established in opening address, "Away thou fondling motley humorist," since both "fondling" and "humorist" suggest comedy. The plot is simple. The humorist says "Come out and see the town." The scholar resists, but then succumbs. So here is complicity. But the mode of comic interaction, of a partnership at first resisted but then rather enjoyed, is developed by the second person address, initially in the intimate form "thee" and "thou." (The second person address will return, quite differently, in "Satyre v.") These two people, the sociable humorist and the reclusive scholar, know and like each other. They are almost married: "For better or worse, take mee, or leave mee: / To take, and leave mee is adultery" (25–26). Once the humorist has persuaded the scholar out into the street he becomes not a "thee" but a "he", but the tone remains affectionate, even protective. "I for my lost sheep stay" (93). The humorist's only fault is too indiscriminate a congeniality. And when he finds himself involved in a duel over his inconstant mistress, he heads back into the scholar's protection: "Directly came to mee hanging the head, /And constantly a while must keep his bed" (111–12). It is almost like the tale of Peter Rabbit.

By the second satire, however, a different emotion is in order: hate–twice mentioned in the first four lines, though clearly set against pity for all "the rest" (4) who are not at the moment the targets of the satirist's dislike. The target is a peculiar convergence, in the figure of Coscus, of bad poetry and bad law. But bad legal scrivening is worse than pretentious or incompetent poetry, because it has consequences. And here begins the characteristically Donnean move: to make one flawed institution the mirror image of another by relating them metaphorically. Thus Coscus "drawes / Assurances, bigge, as gloss'd civill lawes," and because he does not write himself, but uses a professional scrivener (whom he fails to pay), "spares no length" (87–92):

> ... as in those first dayes
> When Luther was profest, He did desire
> Short *Pater nosters*, saying as a Fryer
> Each day his beads, but having left those lawes,
> Addes to Christs prayer, the Power and glory clause.   (92–96)

To translate: Coscus, when he becomes a lawyer, draws up endless documents confirming the titles to land (assurances) and has no need to economize on length because he is freed from the burden of penmanship; *as* Luther, who as a friar favored short prayers (because he had to say them so frequently) when he abandoned the rituals of the Roman church was quite willing to lengthen the Protestant church's most basic and economic ritual, the Lord's Prayer, thereby increasing the number of propositions imposed on the believer. Both sides of the metaphorical divide come off badly. Coscus, as a shifty lawyer, "(unwatch'd) leaves out, *ses heires*" (98) from deeds, thereby short-circuiting the title to the property in question, "As slily," Donne comments, "as ... in Divinity ... controverters, in vouch'd Texts, leave out / Shrewd words, which might against them clear the doubt" (99–102). To translate: Coscus leaves out the crucial phrase from the assurance, *as* theologians, when they cite a scriptural text to support their argument, omit the words that do not support that argument. If anything, religion fares worse in the comparison than does the law. That the law *is*, however, the true subject of the satire, is revealed in the last two lines, where Donne plays with the "feare" he had mentioned to Goodyer as "belonging" to his satires, and reassures himself that his "words none drawes / Within the vast reach of th'huge statute lawes" (111–12).

What statutes? Strictly speaking, neither the Star Chamber decree of 1586 that regulated printing nor the Bishops' Order of 1599 (which had not occurred when the satire was written) were statutes. But Donne may be thinking of the 1581 act (23 Eliz. ca. 2) against seditious publications or of treason law more generally, both of which were notoriously elastic. By "huge" Donne appears to mean "all encompassing in their potential application," a dread he rearticulates in "Satyre IV," when listening to a court libeller makes him feel himself "then / Becoming Traytor," and he imagines he saw "One of our Giant Statutes ope his jaw / To sucke [him] in" (130–33). Milgate is in error when he attributes Donne's momentary sense of immunity to the fact that "all he says is true" (p. 139), for the claim of accuracy was no defense against the charge of seditious libel, and in fact was held to exacerbate the felony. What Donne more likely means by the conclusion to "Satyre II" is that he has immunity because his satires remain unpublished. By the time he comes to write "Satyre IV," that confidence has vanished, and he imagines "one of our Giant Statutes" just about to swallow him up.

The word "hate" appears twice more in "Satyre II" (10 and 107), confirming that its tone is of Juvenalian animosity. But "Satyre III" signals a change, to a much more conflicted range of emotions and motives:

> Kinde pitty chokes my spleene; brave scorne forbids
> Those teares to issue which swell my eye-lids;
> I must not laugh, nor weepe sinnes, and be wise,
> Can railing then cure these worne maladies? (1–4)

Thus the "spleen" of Persius (and Guilpin) and the "railing" of Marston are no longer inappropriate for a modern writer who reflects on the consequences of the Protestant Reformation. Where Hall believed that "the Satyre should be like the Porcupine, / That shoots sharpe quils out in each angry line" (v.3. 1–2) and regretted that his own style was too quiet to live up to the standards of antiquity, and Marston claimed to have found a higher because fiercer style "then wel beseemes a rough-tongu'd Satyres part" (9.9), Donne has preemptively gone beyond classical imitation to question the very notion of a satirical stance. But he has also abandoned the flaccid posture of lament or complaint, the "tears" that had just, in 1595, become the sign of devotional poetry. Thus indictment is replaced by interrogation (a series of intricate rhetorical questions) and the hopeless account of a bad situation with severe recommendations for change (a series of injunctions): "Know thy foes" (33). "Seeke true religion" (43). "Unmoved thou / Of force must one, and forc'd but one allow" (69–70): "Aske thy father which is shee" (71). "Doubt wisely" (77). "Keep the truth which thou hast found" (89). The short passage which looks most like traditional satire, and which introduces the poor confessional decisions of Mirreus (Roman Catholic), Cranz (Genevan Calvinism), and Graius (the newly established English church), is actually less central to the argument than it appears. The most powerful injunction comes towards the end of the poem, where Donne attempts to deal with the facts of state coercion, Erastianism, and inflexible reformism. So law returns as the key to the satirist's distress:

> Foole and wretch, wilt thou let thy Soule be tyed
> To mans lawes, by which she shall not be tryed
> At the last day? (93–95)

In the closing lines, popes and monarchs who insist that they derive from God their power to legislate religious belief and practice are put firmly in their place, and inserting Henry VIII as the coercive monarch instead of Elizabeth would have deceived nobody:

> So perish Soules, which more chuse mens unjust
> Power from God claym'd, then God himselfe to trust. (109–10)

This is strong medicine. I believe it to be motivated by shock at the trial and execution of Robert Southwell, who had the temerity to ignore the series of Elizabeth's proclamations, especially that of 1585, which banished Jesuits and Catholic priests from the country and made it a capital crime to return. Southwell had been captured by the notorious priest-hunter Richard Topcliffe, who wrote to the queen: "I never did take a weightier man, if he be rightly treated," that is, tortured to reveal the names of his associates. Southwell's religious poems were published immediately after his death, and they established a new, lamentable, fashion in devotional poetry on which, incidentally, Joseph Hall commented sardonically in *Virgidemiae* (1.8:"Now Good Saint Peter weeps pure Helicon").[9] In "Satyre IV" Donne, in mocking a lover who keeps saying "By Jesus" to his mistress, initially suggested, sardonically, that "A / Topcliffe would have ravish'd him away / For saying of our Ladies psalter" (216–17). But he was scarcely joking. Later versions substituted "A Pursevant," either for prudence, or because the name would have lost its topicality.

"Satyre IV" is too long for effective summary here, but it is clearly a rewriting, in a much darker tone, of the premise of "Satyre I," the frivolity of the street giving way to the unstable and rumor-ridden political climate of

the court, the unwanted but charmingly seductive companion to the truly
obnoxious one who pours political poison into the poet's ear, and thus makes
him feel guilty by association:

> He like a priviledg'd spie, whom nothing can
> Discredit, Libells now 'gainst each great man.   (119–20)

Thus the satirist becomes aware of what a satirist looks like, sounds like,
from the outside; besides, he is wearing, however threadbare, what is still
recognizably a black velvet jerkin, such as that which Donne himself
is painted wearing in the dilapidated Lothian portrait (although in that
portrait the melodramatic black velvet jacket has sleeves). It is from this
imaginary encounter (with himself?) that the satirist flees to the safety of
home, where, to his horror, "a trance / Like his, who dreamt he saw hell, did
advance it selfe" (157–58) on him, and the negative view of Elizabethan
court society that he has unwillingly received through his ears is now
repeated, as a nightmare, before his eyes. Before long, he is shaking like "a
spyed Spie" (237), the "privileg'd" status of the spy in line 119 having been
withdrawn, the undercover agent having blown his cover.

At the opening of his last satire, which, as I have said, is effectively an
abandonment of the genre, Donne returns to the problem of tone:

> Thou shalt not laugh in this leafe, Muse, nor they
> Whom any pitty warmes; He which did lay
> Rules to make Courtiers ...
> Frees from the sting of jests all who in extreme
> Are wrech'd or wicked.   (1–6)

Thinking of a line of advice in Castiglione's *Il Cortegiano* (*The Courtier*),
Donne now makes a further move away from railing, a partial resolution of
the conflict between pity and spleen, with the conflict resolved in favor of the
former. Critical consensus declares that this poem is weaker than the others.
I believe this to have been intentional. As *satire* it is weaker; as sociopolitical
analysis it is stronger and more coherent, since, like "Satyre III," it insists on
tracing the problems in the institution under review back to their source.
"Powre of the Courts below / Flow from the first maine head" (45–46). And
yet, if the institutions of law and religion have this structure in common, are
seen seriously as formal analogies whose similarity depends on their being
kept conceptually apart, they bleed into each other when it comes to the
legalized harassment of Catholics:

> ... Would it not anger
> A Stoicke, a coward, yea a Martyr,
> To see a Pursuivant come in, and call

> All his cloathes, Copes; Books, Primers; and all
> His Plate, Challices; and mistake them away,
> And aske a fee for comming? Oh, ne'r may
> Faire lawes white reverend name be strumpeted,
> To warrant thefts. (63–70)

These lines echo, but more wittily, Robert Southwell's complaint to the queen in *An Humble Supplication* (written 1591), about "the continuall hell we suffer by the merciles searching and storming of Purseyvants and such needy Officers" (Milgate, pp. 168–69). The governmental obsession about Catholic priests has created a new industry, a new black market, such that even ordinary thieves are profiting from the bad laws by coming with false badges and warrants, "under the pretence of Pursevants, [to spoil] us in our howses, having th'officers to assist them in the Robberies" (Milgate, pp. 168–69). By the end of the satire Donne is once more addressing, as in "Satyre I," a "thee" who is also a "Foole." Now, however, this figure is no mere window-shopper but the prototypical suitor or appellant at law, perhaps Donne himself; and the poem ends by warning against a dangerous illusion, the illusion that there is such a thing as Law and Justice:

> O wretch that thy fortunes should moralize
> Esops fables, and make tales, prophesies.
> Thou'art the swimming dog whom shadows cosened,
> And div'st, neare drowning, for what's vanished. (88–91)

I believe it to be no coincidence that Marston's proem to the *Scourge* ends with the same fable, but in a totally different key: "Yee scrupulous observers, goe and learne / Of Aesops dogge; meate from a shade discerne" (*Ad Rithmum*, 37–38). Although there is no evidence that Marston's satires circulated in manuscript before their publication in 1598, it seems plausible that Donne's more subtle use of the fable of *The Dog and the Shadow* is a response to Marston's, rather than vice versa.

But after "Satyre V" Donne did not give up on satire completely. He must have rethought the hazards he ran when, in 1606, in the case entitled *de libellis famosis*, the Star Chamber defined *seditious libel* (criticism of "great men" or of the government) as a crime because it undermined respect of authority; specifically it casts "scandal" on the government. Hence the truth of any accusation was no defence. As Sir Edward Coke put it, the greater the truth, the greater the libel. Moreover, *de libellis famosis* established that libeling the dead was still seditious, the case in question having to do with Archbishop John Whitgift, who had died in 1604. The ruling must have caused Donne to reconsider his characterization of the rumor-monger in "Satyre IV," especially as his charges would remain pertinent under James:

He ... Libells now'gainst each great man.
He names a price for every office paid;
He saith, our warres thrive ill, because delai'd;
That offices are entail'd, and that there are
Perpetuities of them, lasting as farre
As the last day; and that great officers,
Doe with the Pirates share, and Dunkirkers.   (119–26)

Even before *de libellis famosis* Donne had begun to divert his satirical instincts into new, less immediately recognizable forms. One of these was the inscrutable, undecodable mock-epic entitled "*Metempsychosis*: The Progresse of the Soule," perhaps written in 1601, whose title bemused editors and licensers into thinking it was a religious poem, whereas in fact it was a scurrilous joke. But a more interesting case of adaptiveness was the companion piece to *Pseudo-Martyr*, the mock *Inferno* that Donne called *Ignatius his Conclave*, a satire against Ignatius Loyola, founder of the Jesuits. This prose work, which called itself a satire on the title-page, was clearly acceptable to the new regime; it was published both in Latin and English in 1611, the Latin version licensed under the hand of Bishop Thomas Morton himself. The *Conclave* imagines a competition in Hell for the post of Lucifer's second-in-command, a competition that Loyola wins. The *Conclave* was much more popular than *Pseudo-Martyr*, confirming that satirical works (like the Marprelate pamphlets) often have a market advantage over their dogmatic counterparts. The *Conclave* had three Latin and four English editions during the seventeenth century, whereas *Pseudo-Martyr* was never reissued (Bald, p. 228). Readers today have considerable difficulty, however, in grasping the tone or even following the arguments by which the candidates are evaluated, and the piece probably reflects Donne's ambivalence about having just published *Pseudo-Martyr*, which made public his defection from his own distinguished Catholic origins. At any rate, the *Conclave* allowed him to be witty, and to be witty in print, which may have served as something of a relief.

In the meantime, Donne kept his satires in manuscript. Probably in 1608, he supplied Ben Jonson with a copy of them, and apparently countenanced Jonson sending them on to Lucy, Countess of Bedford, whom Donne had recently met and hoped to impress. Milgate believes (p. lix) that the variants found in three manuscript versions, especially the cluster in "Satyre III," were revisions by Donne for this purpose. We know that Jonson transmitted the satires to the countess because he left us an epigram entitled "To Lucy, Countesse of Bedford, with M. Donne's Satyres," an epigram published in his 1616 *Workes*, which also tells us that very few people choose to read satire, but those who do thereby establish their superiority of character and intellect. More circulation is indicated by another epigram, this time by Thomas Freeman, who in 1614 published the following brief accolade:

> To John Dunne.
> The *Storme* describ'd, hath set thy name afloate,
> The *Calme*, a gale of famous winde hath got:
> Thy *Satyres* short, too soone we them o'relooke,
> I prithee *Persius* write a bigger booke.[10]

Modern readers, who wade through the multiple repetitions of Hall and Marston, may be relieved that he did not.

We can tell that Donne is still thinking seriously about the social function of satire from a letter he wrote to his friend Sir Henry Goodyer in the spring of 1612, shortly after the death of Sir Robert Cecil, James's Treasurer and Secretary of State:

> Nothing in my L. of Salisburies death exercised my poor considerations so much, as the multitude of libells. It was easily discerned, some years before his death, that he was at a defensive war, both for his honour and health, and (as we then thought) for his estate: and I thought, that had removed much of the envy ... But I meane to speake of nothing but the libells, of which, all which are brought into these parts, are so tastelesse and flat, that I protest to you, I think they were made by his friends. It is not the first time that our age hath seen that art practised, That when there are witty and sharp libels made, which not onely for the liberty of speaking, but for the elegancie, and composition, would take deep root, and make durable impressions in the memory, no other way hath been thought so fit to suppresse them, as to divulge some course, and railing one: for when the noise is risen, that libels are abroad, mens curiositie must be served with something: and it is better for the honour of the person traduced, that some blunt downright railings be vented, of which everybody is soon weary, then other pieces, which entertain us long with a delight, and love to the things themselves. *(Letters*, p. 90)

This extraordinary passage tells us more about Donne's theory of satire than any amount of comparison with his Roman models or his Elizabethan competitors. And indeed the passage continues with a still more remarkable defiance of *de libellis famosis*, to the effect that "one may do his Countrey good service, by libellings against a live man. For where a man is either too great, or his Vices too generall, to be brought under a judiciary accusation, there is no way, but this extraordinary accusing, which we call Libelling" (pp. 90–91). And we need to continue:

> But after death, it is, in all cases, inexcusable. I know that Lucifer, and one or two more of the Fathers who writ libellous books against the Emperours of their times, are excused by our writers, because they writ not in the lives of

those Emperours. I am glad for them that they writ not in their lives, for that must have occasioned tumult, and contempt, against so high and Soveraign persons. But that doth not enough excuse them to me, for writing so after their death; for that was ignoble, and uselesse, though did a little escape the nature of libels, by being subscribed and avowed: which excuse would not have served in the Star-chamber, where sealed Letters have been judged Libels. (pp. 91–92)

In this letter Donne (however privately) defied both statutes and the practices of the Star Chamber, outlining a theory of heroic satire that takes on a job that nobody else dare touch.

When he was in his fifties, as Dean of St. Paul's Cathedral and one of James I's most eminent preachers, Donne had achieved the prominence and influence he sought, though not in the political domain, the arena he seemed to have imagined for himself when he wrote at least "Satyre v." At this later stage in his life, he came to speak of satire as a negative state of mind which was bad for both Church and State. Frequently in his preaching he alluded to satire and "libels" as something to be shunned. Nevertheless, even to mention satire in a sermon is to give it a certain negative presence, a shadow in the background, a force still to be reckoned with.

Let us look at two strong examples. One comes from a sermon preached at Lincoln's Inn – that is to say, to an audience of lawyers – in the winter of 1620, probably soon after November 24, when news arrived of the defeat and flight of the Elector Palatine, James's Protestant son-in-law, whose tiny country had been invaded by Spanish forces. This was widely felt to be the fault of James, who had not supported the Elector and his daughter Elizabeth militarily. Donne's text was Matthew 18:7, "Woe unto the world, because of offences," and his objective is to prevent the circulation of criticism against the regime:

All scandals cannot be removed in this life; but a great many more might be then are, if men were not so apt to suspect, and mis-constru, and imprint the name of scandall upon every action, of which they see not the end, nor the way ... To be unsensible of any declination, or any diminution of the glory of God, or his true worship and religion, is an irreligious stupidity; But to bee so umbragious, so startling, so apprehensive, so suspicious, as to think every thing that is done, is done to that end; this is a seditious jealousie, a Satyr in the heart, and an *unwritten Libell*; and God hath a Star-Chamber, to punish unwritten Libels before they are published; Libels against that Law, *Curse not, or speak not ill of the King, no not in thy thought.* (*Sermons*, vol. III, no. 7, p. 183)

Donne's earlier notion of an unpublished satire as having a certain immunity, a certain rectitude, is here cancelled by the assertion that even *unwritten* criticism of the king is seditious libel; and that interesting word *umbragious*, in the shadows, might remind us of that portrait of himself (the Lothian portrait) which he willed to his friend Sir Robert Ker (or Carr), as "that Picture of myne wch is taken in Shaddowes and was made very many yeares before I was of this profession" (Bald, p. 567).

Donne returned to this topic, and to the same quotation from Ecclesiastes 10:20, in 1627, in a sermon preached before the king at Whitehall. By this time, the king was Charles I, with whom Donne was always uncomfortable. The sermon is peculiar for including a personal confession to the effect that Donne is uncomfortable addressing Charles on this topic: "This is the first time, that in the exercise of my Ministery, I wished the King away; That ever I had any kinde of loathnesse that the King should hear all that I sayd" (*Sermons*, vol. VII, no. 16, p. 403). His text is Mark 4:24, "Take heed what you hear," and, as in the 1620 sermon, he attempts to control the rising tide of criticism of the king, caused now by the overt Catholicism of his queen:

> *Take heed what you heare*: Come not so neare evill speaking, as to delight to heare them, that delight to speake evill of Superiours. A man may have a good breath in himself, and yet be deadly infected, if he stand in an ill ayre; ... the heart concludes with his conclusions, whom we have been willing to hearken unto. We make *Satyrs*; and we looke that the world should call that *wit*; when God knowes, that that is in a great part, self-guiltinesse, and we doe but reprehend those things, which we our selves have done, we cry out upon the illnesse of the times, and we make the times ill; so the calumniator whispers those things, which are true, no where, but in himselfe.
>
> (vol. VII, no. 16, p. 408)

This sermon differs from that of 1620 in its attitude to satire in being more profoundly personal. Whereas the earlier indictment spoke to satire as a political undertow, this one speaks from the perspective (we know this, though Donne's audience did not) of someone who had himself not only written satires, but made his darkest adventure into that genre a tale of being infected through the ear. In particular, the denigration of satire as an ostentation of *wit* looks back to the high old days of the 1590s, when Donne and his fellow members of the Inns of Court, put their wit on display for the amusement of a coterie audience, without much thought as to what the social and political consequences might be. Those "we's" are particularly interesting, therefore, both indicating the earlier coterie and drawing in the present audience to be wary of sociopolitical criticism, whether as speakers or listeners. "Self-guiltinesse" therefore has a double valence here; on the one hand, it recognizes the inevitable complicity of the satirist in the abuses he describes (for how can he know about them if he has stayed demurely at home, engaged in his studies); on the other hand, it stands as a judgment on poems that had carried some of Donne's deepest convictions. But the satires survived. They even survived a licensing stay on them while the 1633 edition was in press; and so they have made Donne's canon more interesting, indubitably, than without them it would have been.

NOTES

1 This letter was, perhaps significantly, not included in the *Letters to Severall Persons of Honour* (1651). It derives from the Burley manuscript (Henry Wotton's commonplace book) and has been printed in various selections of Donne's prose, including E. M. Simpson, *A Study of the Prose Works of John Donne* (Oxford: Clarendon Press, 1948), p. 316.

2 For a careful explanation of this episode, see Cyndia Clegg, *Press Censorship in Elizabethan England* (Cambridge: Cambridge University Press, 1997), pp. 198–217.

3 Wesley Milgate (ed.), *The Satires, Epigrams and Verse Letters* (Oxford: Clarendon Press, 1967), p. lii.

4 Thomas Fulton, "Hamlet's Inky Cloak and Donne's *Satyres*," *JDJ* 20 (2001), 71–106.

5 Alvin Kernan, *The Cankered Muse: Satire of the English Renaissance* (New Haven: Yale University Press, 1959), p. 381.

6 J. B. Leishman (ed.), *The Three Parnassus Plays (1598–1601)* (London: Nicholson and Watson, 1949), pp. 111, 121.

7 Lawrence Manley, *Literature and Culture in Early Modern London* (Cambridge: Cambridge University Press, 1995), p. 381.

8 John Marston, *Poems*, ed. Arnold Davenport (Liverpool: Liverpool University Press, 1961), pp. 77, 149.

9 Arnold Davenport (ed.), *Collected Poems of Joseph Hall* (Liverpool: Liverpool University Press, 1949), p. 19.

10 Milgate, p. xlvii; cited from *Rubbe and a great Cast, the Second Bowle* (1614), Epigram 84.

9

ACHSAH GUIBBORY

Erotic poetry

Even after four centuries, Donne's love poetry strikes us as fresh and immediate, with its urgent rhythms, its irregular, frequent stresses communicating the sense that passion cannot be contained within regular iambic feet. He insists that, unlike poets who "have no Mistresse but their Muse" ("Loves growth," 12), he is describing love as it really is. Yet, lines or even poems remain uncertain, endlessly intriguing, like puzzles where a piece seems missing, or where there's a surplus. We try to stabilize his elusive meanings, much as he sought to capture that most unsettling and mysterious experience of human life: love.

The voice is usually male, though a few adopt a female voice. To the extent that men and women experience desire differently, Donne expresses a distinctly male perspective. He writes as if discovering a new emotional world of desire, one whose terrain has never before been explored. Yet women as well as men recognize it at once – most of us have been there, or hope to be. Donne philosophizes about love, trying to define it, but even when he soars, he brings love's philosophy down to earth, grounding it in concrete (if imagined) material experience that prompts him to revise conventional wisdom, and even sometimes his own pronouncements.

Donne's interest in the dynamics of desire extends beyond the love lyrics. Verse epistles to friends and patrons employ a hyperbolic language of love; poems to God draw analogies from secular amatory experience. "Sir, more than kisses, letters mingle Soules," he writes in a poem "To Sr Henry Wotton" (1). A homoerotic note sounds in devotional sonnets that address God as the beloved ("What if this present were the worlds last night") or beg God to "ravish" him ("Batter my heart," 14). Clearly, *eros* was, for Donne, the driving force of life, affecting most relations, and spiritual and sexual desire not as sharply segregated as we might think.

Strictly speaking, Donne's love poetry encompasses the *Elegies* and the *Songs and Sonets*, poems marked by an energetic, often bawdy wit, a new explicitness about sexual desire and experience, and an irreverent attitude towards authority figures. Neither the *Elegies* nor the *Songs and Sonets* were published in Donne's lifetime. Rather, these poems circulated in manuscript among "coterie" audiences that might be expected to understand Donne's wit, specific personal or social references, and even share his values. Donne's reluctance to give his poems to a large, public audience suggests not only gentlemanly reserve but also his recognition that there was a dangerous aspect to his writing, and not only his satires.

Elegies

Perhaps the *Elegies* seemed particularly dangerous, and not just because their sexual explicitness would have been indecorous for a man seeking public office, or, later, for the Dean of St. Paul's. Several were not published in the first editions (1633, 1635) of Donne's *Poems*: "Variety" did not appear until 1650; "Going to Bed," "Loves Progress," and "His parting from her" not until 1669. The number of Donne's *Elegies* is disputed – twenty or fewer poems; some editors have doubted that "Sapho to Philaenis" is by Donne. His *Elegies* are about love (not dead people) and take their generic name from Roman amatory poems written in elegiac meter.

Donne most likely wrote these poems when he was a young man in his early twenties, attached to the Inns of Court. Elizabeth was queen of England and Petrarchan poetry was popular. Petrarch, the fourteenth-century Italian poet, had written a sonnet sequence describing the progress of his love for the unavailable, chaste Laura, and analyzing his interior, emotional life. Later poets found that the narrative of Petrarchan love could express the dynamics of the court, where courtiers served a powerful monarch or patron (remote, distant, elevated), proclaiming their constant "devotion," hoping to receive "grace," and complaining about their lack of "reward." As amorous court-ship became the language of courtiership, Petrarchan language of "service" was used in the court of Elizabeth, the unmarried "virgin" queen, who encouraged her courtiers' devotion while retaining power. But Petrarch was not the only model for love poetry when Donne was coming of age. In the 1590s, witty, ambitious young men at the Inns of Court imitated Ovid, whose wit and detachment in describing the male lover's aggressive pursuit of women and attainment of his goals seemed a more attractive model than Petrarch's submissive, yearning, endlessly devoted, and frustrated lover.[1]

Echoing Ovid's representation of male/female relations and even situations in *Amores*, Donne's *Elegies* are dramatic addresses of a man to his mistress (the exception is "Sapho to Philænis," in which Sapho addresses her absent female lover) – although occasionally other objects are addressed (a perfume rhetoric-ally identified with the woman in "The Perfume," himself in "Variety," Night in "His parting from her," or another man in "The Comparison" and "The Anagram"). The relations depicted are clearly sexual, sometimes illicit or adulterous ("Iealousie," "The Perfume," and the elegy beginning "Natures lay Ideot.") Whereas Petrarchan poetry idealized women and spiritualized desire, Donne's Ovidian *Elegies* flaunt the speaker's sexuality as he describes his escapades.

Mocking notions of constancy and faithfulness, these poems are irreverent, and their anti-authoritarian stance creates ripples beyond the poems. The speaker is often disgruntled or angry. He rails against authority figures – the "Hydroptique father" and "immortall mother" of his mistress who oppose their love ("The Perfume," 6, 13); the "loathsome" husband of his mistress ("Iealousie,"7). Satire intrudes into elegy, as the speaker in "Loves Progress," arguing that only "one thing" in "woman" (10) should be valued, compares his love of woman's body to our love of gold, not for its "wholsomness" or "ingenuitie" or purity but simply because "'tis made / By our new nature (Use) the soul of trade" (13, 15–16). For all the witty glorification of sex and women's "Centrique part" as especially "worthy" of men's love (36, 37), the poem critiques the materialism of English society, presents women as tricksters, and voices disappointment that women are no more "wise and good" (22) than men – that this is an imperfect world.

Donne's *Elegies* disdain the constancy Petrarchan and courtly devotees profess. "Variety" insists that even "The heavens rejoyce in motion" (1). Constancy to one woman is unnatural, and nature is the law according to which man must run. The elegy "Change" seems an exception, as the paranoid speaker rails against his mistress, fearing that she, like "Foxes, and goats," will "change" lovers when she pleases (11). But at the end he changes his opinion (demonstrating the truth that change rules the world), refusing the "captivitie" (29) of monogamy and embracing the serial polygamy of the river which "kisse[s]" one "banke" and then the "next" (33–34).

With their libertine wit asserting (male?) fantasies of liberty,[2] Donne's *Elegies* remove woman from the pedestal on which she had been adored in courtly and Petrarchan poetry. Instead, he compares women to animals, fields, land, and their bodies are imperfect and open, unlike the perfect, classical, closed bodies of statues. "The Comparison" contrasts the "sweat drops of my Mistris breast," which seem "pearle" necklaces, with the "ranke sweaty froth" that "defiles" the brow of his companion's mistress (4, 6, 7). Whereas the Petrarchan blazon described the face and the higher, more spiritualizable parts of the woman's body, Donne focuses on bodily fluids and goes for the vagina, demolishing the statue-like image of woman. The "cherishing heat" of his mistress's "best lov'd part" (38) contrasts with the other woman's genitals, which are like "the dread mouth of a fired gunne" (39).

Repulsion about the female body spills over, contaminating the supposedly beautiful, desirable mistress.

The misogynous wit of these poems expresses frustration about the difficulty of controlling women, even as these speakers seek control. In "Change," he worries that women, like the "sea" which "receives the Rhene, Volga, and Po" (20), are open to multiple men. The speaker in "Natures lay Ideot" is furious that his mistress has used arts she learned from him to find other lovers. These angry diatribes express the man's desire to control women (and perhaps the larger world) and frustration at his inability. The elegy beginning "Come, Madam, come" (commonly titled "Going to Bed") seems different – there is no anger, just the pleasures of a male erotic fantasy. The poem describes the beloved as an "Angel" who brings "A heaven like Mahomets Paradise" (20–21). But within the seductive flattery lies desire for dominance. He asks her, like the Queen, to "License" his "roaving hands" to explore his "new-found" "America" (25, 27). But once license is given, she becomes territory to be possessed and "man'd" as he goes "Before, behind, between, above, below" (28, 26). After a series of arguments offered to convince her to reveal all, he concludes, "To teach thee I am naked first; why than / What needst thou have more covering than a man" (47–48), suggesting (in a witty revision of Paul's words in 1 Corinthians 11:3–7) that she needs no more clothes than he does, and that his body is the only "covering" she needs – an apt image for showing that man should be "on top." All of this mastery may be something hoped for not attained. Still, this poem, like Donne's other elegies, expresses a fantasy of male power that may also have sociopolitical significance, obliquely articulating discomfort with serving a woman monarch in a patriarchal society.

The *Songs and Sonets*

Donne's *Songs and Sonets* express a more diverse range of attitudes towards women and the experience of love. Comprising fewer than sixty poems, it is a highly inventive collection, varied in stance and tone as well as stanza forms. Although we cannot date individual poems, Donne probably wrote most of them over a period from the 1590s into the first decade of the seventeenth century. His friend Ben Jonson insisted that a stable voice is the mark of a virtuous man, constant in a mutable world; but the *Songs and Sonets*, with their variety of personas or "voices," present a self whose identity is fluid. Donne tries on various roles, expressing the mutability of the world and the instability of desire even as he seeks permanence and stability.

Some lyrics adapt Petrarchan conventions. "The broken heart" anato-
mizes the pain of heart-break. "Loves Deitie" complains about loving "one
which did scorne" (4). "The Dampe" imagines himself dead, "Massacre[d]"
(8) by his disdainful mistress. Other *Songs and Sonets* share the *Elegies'*
sensibility, as an arrogant, emotionally detached male speaker flaunts his
sexual freedom, refusing to be tied down. "The Indifferent" responds to a
woman's desire for constancy by insisting that he can love "any, so she be
not true" (9). As in the *Elegies*, satire intrudes when Venus says she had not
heard till now anyone who wanted constancy – as if a constant woman is a
strange aberration in this inconstant world. Inverting traditional values
(political, religious, and amorous), playing with notions of "true" and
"false," Donne's speaker boasts that he is committed to being inconstant
or "false" (27).

Other poems echo the cynicism of "The Indifferent." "Womans constancy" and "Confined Love" embrace inconstancy and change, and feature
women speakers. "Communitie" has a decidedly male speaker who views
women as "indifferent" things (neither "good" nor "bad") – mere commodities that can be "use[d]" by "all" and then discarded (lines 3, 8, 12).
Economics and erotics intertwine, as the speaker envisions a society with
no individual ownership or property. Love is mere appetite, and, far
from being worshipped, woman is demoted beneath the level of the human
or even the animal. As in so many *Songs and Sonets*, the speaker's
impulse is to generalize, to make a definitive statement that will be contra-
dicted by other poems, which also adopt seemingly definitive stances,
and that the poem itself complicates or undermines. Here the speaker
dismisses the possibility of emotional attachment as he strips woman of a
human soul.

"Loves Alchymie" is out to dispel the illusions of men who think they can
find the "Elixar" (7) in loving a woman. Drawing an analogy between love
and alchemy, boasting of his sexual experience as he claims that no one has
"deeper digg'd loves Myne then I" (1), the speaker concludes that there is no
"centrique happiness" (2) or perfection to be found in love. Bitter and mocking, he attacks those who glorify their experience; the "dreame" (11) of love
contrasts with the disappointing reality. Disappointment in love, which is
only sex, produces misogynous dismissal of women as mere bodies, inert
matter, at best medicinal: "Hope not for minde in women; at their best /
Sweetnesse and wit, they'are but *Mummy*, possest" (23–24).

Other *Songs and Sonets*, however, celebrate love as the supremely fulfilling experience. In these lyrics, we seem to have entered another world.
"The good-morrow" and "The Sunne Rising" voice a joy and sense of
fulfillment in intimacy that the speakers of other poems disdain or fear.

Here, the particular, singular woman is essential for the man's fulfillment. In contrast to the libertine poems, poems on "mutual," reciprocal love describe love as an antidote to the impermanence and mortality that characterize the rest of the world. Obsessed with change and decay, Donne desires permanence and stability, and sometimes thinks he has found it in love.

Although it is tempting to try to find a pattern in the *Songs and Sonets*, the poems defeat such an attempt. They are not arranged in a sequence like Sidney's *Astrophil and Stella*, or Petrarch's *Canzoniere*. We cannot certainly say that the libertine, cynical poems are early, and the poems about mutual love later, as if Donne matured into sincerity and stability. Still, we find a notable difference: in Ovidian, libertine poems, where the speaker appears most distant from his desire, women are debased; in those poems where the speaker embraces his desire, woman is specially valued.

Readers have long identified the "mutual love" poems with Donne's secret courtship and marriage to Anne More. Manuscript evidence suggests that some poems had a very limited circulation, as if Donne considered them particularly private.[3] Certain lyrics that privilege the sacred space of clandestine love and describe the world's opposition fit with what we know of Donne's situation at the time. Yet so long as we lack evidence for the dates and occasions of Donne's lyrics, poems like "The Relique" or "The goodmorrow" must frustrate the autobiographical readings they invite.[4]

Love, politics, and the public world

Donne explores the relation between the private experience of love and the public, outer world. Elegies about "love" and erotic desire are often also about politics, and not just the politics of the bedroom. Sometimes the difficult argument and resonant language make us feel the poem is about something other than love. In "The Bracelet," the speaker complains about the loss of his mistress's chain but also about the "bitter cost" of the twelve coins or "righteous Angels" (punning on the name for an English gold coin) which by her "severe Sentence" have to "beare" the "great burden" of his "sins" (8, 9, 17–18). In Donne's language and his depiction of the mistress as a "dread judge" (18) who extracts payment from him, we sense a hidden subtext (Catholic "recusants" who did not attend Church of England services had to pay a fine).[5] The mistress here demands the obedience due only to God; and Donne's description of her unbending will ("thou art resolute; Thy will be done," 79) seems to express reservations about the power claimed by monarchs (or popes?) over religious as well as temporal, secular matters.

Donne brings politics and religion into his erotic poems. This complex intertwining appears in the elegy beginning "Oh, let mee not serve so," where amatory, political, and religious discourses are so interwoven that the reader is challenged to decipher the poem, and determine what Donne might be saying about the service of love and about political and religious service.

The elegy begins with the speaker renouncing his unrewarded service to his cold Petrarchan mistress.

> Oh, let mee not serve so, as those men serve
> Whom honours smoakes at once fatten and sterve;
> Poorely enrich't with gret mens words or lookes; ...　　　(1–3)

Comparing his fruitless devotion to the service of unrewarded court flatterers, his extended analogy collapses the two realms so that it is difficult to tell whether Donne is talking about amorous or political experience. The third term, religion, enters the poem as the speaker refuses to be one of "those Idolatrous flatterers" (5) and speaks of his mistress as his "Purgatory" (13). She has been not only "faithlesse" (13) (inconstant? lacking the true faith?) but "traiterous" (28) and destructive, burning or drowning the victims she lures with her embrace. As he describes her victims, we hear echoes of martyrdom that was a trope for love-suffering but also a reality for some persecuted Catholics, including members of Donne's own family. The speaker ends warning the mistress not to let her "deepe bitternesse [i.e., coldness] beget" "despaire" and "disdaine" in him (35, 36, 38).

> ... I shall
> As nations do from Rome, from thy love fall.
> My hate shall outgrow thine, and utterly
> I will renounce thy dalliance: and when I
> Am the Recusant, in that resolute state,
> What hurts it mee to be'excommunicate?　　　(41–46)

Without her subject's love, the mistress/Prince has no power. The political implications are radical, suggesting that monarchs (like beautiful women) only rule by the consent of their subjects, not by any divine right. Donne's lover envisions himself breaking free. Threatening to rebel, he figures himself as a "Recusant," a term designating Catholics who refused to attend the Church of England (*OED*, meaning A.1). A sharp political and religious stance seems encoded in the flippant hostility of the poem's conclusion. Yet the analogy is confusing, for it identifies the woman with Rome, and the speaker with Protestants breaking from Rome. Knowing something about the political/religious conditions in late sixteenth-century England and Donne's own personal history (he left the Church of Rome in which he was raised), we are left wondering whose service Donne is renouncing and what the religious implications might be. This elegy frustrates our effort to construct a consistent political subtext, even as it raises intriguing possibilities.

In the *Songs and Sonets*, the relation between love and politics shifts to a different register. In "The Indifferent," as in the Ovidian *Elegies*, Donne's speaker adopts a libertinism that makes a political statement, as he refuses to remain the woman's "fixd subject" (18). In the mutual love poems, however, the world of the lovers opposes the public, political sphere, constituting a separate, alternative sphere and locus of value. "The Anniversarie" announces that "All Kings," indeed everything,

> Is elder by a yeare, now, then it was
> When thou and I first one another saw:
> All other things, to their destruction draw,
> Only our love hath no decay. (4–7)

The experience of love – transcendent, durable – contrasts with the mutable public world, dominated by time.

The world of the lovers contrasts with that of "Kings," yet Donne's argument depends on the public analogy. The fact that Donne's private world of love is described in terms of kings, court-apprentices ("The Sunne Rising"), and worldly enterprises ("The good-morrow," "The Canonization") has led some critics to suggest that Donne was attracted to the absolutist ideology of James I.[6] Yet the monarchy of love Donne establishes is oppositional. The harmless lives of lovers contrast with the "Lawyers" and "Soldiers" who "finde out warres" ("The Canonization," 16). Repeatedly, the public world seeks to intrude, like the sun in "The Sunne Rising." The speakers of "The Relique" and "The Canonization" ask to be left alone as they glorify an experience of love that constitutes a world of its own.

The autonomous, private world of love

In presenting the experience of love as the most interesting, important part of life, the *Songs and Sonets* voice ideas that have become so powerful in our modern world that we must remind ourselves how bold and revolutionary they were in Donne's time. Some of his most memorable lyrics argue that personal fulfilment can only be found in love, and that the realm of sexuality is autonomous, private, self-sufficient.[7]

"The good-morrow" begins with a sense of wonder: the speaker, waking in bed with his beloved, has just made a discovery about himself and their relation that makes the discovery of "new worlds" (12) like America pale in comparison. Although Donne's poetry often assumes the inequality between men and women that was part of early modern English culture, here the lovers are "two hemisphaeres" (17), equal, neither sufficient without the other. There is a sense of completion, as if the lover has finally found what was missing from life, his other half.

"Soules" awake as well as the bodies ("The good-morrow," 8), as if called by love from the sleep of ordinary life and mere lust. The experience of loving and being loved offers a feeling of integration that contrasts with the fragmentation and corruption the speaker finds in the world. Hence we find circles, images of perfection and wholeness, in the "mutual" love poems. Love "makes one little roome, an every where" ("The good-morrow," 11); its walls become the "spheare" of the sun, while the lovers' bed remains its "center" ("The Sunne Rising," 30). The public world – of courts, kings, lawyers, adventurers – is worthless compared with the riches these lovers contain. "Looke, and tomorrow late, tell mee," he challenges the sun,

> Whether both the'India's of spice and Myne
> Be where thou leftst them, or lie here with mee.
> Aske for those Kings whom thou saw'st yesterday,
> And thou shalt heare, All here in one bed lay.
> She'is all States, and all Princes I,
> Nothing else is. (16–22)

That last, remarkable line obliterates everything outside. Whereas Donne's libertine poems assert the speaker's autonomy, his self-possession (unruled by either his desire or a woman), here that autonomous sphere expands to include the beloved, as the two lovers constitute a self-sufficient, all-powerful world.

There is an awareness (never entirely suppressed) that this is fantasy, that the outer world has not really disappeared, that the sun, in fact, will not stay in the bedroom, that there are no absolute assurances that love will last forever. And yet Donne brilliantly captures the feeling of those rare moments in (new?) love, when it seems that a world has opened, that nothing else matters, that this is perfection.

It is often said that erotic love, or sexual desire, requires or presupposes a certain lack – the Greek word *eros* denotes "'want,' 'lack,' 'desire for what is missing'."[8] Obstacles, absence, or frustration seem built into desire, for we can only long for what we do not, at the moment, possess – whether it is another person or God. Donne is keenly aware of the instability of desire, of the conflict between our longing to dissolve the boundary between self and other and our impulse to withdraw and reassert the self's separate identity. Yet a few of Donne's love poems imagine desire as fulfilled and, miraculously, persisting, as if in defiance of natural laws. "Loves growth" assures his beloved that his "encrease[d]" love will not "abate" (28), any more than princes "remit" "New taxes" (27). "The good-morrow" argues (by means of a phallic image of undiminished desire) that their love will continue: "if none doe slacken, none can die" (21). The claim is an assertion of faith, in the face of so much evidence of instability and decay in the world.

Despite this brave defiance, fear of death haunts Donne's love poems, even as they claim that love endures, constant, untouched by time. Death, the ultimate rupture of love, stands behind the "Valediction" poems. As the opening of "A Valediction: forbidding mourning" suggests, the parting of lovers is analogous to death. We never know if we'll meet again. Still, Donne has his travelling speaker promise, through his final compass conceit, that the circle won't be broken. Moreover, Donne often gives his lovers a kind of afterlife: the power to affect the world after death. The speaker of "The Relique" imagines that in times to come, his arm bone, encircled with the bracelet of his beloved's hair, will be taken to the "Bishop" and "King," and the lovers "adore[d]" by "all women" and "some men" (19, 15). The last stanza of "The Canonization" envisions a future audience invoking the lovers as saints.

Love and religion

Erotic love here takes on religious significance. Donne overturned conventional pieties with his witty libertinism, but his boldest intervention was representing erotic love as a spiritual experience that provides fulfillment the public world, and even its religious institutions, cannot.

The *Songs and Sonets* flirt with blasphemy, connecting sexual, consummated love with spiritual matters. The elegy "Going to Bed" had compared sexual to spiritual joy, but sexual conquest was the goal, religious analogies simply the means. "The Extasie," however, argues that love engages bodies and souls, and that the body and sex are the medium for the work and union of souls. The first part of the poem describes the conversation of the lovers' "soules," which have "gone out" (15–16) of their bodies as the lovers lie on a "pregnant banke" (2) in spring. In their ecstasy, these lovers learn that their "mixt soules" have been "mixe[d] againe" by "Love," making "both one" (35–36). Were the poem to stop here, we might read it as extolling Neoplatonic transcendence, in which the body and senses are left behind as the lover ascends to the spiritual in the process of loving. Donne, however, challenges the Neoplatonic body/soul dualism at the heart of Petrarchan love, as he argues that the lovers must "turne" to their "bodies" (69). Only through the material ("ayre," 58, or "bodies") can souls "flow" (59) into each other. "Loves mysteries in soules doe grow, / But yet the body is his booke" (71–72).

"Love must ... take a body," as Donne says in "Aire and Angels" (10), recalling the Incarnation of the divine in Christ, which provides justification for his logic. Donne's belief that body and soul are interdependent is not just part of his logic; it even affects the ways his conceits and metaphors work. The literal, bodily "vehicle" of the metaphor is essential to the meaning or "tenor" of Donne's analogies, just as the body is essential to the operation and life of the soul. We might think of the comparison of the lovers to saints in "The Canonization": Donne's figurative language makes sexual love sacred, suggesting that it offers an experience of transcendence, a taste of the divine. In contrast to his Ovidian poems, where sex is a matter of the body and women interchangeable, poems celebrating the sacredness of erotic love depict lovers who are committed to each other in an exclusive relation that doesn't need the church. They are the true clergy of the world, taking the place of ordained priests. In "A Valediction: forbidding mourning," the lovers would profane their love if they were "To tell the layetie [of] our love" (8) by weeping. Donne extends the religious language of Petrarchan poetry, making it ecclesiastical and pushing it to new, provocative heights, as he describes the ennobling power of erotic love.

Religious – and sometimes specifically Catholic – images appear in these poems.[9] In "Aire and Angels," the lover worships the woman as an angel, at least before he embraces her. To imagine the woman as angelic, worthy of worship, is Petrarchan, but the Reformation had rejected the worship of saints and angels. Donne's poems are populated by terms that in post-Reformation England look decidedly Catholic. In "The Funerall" and "The Relique," the bracelet or wreath of her hair and the bones of the dead lover are imagined as "Reliques," worshipped and revered by those who come later ("The Funerall," 20). In "The Canonization," Donne's lovers are saints and martyrs who "at our own coste die" (21); monastics, severed from the world, they have made each other their "hermitage" (38). Future lovers will "invoke" them in prayer, asking them as intercessors to "Beg from above / A patterne of your love" (45). In "The Relique" the lovers perform "miracles" in loving "well and faithfully" (31, 23). "The Canonization" (27) and "The Funerall" identify love with "mystery" – a word that meant in Donne's time not only something "secret" but also something known only through divine revelation, or a rite of the Christian church, specifically the Eucharist (*OED*, meanings 2a, 3, 5a). In all these poems, the experience of love transforms the lovers, conferring on them a kind of grace.

Donne captures the truth that there is something mysterious about intimacy. Love, like birth, feels miraculous. But there is also a historically specific dimension to the fact that Donne made love "sacramental" during a period when the sacraments were contested, a site of religious conflict.

The Reformation had reduced the sacraments from seven to two (Baptism and Communion), redefined them as "signs" rather than instruments of grace, abolished monasteries, got rid of saints, and forbade the worship of saints, relics, and images. All of these appear in Donne's celebrations of love. The experience of intense, reciprocal, committed erotic love offers spiritual fulfillment and access to the divine, much as in the Roman Catholic Church the sacraments provided avenues for grace. Donne's representation of love as both sexual and spiritual is an erotic reworking of the Catholic understanding that body and soul, material and spiritual are inseparably linked in the world, in devotion, and in the Sacrament. His poetic representation of love evokes the Protestant/Catholic conflicts of his time, while suggesting that only erotic love (and the bedroom) is a site of peace and unity, a "temple" ("The Flea.")

This vision of love and his lovers, set against a divisive world, resonates with what we know of the clandestine courtship and marriage between the (formerly?) Catholic Donne and the firmly Protestant Anne, in which secrecy played a role, and in which perhaps he saw a hopeful image of religious unity. Yet the polemically charged religious language of these *Songs and Sonets* raises other intriguing interpretive questions. Did Donne write these poems when he was still a Roman Catholic, or after he had conformed to the Church of England, or was he "between" churches? Is Donne creating what M. Thomas Hester has called a "recusant poetics" in which poetry becomes a safe place for expressing Catholic sentiment?[10] Or is Donne standing apart from all institutions, suggesting that love offers an alternative, providing access to the divine presence, making other clergy unnecessary?[11] We can, as yet, only speculate. But one thing is clear. As erotic love assumes a spiritual function, it takes the place of religion, anticipating the modern privileging of romantic love. The poems are deeply anti-institutional and radical (clergy, kings, universities are unnecessary) as they locate supreme value and happiness in private, interpersonal relations and imagine erotic experience as capable of fulfilling the whole person, soul and body, and spiritual as well as sexual desires.

Donne's celebration of erotic love as a transcendent spiritual experience was boldly revolutionary not only in its anti-institutionalism, but also because it opposed a long-standing Christian tradition that distrusted the body and sexuality. Paul, and later the Church fathers, had associated sin with sexuality and the corruptible body. In the traditional Christian view, *agape* (divine love, God's constant love for "man") contrasts with *eros* (human sexual desire, self-centred and inconstant).[12] In the New Testament, Paul opposed "spirit" to "flesh," defining "spirit" as the essence of the human being, and identifying "flesh" with death, the body, sexuality, and all that draws man from God (see, for example, Romans 8:13). Although Paul valued marriage as a "great mystery … concerning Christ and the Church" (Ephesians 5:32), he exalted celibacy, setting the stage for Augustine and other Church fathers, who identified the Fall with sexuality and forged a link between sex, sin, and death that continued to be influential long after the Reformation supposedly demoted celibacy and placed new value on companionate marriage.

When Donne celebrates sexual love as a spiritual experience, he radically defies this Christian association of sexuality with sin. The lover in "The good-morrow" tells his lover, with amazement, that they have progressed from their former "childish" pleasures to this moment in bed when their "soules" are finally awake: "my face in thine eye, thine in mine appeares" (3, 9, 14). We hear an echo of Paul's description of divine, agapic love: "When I was a child, I spake as a child, I understood as a child, I thought as a child: but when I became a man, I put away childish things. For now we see through a glass, darkly; but then face to face: now I know in part; but then shall I know even as also I am known" (I Corinthians 13:11–12). Something miraculous has happened between Donne's lovers, for his speaker feels what Paul said humans would only experience in heaven with God. At moments like these, moments of physical, sexual, and emotional intimacy, *eros* merges with *agape*. Walls collapse, the veil parts, we know as we are known; our deepest, truest selves exposed.

And yet we sometimes glimpse traces of the negative evaluation of *eros* in Donne's poetry. "Each such Act, they say, / Diminisheth the length of life a day," the speaker in "Farewell to love" says (24–25), repeating the common-place notion that orgasm shortens man's life. Having discovered that there is no "Deitie in love" (2), he seeks to avoid "things which had indammag'd me" (34). Behind the cynicism of this poem, and others, lurks a suspicion that sex and women are dangerous. Even poems exalting love suggest that erotic experience is self-destructive. Although the speaker in "The Canonization" sees his ruined fortune and grey hairs as signs of privileged martyrdom, they also show the self-destructive aspect of a life devoted to erotic love. Here society and physiology are at fault. Yet perhaps Donne did not quite cast off the legacy of a Christian tradition that associated sexual love with sin, and that would assume a more insistent voice in Donne's later sermons and some divine poems, which seem to recant his earlier celebration of erotic love.

Still, for all the moments of uncertainty, Donne's love poetry embraces human sexuality and celebrates the experience of love. And perhaps that is, finally, the most dangerous aspect of his erotic writing, as it strains against the constraints of the Christian society in which he lived and eventually preached as Dean of St. Paul's. One can "moralize" Donne's love poetry,[13] much as the Middle Ages did Ovid – and much as the early rabbis and the

Christian Fathers moralized the Song of Songs – but Donne's *Songs and Sonets* ultimately resist such moralizing.

His conviction (or hope) that erotic love is the fullest expression of a human nature made in the image of God appears even in that desolate poem, "A nocturnall upon S. *Lucies* day." Anatomizing his grief at the death of his beloved, the speaker, in a display of hyperbolic wit, shows the cost of intimacy, when it feels as if another person has become essential to our life, someone we cannot live without. With her death, he has become an object of "study" (10) for surviving lovers, but the lesson is grim,

> For I am every dead thing,
> In whom love wrought new Alchimie.
>   For his art did expresse
> A quintessence even from nothingnesse,
> From dull privations, and leane emptinesse:
> He ruin'd mee, and I am re-begot
> Of absence, darknesse, death; things which are not.

Having created him, Love has now destroyed him. The speaker has been transformed, not into something higher, but lower (though even here Donne finds himself distinguished, unique) – made by her death "the Elixer" of "the first nothing" (29) – the *nihilo* out of which Augustine said God created the universe. The love that made each of them sufficient to the other has left him devoid of life, now that she (his soul) has departed. Perhaps his expression of unrelieved grief suggests that such all-consuming love has left no place for God. At the end of the poem, the speaker turns to heaven, much as Petrarch did at the end of his sonnet sequence. Yet Donne turns not to God but to the beloved woman, now a saint in heaven: "Let mee prepare towards her, and let mee call / This houre her Vigill, and her Eve" (43–44). It seems too narrow to interpret the poem, as some have done, simply as an exposé of idolatrous love. For all its awareness of the Church's teachings that human love can be a fearful, seductive idolatry, "A nocturnall" refuses to give up either the beloved or the conviction that, despite proscriptions by institutions and human authorities, love between two human beings remains, as the biblical Song of Songs 8:6 put it, "strong as death," an inextinguishable "flame," the experience that gives life its meaning and, if anything does, connects us with the divine.

NOTES

1 See Arthur F. Marotti, "'Love is not love': Elizabethan Sonnet Sequences and the Social Order," *ELH* 49 (1982), 396–428; Achsah Guibbory, "'Oh, let mee not serve so': The Politics of Love in Donne's *Elegies*," *ELH* 57 (1990), 811–33; and

Jim Ellis, *Sexuality and Citizenship: Metamorphosis in Elizabethan Erotic Verse* (Toronto: University of Toronto Press, 2003).

2 I am indebted to Joshua Scodel's paper, "'None's Slave': Some Versions of Liberty in Donne's Secular Poetry," presented at the 2003 John Donne Conference, which examined the connection between libertinism and the concern with political liberty.

3 This information comes from Gary Stringer and Ted-Larry Pebworth, editors of the Donne *Variorum*.

4 See M. Thomas Hester (ed.), *John Donne's 'desire of more': The Subject of Anne More Donne in His Poetry* (Newark: University of Delaware, 1996), especially essays by Ilona Bell, "'if it be a shee': The Riddle of Donne's 'Curse,'" pp. 106–39; Dayton Haskin, "On Trying to Make the Record Speak More about Donne's Love Poems," pp. 39–65, and Maureen Sabine, "No Marriage in Heaven: John Donne, Anne Donne, and the Kingdome Come," pp. 228–55.

5 M. Thomas Hester describes the Catholic subtext in "'Over Reconing' the 'Undertones': A Preface to 'Some Elegies' by John Donne," *Renaissance Papers 2000* (Rochester: Camden House, 2002), pp. 137–53.

6 Carey, *Donne*, pp. 113–15; Jonathan Goldberg, *James I and the Politics of Literature: Jonson, Shakespeare, Donne and their Contemporaries* (Baltimore: Johns Hopkins University Press, 1983), 210–19.

7 Anthony Low, "Donne and the Reinvention of Love," *ELR* 20 (1990), 465–86; Richard Halpern, "The Lyric in the Field of Information: Autopoiesis and History in Donne's *Songs and Sonets*," *The Yale Journal of Criticism* 6 (1993), 185–215.

8 Anne Carson, *Eros the Bittersweet* (1986; rpt: Dalkey Archive Press, 1998), p. 10.

9 M. Thomas Hester, "'this cannot be said': A Preface to the Reader of Donne's Lyrics," *Christianity and Literature* 39 (1990), 365–85.

10 Hester, "'this cannot be said,'" 365–85.

11 Achsah Guibbory, "Donne, Milton, and Holy Sex," *Milton Studies* 22, ed. Albert Labriola (Pittsburgh: University of Pittsburgh Press, 1995), 3–21.

12 See Alan Soble, *Eros, Agape and Philia: Readings in the Philosophy of Love* (New York: Paragon House, 1989); Elaine Pagels, *Adam, Eve, and the Serpent* (New York: Random House, 1988); Peter Brown, *The Body and Society: Men, Women, and Sexual Renunciation in Early Christianity* (New York: Columbia University Press, 1988).

13 Moralizing readings include N. J. Andreason, *John Donne: Conservative Revolutionary* (Princeton: University of Princeton Press, 1967), and Judy Sproxton, *The Idiom of Love: Love Poetry from the Early Sonnets to the Seventeenth Century* (London, Duckworth, 2000), ch. 6, pp. 117–42.

10

HELEN WILCOX

Devotional writing

To John Donne, devotion and writing were inseparable. His belief in God was so profoundly word-centred that, in both his theology and his experience, the practice of religious contemplation and spiritual communion with God always and inevitably involved language. The very principle of creation, according to St. John's Gospel, is the divine "Word,"[1] and Donne discerned this "Logos" writ large in every aspect of God. As one of the late sermons explains, God the Father created the world by a spoken word: "God spake, and all things were made." God the Son, the second person of the Holy Trinity, is the Word "made flesh" (John 1:14), the expression of God's sacred text in human form. God the Holy Ghost, completing the Trinity, is the spirit that "enables us to apprehend, and apply to our selves, the promises of God in him" (*Sermons*, vol. VIII, no. 1, p. 52). The actions of the three persons of the Christian God are here understood entirely in terms of linguistic processes: speech, symbolic expression, and interpretation. In this logocentric universe, Donne conceived of the role of human beings in relation to God in an equally and mutually verbal way: "God made us with his word, and with our words we make God" (*Sermons*, vol. III, no. 12, p. 259). This was not a post-structuralist statement before its time – Donne is not implying that God only exists because he is spoken about by us – but it does indicate just how vital *words* are in Donne's sense of the human relationship with God.

It is no surprise, therefore, that Donne felt called to use his own prodigious linguistic gifts for the purposes of religious devotion and instruction. To do so, in his view, was an honor and a responsibility: "Blesse, praise, speake; there is the duty" (*Sermons*, vol. III, no. 12, p. 260). In his poem "To Mr *Tilman* after he had taken orders," Donne advises his newly ordained friend that it is the "prerogative" of preachers to "convey" Christ to others in words (41–42). Nor was it only preachers who were charged to use language in this intensely spiritual way; the ordinary believer, too, was urged by Donne to "delight" in speaking "of God, and with God, and for God" (*Sermons*, vol. VIII, no. 4, p. 119). Donne's devotional writing may in fact be summed up by means of these three prepositions: his religious works in prose and verse all speak *"of* God"; his divine poems and his *Devotions upon Emergent Occasions* are prayerful dialogues *"with* God"; and his sermons take on the awe-inspiring task of speaking *"for* God" (my italics). Any use of language with respect to God, in Donne's view, constitutes a daunting linguistic challenge. As he wrote in his poem "Upon the translation of the Psalmes by Sir Philip Sydney, and the Countesse of Pembroke his Sister," those writers who "dare" (a revealing choice of verb) to "Seeke new expressions" for God face the inappropriate task of thrusting a "cornerlesse and infinite" God into "strait corners of poore wit" (1, 3). The devotional poet knows that God, who is the eternal Word, is more complex than even the most beautiful and profound, yet finite and fallen, human words can express. But the duty to converse "of God, and with God, and for God" does not go away just because it is difficult. How did Donne, whose not-so-poor wit was said by Carew to have won him the highest position in its "universall Monarchy,"[2] respond to the spiritual and linguistic vocation to express the divine? This chapter will pay particular attention to Donne's devotional sonnets, his occasional meditations in verse, his prose *Devotions* and his three Hymns, examining the relationship of writing and devotion in these deservedly renowned works. To what extent, for example, was Donne able to resist the temptation to "seeme religious / Only to vent wit" ("The Litanie," 88–89)? And how did the poet, laboring in what Coleridge called "Wit's Maze" and "Thought's Forge,"[3] find the imaginative way and discover the rhetorical heat sufficient to convey in language the experience of God?

Devotional sonnets

The best known of Donne's divine poems are his sonnets, which fall into two groups: "La Corona," an interlinked set of seven sonnets forming a *"crown of prayer and praise"* (1:1), and the nineteen *Holy Sonnets* (entitled "Divine Meditations" in some manuscripts). It is a sign of the profound interconnection of secular and sacred experience in Donne's work that, while his love poems in the *Songs and Sonets* include no formal sonnets, his devotional poetry embraces this poetic form most closely associated with the Petrarchan tradition of earthly love. In some sense, then, Donne's religious sonnets may be seen as love poems to God: as he writes in "Batter my heart," "dearely 'I love you,' and would be loved faine, / But am betroth'd unto your enemie" (9–10). The sonnets struggle to contain the contraries of desire and despair, passion and preoccupation, trials and triumphs: loving God, Donne's devotional writing suggests, can be as troubled and varied an experience as that depicted in his secular love poetry.

The sonnets in "La Corona" follow the sequence of events in Christ's life from the Annunciation to the Ascension, and this doctrinal focus makes them less intense than the *Holy Sonnets*, which are driven by the urgent concerns of the speaker. However, two key features of "La Corona" introduce us unmistakeably to the world of Donne's divine poems. First, despite the unusually celebratory tone of this short sonnet sequence, the opening sonnet confesses that the poems were woven together "in my low devout melancholie" (2), which is indeed the starting-point and prevailing mood of most of his religious verse. The inseparable partnership of deep devotion and intense anxiety marks Donne's devotional writing; as he writes in "O might those sighes," his religious experience is a "holy discontent" (3). His devotion (or that of his uneasy persona) is driven by the fear of death and ultimate judgment: the *Holy Sonnets* ask, with a deep sense of dread, "What if this present were the worlds last night?" and attempt to discover reassurance for his "blacke Soule" ("Oh my blacke Soule") in the answers produced by his "muses white sincerity" ("La Corona," 1:6). It is utterly in keeping with this perplexed melancholy that the only biblical paraphrase known to have been made by Donne is his poetic rendering of the Lamentations of Jeremiah. However, the lamentational mode of his devotional writing as a whole does not result in a numbing depression; on the contrary, it is the very source of the poems' rational and emotional energy. One holy sonnet, "This is my playes last scene," for example, vividly imagines the drama of "my spans last inch" as death approaches (4); another, "Death be not proud," confronts this "Mighty and dreadfull" force head-on (2); a third, "Spit in my face," sets the sinful speaker on the cross, asking the onlookers to "Buffet, and scoffe, scourge, and crucifie" him in place of the sinless Christ (2). Such extreme audacity of penitential humility is the hallmark of Donne's devotional tone.

This leads us to the second key aspect of Donne's devotional writing of which "La Corona" immediately makes the reader aware: the centrality of paradoxes in Donne's religious language and thought. The first sonnet addresses God as the "All changing unchang'd" (4), and the second envisages Christ as "That All ... Which cannot die, yet cannot chuse but die" (2, 4). At the heart of the Christian faith, and of Donne's fascination with it, are impossible possibilities. The Crucifixion, for instance (when the Son of God was raised up on the cross to die, thereby destroying the power of death) is punningly described by Donne as the moment when, paradoxically, the "Sunne" will "by rising set, / And by that setting endlesse day beget" ("Goodfriday, 1613. Riding Westward," 11–12). In his holy sonnet, "I am a little world," the speaker desires to be burnt up with a destructive yet life-giving "fiery zeale" which "doth in eating heale" (13–14); in "Oh, to vex me," devotional "Inconstancy" gives rise to "A constant habit" and, in a succinct definition of a paradox, "contraryes meet in one" (1–2). The most famous of all Donne's holy paradoxes, the conclusion to his sonnet "Batter my heart," recalls a liturgical text which declares that the "service" of God is "perfect freedom":[4]

> Take mee to you, imprison mee, for I
> Except you'enthrall mee, never shall be free,
> Nor ever chast, except you ravish mee.   (12–14)

Inspired by the paradoxes in the existing language of the Church, Donne's radical imagination takes him further, into the daring clashes of spiritual and physical, masculine and feminine, active and passive, sacred and profane impulses that characterize his devotional writing.

If there is one major biblical precedent for the *Holy Sonnets*, it is surely the figure of Jacob, who "wrestled" all night with God and would not let God go until he received a blessing (Genesis 32: 24–30).[5] The speaker in the sonnets has a similar determination, both emotional and rhetorical; in these poems Jacob's wrestling has become an intense verbal tussle, but the purpose – salvation – remains the same. The persona in "If poysonous minerals" may well say, "But who am I, that dare dispute with thee / O God?" (9–10), but the consciousness of his impudence certainly does not stop his restless questioning. The sonnets are shot through with a desire for debate, however futile such argument may ultimately be,[6] producing intellectually boisterous and passionately argued, often noisy, poems. As Donne aptly comments in one of his last sermons,

> Man is but a voice, but a sound, but a noise ... A melancholique man, is but a groaning; a sportfull man, but a song; an active man, but a Trumpet; a mighty man, but a thunderclap.   (*Sermons*, vol. IX, no. 1, pp. 61–2)

Although each of the speakers in the *Holy Sonnets* is "but a voice," they combine to command, inquire, threaten, rationalize, imagine, and expostulate their way into God's attention, whether by groans or trumpet blasts. There is critical debate about the extent to which Donne speaks autobiographically or dramatically in these poems, as well as a continuing uncertainty concerning their dates and possible clustering at stages of Donne's life; but there is no doubting the poems' brilliant capacity to sound the authentic notes of the human voice on the edge of wonder and despair. As C. A. Patrides wrote, the *Holy Sonnets* represent "the summit" of Donne's art.[7]

The brevity and containment of the individual holy sonnets are important aspects of their cumulative impact. The secular lover in "The triple Foole" needs "Rimes vexation" to purge away his tears, and in a similar way the speakers in the *Holy Sonnets* follow the pattern of the sonnet form that channels and "fetters" (9, 11) the religious emotions they express. As Louis Martz suggested more than fifty years ago, the two quatrains and the sestet of each sonnet can give shape to the three stages of spiritual meditation recommended by Ignatius Loyola, founder of the Jesuits.[8] Donne's sonnet on the Last Judgment, for example, begins with four lines which compose the scene before the mind's eye:

> At the round earths imagin'd corners, blow
> Your trumpets, Angells, and arise, arise
> From death, you numberlesse infinities
> Of soules, and to your scattred bodies goe ...   (1–4)

The almost unimaginable bustle of the "last busie day" ("The Relique," 10) is conjured up in words that simultaneously stimulate the senses ("round earths," "blow / Your trumpets") and stretch the mind ("imagin'd corners," "numberlesse infinities"). With this compact and lively composition of place, the deliberate process of meditation has begun. The logical sequel to this, an analysis of what has been envisaged, follows in the second quatrain:

> All whom the flood did, and fire shall, o'erthrow,
> All whom warre, dearth, age, agues, tyrannies,
> Despaire, law, chance, hath slaine, and you whose eyes
> Shall behold God, and never tast deaths woe.   (5–8)

With exhaustive thoroughness, the causes of death of those "numberlesse infinities / Of soules" are rehearsed: these four lines manage to contain the deaths that have occurred (or will occur) in the whole of biblical history, from Noah's flood to the fires at the end of the world. It is revealing of the penitential mood of the *Holy Sonnets* that water and flames, symbolic of repentance and chastisement, are invoked here; they are also the favored elements in "I am a little world." It is also typical of Donne's radical insecurity that one of the forces at work in slaying human beings, named prominently at the beginning of a line, should be "Despaire."

In the sestet of the sonnet, with a sudden change of direction characteristic of this tightly packed poetic form, the speaker turns to look inwards, responding to the imagined scene and contemplating its consequences at an individual level. As is so often the case in Donne's devotional works, the effect of this final stage of the meditation is to awaken fear, and specifically the dreadful thought that the speaker's sins will be too great to be forgiven:

> But let them sleepe, Lord, and mee mourne a space,
> For, if above all these, my sinnes abound,

'Tis late to ask abundance of thy grace,
When wee are there; here on this lowly ground,
Teach mee how to repent; for that's as good
As if thou'hadst seal'd my pardon, with thy blood.   (9–14)

The paradoxical confidence of this self-doubt is fascinating. The speaker commands God to leave the dead sleeping – indeed, to postpone the Last Judgment – and to concentrate instead on him, in an extremity of self-focus intensified by the alliteration of "mee mourne." There is also a startling assumption in the last lines that the very idea of redemption by the blood of Christ shed on the cross is an optional alternative ("that's as good / As if ...") to the personal attention demanded by the speaker from God. Thus the poem does not end as it began, looking to the future in those far-flung "imagin'd corners" of the earth, but in present and local circumstances, "here on this lowly ground," in the corners of a fearful heart.

What the speaker of this sonnet seeks is the assurance of an "abundance" of grace, but how can that be achieved without the initial inspiration to repent? In his sonnet "Oh my blacke Soule!," Donne highlights what we might call this "Catch-22" of redemption: "Yet grace, if thou repent, thou canst not lacke; / But who shall give thee that grace to beginne?" (9–10). These lines reflect the dilemma of much of Donne's devotional writing and the agonizing complexity of his particular doctrinal circumstances, caught as he was between the active vocation of Catholicism and the predestination of Calvinism. Could the speakers of the *Holy Sonnets* do anything to influence God's final judgment – and if so, what? The implied answer given by the sonnets – their response to these profound personal and doctrinal difficulties – is prayer. The sonnets are themselves a form of dialogue, and their meditations often lead, as in "If faithful soules," to a resolution to pray:

Then turne
O pensive soule, to God, for he knowes best
Thy true griefe, for he put it in my breast.   (12–14)

The "pensive" melancholy expressed in these poems is seen as a gift of God, "put ... in my breast" as a source of grace. The *Holy Sonnets*, with their grief-ridden drama and dynamic debates, are a means of confronting fears, examining both conscience and doctrine, and in these processes they resume dialogue with God. As Donne wrote in a sermon preached before the king in 1628, "to turne upon God, and to pursue this sorrow for our sins" is not a negative action but a means of transforming sorrowful human "sighes" into the breath of God. In this way, the circle is completed: *"the Spirit of man returns to God that gave it"* (*Sermons*, vol. VIII, no. 8, p. 197).

Occasional meditations and *Devotions*

Donne's religious poetry draws the reader into its passionate dialogues with God by means of outspoken wit, dynamic questioning, and an almost tangible sense of "Despaire behind, and death before" ("Thou hast made me," 6). It also intrigues us with the continuing puzzle of Donne's ecclesiastical allegiances. As the sonnet "Show me deare Christ" demonstrates, his devotional poetry concerns, at least in part, a search for the true Church, Christ's "spouse, so bright and clear" (1). Is she the "richly painted" Catholic Church, or the Calvinist faith that "Laments and mournes" (3, 4)? Ironically, even from these short phrases it is clear that both traditions are present in Donne's devotional poems. There is a "richly painted" quality to his work – dramatic, sensual, sacramental – yet it undoubtedly also "Laments and mournes." This doctrinal, functional, and stylistic range may also be found in the variety of religious meditation present in the poems. While the *Holy Sonnets* accommodate the Ignatian practice of "wholsome meditation" ("Wilt thou love God," 2) in their rigorous concentration on the Last Things, Donne's longer devotional poems work largely in the protestant tradition of meditation on specific occasions.[9] These works, at least in their initial inspiration, are more worldly than the sonnets, often set in a specific social or personal context. Donne's extended contemplation of worship and religious language, for example, emerges from his praise of the Sidney Psalm translation, while his poem "To Mr Tilman" becomes a meditation on the nature of the priesthood.

Fundamental to these poems is a view of the world which sees it as always potentially emblematic: events, sights, or experiences, however ordinary or apparently unspiritual, are bearers of the Word if rightly interpreted. As Donne writes in "The Crosse,"

> Who can deny mee power, and liberty
> To stretch mine armes, and mine owne Crosse to be?
> Swimme, and at every stroake, thou art thy Crosse;
> The Mast and yard make one, where seas do tosse;
> Looke downe, thou spiest out Crosses in small things;
> Looke up, thou seest birds rais'd on crossed wings;
> All the Globes frame, and spheares, is nothing else
> But the Meridians crossing Parallels.   (332)

In this list of examples expressive of the poet's range of interests, the reader is reminded that the human body, sea travel, the natural world, and cartography all afford "Materiall Crosses" which serve as images of "spirituall" truths (26). In this sense, to practice divine meditation is to live in the world with an alert awareness of the spiritual dimension of each detail of the creation.

Throughout his writing, Donne is intensely conscious of the dimensions of time and space within which human life takes place. Among his secular poems, for instance, "The Sunne Rising" insists that the sun must cease to define "the rags of time" and simply stand still to "warme the world" contained within the lovers' bedroom (10, 28). Donne is fascinated by the temporal and spatial framework of human existence, yet strives to get the better of them with his witty logic and creative vision. In his religious verse, conjunctions of history and oppositions of geography challenge Donne to produce dazzling meditations on the fundamentals of Christian faith. In "The Annuntiation and Passion," for example, he contemplates the fact that the feast of the Annunciation (March 25) happened to fall on Good Friday in the spring of 1609. This coincidence of the calendar is strange and troublesome to Donne – he does not know whether to "feast or fast" – but it allows him to tell an "Abridgement of Christs story" (6, 20). The doubly holy day demonstrates that the two moments of biblical history, when the angel announces to Mary that she will give birth to the Son of God, and later when Christ dies on Good Friday, can be collapsed into one as a statement of God's saving love:

> All this, and all betweene, this day hath showne,
> Th'Abridgement of Christs story, which makes one
> (As in plaine Maps, the furthest West is East)
> Of the'Angels *Ave*,'and *Consummatum est.*   (19–22)[10]

Fascinatingly, Donne resorts to the dimension of space to explain an apparent impossibility in time: Christ can begin and end his incarnation on the same day, and Mary can be at the same time "almost fiftie" and "scarce fifteene" (14), by the same logic that west and east can meet on a map. Time and space, like God, are circular in Donne's imagining: as "The Annunciation and Passion" states, their emblem is "a circle .../ Whose first and last concurre" (4–5).

Donne's experience on the same day in the Church's calendar four years later led to his greatest occasional poetic meditation, "Goodfriday, 1613. Riding Westward," which is again based on strange relationships of time and space. He is riding to the west, from London to Ludlow, on the very day that the events of the Passion of Christ in Jerusalem, the east, are commemorated liturgically. This geographical contradiction inspires Donne to devise a witty theorem of the relationship of the soul to the body, or rather the mismatch between devotional intentions and actual achievement:

> Let mans Soule be a Spheare, and then, in this,
> The intelligence that moves, devotion is,
> And as the other Spheares, by being growne

> Subject to forraigne motions, lose their owne,
> And being by others hurried every day,
> Scarce in a yeare their naturall forme obey:
> Pleasure or businesse, so, our Soules admit
> For their first mover, and are whirld by it.
> Hence is't, that I am carried towards the West
> This day, when my Soules forme bends towards the East.   (1–10)

Donne's circumstances on Good Friday in 1613 are thus fertile ground for his playfully serious intellect. Conscious of the importance of devotion on this day, he nevertheless excuses his failure by means of an elaborate parallel with the heavenly bodies which from time to time are moved by forces beyond their control. Like Donne himself, the "Spheares" are led astray from their steady easterly movement towards God into "forraigne motions" which whirl them towards the west. A particular occasion has thus led to a brilliant meditation on the direction that a human life should really be taking.

This, however, is only the beginning of an extended poem on the events of Good Friday, and the reader soon discovers that Donne will seek further devotional profit from the contrary movement of his soul and body. He argues that it is, in fact, better that he has his back turned towards the east, since to look at Calvary would be too much for him:

> Yet dare I'almost be glad, I do not see
> That spectacle of too much weight for mee.
> Who sees Gods face, that is selfe life, must dye;
> What a death were it then to see God dye?
> It made his own Lieutenant Nature shrinke,
> It made his footstoole crack, and the Sunne winke.
> Could I behold those hands which span the Poles,
> And turne all spheares at once, peirc'd with those holes?   (15–22)

The rhetorical trick played by Donne here is very successful. He claims to be "glad" that he cannot see that overwhelming sight, Christ's death on the cross, which on the first Good Friday led to a violent earthquake and an eclipse of the sun; yet, while his back is turned on Calvary, he describes its details with intense devotion, seeing them with his "memory" – the faculty required for the meditative composition of a scene – if not with his "eye" (33–34). Until the very last line of the poem, the narrator does not look at God, the "Saviour, as thou hang'st upon the tree" (36). However, this situation is ultimately to the sinner's advantage, since it enables him to be punished, purged and made ready, in the last words of the poem, to "turne my face" to see Christ (42). This is, therefore, a meditation not only on the redemption but also on conversion, the process of turning again to God.

In the course of the poem the spheres turn, and the narrator and his horse turn away from Christ, whose hands meanwhile "turne" the created universe. At the end, once he is assured that he will be saved, the narrator makes that last vital "turne" back to God.

"Goodfriday, 1613" makes clear how meditative writing could function for Donne as a way of converting secular circumstances into a source of spiritual refreshment, as well as of overcoming what he called "the manifold weaknesses of the strongest devotions" (*Sermons*, vol. VII, no. 10, p. 264). Human beings, Donne knows, are vulnerable to distraction, even when – or perhaps especially when – they try to pray:

> I throw my selfe downe in my Chamber, and I call in, and invite God, and his Angels thither, and when they are there, I neglect God and his Angels, for the noise of a Flie, for the ratling of a Coach, for the whining of a doore ...
>
> (*Sermons*, vol. VII, no. 10, pp. 264–65)

The engaging honesty of this passage is akin to that which Donne displays in his devotional writing, especially his works produced during periods of illness where the self-examination is particularly rigorous and unflattering. He confesses that he wrote "The Litanie," for example, while enduring "imprisonment in my bed," and although he calls the poem "a meditation in verse," he adds that the liturgical title he chose "imports no other then supplication" (*Letters*, p. 32). These poetic prayers are addressed to the Trinity, but he also asks for the intercession of the saints and that "universall Quire" of the "Church in triumph" ("The Litanie," 118–19) in order to be delivered from a long list of potential errors and temptations to which he, as mere "mudde walls and condensed dust," is prone (20). The specified sins again confirm the tenor of his devotional verse: he worries about "needing danger, to bee good" (136), a succinct assessment of his *Holy Sonnets* with their productive terror of death and judgment, and he is aware of the danger of being excessive in "seeking secrets, or Poëtiquenesse" (72), recalling his predominant fascination with complexity, paradox, and wit. Perhaps most interestingly, in addressing the martyrs of the church, he admits that "to some / Not to be Martyrs, is a martyrdome" (89–90). Donne's devotional writings leave the strong impression that it would have been a "martyrdome" for Donne himself, had he *not* found himself stretched as a martyr on the rack of uncertainty, contradiction, and fear.

Like "The Litanie," Donne's *Devotions upon Emergent Occasions*, his prose meditations on mortality, were written as a result of a period of illness. He took his own seriously diseased body as the text of the "miserable condition of Man" (*Devotions*, p. 7) on which to practice his meditative exegesis; he called the resulting work an "Image of my Humiliation" (p. 3).

As in his occasional religious verse, the mixture of elaborate rhetoric, pains-taking argument, and the frank details of his melancholic "ridling distemper" (p. 8) creates a peculiarly powerful impact. Each stage of his sickness war-rants a "Meditation," "Expostulation," and "Prayer," a three-part spiritual exploration inspired by a change in circumstances such as the visit of Donne's physicians, their decision to purge the patient, or the application of "Pidgeons, to draw the vapors from the Head" (p. 62). At the height of his suffering, recorded in the seventeenth Devotion, Donne hears a bell "tolling softly for another" (p. 86) and turns this coincidental external event into an unforgettable emblem of human transience. In a justly famous passage, Meditation 17 asserts the interconnected nature of individual lives, using another of Donne's powerful geographical metaphors:

No Man is an *Iland*, intire of it self; every man is a peece of the *Continent*,
A part of the *maine*; if a *Clod* be washed away by the *Sea*, *Europe* is the lesse
... Any Mans *death* diminishes *me*, because I am involved in *Mankinde*;
And therefore never send to know for whom the *bell* tolls; It tolls for *thee*.

(p. 87)

This understanding of the interdependence of human existence asserts the communal nature of the *Devotions*. While rooted in the particularity of Donne's own condition, his text speaks for and is "involved in *Mankinde*." The *Devotions* may be intensely self-focused but their ultimate concern is to analyze the wider human condition and read the relationship of humanity to divinity.

Each of Donne's devotions is carefully structured, moving from contempla-tion through questioning to prayerful acceptance. Meditation 17 analyzes the symbolic significance of an ordinary sound – a funeral bell tolling – in order to demonstrate that no life is separate from any other. Drawing on another favorite source of metaphor, Donne writes that "All *mankinde* is of one *Author*, and is one *volume*" (p. 86), and death does not lead to removal of that volume but simply translation "into a better *language*" (p. 86). The second stage of the devotion, the Expostulation, lives up to its name by entering into an agonized debate with the God whose "*voice*" – indeed, whose "*whole Consort*" (p. 88) – may be heard in the sound of the tolling bell. If "transla-tion" to heaven means transferral to a place of "*glory* and *joy*," why, asks Donne, are we not induced there by "*glorious* and *joyfull* things?" (p. 88). In one of his most outspoken challenges to God, Donne rails against sorrow, death, and mortification, the "*miserable ends*, and *miserable anticipations* of those miseries" (p. 88) which form the way to everlasting life: "Is the *joy* of *heaven* no perfecter in it selfe, but that it needs the *sourenesse* of this *life* to give it a *taste*?" (p. 89). The final section, Prayer, of the seventeenth devotion struggles to recover equilibrium after what Donne calls the "unthankfull rashnesse" (p. 89) of these questions. Serenity is achieved, aptly, through the echoing of words spoken by Jesus on the cross as he, too, faced death. The despair of the suffering Donne is given voice in the biblical cry, "*My God, my God, Why hast thou forsaken me?*" (p. 90), but he also expresses his acceptance that the funeral bell is tolling his own death, by using Christ's last words, "*into thy hands, O my God, I commend my spirit*" (p. 89). This intensely creative juxtaposition of personal experience, rigorous enquiry, and theological resourcefulness is the motor driving Donne's *Devotions*.

The detailed attention paid to his decrepit physical state in the *Devotions* is typical of the boldness of Donne's religious works, in which audacity and humility so often and so strangely overlap. Who but Donne could have turned the spots on his skin into a source of contemplation and, ultimately, comfort? Aware in Meditation 13 that his spots signify a "malignant, and pestilentiall disease" (p. 674), Donne transforms his autobiographical material into a meditation on human imperfection:

> My *God, my God*, thou hast made this sick bed thine *Altar*, and I have no other *Sacrifice* to offer, but my self; and wilt thou accept *no spotted sacrifice?*
>
> (p. 75)

In contrast to the unblemished sacrifice of Christ, who offered himself to God "without spot" (Hebrews 9:14), Donne is all too conscious of the inescapable "spottedness" of the human soul. But his wiry wit refuses to accept defeat even on this point. He argues that sins, "the *spotts* that we hide," are a greater danger in the long run than the superficial blemishes of his disease, and therefore accepts his physical spots as a timely reminder of those within. By the end of the Expostulation, he has turned both into a celebration of the redemption:

> these *spotts* upon my *Breast*, and upon my *Soule*, shal appear to me as the *Constellations* of the *Firmament*, to direct my contemplation to that place, where thy *Son* is, they *right hand*. (p. 70)

A diseased body has been imaginatively transformed into a devotional aid: Donne's spots have become stars in the heavens. Or, as Donne puts it in the Prayer which completes this stage of his *Devotions*, "these spotts are but the letters, in which thou hast written thine own name, and conveyed thyself to me" (p. 70).

Once again we are reminded of the centrality of writing in Donne's religious experience. Not only do his *Devotions* use language with enormous inventiveness to redeem the miserable personal experience of his sickness; they also envisage that illness itself as a text written by God and anticipate death as a process of translation. Words, both literal and metaphorical, lie at the heart of Donne's encounter with the divine. Indeed, in one of the richest passages of the *Devotions*, Expostulation 19, Donne honors God for the variety of his language:

> My *God, my God,* Thou art a *direct* God, may I not say, a *literall God* ... But thou art also ... a *figurative,* a *metaphoricall God too:* A *God* in whose words there is such a height of *figures,* such *voyages,* such *peregrinations* to fetch remote and precious *metaphors,* such *extentions,* such *spreadings,* such *Curtaines* of Allegories, such *third Heavens* of Hyperboles ...   (p. 113)

This exuberant celebration of the divine word as found both in the Bible and in God's "*workes*" (p. 114) is notable for the way in which Donne himself attempts to imitate the grandeur of God's language. Divine metaphors are praised by means of Donne's own metaphors ("*peregrinations* to fetch remote and precious *metaphors,*" "*Curtaines* of *Allegories*") and God's hyperboles are evoked by Donne's exaggeratedly high "*third Heavens.*" The poet succeeds splendidly in representing what he calls "the *majesty* of the Word" as well as its "*reverent simplicity*" (p. 113) – so much so that one might think he is attempting to outdo God with his linguistic brilliance. As in the holy sonnet, "Spit in my face," the intensity of Donne's sense of God's greatness leads the human speaker to take center stage with dramatic panache. However, this displacement of the divine is always only temporary, as a means to greater devotion. The sonnet culminates in admiration of the crucified Christ, who took on "vile mans flesh" in order to be "weake enough to suffer woe" (p. 327). Similarly, Expostulation 19 comes to recognize the inadequacy of human expression – including Donne's – to encompass divine language: "O, what words but thine, can express the inexpressible *texture,* and *composition* of thy *word*" (p. 113). Witty though he is, even here in submission, Donne has met his linguistic match in God.

Hymns

Donne's spiritual experience, as we have seen, found expression in the extended meditations of his occasional verse and the prose *Devotions,* as well as in the vehement brief dramas of his sonnets. However, another devotional mode was available to Donne, who knew full well that the calling of a Christian is to "sing our part" ("Upon the translation of the Psalmes ...," 56). Indeed, as he comments in a sermon, "The greatest mystery of our Religion ... is conveyed in a Song" (*Sermons*, vol. II, no. 7, p. 171), and this was a challenge that Donne could not resist. His three hymns allow us to see (or hear) the devotional Donne at his most lyrical, exploring religious mysteries in relatively simple stanza forms that could be set to music.[11] Each hymn also finely reveals something of the mystery of Donne's own distinctive nature as a devotional poet.

"A Hymne to Christ, at the Authors last going into Germany," probably written in 1619 when Donne went abroad as chaplain to a diplomatic mission, approaches his imminent sea voyage from the emblematic perspective that we have already noted in "The Crosse." Donne's journey, however stormy, is invested in advance with a spiritual significance:

> In what torne ship soever I embarke,
> That ship shall be an embleme of thy Arke;
> What sea soever swallow mee, that flood
> Shall be to mee an embleme of thy bloode;
> Though thou with clouds of anger do disguise
> Thy face; yet through that maske I know those eyes ... (1–6)

These opening lines employ a typological mode of double vision, by which the early seventeenth-century ship is, simultaneously, the ark of Noah. Biblical images and events (the flood, the blood of Christ's passion, the pillar of cloud in Exodus) are all understood to foreshadow Donne's own experience, just as Old Testament figures such as Jonah or David may be seen as anticipatory "types" of Christ. Thus "A Hymne to Christ" not only makes flamboyant use of this scriptural reading of experience, but also draws to our attention the fundamentally biblical nature of Donne's devotional writing. His thinking, praying, meditating, writing, and preaching are steeped in knowledge and exegesis of the biblical "word"; indeed, he produced prose commentaries on parts of Genesis and Exodus in his *Essays in Divinity*, and the *Holy Sonnets* are clearly in the tradition of the penitential Psalms and the Lamentations of Jeremiah. However idiosyncratic we may consider his divine poems to be, they are at the same time profoundly influenced by scripture. "Batter my heart," possibly the most startling and distinctive of all Donne's devotional sonnets, takes its sexual metaphors from the Song of Songs, and its language of destruction and renewal – "breake, blowe, burn" (4) – from Deuteronomy, the Psalms, and the Book of Revelation.[12] To acknowledge Donne's biblical sources is not to diminish his originality; it is to place him properly in the historical and religious context from which he forged his distinctly individual voice.

"A Hymne to Christ," like "Goodfriday, 1613," takes the occasion of an actual journey not only as a source of emblems but also as the spur to devotion. In the same way as in the "Valedictions" of Donne's secular verse, departure – heralding separation or danger – serves (paradoxically) to intensify a relationship. In the case of the hymn, however, it is his spiritual marriage to God that is strengthened, while his worldly partnerships are given up in favor of this superior, "Eternall" (15) love:

> I sacrifice this Iland unto thee,
> And all whom I lov'd there, and who lov'd mee;
> When I have put our seas twixt them and mee,
> Put thou thy sea betwixt my sinnes and thee.　　　(9–12)

The speaker has a wayward soul whose "amorousnesse" (18) has been out of control and must be freed from loving "false mistresses" such as "Fame, Wit, Hopes" (28). As in the holy sonnets, particularly "Batter my heart," the soul must be forced to renounce all other relationships, explicitly referred to as marital agreements: "Seale then this bill of my Divorce to All" (25). The hymn is a major attempt at renunciation: of physical safety (for the seas may well "swallow" him, 3), of home ("this Iland," 9), of past loves, and even of light itself. The concluding lines interpret this in positive terms, since

> Churches are best for Prayer, that have least light:
> To see God only, I goe out of sight:
> 　　And to scape stormy dayes, I chuse
> 　　An Everlasting night.　　　(29–32)

We may wonder, however, to what extent this rejection of the world is a fair conclusion to the hymn. After all, earlier in the poem those "stormy dayes" have been seen as signs of divine immanence, not something to run away from; and the idea of escaping temptations by going "out of sight" still presupposes the world whose "sight" of the speaker is implied. Making himself invisible is not a skill that comes easily to Donne.

In his "Hymne to God my God, in my sicknesse," Donne himself is very much in view – in fact, his ailing body is the central focus of a meditation on mortality and redemption, just as it was in his *Devotions*. Lying "Flat on this bed," he is a "Mapp" of salvation on which (as in the imaginative carto-graphy seen in "The Annuntiation and Passion") the normal principles of place and time are superseded by the dimensions of eternity. All the "straits" on the world map become newly discovered routes to heaven, where west and east meet, and he prays that "the first *Adams* sweat" will be wiped away by the sacrifice of the second Adam, Christ (24–25) as the Old and New Testaments meet in his own feverish face. In addition to its powerful imme-diacy, this hymn is typical of Donne's devotional writing in its anticipatory stance; once again, the certainty of salvation is deferred. This is most clearly stated in the magnificent opening stanza:

> Since I am comming to that Holy roome,
> 　　Where, with thy Quire of Saints for evermore,

I shall be made thy Musique; As I come
I tune the Instrument here at the dore,
And what I must doe then, thinke here before.   (1–5)

Donne's devotional writing is, throughout, a tuning of the instrument at the door: a warming up in the anteroom of heaven. In "At the round earths imagin'd corners," it is suggested that God should "let [the dead] sleepe" a little longer (9) in order to allow the speaker time to get ready for the Last Judgment. In "Goodfriday, 1613," he even defers his conversion and promises to turn his face towards God only in the poem's last half line. Donne's characteristic postponement of judgment and mercy has been excellently summed up by Raymond-Jean Frontain as a "drama of suspended activity."[13]

"A Hymne to God the Father" is perhaps the best known of Donne's poems of deferred certainty. It is a confession of overwhelming sinfulness (the word "sinne" is used eight times within the space of thirteen lines), and the refrain in the first two stanzas sets the poet himself, through the pun on his own name, at the heart of this recurring principle of incompleteness: "When thou hast done, thou hast not done" (5, 11).[14] Even in the final stanza, "Thou hast done" is deceptive, since it depends on God's previously "having done" something (assured the speaker of Christ's saving presence at his own death) which is, at least grammatically, provisional. The poem is a rhetorical tour de force, in which the repeated "sinne" is displaced in the end by its punning close relative, the shining "sonne." By compressing the effects of the redemption into the change of one vowel-sound, the poem's language "*cloyster*[s]" an "*Immensity*" in "little roome" ("La Corona" 2:14, 13). But despite this apparent celebration of salvation, what drives the hymn is fear, not love. The speaker's "sinne of feare" (13) is the last and most dominant sin, and the closing words, "I feare no more," are a promise rather than a statement of present achievement. Indeed, without fear, there would have been very little devotional writing by Donne. Fear of death – or, more accurately, of its consequences – is the impulse behind most of his *Holy Sonnets*, occasional meditations, *Devotions*, and hymns, and it inspires him to religious writing of unprecedented intensity and brilliance. He wrote with great perception, in the sonnet "Oh, to vex me," when he admitted that "Those are my best dayes, when I shake with feare" (14).

"A Hymne to God the Father," poised on a pun before the moment "when I have spunne / My last thred" (13–14), is an appropriate poem with which to conclude this study of Donne's word-centred, fear-focused devotional writing. It reminds us that, though he longs for God's "all-healing grace" ("Father, part of his double interest," 11), Donne prefers to pray for it in places "that have least light" ("A Hymne to Christ," 29), where perhaps the sound of a bell tolling (*Devotions*, p. 87) or the affront of imminent death's swelling pride ("Death be not proud") will goad him into devotion. Even then, his response is not adoration or ecstasy but, rather, a puzzled admiration of God's "strange love" ("Spit in my face," 9) or a consuming "holy thirst" ("Since she whom I lov'd," 8) for greater understanding and reassurance. He knows, in a rational way, the logic of redemption: God has made him and will not want to let his "worke decay" but will "rise" and "fight" for it ("Thou has made me," "As due by many titles," 11). However, this knowledge is not enough; his "devout fitts" are unsteady, unpredictable, coming and going "Like a fantastique Ague" ("Oh, to vex me," 12–13). This association of devotion with temporary illness, metaphoric or actual, is an important clue to the nature of Donne's representation of spiritual experience. It is characterized by shifting moods and contexts, and yet manifests a prevailing discontent; it is full of anxious energy – emotional, linguistic, dramatic, sexual – that nevertheless gives way to passivity as God is asked to "chuse" or even "ravish" the speaker ("As due by many titles," 13; "Batter my heart," 14). These paradoxical and unstable qualities of Donne's devotional writing are, ultimately, the key to its rhetorical power and its implicit hopefulness. For the security of redemption is its promise of – indeed, the necessity of – change; this paradox underlies all those divine riddles of which Donne is so fond. "Inconstancy" may be, perversely, the troubled Christian's "constant habit" ("Oh, to vex me," 2–3), but it is also necessary to salvation, by which the mortal becomes immortal. Donne envisaged this shape-shifting in his *Devotions*: "O my God, my God, what thunder is not a well-tun'd Cymball, what hoarseness, what harshness is not a clear organ, if thou be pleased to set thy voice to it?" (p. 88). The triumph of Donne's sometimes thunderous devotional writing is that it anticipates this transformation – if not into conventionally sweet heavenly music, then into a uniquely "well-tun'd Cymball" sounding through eternity.

NOTES

1 See John 1:1, "In the beginning was the Word." The Greek ('logos') and Latin ('verbum') are also used by Donne in his sermons to refer to this principle of the originating word. See P. G. Stanwood and Heather R. Asals (eds.), *John Donne and the Theology of Language* (Columbia: University of Missouri Press, 1986).

2 Thomas Carew, "An Elegie upon the death of the Deane of Pauls," in Grierson's edition of Donne's *Poems*, p. 378.

3 S. T. Coleridge on Donne's poetry, reworked in "Fragments of an Epistle to Thomas Poole" in J. C. C. Mays (ed.), *The Collected Works of Samuel Taylor Coleridge, Poetical Works I: Poems*, (Princeton: Princeton University Press, 2001), part 1, p. 246.

4 The Collect for Peace from Morning Prayer, in John E. Booty (ed.), *The Book of Common Prayer 1559: The Elizabethan Prayer Book* (Charlottesville: University Press of Virginia, 1976, for the Folger Shakespeare Library), p. 59.

5 See Jeffrey Johnson, "Wrestling with God: John Donne at Prayer," in Raymond-Jean Frontain and Frances M. Malpezzi (eds.), *John Donne's Religious Imagination* (Conway, AR: UCA Press, 1995), pp. 316–17.

6 As Helen Gardner wisely observed, "Over the argument and the wit of the divine poems hangs the knowledge of the futility of argument" (John Donne, *The Divine Poems*, ed. Helen Gardner [Oxford: Clarendon Press, 1952], p. xvi).

7 C. A. Patrides (ed.), *The Complete Poems of John Donne* (London: Dent, 1985), p. 44.

8 Louis L. Martz, *The Poetry of Meditation* (New Haven: Yale University Press, 1954).

9 See Barbara K. Lewalski, *Protestant Poetics and the Seventeenth-Century Religious Lyric* (Princeton: Princeton University Press, 1979).

10 *"Ave,"* "Hail," is the angel Gabriel's greeting to Mary (Luke 1:28); *"Consummatum Est,"* "It is finished," are the last words of Christ on the cross (John 19:30).

11 "A Hymne to God the Father" was turned into an anthem within Donne's lifetime, by John Hilton, and has been set by several other composers from Pelham Humfrey to Benjamin Britten.

12 See Catherine Cresswell, "Reading the Face of God in Donne's Holy Sonnets," *John Donne's Religious Imagination*, p. 190.

13 Raymond-Jean Frontain, "Introduction," *John Donne's Religious Imagination*, p. 16.

14 It is likely that Donne also puns on his wife's surname, More, in the subsequent phrase: "I have more."

11

PETER McCULLOUGH

Donne as preacher

At his death in 1631, John Donne was popularly famous not as a poet, but as a preacher. Even the elegists marshalled to praise Donne in the first editions of the collected *Poems* (1633, 1635) lauded his preaching, not his poetry. Indeed, the author of a dedicatory epigram to the printer of *Poems* was bold to say, "Yet shew I thee a better way;/Print but his Sermons, and if those we buy,/He, We, and Thou shall live t' Eternity."[1] This petition was soon granted. Six of Donne's sermons had already appeared in print during his lifetime, including two by royal command, followed quickly by Donne's last sermon, *Deaths Duell*.[2] Then in folios published in 1640, 1649, and 1661 by John Donne, Jr., there appeared the 156 sermons that still form the basis of the sermon canon (see *Sermons*, vol. X, pp. 402–09). There was little doubt in the seventeenth-century mind that eloquence used for preaching was infinitely superior to penning ephemera like poems. Yet modern taste has inverted these early modern priorities. Donne's sermons have been used primarily either as convenient thematic glosses on the poetry, or for biographical evidence about Donne's theology, politics, and personality. Formal criticism has tended to praise them only when, in selected passages, they approach modern notions of "the poetic." To appreciate properly Donne's sermons requires students first to acquaint themselves with what they are formally and generically.

No early modern sermon can be studied properly using modern definitions of what a sermon is. Even the casual observer will recognize that the length of any complete Donne sermon – averaging twenty modern pages, and requiring at least one hour to deliver – sets it apart from almost anything heard from a pulpit today. Not surprisingly, students frequently assume that the excerpts in anthologies are in fact complete sermons. But sermons as Donne wrote them, and as his auditories experienced them, are best understood as full-scale classical orations adapted through centuries of tradition to a Christian purpose. From early Christian times, sermons were composed following classical rules of oratory and rhetoric. Particularly to Renaissance humanists like Donne, the classical oration provided the perfect model for the Christian sermon. So, with typical Christian humanist bravado, Donne claimed that "the orators, which were used to speake in the presence of the people, to the Romane Emperors" in fact practiced "a way of *Civill preaching*" (*Sermons*, vol. v, no. 10, p. 200).

Donne's sermons, like those of his contemporaries, provide important evidence of Renaissance literature's debt to the *epideictic* branch of rhetoric: the art of persuasively praising virtue or blaming vice, with an emphasis on inspiring voluntary actions by appeal to the auditory's emotions (Latin, *movere*). It is helpful to consider his sermons in the context of other literary genres from the period that exhibit the same rhetorical priorities. Across the whole range of poetic forms practiced by Donne's contemporaries the ideals are *epideictic*: Spenser sets out to "fashion a gentleman" through the appeal of exemplary romance episodes in *The Faerie Queene*, while Ben Jonson in his epigrams praises and blames the Jacobean elite. Like these, Donne's sermons are consummate achievements in eloquent praise and blame. And they are predicated on inspiring actions and feelings rather than dictating them – they persuade by commending the auditors' or readers' emotional, interpretative, and finally active engagement with eloquently presented examples. Far from being prescriptive declamations by a legalistic preacher, they are highly wrought pieces of literary persuasion that, like Spenserian epic or Shakespearean drama, invite emotional and intellectual engagement between author-performer and audience.

What follows is an overview of the salient formal characteristics of Donne's sermons and the conventions associated with their composition and delivery, followed by a brief close reading of one representative sermon to illustrate the importance of form to meaning in the sermons. The majority of recent work on Donne as preacher has focused on his careful negotiation in the sermons of the complexities of Jacobean and Caroline politics, both religious and civil. The issues of religion and politics are carefully treated elsewhere in this volume, and the concerns of this chapter are thus primarily generic. But students should be aware that critics continue to disagree primarily over the extent to which Donne either endorses, or carefully criticizes, both Stuart absolutism and emergent Laudian ceremonialism and sacrament-centred worship.[3] As a result, all who study Donne's sermons need to be vigilantly aware that Donne's preaching career was a long one – 1616 to 1631 – and thus stretches across a period of rapid ecclesiastical and political change in England. In addition, his preaching venues (and thus, his auditories) were quite varied, ranging from the elite intimacy of court, to populist assemblies like Paul's Cross, and private christenings and marriages. In short, the *corpus* of sermons cannot be treated as an undifferentiated whole, but demands careful contextual readings of individual works within it.

Both students and scholars must also resist the temptation to use extracts ripped from the organic structure of individual sermons. Whether analyzing literary qualities or ideological content, analysis must be based on an understanding of sermons as integral wholes. No student could properly analyze a Shakespeare sonnet without reference to its formal conventions of quatrains and couplet, or build an argument on *Hamlet*'s soliloquies without reading the whole play. And early modern sermons observed similarly strict formal conventions that demand comprehensive attention for any proper understanding of Donne's use of them. These should provide students with a crucial first step for understanding this now unfamiliar genre.

Donne's sermons were written in accordance with the classical rules for the proper stages in composing an oration, and for the parts of the oration itself, as these were adapted by Christian tradition to sermons. As rules drummed into every schoolboy's head and recycled in manuals for preachers, these formed as much a part of audience expectation as they did authorial composition. Modern students, like Donne's first hearers, should cultivate a lively awareness of these rules in order to enjoy Donne's creative play with them. The five stages in the composition of an oration (which students might still recognize from rules for writing an essay) were known by their Latin names, which easily correspond to their most obvious English translations: *inventio* ('invention', finding valid arguments), *dispositio* ('disposition', arrangement of those arguments into their best strategic order); *elocutio* ('elocution', the verbal expression of the first two stages); *memoria* ('memory', strategies for memorizing the oration), and *pronuntiatio et actio* ('pronunciation and gesture' in delivery of the oration). By asking how Donne followed these stages when composing and delivering any given sermon, a modern reader can begin to make formal sense of what might otherwise look like twenty pages of undifferentiated prose, and discover profitable lines of analysis and interpretation.

The first three stages result in what a sermon reader finds now on the printed page. The entire sermon will be the product of Donne's *inventio*, his process of researching and selecting valid evidence to support his argument. As in most sermons, by far the largest body of Donne's evidence is from the Bible, which, like all early modern Christians, Donne reverenced as the ultimate revealed authority for faith and salvation. In addition, Donne found the scriptures superior in their aesthetic form as well as their religious content: "there are not so *eloquent* books in the world, as the Scriptures" (*Sermons*, vol. X, no. 4, p. 103). Donne's use of scriptural sources is too vast to survey here (but see *Sermons*, vol. X, no. 4, pp. 111–12). But students should be sensitive to how, for Donne, biblical texts offered a combination of both moral authority and artistic inspiration. Unlike extreme puritan preachers, Donne also responds creatively to non-scriptural evidence; foremost in this category are the early church Fathers, in particular St. Augustine. Medieval and early modern theologians also appear, including not only Protestants like Luther and Calvin, but also Roman Catholics (not always simply for refutation) like St. Thomas Aquinas. Similarly, classical authors such as Seneca can be admitted for illustrative purposes, as can *exempla* (examples, illustrations) from science, philosophy, music, the plastic arts, contemporary politics and anecdote and experience from everyday life. The huge range that Donne allows for himself in *inventio* distinguishes him from other prominent preachers of his day. Lancelot Andrewes (1555–1626), for example, is almost relentless in using only scriptural evidence, or arguments about scripture from the Fathers, making his sermons microscopically scriptural in argument and diction. Donne, however, habitually moves outside scripture to explain scripture, in a movement that, when compared to Andrewes, is expansively macroscopic. From this mass of *inventio*, a careful student of Donne will wish to ask *why* the author reaches for evidence and arguments from any one of these categories to illustrate a particular point.

Some rhetoricians, particularly in the Renaissance, argued for the superiority of *dispositio* for an oration's success. No matter how good an argument was, they insisted, if it was placed at a disadvantageous place in a speech, its worth was lost. Having found ("invented") his arguments, Donne, like any good orator, arranges his material into an order designed to have the greatest possible emotive – and thus persuasive – impact on his auditory. So questions need to be asked and answered not just about *which* arguments and illustrations Donne uses in a sermon, but even more crucially, *where* he puts them within the sermon at large. Students will be familiar with this kind of analysis from the close-reading of poems, and need to apply the same strategies to the sermons. For example, the famous "compass conceit" in "A Valediction: forbidding mourning" (line 28), with its brilliant pun on the alchemical circled-dot symbol for gold, would be far less effective, indeed wasted, if it did not come after stanzas which had first carefully introduced the related symbolic imagery of "the spheares" (line 11), the elements (line 16), refining metals (line 17), and, immediately before the compass, "gold to ayery thinnesse beate" (line 24). Although in sermons the structural units are larger – long sentences and paragraphs, not lines and stanzas – the strategic deployment of arguments, *exempla*, and imagery is just as subtle and significant.

The third stage in composition, *elocutio*, is the aspect of Donne's sermons that received the greatest amount of critical attention in the last century. The actual verbal expression – diction and syntax – of the arguments that have been chosen and arranged (*inventio* and *dispositio*) by Donne gives his sermons what we now call their prose *style*. Rhetorical convention for formal orations like sermons demanded elevated speech (*eloqui*), as opposed to common speech (*loqui*). To achieve this heightened effect, what Erasmus called the "fulness of words and matter" (*copia*), Renaissance verbal artists, whether writing speeches, poems, plays, or sermons, drew upon elaborately codified traditions of figurative language in an effort to find words, and patterns of words, that best conveyed the emotional content of their ideas. These, still known as figures and tropes, constitute the vocabulary of formal stylistic analysis, and are as prominent in Donne's sermons as in his verse: *metaphor* ("this life is a Circle, made with a Compasse," vol. II, no. 9, p. 200), *parison* ("a great Man, and a good Man, a happy Man, and a holy Man," p. 201), *rogatio* ("Is that contract void, and of none effect? Must he not die?" p. 208), *hypotyposis* ("Take a flat Map, a Globe *in plano*, and here is East, and there is West," p. 199), *paronomasia* ("no length, no strength enables us," p. 199), *polyptoton* ("We shall see the death of Death it self in the death of Christ," p. 202), *antithesis* ("We have seen a man recovered after his drowning, and live to hang himselfe," p. 199), *prosopopoeia* ("God answers ... *You shall dye like men*," p. 201). These examples – highly selective, and randomly taken from just one sermon – are necessarily on a small scale. This could be misleading, because in his sermons' *elocutio*, as in their *inventio*, Donne works on a large, sweeping scale quite unlike his most famous poetry. Readers of the sermons looking for the flash of the sharp, quick paradoxes and conceits that we have come to associate with "meta-physical" poetry will be disappointed – in sermon prose, Lancelot Andrewes is infinitely more "metaphysical" in that sense than Donne. If Donne's *Songs and Sonets* and Divine Poems might be compared to the witty painted miniatures by Hilliard or Oliver, his sermons are like vast, dramatic can-vasses by Titian or Rubens. As scholarly studies of Donne's sermon prose style concluded generations ago, Donne prefers rhetorical tropes and figures of amplification like symmetrical periphrasis and analogy, and extended, often paragraph-long elaborations of a single idea in expansive, complex sentences – a style frequently associated with Cicero's long "periods," as opposed to the curt, staccato syntax associated with Seneca and practiced by Francis Bacon and Andrewes.

The two remaining stages of composition, *memoria* and *pronuntiatio et actio*, relate of course to delivery, and, as Brian Vickers points out, "only make proper sense when rhetoric is a performance art."[4] And early modern sermons were indeed performance art – their authors and their audiences competed far more directly than has ever properly been understood with public theatre and courtly masque in Donne's London. *Memoria* might seem unrelated to composition. But Donne's sermons, like almost all others in the period, would have been delivered entirely from memory – auditories took a dim view of any preacher who addressed them from notes, much less read-out a prepared text. Committing so much complex prose to memory would challenge the most skilled modern actor, but even children's education in the early modern period was based primarily on rote memorization of vast amounts of text, mostly in Latin. The intensity of both oral and aural textual culture in the Renaissance produced performers and audiences who could easily perform or attend any four-hour *Hamlet*, as well as one- and two-hour sermons.

The strategies for such feats of memory (the *ars memoria*, or 'art of memory') left important traces in sermon texts. Even if unannounced, a preacher would have the structure of his sermon in his head already from the process of *dispositio*. And since classical times, orators had been trained to imagine a spatial version of their speeches, usually a building, with the various rooms (*loci*, "places") in it "containing" the various parts of the oration, through which the orator would imagine himself proceeding in order. Donne seems to have been fond of this device, for he frequently incorporates it into his sermons' imagery, as in an undated sermon on prayer preached "to the Nobility" (*Sermons*, vol. v, no. 12). He likens the sermon to "a goodly palace" through which he will guide his auditory: together they will "rest a little, as in an outward Court, upon consideration of prayer in generall; and then draw neare the view of the Palace, in a second Court" to consider the Lord's Prayer, and then "passe thorow the chiefest rooms of the palace it self" which contain four principle arguments about how to pray properly, before finally "going into the backside of [the palace]" to refute objections to those arguments (vol. v, no. 12, pp. 231–32). In sonnets Donne built "pretty roomes" ("The Canonization," line 32); in sermons he built palaces.

Pronuntiatio et actio is largely uncharted territory in the study of early modern preaching, including Donne's. But in this category usually lay the success or failure of any preacher. A speaker's *pronuntiatio* manipulated three things: *quantitas* ("quantity," the volume and pitch of the voice), *qualitas* ("quality," the type or tone of the voice, something physiologically unique to any speaker), and *spatium* ("space"; that is, the timing, pace, and rhythm of delivery). To read any Donne sermon (ideally aloud) with these concepts in mind is to take a quantum leap forward in appreciating the animated theatricality which Donne intended when composing, and of course, delivering, his sermons. Nothing kills an oration like a dead-pan, monotone delivery, something all too easily encouraged in the mind's ear when silently reading long passages of complex prose on the page. But it is in delivery (*pronuntiatio*) that oratorical prose style (*elocutio*) best reveals its function, that is, to persuade and prompt action by raising the emotions. The tropes and figures are themselves a signifying language, which imitate, by exaggeration, human emotional states, and they should be delivered, or at least silently imagined in reading, accordingly. A helpful analogy might be the system of expression markings used by composers to aid performers' interpretation of a musical score. Donne's profound climax for a vast prose paragraph on despair, for example, demands a dramatic manipulation of *quantitas* and *spatium* just as the final cadence of a concerto would manipulate tempo and dynamics: "we are waighed downe, we are swallowed up, irreparably, irrevocably, irrecoverably, irremediably" (vol. VII, no. 1, p. 57). The two parallel subject-verb constructions that begin the clause force a slowing of tempo that is then intensified by the repetition of the four similar-sounding adverbs separated only by commas (*similiter desinens* and *articulus*). The difficulty of pronouncing the unfamiliar multi-syllabic adverbs, coupled with the repetition of the negative prefix 'ir-' requires not only the careful, deliberate pronunciation of the words themselves, but also the gradual increase of the length of pauses between each, probably also with a reduction in volume that leads the auditory to a perfect emotional sense of having dwindled to nothingness in the absence of faith in God. Immediately after this, Donne quickens the pace with a pithy summary (*acclamatio*): "This is the fearfull depth, this is spirituall misery, to be thus fallen from God." A rapid succession of rhetorical questions (*rogatio*) – "But was this *David's* case? was he fallen thus farre, into a diffidence from God?" – continues the acceleration in delivery that mimics the preacher's thematic attempt to snatch the auditory out of despair and into hope. This is completed, in a brilliant contrast to the page-length paragraph on despair which preceded it, with a single-syllable sentence that transforms the whole theme of negativity with the triumphant answer: "No." (vol. VII, no. 1, p. 57). Again, this is an example on a small scale, but it could be used as an analogy for the shape, in delivery, of entire sermons, which use rhetorical devices to imitate and thus engage, in a carefully plotted design, a huge dramatic range of contrasting emotions.

To this aural range was added significant gesture – primarily with the hands, but also facial expression. The aim was for these elements – speech and gesture – to animate or embody for the auditory's visual apprehension the words they simultaneously apprehended aurally. In pre-modern psychology, intellection and the control of the will was not purely mental or rational, but required the cooperation of the physical. Hence the urgency to stir emotions not just in the modern metaphorical sense, but in a truly physiological sense of "moving": the emotions moved the mind. Was Donne, though, an egotistical, emotional manipulator in the pulpit? Some influential modern critics of his sermons have thought so, treating Donne's emotionalism with suspicions of insincerity. The first was T. S. Eliot, who in the course of praising his favorite Jacobean preacher, Lancelot Andrewes, sketched this famously damning character of Donne in the pulpit:

> About Donne there hangs the shadow of the impure motive; and impure motives lend their aid to a facile success. He is a little of the religious spellbinder, the Reverend Billy Sunday of his time, the flesh-creeper, the sorcerer of emotional orgy ... Donne had a trained mind; but without belittling the intensity or profundity of his experience, we can suggest that this experience was not perfectly controlled, and that he lacked spiritual discipline.[5]

But an understanding of Renaissance oratorical practice, and consideration of eyewitness accounts of Donne in the pulpit should qualify Eliot's criticism, and take us closer to understanding Donne's unique pulpit persona. Izaak Walton paints a vivid picture of Donne the preacher:

> a Preacher in earnest; weeping sometimes for his Auditory, sometimes with them: always preaching to himself, like an Angel from a cloud, but in none; carrying some, as St. *Paul* was, to Heaven in holy raptures, and inticing others by a sacred Art and Courtship to amend their lives; here picturing vice so as to make it ugly to those that practised it; and a vertue so, as to make it be beloved even by those that lov'd it not; and all this with a most particular grace and an unexpressible addition of comeliness.[6]

Walton's assessment uses the rules for rhetoric outlined above, including a concise definition of sermons as *epideictic* rhetoric that pictures vice and praises virtue. But most striking is the emphasis he places on Donne's *pronuntiatio et actio* ("weeping," "grace," "comeliness"). Jasper Mayne's elegy comes even closer to describing exactly how Donne furthered his spoken words with significant gesture and facial expression:

> Yet have I seene thee in the pulpit stand,
> Where wee might take notes, from thy looke, and hand;
> And from thy speaking action beare away
> More Sermon, then some teachers use to say.
> Such was thy carriage, and thy gesture such,
> As could divide the heart, and conscience touch.
> Thy motion did confute, and wee might see
> An errour vanquish'd by delivery.
> ("On Dr. Donne's death: By Mr. Mayne of Christ-Church
> in Oxford," 57–64, in Grierson [ed.], *Poems*)

And an Oxford don of the time made a memo to himself about Donne's success in the pulpit that entirely equates Donne's power with his delivery: "Dr Donne deane of Pauls, his powerful kinde of preaching by his gestur and Rhetoriquall expression."[7] These accolades suggest not that Donne was Eliot's egotistical maniac in the pulpit, but that he epitomized the agreed ideals for the fifth stage of composition of an oration. Cicero insisted that "impulse of spirit" and "emotion" won more arguments than "judgement or deliberation"; St. Augustine thought affective persuasion more important than doctrine; the author of the most prominent early modern preacher's manual, Andreas Hyperius, insisted that "the preacher ... standeth of no one thing more in neede" than "of moving the affections"; and Donne himself declared that "a Sermon intends *Exhortation* principally and *Edification*, and a holy stirring of religious affections."[8]

The model of joining signifying gesture with emotive language is of course a theatrical one, something acknowledged by rhetoricians. Aristotle conceded that tragedians first came up with these methods. Thomas Wright, in his *Passions of the Minde in Generall* (1630), argued that "in the substance of externall action for most part oratours and stage plaiers agree."[9] Donne, we know, was, at least in his youth, an avid theater-goer. And considering the sermons as staged dramatic monologues is another valid means of approach to them *via* a more familiar literary genre. Whether from pulpit or on stage, the dynamic between speaker and auditor is a participatory one: the preacher or actor must first manifest in his body, as well as with his words, the emotions he wishes to raise in the audience hearing and seeing him. So, far from being himself or indecorously parading his own personality in the pulpit, as many have too easily assumed, Donne may never have been *less* himself than when preaching. Good emotive preaching as Donne understood it had to impersonate a huge range of emotional states and personalities in order to offer the variety of emotional experience necessary to provide an hour's preaching that was not monotonous, or uniform, and – crucially – that spoke to the huge range of social, emotional, spiritual, and human conditions assembled before him. Just as Shakespeare or Jonson had to please both nobility and groundlings, Donne composed sermons that were usually attended by audiences that were highly mixed. The thousands who flocked to hear him at Paul's Cross ranged from the Lord Mayor to apprentices, and even in the Chapel Royal, he could expect to address anyone from the king to his household servants. Hence Walton's observation that Donne could shift from meditational "holy raptures," to worldly vocabularies of "Art and Courtship," to lurid pictures of "vice," and then convincing images of "virtue." Such variety was admired because it engaged the greatest possible range of listeners. To achieve this requires the combined skill of both playwright and actor – to both script and perform.

Donne practiced perhaps better than any preacher of his age the lessons of the preaching manuals for achieving this aim: "Before all things it is very necessary that hee which speaketh, doe conceyue such lyke affections in his minde, and rayse them upp in himselfe, yea, and (after a sorte) shewe them forth to be seene unto others, as he coueteth to bee translated into the myndes of his auditors" (Hyperius, p. 43r). A modern person might compare these strategies to those of "method acting"; a less anachronistic comparison would be to the emotive meditative strategies of St. Ignatius' *Exercises*, which we know influenced Donne's holy sonnets. Compare Hyperius's further advice to the preacher to prepare for a sermon's delivery "by the dilligent consideration of the things [that] are before his eyes," even "a vehement imagination or fantasy [that] depaynteth to himself the formes of the things whereof he entreateth" (p. 43v). With this we can better understand anecdotes like that from Donne's 1625 correspondence with Sir Robert Ker, in which Donne reveals that before a sermon at court he needed an hour to "collect his thoughts," no doubt to work himself into a meditative state that enabled him to raise and then carry into the pulpit the emotions he wished to raise in his auditory.[10] One thing that we can safely argue that the author of the poetry imported into his preaching was his mastery of assuming a myriad number of dramatic voices and personae so convincing that critics have too quickly assumed they are all autobiographically his own. The "I's" of Donne's sermons are often hypothetical, fictional creations in the Sidneyan sense of "poesy" – they "affirm nothing" in the autobiographical or historical sense, but convey truth through what Hyperius called "vehement imagination or fantasy."

But of course Donne would insist that what he called "the dignity of so great a service" (vol. II, no. 7, p. 171) distinguished the preacher from any mere stage-player. If we ever see the "real" Donne in the pulpit, it is in disarming moments of his astonishment at the duty and power of his office to proclaim nothing less than God's salvation to his hearers: "That when I call to God for grace here, God should give me grace for grace, Grace in a power to derive grace upon others ... That when mine eyes looke up to Heaven, the eyes of all should looke up upon me, and God should open my mouth, to give them meat in due season." Donne is certainly mesmerized by this power, but we make a mistake if we only see, with Eliot, egotistical solipsism, or, with John Carey, "power lust" here.[11] Donne is more usually reaching out of himself to offer his auditory what he believes to be saving truth.

On the first Friday in Lent, 1623, Donne stepped into the pulpit at Whitehall palace – probably the outdoor pulpit erected by Henry VIII which, like Paul's Cross, accommodated thousands of all social ranks around it, with the king and nobility listening from upper-story windows and galleries. Donne always calculated his performances to appeal to the given time, date, and occasion of preaching. The occasion for this sermon was the great court Lent sermon series – three royally sponsored sermons preached in each of the six weeks of Lent by the most famous preachers in the kingdom. After the crowd was hushed by his ascent into the pulpit, Donne would have first uttered a statutory prayer for Church and State, and then begun his sermon with the declamation of his scriptural text. Whereas a classical oration expounds a given theme or subject, early modern sermons required as their subject a specific, quoted text from the Bible. The opening paragraphs of both classical orations and early modern sermons were known as the *exordium*, from the Latin *exordior*, "to lay a warp, to begin to weave," hence, the beginning, or introductory part of the speech or sermon's text (itself from the Latin *textus*, "web"). Here the orator introduces the occasion, justifies his presence before the auditory, and begins the crucial work of engaging its sympathy. But in sermons, a preacher started to weave a text *from* a text. And the best preachers, like Donne, integrated their chosen biblical text with their own sermon text from the very start. Appreciating the artistry of this process of "weaving" the *exordium* is the beginning of a sound reading of a Donne sermon.

In delivery, as in reading, the first words of a sermon are thus not the preacher's own, but the Bible's. But they are part of the sermon, and the lively game of interpretation played between preacher and auditory begins, often with a great deal of wit, here. On this February morning Donne must have inspired knowing smiles by proclaiming only two words as his text: "John 11.35: Jesus wept" – famously, the Bible's shortest verse. Before uttering any words of his own, Donne thus holds his audience captive through their desire to know how he will, with Renaissance *sprezzatura*, spin an hour's sermon out of only two words. To raise the stakes of the game, Donne at first ignores the obvious by beginning not with clichés about the Bible's shortest verse, but by embroidering a recondite pun that flatters the auditory as a privileged "in-group": "I am now but upon the Compassion of Christ. There is much difference betweene his Compassion and his Passion, as much as between the men that are to handle them here" (*Sermons*, vol. IV, no. 13, p. 324). The first sentence clearly alludes to Christ's compassionate weeping in the set text. But the distinction between "Compassion" and "Passion" introduces a calendrical allusion to Good Friday, the day of Christ's "Passion" on the cross. Thematically the allusion is justified by introducing on this, the first Friday in Lent, the appropriate theme of tears, but at the very first instant of doing so, also anticipating the last Friday of Lent (Good Friday) and Christ's crucifixion. But Donne then refers to two men who will "handle" these themes "here" in the Whitehall pulpit. Donne's audience followed the Lent sermon series with the eagerness which we might associate with a hit television series or sporting competition, and they knew that Donne always preached on the first Friday in Lent, and that the climactic sermon fixture on Good Friday was always taken by the Dean of Westminster. In 1623 this was Dr. John Williams, a preacher who emulated in the pulpit his Cambridge tutor Thomas Playfere, famous (like Donne) for weeping during his sermons. So the thematic imagery of tears is now also linked to the pulpit personalities of Donne and another preacher. But it then melts into an even more heightened pun that glosses Donne's own sermon and pays a gracious compliment to the forthcoming sermon by Williams, one of whose state offices was Lord Keeper of the Great Seal: "Let me chafe the wax, and melt your soules in a bath of his Teares now, Let him set to the great Seale of his effectuall passion, in his blood, then." Within three sentences, Donne has caught his auditory in a web of allusion that knits together transcendent spiritual, scriptural, and calendrical themes with the immediate material context of personality, place, and occasion.

The opening paragraph then concludes with Donne carefully positioning his authorial self in his desired relationship with his auditory. Moving away from the autobiographical "I" of the courtly allusions to himself and Williams, he reaches for a quotation from a church Father, St. Bernard, to gain both authority and distance by referring to himself in the third person in order to resolve the whole paragraph by again quoting his biblical text, but in such a grammatical way as to conflate auditory, preacher, and Christ himself: "bring S. Bernards patience ... be willing to heare him [Donne], that seeks not your acclamation to himselfe, but your humiliation to his and your God ... to make you weepe with them that weepe, And Jesus wept" (Sermons, vol. IV, no. 13, p. 324). Only then does Donne quickly acknowledge the well-known statistic of this being the Bible's shortest verse, concluding his exordium with a summary that yet again quotes his text, as he will continue to do throughout the sermon like the most skilfully deployed refrain in any lyric: "This is the season of generall Compunction ... and no man priviledged, for Jesus wept."

After this strategically brilliant exordium, Donne proceeds to the next structural part found in every early modern sermon, the divisio, or "division" of the arguments that will follow. Many readers might be tempted to put a sermon down at this point, because thematic imagery, tropes and figures, and most wit evaporate while the preacher offers a detailed structural outline of the sermon. Again, impatience should be qualified by an understanding of function. As in the corresponding part of a classical oration, the partitio (partition), the sermon divisio is by design schematic – these must be skeletally clear outlines in order to aid both the preacher and auditory. For the former, it is a crucial aide memoir; for the latter, it offers a road-map marked with the milestones which an audience (who themselves often took notes) will want to watch and listen for. Although not rhetorically flashy, readers should always pay particularly close attention to this part, which is almost always marked (*"Divisio"*) in the margin of Donne's printed texts. Donne and his contemporaries usually preferred a three-part division of their argument, but usually with subdivisions within those parts. The importance of structure to interpretation here can again be compared to sonnet structures. Few exercises can be as helpful to the critic as outlining the parts of the sermon or sonnet in order to see not only how the argument progresses, but how the deployment of examples and evolution of thematic imagery in each part furthers the author's meaning.

Donne's *divisio* in "Jesus wept" is based on the observation that in the Bible, Christ "wept thrice": for Lazarus, for Jerusalem, and at his Passion (lines 30–37). Already, Donne has here a narrative biographical trajectory from Christ's life, but also a thematic climax for his sermon that stretches from weeping for an individual, a nation, and finally humanity. These three kinds of tears – "Humane" "Propheticall," and "Pontificall, appertaining to the Sacrifice" (p. 325) – are thus announced as the three parts of the sermon, which Donne refines further in the *divisio* by noting for each of the three kinds of tears, Christ's intentions in shedding them, and the occasions for his doing so; finally, Donne assigns a governing symbolic metaphor to each of the three kinds of tears ("a Spring," "a River," "the Sea"; p. 326). The result, very clear if outlined on paper, is a three-part sermon with three subsets of three subsidiary arguments each – three "threes" that in their very numerical structure symbolize the Trinity and figure symmetrical perfection. And the *divisio* exploits its final section's reintroduction of metaphor to create from preacher, auditory, and Christ a pool of rhetorically redemptive tears:

> because the Spring flowes into the River, and the River into the Sea, and that wheresoever we find that Jesus wept, we find our Text ... we shall looke upon those lovely, those heavenly eyes, through this glasse of his owne teares, in all these three lines ... For so often Jesus wept. (p. 326)

The sermon, then, unfolds along these announced lines like the three-quatrain progression of a Shakespearean sonnet, as Donne considers the three kinds of tears in a whole range of contexts – physical, familial, social, political, soteriological. Through this process, the imagery of tears remains constant, but it also evolves to gather, like a stream, new depths and shapes until it emerges, transformed in the conclusion into something wholly different from, but related to its source, and greater than the sum of its parts. The *conclusio* (again, a term shared by classical orations and sermons) includes an emotionally clenching *peroration* designed to summarize the whole of the exercise with the aim of inspiring action on the part of the hearers. Donne's strategy here is almost always the same – to open-out, to expand the range of meaning toward universals, but with the added immediacy of the first person, toward consolation and joy. The three "exemplar bathes of Christs teares" have shown the value of weeping for oneself, one's nation, and one's sins (p. 343). The water imagery then leaps from tears to the saving immersion of baptism, which, like proper pentitential tears, holds out the promise of eternal life in heaven. Only then – though, given the exhaustive treatment of so many biblical examples of tears, the audience must have been wondering when it would finally appear – Donne concludes the sermon with the triumphantly hopeful quotation of Revelation 7:17: "*The Lord shall wipe all teares from thine eyes*, that is, dry up the fountaine of teares; remove all occasion of teares hereafter, in the triumphant Church" (p. 344). Like the concluding couplet of a Shakespearean sonnet, this conclusion uses the image system that has evolved throughout the preceding hour both to suggest a new, climactic meaning, and to take the reader or auditor back to the first introduction of that imagery in a conscious summary of how it has metamorphosed in the course of the text. Revelation 7:17 suddenly transforms tears from marks of worldly sorrow to, in their heavenly absence, emblems of grief exchanged for joy. The verse however actually reads "wipe away all teares from *their* eyes" [emphasis added]. By the deft substitution of the second person singular for the plural, Donne sends his auditory away thinking of the application of his sermon to themselves as individuals, having achieved in the end the aim stated in his witty opening: he "seeks not your acclamation to himselfe, but your humiliation to his and your God."

NOTES

1 The prefatory epigrams and concluding "Elegies upon the Author" from *Poems* are included in Grierson (ed.), *Poems*, vol. I, pp. 371–95. Only Thomas Carew's prioritizes Donne's poems over his sermons (Grierson [ed.], *Poems*, vol. II, pp. 378–80).

2 *Sermons*, vol. IV, no. 7; vol. IV, no. 10; vol. IV, no. 15; vol. VI, no. 12; vol. VII, no. 2; vol. VIII, no. 2; vol. X, no. 11.

3 Contrast, for example, the approaches of Jeanne Shami, *John Donne and Conformity in Crisis in the Late Jacobean Pulpit* (Cambridge: D. S. Brewer, 2003), and Debora Shuger, *Habits of Thought in the English Renaissance: Religion, Politics, and the Dominant Culture* (Berkeley and Los Angeles: University of California Press, 1990), ch. 5.

4 Brian Vickers, *In Defense of Rhetoric* (Oxford: Clarendon Press, 1988), p. 65.

5 T. S. Eliot, "Lancelot Andrewes," in *Selected Essays*, new edition (New York, Harcourt, Brace and World, 1950), p. 302. This first appeared in the *Times Literary Supplement* no. 1286 (Sept. 23, 1926), pp. [621]–22.

6 Walton, *Lives*, p. 49.
7 Thomas Crosfield, quoted in Bald, *Donne*, p. 412, n. 3.
8 See Neil Rhodes, *The Power of Eloquence and English Renaissance Literature* (Hemel Hempsted: Harvester Wheatsheaf, 1992), Part I; St. Augustine, *On Christian Doctrine*, trans. D. W. Robertson (Indianapolis: University of Indiana Press, 1958), esp. Bk. IV; Andreas Hyperius, trans. John Ludham, *The Practise of Preaching* (London, 1577), p. 41; Donne, *Sermons*, vol. VIII, no. 3, p. 95.
9 Quoted in David Bevington, *Action is Eloquence: Shakespeare's Language of Gesture* (Cambridge, MA: Harvard University Press, 1984), p. 70.
10 *Letters to Severall Persons of Honour* (1651), pp. 313–14; this was before the first sermon preached to King Charles, so calming Donne's nerves might have been just as important as raising his emotions on this occasion.
11 John Carey, *John Donne: Life, Mind and Art*, new edn. (London: Faber and Faber, 1990), p. 108.

12

LYNNE MAGNUSSON

Donne's language: the conditions of communication

While no one would dispute that Donne was a man of many abilities, it is clear that Donne's linguistic gift was his principal talent and his most significant asset. He may have come from a good family, but he inherited neither property nor titles. He absorbed himself in learning, but while law, medicine, astronomy, and other new sciences provided material for his verbal creativity in poetry and prose, he is not remembered for any distinctive contribution to knowledge. He is remembered as a preacher, but does not figure as an important theologian. What he had was an exceptional verbal ability: the "talent" he could most readily put out to "use" was his linguistic capital. It is what enabled his poetry, his sexual conquests, his literary friendships, his relative success as a secretary, his access to patrons like the Countess of Bedford, his notice by King James, and his power to preach sermons with the golden tongue of St. Chrysostom. His tongue probably also got him into lots of trouble – witness the cockiness of his first letter to Sir George More after eloping with his daughter, which helped to land him in prison; Sir Thomas Egerton's reported satisfaction, after Donne was forced out of his service, with an inferior secretary who was not so clever at finding things to correct in his dictation or written drafts; Donne's concern about potential political danger if his *Satires* were to be published and the actual brief scare when a sermon preached in 1627 offended Charles I.[1] Not merely Donne's poetic career but his entire life was marked off by his virtuoso performances in words. Whether crafting poems, pouring out letters to friends or sustaining the discipline of weekly sermons, Donne's fertility of verbal invention as he turned his favorite topics and "master-images"[2] to fresh applications epitomized that quality of Renaissance rhetorical culture that Erasmus recommended as "copia" and imagined as equipment for a meaningful and active life. Indeed, for Donne, the abundant flow of words is a testimony of life: "in bodily, so in spirituall diseases," he writes in one sermon, "it is a desperate state, to be speechlesse" (*Sermons*, vol. V, no. 12, p. 233).

The tradition of criticism on Donne's language has focused on poetic devices in particular poems, such as the striking form of comparison that has come to be known as the "metaphysical conceit," metaphors, paradox, wordplay, and other forms of ambiguity; or critics have focused, more generally, on the distinctive quality of "wit" on display in his literary works.[3] While this chapter will not ignore these features, it will build an argument about how Donne used his gift with language as equipment for poetry and as equipment for living. It will employ methods of close reading that engage the complexities of Donne's practical, non-literary language with something of the same care and energy that has been traditionally reserved for the poetry. Analysis of the linguistic preoccupations in Donne's religious prose and his practical correspondence can cross-fertilize analysis of the poetry.

Donne's verbal genius was not abstracted from the social, religious, and political contexts of his time[4] or from the historical particularities of early modern English. Linguistic virtuosity in life inevitably runs up against the pressures and resistances of real-world communication, which are caught up in the political and social arrangements of the times. For language is a form of action, whether social, political, performative, or aesthetic. The French sociologist, Pierre Bourdieu, has emphasized that "language is ... an instrument of power. A person speaks not only to be understood but also to be believed, obeyed, respected, distinguished." In social interaction, linguistic capital is never more than one among many forms of symbolic capital that help to determine how one's discourse may be valued: whether or not it gets a hearing, is admired, believed, granted authority, and acted upon. Linguistics (and by extension also formalist poetics), in Bourdieu's view, has gone wrong by taking "the *conditions for the establishment of communication*," for gaining a hearing, "as already secured, whereas, in real situations, that is the essential question."[5]

These may not be the terms in which we usually discuss a poet's language. But Donne was a poet whose language was continually coming up against the trials and frustrations of life in a hierarchical social world and a monarchic state. Coterie communities like Lincoln's Inn and manuscript circulation among friends may have provided a buffer zone, but, at least until he embraced his religious vocation, access was always an issue for him. Poetic fame was no more certainly his goal than gaining a hearing in circles that mattered to him and then using pre-eminent place effectively to give his words credit and authority. Throughout his career, Donne shows a fascinated engagement with what we now call "pragmatics" – the study of the practical conditions of communication or how language works in its contexts of use. The circumstances of social access and interaction affect both the central themes and the linguistic performances of his sermons, letters, and poems. The linguistic code itself – the particularities of early modern English and especially of its grammar – is an important part of the context shaping Donne's verbal performance. Donne makes art in his prose and verse writings out of the friction in language. His writings highlight the static involved not only in structures of social interaction but also in the grammatical structures of early modern English, especially those aspects relating to the logical and theological disputes that most captivated his attention.

Poems like "The Extasie" put on display Donne's self-reflexive awareness of linguistic action. He highlights how the premises of a language constantly condition and constrain not only mimesis, or how anything so unusual as an "extasie" can be represented, but also communication, or how intersubjective dialogue can be effectively conducted. The conditions of communication are foregrounded by setting "body" talk, or normal conversation, in comparison with "soul" talk. While the "we" of ordinary discourse "sat" face-to-face and "said nothing, all the day" (4, 20), Donne's talking souls, in their refined "dialogue of one," forego the "I" and "thou" of ordinary conversational exchange, to address one another reciprocally and simultaneously as "we." Even in a poem on a more worldly subject like "The Storme," a verse epistle to Christopher Brooke, Donne suggests that the true quality of his social relation with a beloved friend is falsified by the linguistic requirement to separate out a writing (or speaking) "I" from an addressed "you" or "thou": "*Thou* which art *I*, ('tis nothing to be soe) / *Thou* which art still *thy selfe*, by these shalt know / Part of *our* passage" (1–3, emphasis added). But it is not only in poetry that Donne innovates by resisting or highlighting the ways in which language or social context constrains the possibilities for communication. In what follows, I will look, first, at a sermon in which Dr. Donne sets an idealized form of dialogue, Protestant prayer, in relation to the actual conditions of a Jacobean courtly suitor's request-making. Second, I go backward in time to consider two letters that Jack Donne wrote to his father-in-law, Sir George More, after eloping with Anne More. Here we can see how two competing types of interaction theorized in the sermon, one of direct reasoning and the other of courtly negotiation, actually played out in his practical affairs. Finally, after a brief look at some general qualities of Donne's poetic diction and grammar, I turn to "Lovers infinitenesse" to illustrate how the two patterns of interaction figure in a poem.

The pragmatics of prayer

In an undated sermon *"Preached to the Nobility"* on Luke 23:34, Donne explicates Christ's utterance upon the cross, *"Father, forgive them, for they know not what they do*," as a pattern for Protestant prayer by means of an analogy to the courtly suitor's plea.[6] The complex working out of the analogy illuminates courtly communication as fully as it does prayer, and it makes apparent how the conditions for establishing and sustaining communication are always embedded in social and political relationships. As Donne asks his auditors to imagine the "outward Court" of a "goodly palace" (*Sermons*, vol. v, no. 12, p. 231) and the conditions for entry, it appears that the analogy will be worked out primarily by contrast, the direct access of prayer set against the highly mediated situation of courtly request. Entrance into prayer is regulated only by such axioms of easy and unrestricted approach as "*Ask and it shall be given*" and "*Knock and it shall be opened*" (p. 232). By contrast, in worldly princes' palaces, the access of most ordinary suitors is limited to negotiation through patrons and mediators, and even powerful nobles who are able to get past the guards and ushers and to bear up under the "examination of [their] degree or habit" (p. 234) are met with further exasperating hindrances:

> How much the favourites of Princes, and great personages labour, that they may be thought to have been in private conference with the Prince. And though they be forced to wait upon his purposes, and talk of what he will, how fain they would be thought to have solicited their own, or their Dependants businesse.
>
> (p. 232)

But in God's court (which may be in any chamber), every suitor has immediate access – "O my unworthy soule, thou are presently in the presence" (p. 234). Even a whisper gains an attentive hearing, with no barriers associated with the Prince's own business or leisure: "Here we may talk long, welcomely, of our own affaires, and be sure to speed" (p. 232). In Donne's description of this "easie" speech with God, the normal temporal sequencing of speech acts is suspended: "Before we call, he answers, and when we speak, he heares" (p. 233), and even the difference of persons in the dialogic exchange is collapsed: "it is the Holy Ghost it selfe that prays; and what can be denyed, where the Asker gives?" (p. 233).

Here the analogy begins to get more complicated, as if in recognition of a possible downside to this idealized simultaneity of demand and response. Suddenly, instead of prayer conceived as private communion, Christ's petition-making to the Father has for audience "that faithfull company of departed Saints" and the speech action of prayer recovers both the suspense of an unfolding situation and the pleasures of performance. The Saints "stand all attentive, to heare what thou wilt aske of this Father. And what shall they hear? what doest thou aske? *Forgive them*, forgive them?" (p. 235). The significance of the analogy is further complicated by the self-reflexive conditions of its performance, for it is important to remember that Donne is in the midst of his own performance, delivering a sermon preached "*to the Nobility*" (p. 231). It is very clear that Donne prized the performative dimension of linguistic exchange. Such an enjoyment is in keeping with an understanding of language as symbolic capital but it can pull against models Donne likes to promote of unhindered communion and reciprocal dialogue. In quite different circumstances in a letter to a friend (probably Sir Henry Goodyer in 1604), Donne promotes the mutual exchange of letters as the best conveyance "for knowledge, or love" and then, immediately, demands attention for *his* monologue, putting on hold the dialogic response of the other as he highlights his own performance: "Since then at this time, I am upon the stage, you may be content to hear me" (*Letters*, pp. 105, 107). Highlighting the performance moment in Christ's petition-making, Donne reintroduces an element of courtly ceremony into the ideal model of prayer.

Donne turns to his interpretation of Christ's language, based primarily on how grammar illuminates its speech action. Accenting the imperative form of the verb, he underlines the bold forcefulness of a demand to forgive "murderers" (p. 235) and characterizes the Son's as a direct and plain-speaking style. However, even as he applauds its unconstrained reasonableness, he begins to distinguish between Christ's direct style and a more self-limiting style of prayer it turns out is better suited to the "private man" (p. 236): "We must pray for our selvs *limitedly*, forgive us, as we forgive. But thou wilt have their forgivenes *illimited* and *unconditioned*" (p. 236, emphasis added). In the Son's language, there need be neither qualifications nor conditionals, yet the request is not thereby merely willful, since it is concluded with reason-giving: "He hath a *For*, for his Prayer: *Forgive them, for, &c.*" (p. 236). Reasonable and to-the-point though this speech style may be, Donne further distinguishes it from his recommended script for Protestant prayer: "he gave us a convenient scantling for our *fors*, who prayed, Give me enough, for I may else despair, give me not too much, for so I may presume" (p. 237). The auxiliary verb "must" associated with Christ's command imposes obligation while "I *may*" registers concern about permission. Surprisingly, Donne recuperates, as a suitably self-limiting model for prayer, something very like the courtly logic of deference, language that inscribes and displays the superior power of the interlocutor: while "Things absolutely good ... we may absolutely beg," with "mean and indifferent things, qualified by the circumstances, we must aske conditionally and referringly to the givers will" (p. 237). Interconnected with the competition between styles of reasoned plainness and social deference is a perplexing question Donne raises deriving from his reading of "Schoolmen" (that is, scholastic theologians) about whether prayer is an act "of our understanding" or "an act of our will" (p. 237). Ideally, understanding and will should be able to come together without problem in the reasoned action of prayer, but here they play interference with one another. Given the perfection of the Son's will and its unity with the Father's, understanding can take center stage in his exemplary speech act, but, given the imperfections of the human will, negotiation between the asker's and the giver's will must play a more prominent role and make plain speech problematic.

The syntax being recommended for human prayer is what the Renaissance called courtesy or civility and modern-day discourse analysis calls "negative politeness"[7]: strategic rhetorical maneuvering to avoid coercing or imposing upon the prerogative or actions of the superior and to avoid presumptions about the desires or willingness of the superior. Finally, the homiletic lesson of a sermon that begins by asserting the direct and unlimited access of prayer is how to curb, limit, and conform one's will in prayer to God's will. The physical obstacles to courtly access derided in the working out of the sermon's analogy may appear to be gone, but the praying subject has internalized the limitations in the self-censoring courtliness of his language. As a pattern for human prayer, Donne finally substitutes the Lord's prayer, the Church's prayer "*of Precept*" for Christ's "*Prayer of Example*" (p. 244). But his grammatical analysis makes clear that the pattern is also the Elizabethan and Jacobean courtesy language on which the Lord's Prayer in the vernacular – with its tropes of deference and humility – was molded, a power-inflected language of social negotiation caught up in the political arrangement of monarchical government and social hierarchy.

The performance of letters

Donne placed letters and poems on an equal footing when he explained why he loved to preach sermons on the Pauline epistles and the Psalms: "they are Scriptures, written in such forms, as I have been most accustomed to; Saint *Pauls* being Letters, and *Davids* being Poems" (*Sermons*, vol. II, no. 1, p. 49). I propose to interpret both letters and poems through the lens of analytical categories suggested by Donne's own sermon on prayer, beginning with two letters Donne writes in February 1602 to his father-in-law, Sir George More, after eloping with his daughter. In a first failed request for acceptance and assistance, despite his use of Henry Percy, ninth Earl of Northumberland as his messenger and mediator, Donne presents himself like the Son, trying out a style of plain speech and uncensored argumentation. This strategy misfires drastically, and helps to land him in prison. In a second letter, he grasps the need to bend his own petitioning will to the "giver's will" and employs, apparently to more favorable effect, the complicated and self-limiting courtly rhetoric of subordination and submission.

It is probably not a religious disposition but an intellectual's claim to rational discourse that makes for his bold approach after opening with a perfunctory deferential bow to More's displeasure as a condition joining with Donne's sickness to prevent personal access:

> If a very respective feare of your displeasure ... did not so much increase my sicknes as that I cannot stir, I had taken the boldnes to have donne the office of this letter by wayting upon yow myself to have given yow truthe and clearnes of this matter between your daughter and me, and to show yow plainly the limits of our fault, by which I know your wisdome wyll proportion the punishment.[8]

The sentence's insistent claim to plainness begins the letter's disastrous, though inadvertent, display of how the syntax of truth-telling can clash or conflict with the real-world demands of social negotiation. To begin one's plea in a high-risk speech act to a superior by putting into words a fore-knowledge of the other's judgments is not a strategy calculated to gain favor.

Donne proceeds with confidence to advance his Christ-like "for":

> The reasons why I did not foreacquaint yow with it (to deale with the same plainnes that I have usd) were these. I knew my present estate lesse than fitt for her, I knew (yet I knew not why) that I stood not right in your opinion. I knew that to have given any intimacion of yt had been to impossibilitate the whole matter.   (p. 113)

What is foregrounded here is the speaker's certitude in advancing his acts of "understanding," accented by the repetitive train of unqualified "I knew ... I knew ... I knew." As Dr. Donne also showed in the Son's prayer, the speaker does nothing to hedge his requests or qualify his assumptions: "No suspicion of ignorance, as there, (*If it be possible*)" (*Sermons*, vol. v, no. 12, p. 233), no "I worried that you might prevent it." Even if we can recognize Donne adopting a stylistic register justified in his own mind either by the scholar's conception of the ideal level playing field for argumentation or by a naïve view that his linguistic and intellectual capital are a fit match to social privilege, his repeated description of his style as "plainnes" must have an element of disingenuousness. The vociferous puritan advocates of a "plain style" would certainly not have recognized plainness in Donne, for Donne's plainness is virtually always crossed with performative virtuosity. In the poetry, the complex "metaphysical conceit," paradox, or wordplay are often its markers. Here we can recognize it in the choice of the rare and clever word, "impossibilitate," to highlight his plight. We can recognize it, furthermore, in his failure to resist the dangers of a pun at precisely the moment in the letter where he is making his riskiest assertion:

> I know this letter shall find yow full of passion; but I know no passion can alter your reason and wisdom, to which I adventure to commend these particulers; that *yt is irremediably donne* ... (p. 113, emphasis added)

Here Donne's rhetorical strategy challenges both of the chief principles of negative politeness. Not only does he presume to know how More feels and will respond ("I know this letter shall find yow full of passion"), but he makes it clear that his father-in-law is being coerced, that the speaker is limiting or has limited his possibilities for action ("yt is irremediably donne"). Not only is coercive insistence on the finality of the marriage a foolish strategy of social negotiation, but, when Donne writes, the legality of his marriage is potentially controversial, so that the absolute claim is as much bravado as truth-telling.

Unemployed and imprisoned in the Fleet nine days later, Donne writes more "limitedly," in this prayerful style of deference:

> And since we have no meanes to move God, when he wyll not hear our prayers, to hear them, but by prayeng, I humbly beseech yow to allow by his gracious example, my penitence so good entertainment, as yt may have a beeliefe and a pittie. Of nothinge in this one fault that I hear sayd to me, can I disculpe myselfe, but of the contemptuous and despightfull purpose towards yow, which I hear ys surmised against me. But for my dutifull regard to my late lady, for my religion, and for my lyfe, I refer my selfe to them that may have observed them. I humbly beseech yow to take off these waytes ... [9]

Beyond the obvious abjection of pleas cast as "I humbly beseech yow," Donne avoids any direct assumptions about his father-in-law's will or reactions. The mitigating auxiliary "may" replaces the "shall" of his first letter to qualify any assumption about reception: he merely prays his penitence "may have a beeliefe and a pittie." Gone is the self-certain "I know" that served for a whole range of knowledge claims, replaced by highly attenuated expressions like "I hear sayd to me," which position him merely as the recipient of uncertain information which must be confirmed by others. Replacing "irremediably donne," his apparent reference to his wife as "my late lady"[10] defers to Sir George More's construction of the illegitimacy of the marriage, and the same sentence configures even knowledge of his own "dutifull regard" for lady, religion, and life as unascertainable without the confirmation of hypothetical others: "I refer my selfe to them that may have observed them." Modal auxiliaries in the letter highlight the necessity of permission-granting by the other ("may") and the incapacity of the self ("I can present nothing.") In a final transformation of his former "I know" into "as you will," Donne transfers the trait of foreknowledge to his addressee: "I can present nothing to your thoughts which yow knew not before, but my submission, my repentance, and my harty desire to do any thing satisfactory to your just displeasure" (p. 115).

Thus, whether imagining spiritual communion or negotiating worldly affairs, Donne oscillates between two conceptions of linguistic action: as disputation or as courtship. Undecided whether prayer should be construed primarily as an act of "understanding" or as an act of "will," he also wavers at a critical moment in his life between approaching his irate father-in-law by means of logical appeal or by means of social (and power) negotiation. One of the remarkable qualities of Donne's poetic language, as we shall see later in this essay, is the intermingling of these two registers.

"*Sinewes* even in thy *milke*": grammatical Donne

Before turning to the competition between dialectical reasoning and social dialogue at work in the poetry, it is necessary to emphasize the importance of small words in Donne's poems. In reading Donne, special attention needs to be given to the monosyllables: to conjunctions like "if," "yet," "but," and "for," which mark off reasoning operations; to pronouns like "thou," "ours," "they," and "I" and to other indexical words like "here," "there," "now," and "then," which situate discourse and speaker subjectivity within social and spatial relations; and to auxiliary verbs, especially those like "shall," "would," "can," "must," and "may," which – as we shall see – play a role both in reasoning and social negotiation. Only very occasionally in his poetry does Donne highlight long, flashy lexical words like "impossibilitate," the rare verb vaunted at the climax of the first letter discussed above. Anyone looking for picturesque poetic diction will not find it in such characteristic lines as

(1) They are ours, though they are not wee, wee are ("The Extasie," 51)
(2) When thou knew'st what I dreamt, when thou knew'st when ("The Dreame," 17)
(3) If they were good it would be seene ("Communitie," 13)
(4) For the great soule which here amongst us now ("*Metempsychosis*: The Progresse of the Soule," 61)
(5) So though some have, some may some Psalmes translate ("Upon the translation of the Psalmes," 49)

However pared down their diction, these lines are not unornamented. Together with the monosyllables, one finds rhetorical figures. Apart from metaphor and simile, one finds especially those figures known as schemes of repetition and word order. Illustrated in the lines quoted are *epanalepsis*, a scheme repeating a word at beginning and end of line or clause ("when" repetition in example 2); *anadiplosis*, a scheme repeating a word ending one clause at the start of the next ("wee" in example 1); *antimetabole*, repeating words in converse order ("are" and "wee" in example 1); and more generally, *ploce*, word repetition with intervening words ("some" in example 5). Surprisingly, what the rhetorical schemes of repetition set on display are not – as in many other poets – the lexical nouns but instead the small words and grammatical particles. Thus, Donne's rhetoric accents seemingly inconsequential words and grammatical operators.

Donne is more a poet of grammar and syntax than he is a poet of diction. In a period in which the lexicon of early modern English is expanding at an extraordinarily rapid rate and when literary works like Shakespeare's *Love's Labour's Lost* are calling attention to new, rare, and long words, Donne seldom makes word choices that are calculated to impress in such a way. Whereas Shakespeare heightens his language and achieves some of his admired effects with complicated noun phrases, involving modifiers, qualifiers or both, such as "The deep damnation of his taking-off" (*Macbeth* I.vii.20),[11] "My speculative and officed instruments" (*Othello* I.iii.269), or "the pangs of barred affections" (*Cymbeline* I.i.83), Donne has a strong preference for uncluttered nouns, or adjectives coming rather singly than in battalions. He praises God's language, in the *Devotions*, for having "such *things* in thy *words*" (p. 113). His own simple nominal phrases throw the nouns into stark relief, as if granting concrete "thingness" even to abstractions. His habitual wordplay, however, playing brilliantly upon the fluidity of unstandardized early modern English, makes it clear that he is in no danger of mistaking words for things.

Given Donne's stylistic range, it is easy to find exceptions. "Like Proserpine's white beauty-keeping chest" (the elegy "The Comparison" beginning "As the sweet sweat," 23), for example, might be a line from Shakespeare's *Venus and Adonis* or *The Rape of Lucrece*. That, however, is because Shakespeare's early poems participate in precisely the conventions of poetic diction and comparison that Donne is parodying in the diction and "odious" comparisons of this elegy. Other poems in which Donne deliberately mocks linguistic fashion show that he is attuned to voguish diction. Describing a foolish courtier's language (as well as his clothes), the speaker in "Satyre IV" comments on how his "Velvet" has become "Tufftaffatie" (32–33) and how his macaronic style incorporates "Mountebankes drugtongue" (41). But even more striking is Donne's parody of the courtier's faddish grammar, especially his possessive pronouns:

> He smack'd, and cry'd, He's base, Mechanique, coarse,
> So are all *your* Englishmen in their discourse.

Are not *your* Frenchmen neate? *Mine?* as you see,
I have but one Frenchman, looke, hee followes mee.

(81–84, emphasis added)

In the *Devotions*, Donne identifies as exemplary not only the "things" in God's words but also the "*sinewes* even in thy *milke*" (p. 113), a trait replicated in the strong grammatical sinews of Donne's poetry. Why, when poets like Spenser and Shakespeare are celebrating the rapidly expanding lexicon as a marker of the coming of age of the English vernacular, does Donne focus on its grammar? Sir Philip Sidney, in his *Defence of Poesie*, goes so far as to applaud the fact that English grammar can be ignored: "for grammar it might have, but it needs it not, being so easy in itself, and so void of those cumbersome differences of cases, genders, moods, and tenses, which I think was a piece of the Tower of Babylon's curse."[12] Donne's focus on grammatical analysis in his sermon on prayer may yield a clue. Creative though this may seem now, it was in line with the "literal" method of interpretation in biblical exegesis, practiced not only by the medieval scholastic theologians Donne studied but also by the reforming Protestants newly insistent upon the literal meaning of God's word. Brian Cummings has recently called attention to the grammatical culture of learning over this long period in which grammar remained a corner-stone of an education system based on the *trivium*, three interdependent disciplines with logic and rhetoric building upon Latin grammar. Grammar figured large in medieval theology, but, as Cummings makes clear, the Reformation made grammatical study newly controversial and significant in sixteenth-century Europe. It meant comparing the Latin Vulgate with the original Hebrew and Greek of scripture, and it meant translating the Bible into vernacular languages. These activities highlighted intractable differences among languages and cast into doubt the universality of grammatical categories derived from Latin.[13] Donne's sermons repeatedly treat these differences, as in discussing verb tenses in his Second Prebend Sermon: "That language in which God spake to man, the Hebrew, hath no present tense; They forme not their verbs as our Westerne Languages do, in the present, *I heare*, or *I see*, or *I reade*, But they begin at that which is past, *I have seene* and *heard*, and *read*" (*Sermons*, vol. VII, no. 1, p. 62). In such circumstances, English grammar and, especially, the bewildering array of auxiliary verbs developing in early modern English to take the place of inflected forms for Latin verbs, did matter. It is generally accepted that Donne's religious sensibility informs the imagery and metaphors of the *Songs and Sonets*, with their saints canonized for love, their disputes about air and angels, and the mysticism of out-of-body "extasies." It is also important to recognize that his theological studies encouraged the strong grammatical accent of Donne's poetic eloquence.

Knowledge and power: the example of "Lovers infinitenesse"

The knowledge/power or intellectual/courtly opposition so evident in Donne's sermons and letters is also apparent in "Lovers infinitenesse," a poem that may seem inconsequential insofar as it is built up out of small words and grammatical dilemmas. The logical register – the poetic act cast as an act of "understanding" – is certainly in the foreground in the opening movements of "Lovers infiniteness." The social register enters insofar as the poem, like most of Donne's, announces itself by means of the address term "Deare" and the pronoun "thou" as addressed in a particular situation to another person:

> If yet I have not all thy love,
> Deare, I shall never have it all,
> I cannot breath one other sigh, to move,
> Nor can intreat one other teare to fall,
> And all my treasure, which should purchase thee,
> Sighs, teares, and oathes, and letters I have spent.
> Yet no more can be due to mee,
> Then at the bargaine made was ment,
> If then thy gift of love were partiall,
> That some to mee, some should to others fall,
>   Deare, I shall never have Thee All.   (1–11)

But the overall logical apparatus of "If ... then" hypotheses, with developing arguments and sub-arguments signaled by such markers as "Yet," "Or if," "But if," "For," "And yet," mutes the language of social negotiation, surprisingly, given that the poem responds to the beloved's gift or vow of her love to him. The speaker also casts his current manner of self-expression in contrast to Petrarchanism, representing his capital or store of conventional poetic love persuasions as exhausted or "spent" and avoiding picturesque diction and comparisons. Instead of sensual or pictorial diction, the poem is built on a base of "small" words. Of thirty-three lines, ten consist only of monosyllables, fourteen consist of monosyllables plus one dissyllabic word, and five of monosyllables plus two dissyllabic words. Only four lines contain single words as long as three syllables: "partiall" (9), "generall" (20), "liberall" (31), and "anothers" (33). The first three we would expect to be pronounced as dissyllables. But the metrical scheme stretches them out to three syllables, as if it were Procrustes' bed, supplying stress to a first and third syllable. By this means and their symmetrical placement in each stanza, Donne positions "partiall," "generall," and "liberall" as key words. Even then, these terms are made to chime with the theme word "All" that finishes each stanza, so that the polysyllable calls attention to the monosyllable, intensifying the focus on the speaker's preoccupation with having her "all."

The speaker reasons himself in and out of a series of logical dilemmas that are, in essence, grammatical dilemmas. Brian Cummings explains how Donne's expositions of Scripture in the sermons struggle with the ways "'Gods grammer' plays havoc with human tenses" (*Literary Culture*, p. 414), for, as Donne puts it, "God himself is eternall and cannot bee considered in the distinction of times" (*Sermons*, vol. IX, no. 15, p. 335). In contrast, the speaker of this poem subjects his beloved's vow to "the distinction of times," getting himself tangled in convoluted word order as he queries how a vow in the past tense can stand up to present and future:

> Or if then thou *gavest* mee all,
> All *was* but All, which thou *hadst* then;
> But if in thy heart, since, there *be* or *shall*,
> New love *created bee* . . .
> This new love was not vowed by thee.
> (12–15, 18, emphasis added)

Later the speaker broods over a dilemma related to grammatical "aspect" (that is, perfect versus progressive verbal action), when he worries that the gift of love, as a completed action, cannot also be ongoing:

> Thou canst not every day give me thy heart,
> If thou canst give it, then thou never gavest it. (27–28)

As the speaker perseveres in this register of reasoned knowledge, the reader can hardly avoid protesting – as Sir George More may well have protested when the Earl of Northumberland delivered Donne's letter – that his subject matter and his manner are ill-matched. The logical disquisition seems to make this a very unsociable poem about love. The speaker's focus is almost entirely on his *taking* and the supposed limitations of her *giving*, with his seemingly exhaustive logical analysis blinding him to his own failure – if he must reason according to this commercial arithmetic of exchange – to calculate the return *she* should expect on her investment. Reaching towards resolution, the final stanza shifts registers. Paradox counterbalances logic:

> Loves riddles are, that though thy heart depart,
> It stayes at home, and thou with losing savest it: (29–30)

Thus, a new economy echoing scripture is posited in which giving is, at the same time, keeping. The poem seems resolved, with a means found for continuous giving. But Donne discards this potential resolution, proffering one last "But":

> But wee will have a way more liberall,
> Then changing hearts, to joyne them, so wee shall
> Be one, and one anothers All. (31–33)

Although fusion or becoming "one" is a favorite or "master-image" for Donne, it may not be immediately clear why the speaker prefers the joining of hearts to the paradoxical exchange of hearts. Donne's subtle pun on "*changing* hearts" may explain the shift. It seems to imply that "changing" hearts – in the expected sense of *ex*changing hearts – is co-extensive with the problem of *change* – and those problems the temporal logic of the vernacular runs up against in its imbrication with grammatical verb tense and aspect. Apparently, the poem rejects the logic of the market together with the one-sided acquisitiveness that seems insistently to get caught up in calculations of "exchange," however reciprocal and interactive the commercially laden concept of "exchange" may initially sound. Ostensibly, joining does away with the "I" and "thou," putting the lovers as "wee" on the same footing and suggesting some such "dialogue of one" as is anatomized in "The Extasie." Yet a look at the poem's modal auxiliary verbs will give a different picture of the power relations.

Our close reading of linguistic detail in Donne's sermon and letters suggests that the knowledge/power antithesis is strongly evident in his use of grammatical modality and especially in the modal auxiliary verbs that are also extremely prominent in his poems. Modal auxiliary verbs such as *can / could, may / might, (mot) / must, shall / should,* and *will / would* serve in early modern English to help express a speaker's subjectivity by registering opinion or attitude in relation to a proposition or statement. Based on a group of main or lexical verbs from Old English, a gradually developing set of auxiliary verbs with modal characteristics culminated in early modern English in a system with a curiously double register of meanings. Modern-day linguists have distinguished *epistemic* modality, concerned with gradations of knowledge or belief about the truth of propositions, from *deontic* modality, concerned with duty, obligation, and permission.[14] Thus, depending on context, a speaker saying "he *may* come tomorrow" could be articulating as possible rather than certain his or her reasoned prediction (epistemic) or exercising his or her power to grant permission (deontic). Disputes in Reformation theology are closely caught up with the baffling overlap between these two uses for one system of auxiliary verbs, for "will" and "must" in biblical translations can, for example, leave entirely open the critical matter of whether God's foreknowledge (epistemic) or predestination (deontic) is at issue (Cummings, *Literary Culture*, p. 217). Roughly speaking, epistemic modality maps onto logical operations, Donne's acts of "understanding," whereas deontic modality maps onto social negotiations of power, Donne's acts of "will."

In "Lovers infinitenesse," Donne sets in motion a whole train of modal auxiliaries: "I *shall* never have" (2); "no more *can* be due to mee" (7); "I *shall* never have Thee All" (11); "This new love *may* beget" (18); "what ever shall / Grow there ... I *should* have it all" (21–22, emphasis added). As the first two stanzas unfold, the modals reinforce the discourse of knowledge, and when the speaker claims that his beloved's gift "being generall," he "*should*" have all the love growing there (lines 20–22), the reader is encouraged to interpret his modal auxiliary as epistemic. But the ambiguity of grammatical modality catches up with Donne's speaker. Having predicted as probable his own future possession of the beloved's "all," the speaker does a surprising and seemingly contradictory about-turn:

> Yet I *would* not have all yet,
> Hee that hath all can have no more,
> And since my love doth every day admit
> New growth, thou *shouldst* have new rewards in store;
>
> (23–26, emphasis added)

Suddenly, knowledge discourse gives way to power discourse. This is not about logic. This is about what the speaker *wants* and how she is *obliged* to satisfy his will. In a reversal of the power relations in prayer, where a man must defer, what is quietly unleashed is the speaker's verbal performance of control and mastery. A will to power has been masquerading as a show of knowledge, and the modal auxiliary verbs – with their double register – collude in the masquerade. To get at the gender politics of Donne's love poetry, it helps to focus on the doubleness or grammatical punning between discourses of knowledge and power that happens in "small words" like the modal auxiliaries. It is hard not to read the virtuoso linguistic performance that resolves the poem, ostensibly dissolving the differences of the "I" and "thou" into a mutual "wee," as itself a further assertion of masculine control.[15]

Though devoid of the startling comparisons that are definitely among Donne's trademark figures, this grammatical poem, with its competition between early modern dialogue scripts for reasoning and social negotiation, takes us to the heart of important qualities of Donne's poetic language. We can see how deeply ingrained are its habits of language if we look briefly at how they resurface in the preoccupations of one of Donne's later divine poems, "A Hymne to Christ, at the Authors last going into Germany":

> In winter, in my winter now I goe,
> Where none but thee, th'Eternall root
> Of true Love I may know.

Nor thou nor thy religion dost controule,
The amorousnesse of an harmonious Soule,
But thou would'st have that love thy selfe: As thou
Art jealous, Lord, so I am jealous now,
Thou lov'st not, till from loving more, thou free
My soule: Who ever gives, takes libertie:
    O, if thou car'st not whom I love
        Alas, thou lov'st not mee.   (14–24)

Here, again, we have the arithmetic and the logic of love's gift interrupted by puns and paradox. Reversing the logic of "Lovers infiniteness," the speaker calls upon God for limits to be placed on the growth of his loving. Donne's secular poem may pun on his wife's name as the speaker complains, "Hee that hath all can have no *more*" (24, emphasis added). The hymn certainly puns on Anne More's maiden name where the speaker prays, as a proof of God's love – so that "I may know" "th'Eternall root / Of true Love" (15–16) – to be freed from "loving more" (21). The hymn's almost perverse paradoxical reasoning – "Who ever gives, takes libertie" (22) – reverses the demand in "Lovers infinitenesse" to be endlessly given to. But, just as in "Lovers infinitenesse," the rational undertaking to establish proof of love becomes entangled in a struggle of will that casts the protagonists in a competition for control. God is not exempt from participation in this contest of will. First, sedately, the speaker – having some sense that love needs to be freely given, unconstrained – claims that God is not controlling: "Nor thou nor thy religion dost controule, / The amorousnesse of an harmonious Soule" (17–18). It is once again the modal auxiliary verb in the next line that draws God into the position of willful control occupied by the speaker of the secular love poem: "But thou *would'st* have that love thy selfe: As thou / Art jealous, Lord, so I am jealous now" (19–20, emphasis added).

Thus, Donne's language across many genres wrestles with and plays upon an ambiguous relation between the discourse of knowledge and the discourse of power. No one can fully explain why linguistic change happens as it does, delivering at any one time competing forms for some uses and competing uses for some forms. Present-day linguists claim that there is no necessary or special connection between epistemic modality and deontic modality, the competing uses of modal auxiliary verbs still present in English today. Nonetheless, when linguistic formations of this sort take shape, it is critical to consider the extent to which they become embedded in social, political, or religious arrangements of the time, the ways in which they are evaluated by language users and their addressees in ordinary life, and their potential for artistic expression. Donne's performances in language – with their jostling registers – offer us some dramatic insight.

NOTES

1 Bald, *Donne*, pp. 134–35, 126, 121–22, and 491–94.
2 John Carey's term in *Donne*, p. 3.
3 The heyday of criticism on Donne's language was the early and mid-twentieth century, with the New Criticism following upon key statements by Samuel Johnson, Samuel Taylor Coleridge, Sir Herbert Grierson, T. S. Eliot, and Cleanth Brooks. The advent of New Historicism has resulted in a relative hiatus in language-oriented discussion since about 1985. For selected criticism, see such older anthologies as Arthur L. Clements, ed., *John Donne's Poetry*, A Norton Critical Edition, 2nd edn. (New York: W. W. Norton, 1992), and John R. Roberts, *Essential Articles for the Study of John Donne's Poetry* (Hamden, CT: Archon Books, 1975).
4 Arthur F. Marotti's important study, *John Donne, Coterie Poet* (Madison: University of Wisconsin Press, 1986), led the way in reading Donne's poetry in relation to the social, political, and economic contexts of his time.
5 Pierre Bourdieu, "The Economics of Linguistic Exchanges," trans. Richard Nice, *Social Science Information* 16 (1977), 645–68, at 648.
6 *Sermons*, vol. v, no. 12, pp. 231–44. Notable studies of the relation between Renaissance courtship and prayer or divine poetry include Michael Schoenfeldt, *Prayer and Power: George Herbert and Renaissance Courtship* (Chicago: University of Chicago Press, 1991) and Richard Strier, *Love Known: Theology and Experience in George Herbert's Poetry* (Chicago: University of Chicago Press, 1983). Paul Stevens discusses Donne's conflicted attitudes to courtship and direct access in "Donne's Catholicism and the Innovation of the Modern Nation State," *JDJ* 20 (2001), 53–70.
7 Penelope Brown and Stephen C. Levinson, *Politeness: Some Universals in Language Usage* (Cambridge: Cambridge University Press, 1987), p. 70.
8 John Donne to Sir George More, February 2, 1602, in *John Donne, Selected Prose*, chosen by Evelyn Simpson, ed. Helen Gardner and Timothy Healy (Oxford: Clarendon Press, 1967), pp. 112–14 (p. 112–13).
9 John Donne to Sir George More, February 11, 1602, in *Selected Prose*, pp. 114–15 (p. 114).
10 Alternatively, the phrase could refer to Anne More's deceased aunt, Sir Thomas Egerton's second wife, born Elizabeth More, if Donne had heard of some ill report questioning his respect for her.
11 Shakespeare's works are quoted from *The Norton Shakespeare*, gen. ed. Stephen Greenblatt (New York: W. W. Norton and Company, 1997).
12 *A Defence of Poetry*, ed. J. A. Van Dorsten (Oxford: Oxford University Press, 1966), p. 72.
13 Brian Cummings, *The Literary Culture of the Reformation: Grammar and Grace* (Oxford: Oxford University Press, 2002), pp. 20–23.
14 Matti Rissanen, "Syntax," in *The Cambridge History of the English Language*, Volume III 1476–1776, ed. Roger Lass (Cambridge: Cambridge University

Press, 1999), pp. 187–331 (pp. 231–38); John Lyons, *Semantics*, 2 vols. (Cambridge: Cambridge University Press, 1977), vol. II, pp. 787–849; F. R. Palmer, *Mood and Modality* (Cambridge: Cambridge University Press, 1986), esp. pp. 51 and 96.

15 For an analysis of the language of male mastery and control in Donne's elegies, see Achsah Guibbory, "The Politics of Love in Donne's *Elegies*," *ELH* 57 (1990), 811–33.

13

ILONA BELL

Gender matters: the women in Donne's poems

For Donne as for us, gender matters, deeply, passionately, disturbingly. Donne is constantly writing about women and gender roles, both explicitly and indirectly through analogy and metaphor. Yet unlike his immediate predecessors and contemporaries, Sidney, Spenser, and Shakespeare, Donne rarely lingers over the woman's physical appearance. For this and other more theoretical or ideological reasons, twentieth-century critics generally assume that the woman in Donne's poems is a shadowy figure, the object or reflection of male desire, a pretext for self-fashioning, a metaphor for the poet's professional aspirations, a sex object to be circulated for the titillation and amusement of Donne's male coterie. In the last two decades, as feminist critics have re-examined Donne's attitudes towards women, it has become clear that it was not Donne but the critics who disembodied and disregarded the women in Donne's poems.

Donne has been termed many things: a misogynist who loathed women's bodies and scorned their minds; a metaphysician less interested in emotion than intellection; an egotist and careerist who used women for his own advantage; a wit willing to say anything for the sake of the poem or a rhetorician undone by his own verbal power; and a poet/lover (I wish to stress) who was supremely attentive to the woman's point of view.[1] Donne's poetry and prose contain such a wide variety of genres, viewpoints, and personae, his language is so enigmatic and metaphorical, his attitudes towards women shift so quickly, sometimes within a single poem or line, that it is difficult to say exactly what Donne himself thought, all but impossible to identify an abiding or systematic view of women or gender.

Donne's poetry is obsessed with women. It both echoes and challenges the gender stereotypes of his day. Some of the *Elegies* and *Songs and Sonnets* mock or disparage women as deceitful, inconstant, ugly, or irrational: "Hope not for minde in women" ("Loves Alchymie," 23). Other poems delight in women for their emotional, intellectual, and spiritual vitality: "all my soules bee, / Emparadis'd in you, (in whom alone / I understand, and grow and see)" ("A Valediction: of my name, in the window," 25–27). Donne wooed a number of women in poetry, first as sexual partners and later as patrons, but he loved one woman, Anne More, abidingly and over-whelmingly. By eloping with her, Donne may also have hoped to improve his social, professional, and economic situation. Unfortunately, the marriage infuriated her father, Sir George More, alienated her uncle and Donne's boss, Sir Thomas Egerton, and ruined Donne's career as a lawyer and civil servant.

Some critics argue that because Renaissance love poetry is monologic, because the male poet/lover formulates and speaks the words, he inevit-ably subordinates the woman to his "masculine persuasive force."[2] Stanley Fish has argued that Donne was his own most important and discrimin-ating reader, and indeed Donne often seems to be thinking to himself, moving from one dazzling, dissolving formulation to another: "Our two soules, therefore, which are one ... If they be two, they are two so" ("A Valediction: forbidding mourning," 21–25). Yet even when Donne seems to be exploring his own thoughts as a poem unfolds, he is usually engaged in a dialogue with the person whom the poem addresses: a male friend, a female patron, a lover, God, posterity.[3] In the Latin epitaph written upon his wife's death, Donne describes her as the most important subject and reader of his poems, and it is my belief that many of his love poems were written to and for her.[4]

Most of Donne's poems circulated in manuscript, remaining within Donne's private circle for years after they were written and not appearing in print until after Donne's death. Reading the poems today in an anthology or a collection of Donne's poetry, we may forget that we are eavesdropping on one side of a conversation that was both deeply private and culturally situated, both permeated with personal allusions and imbued with society's norms and expectations.

Donne's attitude toward women and gender roles varies considerably, depending on the audience the poem envisions and the situation it inherits, comprises, or seeks to bring about. Some of Donne's poems are verse letters sent to a friend or patron knowledgeable and astute enough to understand Donne's difficult language and veiled meaning: "darke texts need notes." In praising the Countess of Bedford for her "Vertue, Art, Beauty, Fortune," Donne invites her judgment and support of his poetry: "These are *Petitions*, and not *Hymnes*" ("MADAME, You have refin'd mee," 11, 2, 33).

Some of the elegies and lyrics are also epistolary, but most are dramatic, colloquial, conversational; they sound as if they were written to be recited or read aloud by Donne himself, and most likely they were. A few, addressed to a male peer, answer objections – "For Godsake hold your tongue, and let me love" ("The Canonization," 1) – or invite a knowing chuckle: "Thou, when thou retorn'st, wilt tell mee … No where / Lives a woman true, and faire" ("Song: Goe, and catche," 14, 17–18). But most seek to entertain, converse with, and yes, even seduce, a mistress: "Enter these armes, for since thou thoughtst it best, / Not to dreame all my dreame, let's act the rest" ("The Dreame," 9–10). Some of Donne's most intriguing and challenging poems support multiple, contradictory interpretations, meaning one thing to his mistress, something quite different to "prophane men … Which will no faith on this bestow, / Or, if they doe, deride" ("The undertaking," 22–24).[5]

Most of Donne's poems are not only designed for a particular occasion and audience or audiences but also for a specific genre which had its own set of rules known both to the poet and his readers. The epigrams, among Donne's earliest poems, provide a useful introduction to gender matters because, according to literary convention, the epigrammatic poet speaks in his own voice, addressing the world he both critiques and inhabits.[6]

"A selfe accuser," a pithy hexameter couplet, describes a mistress who chides her lover for following whores:

> Your mistris, that you follow whores, still taxeth you:
> 'Tis strange that she should thus confesse it, though'it be true.

Donne satirizes the man for failing to confront the infidelity they both pretend to conceal. He also implies that the woman's relentless nagging is driving her husband or lover to visit whores. The final epigrammatic twist further hints that she may herself be a floozy and a hypocrite. "*Klockius*" makes a similar point:

> *Klockius* so deeply hath sworne, ne'er more to come
> In bawdie house, that hee dares not goe home.

Klockius has sworn off whores only to discover – as we ourselves discover in the witty epigrammatic turn – that his own home is little better than a bawdy house.

Donne's epigrams play with words, but in a poem as in life, play can have serious consequences:

> Thy sinnes and haires may no man equall call,
> For, as thy sinnes increase, thy haires doe fall.
> ("A licentious person")

The absurd mathematical ratio, combined with the wordplay on hair, heirs, and (less exactly) whores, exposes the miscalculations that give the licentious man venereal disease, threatening his life and heirs.

According to literary convention, the epigram gives us direct access to the author's own views, so what, if anything, do these epigrams reveal about Donne's attitude toward women and gender? Who is the licentious person, the man or the woman? Who is being mocked, Klockius or his mistress? Is Donne affirming the conventional code of ethics, preaching chastity and marital fidelity? Is he endorsing antifeminist stereotypes that scorn women as shrewish, deceitful, and inconstant? Perhaps, but I doubt it, for these men are no less contemptible than the women. Donne's epigrams satirize individuals like Klockius or types like "A licentious person," but they do *not* generalize about men or women.

The epigrams invite us to measure these sketchy characters against clandestine lovers whose daring and devotion triumph over the death they incur:

> Both rob'd of aire, we both lye in one ground,
> Both whom one fire had burnt, one water drownd.
>
> ("*Hero and Leander*")

> Two, by themselves, each other, love and feare
> Slaine, cruell friends, by parting have joyn'd here.
>
> ("*Pyramus and Thisbe*")

The plural nouns and pronouns, the interactive diction, and densely interwoven syntax celebrate the mutuality of love which turns "both" into "one," or which presents "two" paradoxically "joyn'd" by their "parting." As these miniature love stories show, even the briefest of poems and loves can achieve abiding value, drawing the lovers together first in life, then in death, and finally in poetry and myth.

As a group, the epigrams show Donne immersed in London life with its sexual temptations and sexually transmitted diseases, its vanity and self-deceptions, its antagonisms and greed; but they also show him living in a world of books where timeless truths trump earthly failings. While the first three epigrams satirize men and women who delude themselves even more than they deceive each other, the last two eternize lovers so involved in each other that whatever they do "by themselves" has an immediate impact on "each other." Even as Donne's satiric, worldly wit impresses and amuses his male coterie, his incisive intellect and moral severity mocks those who are too dull or complacent to recognize and root out the lies, the self-deception, and corruption that propel their sleazy lives. Donne himself stands above it all, implying that *his* mistress is or will be a very different sort of woman, and that *his* love, when he chooses to express it, will be a very different sort of love, one that he is prepared to fight for against all odds.

Like the epigrams, the *Satires* also show Donne deeply immersed in city life, negotiating the allures of sex, money, and power. Surprisingly, it is "Satyre III," the search for the one true church, that makes the clearest declarations about women and gender.[7] "Satyre III" presents ascertainable truths about women as a way of discovering less easily ascertainable truths about the church: "but unmoved thou / Of force must one, and forc'd but one allow" (69–70). The poem never determines the one true Church, but on two key points about women it leaves no room for ambiguity or doubt. First, it asserts that finding the one true mistress is vitally and undeniably important. Second, it declares that it is stupid and morally wrong to generalize about all women on the basis of particular women. "Carelesse Phrygius" is satirized because he "doth abhorre / All, because all cannot be good, as one / Knowing some women whores, dares marry none" (62–64). Graccus makes the opposite decision, but he is also mocked for failing to make distinctions among women: "Graccus loves all as one, and thinkes that so / As women do in divers countries goe / In divers habits, yet are still one kinde" (65–67). By foolishly assuming all women are the same, Graccus shows himself to be both intellectually unsophisticated and morally undiscriminating.

Written in the 1590s when Donne was studying at the Inns of Court or working for Sir Thomas Egerton, the *Elegies*, like the *Satires*, represent Donne as an upwardly mobile but principled lawyer and civil servant, a seductive and persuasive lover, and an increasingly authoritative poet. Some of the *Elegies* express revulsion for the female body: a "grave, that's dust without, and stinke within." Others revel in intimacy or sexual pleasure that contains its own spiritual glory and intellectual joy: "Here take my Picture; though I bid farewell, / Thine, in my heart, where my soule dwels, shall dwell."[8]

"The Comparison" is entirely devoted to making distinctions, not between one kind of woman and another, but between one particular woman and another: "As the Almighty Balme of th'early East, / Such are the sweat drops of my Mistris breast ... Ranke sweaty froth thy Mistresse's brow defiles, / Like spermatique issue of ripe menstruous boiles" (3–4, 7–8). No doubt Donne's male coterie found this gross physicality amusing. No doubt some men, and even some women, still find it amusing, but ultimately Donne's language is less playful than unsettling.

Although the two women are alike in having female bodies, the poem, and especially the conclusion, draws important distinctions between them. The friend apparently chose his mistress for one reason: sex. Ironically, the friend's single-minded pursuit deprives him of pleasure: his "last act," the sex act, is "harsh, and violent, / As when a Plough a stony ground doth rent" (47–48). Because he thrusts himself into his mistress without first preparing the ground, intercourse is aggressive and laborious. The descriptions of Donne's mistress are also grounded in the flesh, in sexuality that joins spirituality with its own earthy purposes. Donne's imagery demystifies his mistress by comparing her to "th'earths worthlesse durt" (37) but it also elevates her by comparing her to Christ's body and blood:

> So kisse good Turtles, so devoutly nice
> Are Priests in handling reverent sacrifice,
> And such in searching wounds the Surgeon is,
> As wee, when wee embrace, or touch, or kisse.   (49–52)

Since these surgical wounds recall the "ripe menstruous boils" marring the friend's mistress, conflating face and genitals, Achsah Guibbory concludes that Donne's loathing for the female body extends to his own mistress, and betrays a misogyny that pervades the *Elegies* as a whole. And so it may.[9] But I think the poem invites discriminations rather than generalizations, discriminations that yield an enlightening, non-judgmental account of explorative, reciprocal sexuality.

Unlike the friend's rough and unsatisfying copulation, Donne and his mistress share the tender kisses of turtle doves, the reverence and delicacy of a priest handling Christ's body and blood, and the openness of a surgeon, ready to explore the body with a beneficent, knowing touch. Whereas the friend feels revulsion "as a worme sucking an invenom'd sore" (44), Donne and his mistress explore each other's anatomy with a clinical gaze and careful touch, like a surgeon examining a wound without disgust. Donne doesn't quite say where they "touch, or kisse" (52), but the image of the wound evokes the body's apertures, suggesting not only French kisses but also oral sex and genital foreplay.[10] As Katherine Park has demonstrated, this was the period when the rediscovery of the clitoris placed renewed emphasis on women's capacity to reach orgasm, which explains why, her passion being equal to his, the "best lov'd part" (38) is the female sexual part, filled with the heat of Donne's "masculine equall fire" (35). For Donne and his mistress, love-making, replete with touches and kisses on mouth and genitals, is reciprocal, attentive, and highly pleasurable.

Since "The Comparison" is addressed to a specific lyric audience, Donne's male friend, it places us in the position of eavesdroppers. Regardless of which perspective we take, the poem invites us to join the debate. Since Donne attacked first, he is morally culpable if the poem initiates a cycle of degrading attacks against women. If all the friend hears is criticism of his mistress, he may respond with a counterattack on Donne's mistress. But if the poem provokes Donne's interlocutor and us to think more seriously about what constitutes sexual attraction and how sexual and spiritual bliss merge, then it serves a more positive and far-reaching rhetorical purpose.

"The Comparison" explores the subjectivity of desire, the difference of opinion that makes one man's desire another man's loathing. Nasty as some of its similes are, "The Comparison" urges its lyric audience not to construe Womankind in the abstract but to look closely at each woman in all her specificity and corporeality. Making distinctions between one woman and another or one love affair and another – between rough, aggressive copulation and reciprocal, tender love-making – not only questions antifeminist stereotypes that condemn all women as shrews and whores; it also questions social norms that divide women into angels and whores. As I read the poem, Donne's mistress is laudable and loveable precisely because she is sexually active and emotionally responsive.

In the elegy beginning "Who ever loves" (commonly known as "Loves Progress") the speaker argues that the "right true end of love" (2) is not idealized, unrequited Petrarchan desire or Neoplatonic heavenly beauty but sexual consummation:

> Can men more injure women then to say
> They love them for that, by which they're not they?
> Makes virtue woman? must I cool my bloud
> Till I both be, and find one woman wise and good?
> May barren Angels love so. But if we
> Make love to woman; virtue is not she:
> As beauty'is not nor wealth. (19–25)

Petrarchan poets exalt the beloved as a heavenly, angelic creature with hair like gold and skin like alabaster, forever adored and forever unattainable. In seeking a wife, Donne argues, men are more likely to measure a woman's worth by her beauty and wealth. Yet contrary to poetic and social convention, Donne argues that it is "the Centrique part" (36), the sexual part, that makes women, women. From one point of view, this is critical and demeaning to women, reducing them to sex objects, or commodities to be traded among men. From another point of view, it is a matter of fact – or biology. From yet another point of view, it is liberating to women, challenging the double standard. Early modern English homilies, sermons, and marriage manuals all insist that men and women alike are bound to chastity; in practice, however, men were allowed much more sexual freedom. Like contemporary feminist criticism, Donne's *Elegies* question patriarchal ideology that equates female honor with virtue and chastity, subordinating the daughter to the father, and the wife to the husband. In the elegy beginning "Once, and but once," the speaker convinces a young unmarried woman to make love with him under her father's roof. In the elegy beginning "Natures lay Ideot" the speaker teaches a married woman to evade her husband's watchful eye and to enjoy the erotic pleasures of clandestine love.

The *Elegies* encourage women's sexual freedom, and challenge the patriarchal control of women by fathers and husbands. Yet they also seek to use
the poet's "masculine perswasive force" ("By our first strange and fatall
interview," 4) to assert his power over his mistress. In the elegy beginning
"Come, Madam," Donne conducts a hot and heavy sexual seduction as if it
were a military campaign. The language becomes increasingly graphic as the
poem unfolds, culminating in an image of geographical exploration that is as
unconventional as it is audacious:

> Licence my roaving hands, and let them go,
> Before, behind, between, above, below.
> O my America! my new-found-land,
> My kingdome, safeliest when with one man man'd,
> My Myne of precious stones, My Emperie ...   (25–29)

Having politely asked permission to explore every part of her naked body,
Donne gets carried away. The outpouring of prepositions, one following
another in quick, rhythmic succession, says it all. As the thrill of discovery
tears the sentence apart, making the rules of grammar seem as constraining
and irrelevant as the clothing the lovers discard, the rhetoric is almost irresis-
tible. At the same time, however, the imagery betrays Donne's masculine desire
to conquer and control.[11] If the woman is his kingdom and his empire, he is her
king and emperor, reveling unabashedly in his masculine dominion over her.

In "Sapho to Philænis" Donne speaks in the voice of a woman, the classical
Greek poet, Sapho, author of astonishingly passionate lesbian love poetry. The
poem has provoked considerable critical controversy. Some critics have
argued that Donne could not have written a lesbian love poem. Others have
argued that it is an exploitative male fantasy of female sexuality. I think Donne
finds in Sapho a classical antecedent and a poetic guise through which he can
represent female self-expression, artistic, emotional, and sexual.

Sapho's verse letter is addressed to her current but absent female lover,
Philænis, whose name is the Greek word for female friend.[12] In a moment of
jealousy, Sapho imagines Philænis with a new lover, a young boy:

> Plaies some soft boy with thee, oh there wants yet
> A mutuall feeling which should sweeten it.   (31–32)

To forestall the competition, Sapho reminds Philænis that this faceless,
archetypal young boy lacks the "mutuall feeling" that enables Sapho and
Philænis to give each other such sweet pleasure.

Traditional Renaissance poets catalogue and metaphorize each body
part,[13] but Sapho abjures comparisons as trite and tedious distractions
from the frank and open relationship she and Philænis share:

> For, if we justly call each silly *man*
> A *little world*, What shall we call thee than?
> Thou art not soft, and cleare, and strait, and faire,
> As *Down*, as *Stars*, *Cedars*, and *Lillies* are,
> But thy right hand, and cheek, and eye, only
> Are like thy other hand, and cheek, and eye.   (19–24)

The bare, unadorned nouns – hand, cheek, and eye – dismiss the elaborate poetic tropes by means of which male poets objectify female love objects. It is the female body in and of itself that moves Sapho to poetry and sexual ecstasy.

At the climax of the poem Sapho gazes at herself in a mirror:

> Likenesse begets such strange selfe flatterie,
>   That touching my selfe, all seemes done to thee.
> My selfe I embrace, and mine owne hands I kisse,
>   And amorously thanke my selfe for this.
> Me, in my glasse, I call thee; But alas,
>   When I would kisse, teares dimme mine *eyes*, and *glasse*. (51–56)

In the famous and the oft-imitated 45th sonnet of the *Canzoniere*, Petrarch chastizes Laura for a narcissism that is the poetic reflection of his own self-absorption. Trapped by the male gaze and male discourse in an infantile stage of self-absorbed narcissism, Laura is objectified and subjugated by the Petrarchan tropes of adoration and frustration. Donne's revision of the conventional Petrarchan mirror image is shockingly erogenous: abjuring the "likenesse" of metaphor for the "likenesse" of their unadorned female bodies. Sapho brings herself to sexual climax by imagining that she is touching Philænis.

Let's face it, this is hot stuff. Clearly, Donne knew that male readers would be aroused by Sapho's sexuality. Some critics argue that Donne's ventriloquized female voice objectifies Sapho, turning her into the reflection of male desire, making her a fetish to be circulated among Donne's male coterie, much as today's pornographers frame lesbian lovers for the voyeuristic pleasure of male viewers. Yet, while anti-pornography feminists argue that pornography violates and degrades women, an opposing feminist discourse staunchly defends both male and female freedom of speech, advocates women's sexual liberation, and celebrates lesbian sexuality as the purest and least oppressive form of female sexual pleasure; and that, I think, is much closer to Donne's position in "Sapho to Philænis."[14]

After masturbating, Sapho tells Philænis, "So may thy mighty, amazing beauty move / *Envy*'in all *women*, and in all *men*, *love*" (61–62). Of course men will desire Philænis; as Sapho acknowledges, Philænis is beautiful, amazingly sexy, and mightily charismatic. Women envy Philænis because she is so powerfully attractive to men. At the same time, however, the poem suggests, women should also admire Philænis because she lives in a world (or at least in a poem) that allows her the strength and freedom to make her own decisions and fulfill her own desires. Bursting into tears, Sapho addresses Philænis directly – "And so be *change*, and *sicknesse*, farre from thee, / As thou by comming neere, keep'st them from me" (63–64). Rather than reveling in the narcissistic pleasure that transforms the loved object into material for poetry, Sapho acknowledges Philænis's independent agency – and that, I think, is Donne's position in "Sapho to Philænis."

Philænis is the object of male desire, but she is also "mighty" and "amazing" because she is neither defined nor controlled by men. According to my reading, the poem celebrates both Sapho and Philænis as strong, independent, creative, and sexually liberated women – as role models not only for male poets, readers, and lovers but also for female poets, readers, and lovers. Men and women alike have a lot to learn from the "mutuall feeling" "Sapho and Philænis" expresses with such *feminine* "perswasive force." Unimpeded by the ideology of Renaissance poetry and society, independent of male control, Donne's Sapho is gloriously erotic, boldly outspoken, and brilliantly persuasive.

If Sapho is the archetypal female poet/lover who forges her own distinctly female poetic voice, Philænis is the archetypal private female lyric audience. For what could be more private than a verse letter conceived during the act of masturbation? Towards the very end of the poem, when Sapho snaps out of her erotic reverie to realize that Philænis is, oh, so painfully absent, I think Donne is hinting that he wrote the poem for his own private female lyric audience, Anne More, whose last name appears carefully encoded at two climactic moments in the poem:

> My two lips, eyes, thighs, differ from thy two,
>   But so, as thine from one another doe;
> And, oh, no more; the likenesse being such,
>   Why should they not alike in all parts touch?
> . . .
> O cure this loving madnesse, and restore
>   Me to mee; thee, my *halfe*, my *all*, my *more*. (45–48, 57–58)

Punning allusions to a lover's real name were a common feature of Renaissance love poetry, famously illustrated by Sidney's puns on Penelope Rich's name in *Astrophil and Stella* or Shakespeare's puns on his own name, "Will," in the sonnets. Donne often puns on his and Anne More's last names. In the letter informing Anne's father of their clandestine marriage, Donne declares, "it is irremediably donne." In "A Hymne to God the Father," he tries but cannot get beyond his love for his deceased wife: "thou hast not done, / For I have more." But most interesting for "Sapho to Philænis," in

"A Valediction: of my name, in the window" where "love and griefe their exaltation had" (38) and Donne fears Anne may be tempted to accept another suitor, he writes his name in the window (or at least in the poem) in the hope that the words will preserve their love during his absence: "'Tis more, that it shewes thee to thee ... Here you see mee, and I am you" (9, 12).[15]

In "Sapho to Philænis" the possible biographical allusion is just a hint, two words "do" and "more," not likely to have been noticed by anyone but Anne More herself. While the sparse, unadorned diction, "lips, eyes, thighs" (45) disguises their identities, the pun quietly suggests that Donne may have secretly sent the poem to Anne after her father, hearing of their affair, tried to separate them.[16] The exclamation, "oh, no more," asks, oh, am I never again, to enjoy the "mutuall feeling" which gave us both "alike" such pleasure? Or "oh, no More," have I lost my beloved More forevermore? Afraid that Anne might succumb to her father's pressure to marry "some soft boy" who was both more socially appropriate and more malleable, the poem strives to keep alive the "mutuall feeling" which made John Donne's and Anne More's love sweeter than anything he had ever before experienced.

As I read the poem, the poignant final rhyme – restore my More – transforms Sapho's passionate outcry to an intensely private plea, begging Anne More not to be tempted by all the men who are bound to fall in love with her. (Perhaps Donne was also hinting that Anne should keep their love alive by touching herself while reading the poem and thinking of their "mutuall feeling," much as Sapho brings herself to sexual climax while writing the poem and thinking of Philænis). Please, Donne implores in a state of "loving madnesse," don't destroy both your well-being and mine; I cannot continue to be "mee" without you, "my *halfe*, my *all*, my *more*" (58). Wait for me; hold out until we can find a way to be reunited. The dramatic fiction, with its historical displacement and its emphasis on the physical "likenesse" of lesbian love, provides a protective veil that preserves this most private subtext for the lovers themselves.

"Sapho to Philænis" ends not with a recollection of past love or a declaration of present oneness but with an anxious plea for a future reunion – "And so be *change*, and *sicknesse*, farre from thee, / As thou by comming neere, keep'st them from me" (63–64). By adopting the persona of female poet/lover, Donne moves beyond the egotism and narcissism of Petrarchan poetry. Having made a passionately persuasive argument, both Sapho and Donne must await the response only the female lyric audience can provide.

Although Donne clearly wished he could control the women he wooed, especially when he was feeling libidinous or bereft, he was also forced to confront the limits of his poetic power. Poetry of courtship and seduction is one side, but only one side, of an ongoing dialogue between poet/lover and beloved. In the end, poetry of courtship is always dependent on an answering response; the poet/lover can no more force the woman to respond positively to his poem than he can force her to reach sexual climax through his touch.

"Sapho to Philænis," the first female homosexual love poem in English, expresses female sexuality with a boldness and openness that is unsurpassed in English Renaissance poetry. If we imagine "Sapho to Philænis" written by a sophisticated, witty male poet for a coterie of lusty young men, its explicit sexuality may look exploitative, objectifying, and demeaning to women. But if we imagine it written for and read by a private female lyric audience – by Philænis, or Anne More, or "some lover, such as wee" ("The Extasie," 73) – it becomes breathtakingly intimate and extremely moving. If we then try to make ourselves into the ideal lyric audience, the elegy looks more like "The Canonization," where Donne provides a "patterne of your love" – a model for a radical new vision of sexuality, poetry, and society:

> You, to whom love was peace, that now is rage;
>   Who did the whole worlds soule contract, and drove
>   Into the glasses of your eyes
>   (So made such mirrors, and such spies,
>   That they did all to you epitomize,)
>   Countries, Townes, Courts: Beg from above
>   A patterne of your love!   (39–45)

The odd displacement which posits an ideal sonnet reader who then becomes both lyric speaker and lyric audience mimics the displacement Donne achieves by speaking to his private female lyric audience through "Sapho and Philænis." Moreover, the image of "glasses" and "mirrors" recalls both "Sapho and Philænis," "Me, in my glasse, I call thee," and "A Valediction: of my name, in the window," "Here you see mee, and I am you."

The conclusion of "The Canonization" alludes to the Neoplatonic notion that a beautiful woman can provide a "pattern" of ideal, transcendent love, but here too Donne rewrites the conventional trope. Whereas the Neoplatonic lover leaves the woman's earthly body behind as he climbs up the ladder to heavenly love, Donne immortalizes the intersubjective union of man and woman: "and thus invoke us." By driving the whole world into their eyes, Donne creates a pattern for future lovers that is both immortal and fully embodied, both spiritual and sexual:

> And wee in us finde the Eagle and the Dove.
>   The Phoenix ridle hath more wit
>   By us, we two being one, are it.
> So to one neutrall thing both sexes fit,
>   Wee dye and rise the same, and prove
>   Mysterious by this love.   (22–27)

The surface meaning of "we dye and rise the same" suggests that to the world Donne and his mistress look "the same" after lovemaking as they did before. The deeper, more revolutionary meaning suggests that they "rise the same," no longer male and female but something entirely new, a phoenix, a mythical creature that, dying to be reborn from its own ashes, is simultaneously male and female: "So to one neutrall thing both sexes fit." The phoenix endows Donne's heterosexual lovers with the "likenesse," the similarity and mutuality, that makes Sapho and Philænis's same-sex love so wondrous. The pun on "die," meaning both to expire and to reach sexual climax, suggests that sexual ecstasy is transformative, miraculously dissolving sex differences and reshaping traditional gender roles.

"The Canonization" spells out what I think "Sapho to Philænis" implies: Donne's mutual, egalitarian love may be too far out for his own day, but, the poem prophesies, it will be admired and copied in times to come. Hampered by the limits of his own society, Donne can only "build in sonnets pretty roomes" (32), but someday "Countries, Townes, [and] Courts" will be ready to institute the radical new vision of poetry, sexuality, and society that Donne and his mistress represent.

In "The Anniversarie" Donne creates another image of heavenly transcendence, but unlike Neoplatonists Donne unites the lovers and, after imagining their heavenly ascent, quickly returns them to earth: "then wee shall be throughly blest, / But wee no more, then all the rest; / Here upon earth, we'are Kings, and none but wee / Can be such Kings, nor of such subjects bee." Donne's imagery restructures the patriarchal polity that subordinates subjects to their king, as it subordinates women to their fathers and husbands. Unlike the elegy beginning "Come, Madam," which asserts the speaker's male dominion over his female lover, "The Anniversarie" makes both lovers both kings and subjects, both rulers and ruled. This relationship is all the more wondrous because it is unparalleled and unprecedented on earth – and in poetry.

So what can we conclude? Yes, gender does matter. When we give Donne's ambiguous, enigmatic language the close attention it demands, his attitude towards women, sexuality, and gender becomes more multi-faceted, more complicated, and less predictable than it might at first seem. The interanimation or cross-pollination of sacred and profane, the refusal to simplify or suppress thoughts or feelings for the sake of clarity or consistency, the readiness to challenge orthodoxy and to shock the reader into a more open, inquiring, unconventional point of view – these impulses continue to disturb and unsettle any position Donne might take on love, women, and gender. Depending on which poems or lines one chooses to quote and, even more importantly, depending on how one chooses to interpret and evaluate the lines one selects, one can see Donne as a witty misogynist, a great devotee of women, or a lover willing to risk everything for the woman he adores.

Readers and critics can choose to ignore the women in Donne's poems, focusing instead on Donne's self-analysis or self-fashioning. They can allegorize the woman, turning her into a metaphor for Donne's professional advancement, or they can objectify her, turning her into a sex object to be circulated among Donne's smirking male coterie. Nonetheless, a remarkable number of Donne's love poems are, first and foremost, poems for and about women and the relations between men and women and the social roles played by men and women. Misogyny and male domination are fundamental to Donne's poetic and cultural inheritance. Not surprisingly, therefore, Donne's poems acknowledge the sexual stereotypes and the gender hierarchy that subordinated early modern women to men through primogeniture and marriage; however, his poems also dramatize the ways in which Donne and his mistresses – above all and most importantly, Anne More – challenged, even if they were powerless to overturn, the patriarchal polity and society into which they were born and died. Donne's most daringly innovative poems describe not only male desire but intimacy itself, the ecstatic "mutuall feeling" that embodies and constitutes an extraordinary, unprecedented "dialogue of one" ("The Extasie," 74).

When Donne argues that it is not virtue or honor but the "Centrique" part that makes women, women ("Loves Progress"), when he "forget[s] the Hee and Shee" ("The undertaking") and reminds us that women like men have "two lips, eyes, thighs" ("Sapho to Philænis"), he is anticipating the modern conception of gender which argues – biology being one thing and gender another – that sex differences are not natural or universal but culturally constructed and constantly changing. Inevitably, the rules of the genre, the demands of the situation, and the beliefs of early modern English society shape what Donne writes about women and gender; at the same time, however, his poems, "In cypher writ, or new made Idiome" ("A Valediction: of the booke," 21), also reconfigure poetic and social conventions, thereby reconstituting what poets and readers can say, even as the poems prophesy what poetry and society will one day do.

NOTES

1 For these respective critical positions, see Achsah Guibbory, "'Oh, let mee not serve so': The Politics of Love in Donne's *Elegies*," originally published in *ELH* (1990), and reprinted in abridged form in Andrew Mousley (ed.), *John Donne* (Houndsmills: Macmillan, 1999), pp. 25–44; T. S. Eliot, "Metaphysical Poetry," in *Selected Essays* (New York: Harcourt Brace, 1960), pp. 241–50; Carey, *Donne*; Judith Scherer Herz, "'An Excellent Exercise of Wit that Speaks so Well of

Ill': Donne and the Poetics of Concealment," in Claude Summers and Ted-Larry Pebworth (eds.), *The Eagle and the Dove: Reassessing John Donne* (Columbia: University of Missouri Press, 1986), pp. 3–14; Stanley Fish, "Masculine Persuasive Force: Donne and Verbal Power," reprinted in Mousley, *John Donne*, pp. 157–81; and Ilona Bell, "The Role of the Lady in Donne's *Songs and Sonets*," *SEL* 23 (1983), 113–29.

2 Fish, "Masculine Persuasive Force," pp. 161ff; Janet E. Halley, "Textual Intercourse: Anne Donne, John Donne, and the Sexual Poetics of Textual Exchange," in Sheila Fisher and Janet E. Halley (eds.), *Seeking the Woman in Late Medieval and Renaissance Writings: Essays in Feminist Contextual Criticism* (Knoxville: University of Tennessee Press, 1989), pp. 187–206, makes an analogous argument.

3 Arthur F. Marotti, *John Donne, Coterie Poet* (Madison: University of Wisconsin Press, 1986), privileges Donne's male coterie; Dennis Flynn, "Donne and a *Female Coterie*," *LIT* 1 (1989), 127–36, responds by emphasizing Donne's female coterie.

4 M. Thomas Hester makes this argument in "'*Faeminae lectissimae*': Reading Anne Donne," in Hester (ed.), *John Donne's "desire of more": The Subject of Anne More Donne in His Poetry* (Newark: University of Delaware Press, 1996), pp. 17–34.

5 See readings of "The Flea" by Theresa M. DiPasquale, *Literature and Sacrament: The Sacred and the Secular* (Pittsburgh: Duquesne University Press, 1999), pp. 173–86; and Bell, "Courting Anne More," *JDJ* 19 (2000), 59–86.

6 See J. Thomas Hester, "Donne's Epigrams: A Little World Made Cunningly," in Summers and Pebworth (eds.), *Eagle and the Dove*, pp. 80–91.

7 For gender matters in Donne's religious poems, see DiPasquale, *Literature and Sacrament*, and Elizabeth M. A. Hodgson, *Gender and the Sacred Self in John Donne* (Newark: University of Delaware Press, 1999).

8 Quoted from the elegy beginning "As the sweet sweat," henceforth referred to as "The Comparison" (26); a different elegy begins with this quote.

9 Fish, "Masculine Persuasive Force," thinks the poem "triumphs at the expense of the two women who become indistinguishably monstrous when the poet makes it impossible for us to tell the difference between them" (159).

10 Heather Dubrow, "Donne's Elegies and the Ugly Beauty Tradition," *Donne and the Resources of Kind*, ed. A. D. Cousins and Damian Grace (Madison: Fairleigh Dickinson University Press; London: Associated University Presses, 2002), p. 65, notes that Donne describes the genitals in "androgynous terms."

11 This reading is indebted to Guibbory's compelling postcolonial critique of the poem, "'Oh, let mee not serve so,'" 32–33.

12 C. A., Patrides (ed.), *The Complete English Poems of John Donne* (London: Dent-Everyman, 1985), p. 188.

13 Nancy Vickers, "Diana Described: Scattered Woman and Scattered Rhyme," *Critical Inquiry* 8 (1981), 265–79, offers the classic feminist critique of this conventional strategy.

14 For diametrically opposed responses to the poem, see Halley, "Textual Intercourse"; James Holstun, "Will You Rent our Ancient Love Asunder?: Lesbian Elegy in Donne, Marvell, and Milton," *ELH* (1987), 835–68 ; Janel Mueller, "Lesbian Erotics: The Utopian Trope of Donne's 'Sapho to Philænis,'"

Journal of Homosexuality 23 (1992), 103–34; H.L. Meakin, *John Donne's Articulations of the Feminine* (Oxford: Clarendon Press, 1998), pp. 84–138; and Ronald Corthell, *Ideology and Desire in Renaissance Poetry: the Subject of Donne* (Detroit: Wayne State University Press, 1997), pp. 70–74.

15 On Donne's name puns, see Julia M. Walker, "Anne More: A Name Not Written," in Hester (ed.), *Desire of More*, pp. 89–105. For Donne's letter to his father-in-law, see *Original Letters of John Donne Relating to his Secret Marriage*, John Donne Papers, Folger Library.

16 For the full story, see Bell, "Under Yᵉ Rage of a Hott Sonn and Yʳ Eyes: John Donne's Love Letters to Ann More," in Summers and Pebworth (eds.), *Eagle and the Dove*, pp. 25–52.

14

RAMIE TARGOFF

Facing death

John Donne spent much of his life anticipating his death. Although similar claims could be made for many seventeenth-century English men and women, for whom death was a constant presence, Donne had an unusually active relationship to his mortality. As readers of his poems and prose immediately understand, Donne was gripped by a tremendous fear of death, and his writings return again and again to strategies for conquering this fear. However, at the same time that Donne dreaded the moment of death, he also repeatedly seemed to invite it. Donne was a deeply theatrical person, and he was perhaps at his most theatrical when he attempted to stage the actual instant when his soul would depart from his body. From his *Holy Sonnets*, which begin with lines like "This is my playes last scene," or "What if this present were the worlds last night?"; to his meditations on the tolling church bells outside his window as he lay in his sick-bed in *Devotions*; to his innumerable letters anticipating his imminent death; Donne positioned himself again and again on the threshold between this world and the next. What can explain this singular obsession with confronting death? And why was it, as his collected works attest, so powerful an imaginative tool?

There are, needless to say, no simple answers to these questions. But certain preoccupations about death and the afterlife appear repeatedly throughout Donne's works, among which we might emphasize the following: an urge to battle death directly; a desire to take death into one's own hands; a loathing of the separation of body and soul; an overwhelming concern for the material decay of the corpse; an anxiety about the mixing of remains in the grave; a longing above all for resurrection. These preoccupations hardly reflect a consistent, coherent position – indeed, they often seem contradictory – and each represents a different strand of Donne's life-long struggle with mortality. Taken together, however, they make clear what is perhaps most crucial to understand, and most surprising, about Donne's fear of death: it does not primarily reflect an attachment to mortal life.

However attached Donne may seem at moments to his earthly existence, he does not long to perpetuate his life on earth so much as to ensure his redemption after death. Hence death was simultaneously a dreadful prospect and an essential phase in his path to eternal salvation. In his most famous confrontation with death – the holy sonnet beginning "Death be not proud" – Donne boldly affirms his eventual triumph over mortality: "One short sleepe past, wee wake eternally / And death shall be no more; death, thou shalt die" (13–14). This confidence in the "short sleepe," however, was more wishful than deeply felt. For Donne, even the idea of damnation paled in imaginative horror before the ghastly interval between death and rebirth.

Dying

In a letter to his close friend Henry Goodyer, Donne confides that he is frequently overcome with the desire for the next life. "Two of the most precious things which God hath afforded us here," Donne writes,

> are a thirst and inhiation after the next life, and a frequency of prayer and meditation in this ... With the first of these I have often suspected my self to be overtaken; which is, with a desire of the next life: which though I know it is not meerly out of a wearinesse of this, because I had the same desires when I went with the tyde, and enjoyed fairer hopes then now: yet I doubt worldly encombrances have encreased it. (*Letters*, pp. 49–50)

This undated letter was almost certainly written during the years of unofficial social exile following Donne's marriage to Anne More, years in which Donne found himself surrounded by an ever-expanding family and few prospects of professional advancement. However, Donne confesses that, even before these "worldly encombrances," he was already plagued with a similar "thirst and inhiation" – the latter is a term that Donne seems to have introduced into the English language, and suggests an overwhelming, even greedy, act of longing.[1]

Donne's expression of his desire to pass from this life to the next does not directly acknowledge the inevitable, intermediary phase of death. The sentences that follow register the omission, as Donne turns to contemplate the manner in which he would like to die:

> I would not that death should take me asleep. I would not have him meerly seise me, and onely declare me to be dead, but win me, and overcome me. When I must shipwrack, I would do it in a Sea, where mine impotencie might have some excuse; not in a sullen weedy lake, where I could not have so much as exercise for my swimming. (*Letters*, p. 50)

The notion of death as a form of active struggle between two agents speaks to Donne's interest in establishing an agonistic and not merely submissive relationship to his mortality. This is the force of the shipwreck analogy: Donne acknowledges that the shipwreck cannot be avoided – it is something he "must" do – but he would like it to reflect as much resistance on his part as possible.

In this letter to Goodyer, Donne expresses his attraction to the idea of battling against death. However, more frequently in his works we find expressions of the opposite sentiment: a desire to embrace death actively, to submit voluntarily and willfully to his own demise. If one strategy for conquering death is to combat it as an enemy, a second strategy is to determine the time and nature of death oneself. This second position receives its fullest articulation in Donne's polemical defense of suicide, *Biathanatos*. In the preface to *Biathanatos*, whose subtitle reads, "a Declaration of that Paradoxe or Thesis, that Selfe-homicide is not so naturally Sinne, that it may never be otherwise," Donne confesses his own temptation to suicide, and offers a range of explanations. His desire for self-slaughter might be traced to his "first breeding, and conversation with Men of a suppressd and afflicted Religion, accustomed to the despite of death, and hungry of an imagin'd Martyrdome," or it may derive from the fact that the devil finds Donne less protected against his entrance – the "dore worst lockd against him, in mee." It may also be attributed to more positive causes: that there is nothing so inherently sinful about suicide that his conscience should rebel against it. Whatever the explanation, Donne's conclusion is the same: "whensoever my affliction assayles me, me thinks I have the keyes of my prison in myne own hand, and no remedy presents it selfe so soone to my heart, as mine owne sword" (*Biathanatos*, p. 29).

Biathanatos is by no means an unqualified endorsement of suicide. Donne argues that only those suicides motivated entirely by the desire to promote God's glory, and not by self-interests of any sort, deserve to be exempted from the general injunction against them. But what is crucial is Donne's insistence that the desire to end one's own life is not against the law of nature. Donne builds his defense upon a long list of both biblical martyrs and classical figures who pursued selfless and heroic deaths, and his example *par excellence* is none other than Christ himself. In claiming Christ as a suicide, Donne emphasizes the fact that Christ surrendered voluntarily to his death:

> And therefore as himselfe sayd *No man can take away my soule* And *I have power to lay it down*e So without doubt, no man did, nor was there any other then His owne Will, the cause of His dying at that tyme; Many Martyrs having hang'd upon crosses Many days alive: and the theeves were yet alive; And therefore *Pilate* wonder'd to heare that *Christ* was dead. (*Baithanatos*, p. 129)

Because Christ released or emitted his soul "before his Naturall tyme," Donne contends that this "signif[ies] more than a yeilding to death when it comes" (*Biathanatos*, p. 130). The theological grounds for this argument are highly complex, and need not concern us here. But what matters is that Donne admires Christ precisely for achieving what Donne often seems to want for himself: an active and voluntary embrace of death.

The fantasy of willing the emission of his soul instead of allowing himself to be conquered by death does not surface regularly in Donne's writings, but in "A Hymne to Christ, at the Authors last going into Germany," he comes close to articulating such a wish. As John Carey has aptly noted, the gloomy and solitary mood of this poem hardly matches the occasion it describes: a state visit to Germany and Bohemia led by Viscount Doncaster in 1619 for which Donne served as the official chaplain.[2] But Donne's tone is dark and valedictory, and he imagines the journey as a dramatic – and voluntary – farewell to the world. Although the danger he anticipates is one of shipwreck (a reminder of the letter to Goodyer in which he hopes for a shipwreck at sea and not a drowning in a "weedy lake"), Donne frames this catastrophe as one conjured by himself.

The "Hymne" is filled with suggestions of a willed departure from mortal life. The second stanza opens with the affirmative declaration, "I sacrifice this Iland unto thee" (9) and invites the arrival of a "winter" – "in my winter now I goe" (14) – that matches neither the season of the voyage (late spring) nor necessarily the period of Donne's own life (he was forty-seven years old, and in good health). In the third stanza Donne accuses God of loving him not, "till from loving more, thou free / My soule" (21–22). But in the final stanza, the suicidal impulse underlying the poem becomes explicit:

> Seale then this bill of my Divorce to All,
> On whom those fainter beames of love did fall;
> Marry those loves, which in youth scattered bee
> On Fame, Wit, Hopes (false mistresses) to thee.
> Churches are best for Prayer, that have least light:
> To see God only, I goe out of sight:
>   And to scape stormy dayes, I chuse
>   An Everlasting night.   (25–32)

The final two lines declare a clear and unambiguous decision: "I chuse / An Everlasting night." Donne asks to be divorced from all worldly encumbrances in order "to see God only," a choice of self-sacrifice that will plunge him into a world of eternal darkness. This imagery is complicated by its invocation of classical notions of death – "everlasting night" is a straightforward translation of *nox perpetua*, which connotes an eternity marked by nothingness rather than by rebirth.[3] But the important contrast in the poem is between the "stormy dayes" and the "everlasting night," between a tumultuous mortality and a tranquil immortality, between a world full of people and a world – likened to a dark church – in which Donne anticipates that he will "see God only." One of the most remarkable achievements of the "Hymne" is its total erasure of death as a force of its own: "death" is not named once over the course of the poem. Perhaps this above all is what it means for Donne to imagine an active mode of dying: he wants to replace Death as an actor in his own drama so that Donne plays the roles of both agent and victim at once.

Rotting

Had Donne been able to control his own fate, he would have numbered himself among those still alive on the Last Day, those whom St. Paul promised would die and be reborn in an instant.[4] For the possibility of instant death and rebirth eliminates the period of time Donne dreads most of all: the period that the corpse spends in the grave. More than anything else, it is on this account that Donne fears death so intensely: he cannot bear to imagine the processes of dissolution and putrefaction to which his body will be subjected. Although some of this anxiety for the fate of the body no doubt stems from an attachment to his earthly self, the depth of his concerns can be traced to his worries over the logistical problems of returning from so decayed a condition to the necessary perfection of the resurrected body.

Donne's preoccupation with how the processes of death will affect his chances of being materially recollected surfaces in the *Songs and Sonets*. In "The Funerall," Donne begins by speaking from the position of the dead, issuing instructions to those who will bury him:

> Who ever comes to shroud me, do not harme
> > Nor question much
> That subtile wreath of haire, which crowns my arme;
> The mystery, the signe you must not touch,
> > For'tis my outward Soule,
> Viceroy to that, which then to heaven being gone,
> > Will leave this to controule,
> And keep these limbes, her Provinces, from dissolution.   (1–8)

Because Donne accepts the general belief that the body begins to deteriorate the moment that the soul departs, he attempts to provide for an alternative arrangement. The "subtile wreath of hair" taken from his lover becomes a substitute or "viceroy" for his soul, appointed to prevent the dissolution of the flesh until the soul returns on the Last Day to reclaim its body.

In "The Relique," Donne once again imagines himself and his beloved as a posthumous arm and lock of hair, but the hair serves a different purpose. The poem opens with Donne's fretting over future disruptions to his grave:

> When my grave is broke up againe
>   Some second ghest to entertaine,
>   (For graves have learn'd that woman-head
>   To be to more then one a Bed)
>   And he that digs it, spies
> A bracelet of bright haire about the bone,
>   Will he not let'us alone,
> And thinke that there a loving couple lies,
> Who thought that this device might be some way
> To make their soules, at the last busie day,
> Meet at this grave, and make a little stay?   (1–11)

Here the strand of hair does not keep the body intact, but is wrapped around Donne's bone from which the flesh has already rotted. The grim reduction of Donne and his lover to a "bracelet of bright hair about the bone" is not a randomly chosen synecdoche: hair and bones were, along with nails, the only parts of the body known to withstand decay. The idea behind "this device" is to ensure a final reunion before Judgment. Donne keeps his mistress's hair in order to guarantee that when she rushes to retrieve her missing parts on the "last busie day" she will be forced to return to Donne's grave, and their souls will meet once again.

Donne's playful conceits about the consequences of death in the *Songs and Sonets* are more seriously considered – and more anxiously expressed – in his devotional writings. Preaching in 1620 on one of his favorite verses from scripture, Job 19: 26 – "And though, after my skin, wormes destroy this body, yet in my flesh shall I see God" – Donne describes the corpse's material decay in gruesome terms:

> Painters have presented to us with some horrour the *sceleton*, the frame of the bones of a mans body; but the state of a body, in the dissolution of the grave, no pencil can present to us. Between that excrementall jelly that thy body is made of at first, and that jelly which thy body dissolves to at last; there is not so noysome, so putrid a thing in nature.   (*Sermons*, vol. III, no. 3, p. 105)

This picture of the dissolved corpse – composed of "excrementall jelly," and reeking with the "putrid" smells of rotten flesh – poses the central challenge to Donne's belief in the certainty of resurrection when the flesh shall assume its perfected form. Minutes later in the sermon, he attempts to reassure both his congregation and himself that however far the body may be scattered, God will effortlessly reunite its pieces. "Shall I imagine a difficulty in my body," he asks, because I have lost an Arme in the East, and a leg in the West? because I have left some bloud in the North, and some bones in the South? Doe but remember, with what ease you have sate in the chaire, casting an account, and made a shilling on one hand, a pound on the other, or five shillings below, ten above, because all these lay easily within your reach. Consider how much lesse, all this earth is to him, that sits in heaven, and spans all this world, and reunites in an instant armes, and legs, bloud, and bones, in what corners so ever they be scattered. (*Sermons*, vol. III, no. 3, p. 109)

Donne regularly presents his congregation with familiar images, as here where he compares God's re-collection of the self to a merchant sitting in a chair, gathering the appropriate change to make a payment of one sort of another. He does this, it would seem, in order to intensify the strangeness of the second conceit – the wild, potentially terrifying vision of arms, legs, blood, and bones rising from the corners of the earth.

As these passages in the sermon suggest, Donne's anxiety about the fate of the body has nothing to do with an anxiety about damnation. Even when Donne feels most assured of his salvation, his concerns for his posthumous body persist. In *Devotions upon Emergent Occasions*, Donne's prose meditation on the serious illness he suffered in the fall of 1623, he assures us that the soul will proceed to "everlasting *rest*, and *joy*, and *glory*" in the immediate aftermath of death. "But for the *body*," he reflects, "how poore a wretched thing is *that*?"

Wee cannot expresse it *so fast*, as it growes *worse* and *worse*. That *body* which scarce *three minutes* since was such a *house*, as that that *soule*, which made but one step from thence to *Heaven*, was scarse thorowly content, to leave that for *Heaven*: that *body* hath lost the *name* of a *dwelling house*, because none dwells in it, and is making haste to lose the name of a *body*, and dissolve to *putrefaction*. (*Devotions*, pp. 104–05)

The notion that the soul was "scarse ... content" to leave the body for heaven was hardly a conventional Protestant position, even if it reflected an existential truth – anyone who has been in the presence of someone dying, as Donne was many times, would have perceived the apparent resistance of the spirit, the holding on *in extremis* that often precedes the moment of death. Whatever the actual experience of death, however, English Protestants were meant to regard the body as a prison house for the soul, and to rejoice in the soul's liberation. In this sense, Andrew Marvell's description of the soul's plaintive cry for release from the body in "A Dialogue between the Soul and Body" is entirely paradigmatic: "O who shall, from this dungeon, raise / A soul inslaved so many ways?"[5]

For Donne, however, pathos is entirely with the body. The passage from *Devotions* continues:

> Who would not bee affected, to see a cleere and sweet *River* in the *Morning*, grow a *kennell* of muddy land water by *noone*, and condemned to the saltnesse of the sea by *night*? And how lame a *picture*, how faint a *representation* is that, of the precipitation of mans body to *dissolution*?   (*Devotions*, p. 105)

The metaphor for the body as a "clear and sweet *River*" conveys Donne's loving attachment to the beauty of the flesh, a beauty that is horribly altered by the soul's hasty departure. "*Now* all the parts built up, and knit by a lovely *soule*," he concludes, "*now* but a *statue* of *clay*, and *now*, these limbs melted off, as if that *clay* were but *snow*; and *now*, the whole house is but a peck of rubbish, so much bone" (p. 105).

What solaces Donne is not the thought of the immortal soul traveling to heaven, but the recollection that the body will also ultimately ascend. Later in this same chapter of *Devotions*, Donne concludes his "Prayer" by imploring God to return the soul as quickly as possible to the body:

> That therefore this *soule*, now newly departed to thy *Kingdome*, may quickly returne to a joifull *reunion* to that *body* which it hath left, and that *wee* with it, may soone enjoy the full *consummation* of all, in *body* and *soule*, I humbly beg at thy hand.   (p. 110)

Not only the body, but also the soul will take pleasure in the "full *consummation*." For unlike the angels, whose bodiless condition Donne seems at times to pity, human souls are blessed with the gift of corporeality.[6] "I shall be all there," Donne declares triumphantly at the end of the sermon on Job 19.26, "my body, and my soul, and all my body, and all my soul" (*Sermons*, vol. III, no. 3, pp. 109–10). Then, and only then, will death be fully vanquished: when Donne can affirm the integrity of his first person "I" wrested from the disruptions of the grave.

Rising

If we knew none of the details surrounding Donne's preparations for death and we fabricated a dramatic narrative for him, it could hardly surpass the biographical account we have in fact inherited. According to his first biographer and personal acquaintance, Izaak Walton, during the final weeks of his life Donne not only followed a serious regimen of spiritual exercises to prepare his soul for the afterlife, but also found time to rehearse, as it were, what it might feel like to be dead. In a theatrically captivating passage,

Walton describes how Donne not only designed, but also posed for his own funeral monument:

> A Monument being resolved upon, Dr. *Donne* sent for a Carver to make for him in wood the figure of an *Urn*, giving him directions for the compass and height of it; and to bring with it a board of the just height of his body. These being got: then without delay a choice Painter was got to be in a readiness to draw his Picture, which was taken as followeth. Several Charcole-fires being first made in his large Study, he brought with him into that place his winding-sheet in his hand, and, having put off all his cloaths, had this sheet put on him, and so tyed with knots at his head and feet, and his hands so placed, as dead bodies are usually fitted to be shrowded and put into their Coffin, or grave. Upon this *Urn* he thus stood with his eyes shut, and with so much of the sheet turned aside as might shew his lean, pale, and death-like face, which was purposely turned toward the East, from whence he expected the second coming of his and our Saviour Jesus.　　　　　　　　　(Walton, *Lives*, p. 78)

In addition to this private rehearsal of death in his bedroom, Donne also arranged for a public performance, albeit of a different sort. On the first Friday of Lent in 1630/31, when Donne was already deeply stricken with his fatal illness, he preached before his king and probably several hundred listeners what would be his final sermon. This sermon, delivered in the chapel at Whitehall, was posthumously entitled *Death's Duell.*[7] Walton describes the reaction of those present to seeing the sickly dean enter the chapel as comparable to encountering a ghost:

> many of them thought he presented himself not to preach mortification by a living voice, but mortality by a decayed body, and a dying face. And doubtless many did secretly ask that question in *Ezekiel: Do these bones live?* ... Many that then saw his tears, and heard his faint and hollow voice, professing they thought the Text prophetically chosen, and that Dr. Donne *had preached his own Funeral Sermon.*　　　　　　　　　(Walton, *Lives*, p. 75)

The notion that Donne might have "preached his own funeral sermon" is obviously fantastic, but the fantasy did not belong to the listeners alone. In a letter composed during this illness in which Donne responds to rumors that he had already passed away, he articulates the desire to die while preaching. "It hath been my desire," he writes, "(and God may be pleased to grant it me) that I might die in the Pulpit; if not that, yet that I might take my death in the Pulpit, that is, die the sooner by occasion of my former labours" (*Letters*, pp. 209–10). There is an obvious continuity here with the hopes that Donne expressed earlier in his life for an active and voluntary death. In place of dying through willful shipwreck, however, he now imagines dying through the act of preaching.

Our impression that both Donne and his listeners understood *Death's Duell* as his final performance is confirmed by the content of the sermon. Nowhere else in his writing does Donne offer so sustained a contemplation of death, and nowhere else does he involve his listeners so directly as participants in the drama he unfolds. Preaching on a verse from the Psalms, "And Unto God the Lord Belong the Issue of Death" (Ps. 68: 20), *Death's Duell* is structured around three alternative interpretations for the phrase, "the issues of death" *(exitus mortis)*. Donne begins the sermon by overwhelming his listeners with arguments for the pervasiveness of death. Here we find a marked departure from the other materials we have examined. For whereas Donne normally regarded death as a highly marked transition between one world and the next, he insists in *Death's Duell* that what we regard as life is indistinguishable from death. The entire life cycle is rewritten as a continuous act of dying, beginning with conception itself. "In our mothers wombe," he declares, "we are dead so, as that wee doe not know wee live." If the womb is a place of death, it would seem naturally to follow that our birth into the world would be an exit from death. But Donne explicitly rejects this position. "This *exitus a morte*," he continues, "is but *introitus in mortem*, this *issue*, this deliverance *from* that *death*, the death of the *wombe*, is an *entrance*, a delivering over to *another death*, the manifold deathes of this *world*." The occasion of birth now becomes the occasion of death: "Wee have a winding sheete in our Mothers wombe, which growes with us from our conception, and wee come into the world, wound up in that *winding sheet*, for wee come to *seeke a grave*" (*Sermons*, vol. X, no. 11, p. 233).

This crushing negation of the joy of birth suggests a new – and we might say perverse – strategy for conquering the terrors of death. By imagining the phases of our life to be nothing other than a series of deaths, death becomes an entirely familiar, and hence perhaps even meaningless, ontological category. "The whole world is but an universall church-yard, but our common grave," Donne claims, "and the life and motion that the greatest persons have in it, is but as the shaking of buried bodies in their graves by an earth-quake" (p. 234). This startlingly bleak image in which the bustle and activity of life are reduced to the rattling of bones underground empties all meaning from human vitality and achievement. In emphasizing the lack of distinction between life and death, Donne not only seeks to minimize the significance of death. He also confers ever more meaning upon the transition between death and rebirth. The miracle of life no longer comes with creation, but with resurrection.

Before Donne can celebrate resurrection, however, he must confront the period of bodily deterioration that follows upon death – the period, as we have already seen, which Donne fears most intensely. After affirming his "deliver[y] from the manifold deaths of this world ... by that *one death*, the *final dissolution* of body and soule," Donne questions whether this dissolution is truly the "end of all." The answer, not surprisingly, is "it is not":

> Though this be *exitus a morte*, it is *introitus in mortem*: though it bee an *issue from* the manifold *deaths* of this *world*, yet it is an *entrance* into the *death of corruption* and *putrefaction* and *vermiculation* and *incineration*, and dispersion in and from the *grave*, in which every dead man dyes over againe.
>
> *(Sermons,* vol. x, no. 11, pp. 235–36)

The newly coined English term "vermiculation" – the condition of being eaten by worms – is used regularly in Donne's devotional writings, and, along with his other Latinate nouns ("corruption," "putrefaction," incineration," "dispersion"), forces our attention upon the gritty details of the corpse's remains.[8]

Why is Donne so preoccupied with the posthumous state of the body? As we have seen, one answer lies in his obsession with the difficulties of resurrecting the flesh after it has suffered such decay. But another answer emerges in *Death's Duell*, one that we have not encountered in Donne's other works, although we find hints of it in the opening lines of "The Relique" where he anticipates a "second ghest" being buried in his grave. This second explanation turns on the violation of bodily integrity whereby one person's remains become confused with another's. Hence Donne describes with real horror the mingling of family remains:

> When those bodies that have beene the *children* of *royall parents*, and the *parents* of *royall children*, must say with *Iob, to corruption thou art my father*, and to *the Worme thou art my mother and my sister. Miserable riddle*, when the *same worme* must bee *my mother*, and *my sister*, and *myselfe. Miserable incest*, when I must bee *married* to my *mother* and my *sister*, and bee both *father* and *mother* to my *owne mother* and sister. *(Sermons,* vol. x, no. 11, p. 238)

Always mindful of his audience, Donne aimed to engage his most prominent listener, Charles I, by describing royal parents and children. But he moves almost immediately from the fate of future kings and queens to a more personal family incest. The commingling he envisions entails a total negation of discrete, individuated roles within the familial structure: the worm is simultaneously Donne's mother, his sister and himself; Donne is at once husband and parent to both mother and sister.

Of course, the contamination wrought by death is not limited to family members. Death knows no limits, Donne argues, in its disruption of personal identity. Once again beginning with a direct appeal to Charles's attention, Donne imagines the horrible dispersal of the king:

> That that *Monarch*, who spred over many nations alive, must in his dust lye in a corner of that *sheete of lead*, and there, but so long as that lead will laste, and

that private and *retir'd man*, that thought himselfe his owne for ever, and never came forth, must in his dust of the grave bee published, and (such are the *revolutions* of the *graves*) bee mingled in his dust, with the dust of every high way, and of every dunghill, and swallowed in every puddle and pond.

(*Sermons*, vol. X, no. 11, p. 239)

Donne's real sympathies here lie not with the imagined "Monarch," however, but with the plight of the "private and *retir'd man*," who poignantly "thought himselfe his owne for ever." Death does nothing less, Donne argues, than take us away from ourselves – it strips us of self-possession. "This is the most inglorious and contemptible *vilification*," Donne concludes, "the most deadly and peremptory *nullification* of man, that we can consider ... in this death of *incineration*, and dispersion of dust, we see *nothing* that we can call *that mans*" (p. 239). The most devastating blow dealt by death is the collapse of distinctions between persons, the complete erasure of individuality. For Donne, nothing could approximate the horror of losing himself within the collective mass of the dead.

Having reached this absolute nadir in what has been an altogether despairing sermon, Donne thankfully begins his resurrection – in more ways than one. For the experience of the sermon reproduces the experience of moving from death to rebirth, as Donne redirects his focus from the natural horrors of the grave to the supernatural wonders of the divine. "This death of *incineration* and dispersion is, to naturall *reason*, the most *irrecoverable death* of all," he declares,

And yet, *Domini Domini sunt exitus mortis, unto God the Lord belongs the issues of death*, and by *recompacting* this *dust* into the *same body*, and *reanimating* the *same body* with the *same soule*, hee shall in a blessed and glorious *resurrection* give mee such an *issue from* this *death*, as shal never passe into any other death, but establish me into a life that shall last as long as the Lord of life himself. (pp. 239–40)

However debilitating the effects of death may seem to be, Donne reassures us that God will effortlessly overcome them – "*recompacting* this *dust* into the *same body*, and *reanimating* the *same body* with the *same soule*." It is striking that Donne specifies here his own and not his listeners' resurrection: notice the exclusive use of the pronoun "me" ("give mee such an *issue*"; "establish me into a life"). Donne personalizes, in other words, the prospect of rising, a rhetorical choice that must have had a particular resonance coming from the mouth of one so visibly near death.

This affirmation of resurrection concludes the first of the sermon's three explications for the phrase the "issues of death": namely, that God delivers us from death. Donne enters now on a much abbreviated discussion of the second possibility – that the manner of our death should be judged by God alone. Here he contends that a man's salvation cannot be determined by whether he died peacefully or violently, suddenly or slowly; whether he seemed loath to die or embraced his death willingly. Although elsewhere Donne thinks extensively about how he himself would like to die, he dismisses the significance of this subject here, and moves quickly to the third part of the sermon: "this *issue of death* is *liberatio per mortem*, a *deliverance by the death* of another, by the *death of Christ*" (p. 242).

It is difficult to imagine how Donne's audience would have responded to the performance that ensues, a performance that simultaneously narrates the last day of Christ's life and compares it with the activities of Donne's listeners. After characterizing Christ's death once again in the language of suicide – "there was nothing more free, more voluntary, more spontaneous then the death *of Christ*" (p. 244) – Donne declares his intention to "*dwell here*, in this *consideration* of his *death*." "Take in the *whole day*," Donne begins,

> from the *houre* that *Christ received* the *passeover* upon *Thursday unto* the *houre* in which hee *dyed* the *next day*. Make *this* present *day* that *day* in thy *devotion*, and consider what *hee did*, and remember what *you have done*.
>
> (p. 245)

"Remember what *you have done*": each step of Christ's becomes a measure against which those present judge themselves. "*At night* hee *went into the garden* to *pray*," Donne continues, "and he prayed *prolixius*; he spent *much time* in prayer." "I dare scarce aske thee *whither* thou *wentest*," he retorts, "or *how* thou *disposedst* of *thy self*, when it *grew darke* and after *last night*." At times – with palpable irony – Donne connects the two sets of events. "About midnight he was *taken* and *bound with a kisse*," he begins, and then immediately accosts his audience: "art thou not *too conformable* to him in that? Is not that *too literally*, too exactly thy case? at *midnight* to have *been taken* and *bound with a kisse*?" (p. 246)

As we approach the hour of the Crucifixion, Donne makes a dramatic shift in his narration: he moves from the past to the present tense. After reporting that "Towards *noone Pilat* gave *judgement*, and they made such *hast* to execution, as that *by noone* hee was *upon the Crosse*," he conjures the scene for his listeners as if it were transpiring before their eyes. "There now hangs that *sacred Body* upon the *Crosse*," Donne declares, "*rebaptized* in his owne *teares* and *sweat*, and *embalmed* in his *owne blood alive*" (247). The chapel at Whitehall in London becomes the slope of Mount Calvary as Donne indulges in the fleshly details of Christ's body:

> There are those *bowells of compassion*, which are so conspicuous, so manifested, as that you may *see them through his wounds*. There those *glorious eyes*

grew faint in their light: so as the *Sun ashamed* to survive them, *departed with his light too.* (pp. 47–48)

Having fixed his listeners' gaze upon the bowels and eyes of their savior, Donne turns now to bid a strange form of farewell. "There wee leave you in that *blessed dependancy*," he exclaims,

> to *hang* upon *him* that *hangs* upon the *Crosse*, there *bath* in his *teares*, there *suck* at his *woundes*, and *lye downe in peace* in his *grave*, till he vouchsafe you a *resurrection*, and an *ascension* into that *Kingdome*, which hee *hath purchas'd for you*, with the *inestimable price* of his *incorruptible blood*. AMEN. (p. 248)

Death's Duell was preached at the beginning of Lent, and was meant in part to prepare its listeners for taking Holy Communion – the body and blood of Christ. However, the overwhelmingly physical interaction that Donne invokes would have been anathema to mainstream English Protestants, for whom the prospect of hanging on the cross and sucking Christ's wounds would have represented a grotesquely literal participation in the Passion. Although in certain respects Donne left his Catholic roots behind, they seem very close to the surface here. And yet, at the same time that this meditation on Christ's flesh seems indisputably Catholic, the achievement is in some sense also profoundly Protestant. For Donne does nothing less than transform a Catholic altarpiece of a crucified Christ into verbal signs. Like a good Protestant, he replaces the image with the word.

The important question for our purposes, however, is not whether the image is predominantly Catholic or Protestant, but why Donne would choose to end his career on a note so overwhelmingly corporeal. Yet perhaps we could pose the question in reverse. For what conclusion could be more fitting for a man so consumed with anxieties about his body, so troubled by the fate of the corpse after death, so desperate with longing for resurrection? Donne envisions not simply an immersion in Christ's wounds, but even a substitution for Christ's own corpse: he instructs his listeners to "lye downe in peace in his grave, till he vouchsafe you a resurrection." To lie in Christ's grave might mean to avoid some of the dreadful consequences of mortality – to escape the decay of the flesh and the mingling of bodies against which ordinary graves afford no protection. Or Donne may imagine that the holiness of the grave itself provides a level of "peace," a tranquility that conquers the machinations of death.

But where in this scene is Donne? "Wee," he began, "leave you in that *blessed dependancy*," but who constitutes this "wee"? And given Donne's own near-death condition, why does he not include himself among the "*blessed dependan*[ts]"? English preachers often speak in the collective, clerical "we" – this is the voice of the church's authority comparable to the "royal we" of the King – and we could easily assimilate Donne's voice to this conventional model. The particular circumstances of *Death's Duell*, however, invite other interpretations. Remember that earlier in the sermon Donne had singled himself out as he who would be resurrected, using the singular "me." Remember also that Donne desired nothing more than to anticipate death, to leap from one world to the next without falling prey to death's ravaging hands. In his final theatrical coup, Donne stages his own departure by assuming a voice that he has long denied himself: the "wee" of himself and his God. This voice is only conceivable, of course, for those who have completed their *exitus a morte*, those who have arrived triumphant on the other side of the grave.

NOTES

1 The OED lists Donne's letter as the second usage; it assigns the letter's date to 1651, when the letter was first published, but long after it was written. The first entry in the OED is from 1620, and Donne's letter was certainly written before this.

2 Carey, *Donne*, pp. 216–17.

3 See Carey, p. 219. Donne possibly borrowed "everlasting night" from Sir Walter Ralegh's *History of the World*, first published in 1614, in which Ralegh translates some lines of Catullus as follows: "The sun may set and rise / But we, contrariwise / sleep, after our short light / One everlasting night" (C. A. Patrides [ed.], *The History of the World*, [Philadelphia: Temple University Press, 1971], p. 129.

4 See 1 Corinthians 15: 51–52: "We shall not all sleep, but we shall all be changed, in a moment, in the twinkling of an eye, at the last trump."

5 Nigel Smith (ed.), *The Poems of Andrew Marvell* (London and New York: Longman/Pearson Education, 2003), p. 63.

6 See, for example, *Sermons*, vol. IV, no. 1, pp. 47–8.

7 Bald, *Donne*, p. 526. For an overview of the church's Lent sermon series, which were large, court-sponsored events, see Peter McCullough, *Sermons at Court: politics and religion in Elizabethan and Jacobean Preaching* (Cambridge: Cambridge University Press, 1998), pp. 64–70 and passim.

8 Donne is listed in the OED as the second author to use this word (*OED*, meaning 1).

15

DAYTON HASKIN

Donne's afterlife

"One short sleepe past, wee wake eternally": this line from the sonnet, "Death be not proud," has been inscribed on the tombstone of various devotees of John Donne, none of them so fictional as the Victorian poet Randolph Henry Ash, the creation of A. S. Byatt in *Possession* (1990). In Byatt's romance, Ash's widow, Ellen, incorporates the line into a longer inscription that utters her wish for husband and wife to be joined together at the resurrection, "where there will be no more parting."[1] Her choice of the quotation pays silent tribute to something revealed in her journal, that in the last days of Ash's life they had been reading Donne's poems together, in particular "The Relique." Ellen's *fin de siècle* fantasy seems just Victorian enough to prompt a pedant to observe that we have no record of any nineteenth-century readers invoking Donne's poetry in this way. Yet, when we consider that in forty-five years of cohabitation Randolph and Ellen never consummated their marriage, the fantasy is just outrageous enough to have interested Donne as a species of the "mis-devotion" (13) that might attend his writings after he died. Donne's explicit inscription in "The Relique" and other works of an interest in what future audiences might make of his writing suggests a deep longing ultimately to be known and understood.[2]

The belated appearance of a Cambridge Companion to Donne – after the publication of Companions to Spenser and Shakespeare, Jonson and Milton – aptly dovetails with the fact that, although the poetry for which Donne is most valued today was popular in his own century, it took him much longer than the others to be accorded prominence in accounts of literary history. Even contemporaries who knew Donne's poetry well feared for its future – though on quite different grounds. Ben Jonson, who esteemed Donne as "the first poet in the World in some things," pronounced that for his metrical irregularities he "deserved hanging" and predicted that "for not being understood [he] would perish." He also opined that Donne wrote "all his best pieces" by his mid-twenties and attested to Dr. Donne's desire to "destroy" his own poems.[3] Similarly, Izaak Walton, Donne's first biographer, claimed that Donne had "scattered" most of his poems in youth and then "wish't they had been abortive, or so short liv'd, that his own eyes had witnessed their funerals" (Walton, p. 61).

Like other artists, Donne began his this-worldly afterlife when the artifacts that he produced and the reputation that he spawned escaped his control and survived him. His contemporary reputation was summed by Sir Richard Baker in the 1640s: in his young manhood he was "not dissolute, but very neat; a great visiter of Ladies, a great frequenter of Playes, a great writer of conceited Verses," who later, with prodding from King James, "betooke him to the study of Divinity, ... was made Deane of *Paules*, and became so rare a Preacher, that he was ... admired by all that heard him" (*CH*, p. 126). Today we can think of Donne's afterlife as being defined by three principal carriers: (1) the documents in manuscript and print that preserve, imperfectly, what he wrote; (2) the accumulating pronouncements by which he has been dismissed or praised, resisted or tamed, and sometimes appreciatively understood; and (3) the reinvention and creative deployment of his writings by the likes of Byatt, in artful works that evince a continuing power of fecundation. These various legacies were, like children, already busily in motion during Donne's lifetime. Often he sought to exercise control over them. He published little and expressed regret after the "descent" of his poetry into print. Yet he circulated many poems in manuscript, he had the *Devotions* printed, and he scrupulously prepared his sermons for posthumous publication. It may be debated whether the instructions for *Biathanatos* that he gave Sir Robert Ker – to recognize that "it is a book written by *Jack Donne*, and not by D. *Donne*" and to keep it on the one hand from "the Presse" and on the other from "the Fire" – reveal, analogously, his intentions for his poems (*Letters*, p. 22).[4] In any event, the grounds on which his reputation developed shifted decisively in the decade after his death, first with the publication of *Poems by J. D.* (1633) and then with the appearance of *LXXX Sermons*, replete with Walton's account of the preacher's life and death (1640). These publications reinflected the name of a man who was remembered as a public figure: they made "Donne" to signify an author.[5] The publication in the next three decades of more poems and sermons and prose letters, and of *Biathanatos* and the writer's juvenilia, reinforced the identification of the name with the writings. When, later in the century, the literary culture of England altered radically, Donne's desire for his writings to be understood was frustrated; and for most of two centuries he went unread. Yet the roots of a significantly different conception of Donne, one that made his writings incidental to his enduring significance, had taken hold underground. Over a period of thirty-five years Walton revised and augmented his narrative. He disconnected it from the *Sermons* and cast it as the first in a series of tributes to exemplary Englishmen that were meant for readers who rarely opened books of poetry, or sermons.

Questions about the relation between the writer of the poems and the man people remembered as John Donne were inchoate from the first publication of "Elegies on the Authors Death" in 1633. Thomas Carew, in the best of them, declared Donne *"King"* of the *"universall Monarchy of wit"* and acknowledged his pre-eminence in the twin spheres of poetry and preaching (*CH*, pp. 95–96). Thomas Browne was less sanguine, however, about the compatibility of erotic passion and Christian religion. His elegy, subtitled "Upon the *Promiscuous* printing of his Poems, the *Looser sort*, with the *Religious*" (*CH*, p. 88), perhaps alluded simply to the haphazard organization of the volume; the poem was omitted when the 1635 edition reorganized the materials into generic groups. The new arrangement apparently suggested a life that had moved through the sorts of experiences represented in the *Songs and Sonets* to ones thought more befitting the late Dean of St. Paul's. This implication was spelled out in a new epigram by Walton, which was placed beneath an engraved portrait of the author. It explained that the book "begins / With Love; but endes, with Sighes, and Teares for sins" (*CH*, p. 115).

Through the middle decades of the century Donne came to be remembered especially as a poet. Five more editions of the *Poems* appeared by 1669. And the poetry continued to be copied into manuscript miscellanies: the remarkable manuscript compiled by Robert Overton, for instance, shows how both the love poetry and the funeral poems could be made to serve highly personal purposes.[6] Moreover, many practicing poets – Sir John Suckling and other Caroline court writers, Abraham Cowley, Katherine Philips, Andrew Marvell, and young John Dryden – produced love poems or obsequies reminiscent of Donne's. In this large body of poetry Donne continued to be an object of emulation; as his poetry inspired imitators, its originality became more apparent. When, with Edmund Waller and John Denham, the normative poetic style shifted and the importance of the lyric was diminished, Donne was remembered as "the greatest Wit, though not the best Poet of our Nation" (*CH*, p. 150). Dryden, who thus praised him, proposed that his poetry was worth "translating" into verse – and English! Although Jonson's famous interlocutor, Drummond of Hawthornden, may have been the first to refer to the poems as "metaphysical," it was Dryden who made the term stick. When he complained that Donne "affects the Metaphysicks, not only in his Satires, but in his Amorous Verses, where Nature only shou'd reign; and perplexes the Minds of the Fair Sex with nice Speculations of Philosophy, when he shou'd ingage their hearts" (*CH*, p. 151), he indicted Donne for unnaturalness and insincerity and sent his poems packing on a road heading to oblivion.

In the eighteenth century Donne's writings and Walton's biography were generally out of print, and Donne fell almost entirely off the literary map. Between 1669 and 1779 only one edition of the poetry was published. Individual poems rarely appeared in anthologies. Few personal libraries contained a copy either of the *Poems* or of the *Sermons*. By the 1770s Donne was altogether absent from the group of writers for whom Samuel Johnson was hired to write his *Lives of the Poets*. What Andrew Kippis remarked in 1793 – that none of Donne's works were known except his *Satires* – had been true for decades. And yet he had not been entirely forgotten. The task of "translating" two of Doctor Donne's *Satires* had been taken up by Alexander Pope, who gelded the verses to make them easy and inoffensive to Augustan ears. Pope had sufficient respect for his predecessor, whom he figured as the head of a "minor" school, to print the originals alongside his "versified" renditions. Moreover, entries on Doctor Donne regularly appeared in biographical dictionaries, where his unread productions were referred to as characteristic of an earlier, more barbaric phase of English, when unnatural and extravagant displays of wit infected both poetry and pulpit oratory. The clear implication was that such excesses had been quite eclipsed in more enlightened times.

In his *Life of Cowley*, Johnson treated Donne at length and gave new currency to the same old tired criticisms – against the rough style, the unmusical numbers, the far-fetched conceits. "The metaphysical poets," Johnson wrote, "were men of learning, and to shew their learning was their whole endeavour" (*CH*, p. 217). Yet even as Johnson cited the lines from "A Valediction: forbidding mourning" that compare parting lovers to the two feet of a compass, the better to illustrate the "violence" by which metaphysical poets forced the "most heterogeneous ideas ... together" (*CH*, p. 218), he acknowledged that occasionally their work displayed a "fertility of invention" (*CH*, p. 230). This was hardly unmitigated praise. Johnson was of his age in disapproving of this earlier practice as a willful deviation "from nature in pursuit of something new and strange" (*CH*, p. 231). His perspective virtually insured that he would isolate within any given poem mere fragments. Still, the striking bits that he cited put Donne back on the map, albeit in a tiny corner, and made him an object of attention. In the early nineteenth century, a twelve-year-old Ralph Waldo Emerson chanced on Johnson's snippet from the St. Valentine's Day epithalamion and expressed a longing to see the whole poem (*CH*, p. 302). And in 1811, when Samuel Taylor Coleridge filled the margins of an old edition of the *Poems* with personal commentary, he expressed delighted surprise at having come to see how Donne fashioned a conceit to organize and unify an entire poem (*CH*, p. 268). Coleridge made a decisive breakthrough in reading "metaphysical" poetry; yet it took another hundred years and more until that poetry was widely read. If we could allow our narrative to race ahead to the period when an appreciative regard for "metaphysical" poems was taken as a mark of a genuinely modern sensibility, we might conclude with the self-consciously "new" critics of the mid-twentieth century that the cult of Donne was proof that true genius would, inevitably, be recognized at last. In this period Donne was installed as a precursor of modernism, and it was widely believed that T. S. Eliot "discovered" him.

The revival of Donne as a writer was contingent, however, upon a prior set of biographical interests that in the nineteenth century, drawing on inform-ation from Walton's *Lives*, made Dr. Donne significant because he had married for love and because he had played a role in consolidating the nation's transfer of allegiance to Protestantism. Interest in Donne was rekindled in a climate in which Walton's *Compleat Angler* was greatly beloved. Johnson had called for the republication of the *Lives*, which was one of his favorite books; and in 1796 Thomas Zouch responded by publish-ing a large folio edition with footnotes that identify dozens of persons and events from the seventeenth century. Less elaborate editions followed, and by 1813 the book was again said to be "in the hands of every reader."[7] A decade later the foremost poet of the era endorsed "Walton's Book of Lives" in his *Ecclesiastical Sketches*; thereafter Wordsworth's sonnet regularly appeared in the proliferating editions of Walton's book. In 1846 a writer in *Lowe's Edinburgh Magazine* ventured the opinion that for every reader of Donne's poems, there had been a hundred readers of Walton (*CH*, p. 403).

Two aspects of *The Life of Donne* were of greatest interest: the story of his clandestine marriage, presented by Walton as "a flattering mischief" (p. 27) and "the remarkable error of his life" (p. 60), and the implications about Donne's youthful behavior that seemed to be lodged in the proposal that he was a second St. Augustine. Both components of the *Life* eventually pro-moted interest in the poetry and delimited powerful narrative frameworks within which it was interpreted. Each also had a substantial life of its own, however, apart from the poems. In her much reprinted *Loves of the Poets* Anna Jameson, for instance, told a romantic tale about Donne's marriage to Anne More, acknowledging that he had once been celebrated as a writer, only to observe that he was now "more interesting for his matrimonial history ... than for all his learned, metaphysical, and theological produc-tions" (*CH*, p. 351). Meanwhile, since Walton had depicted Donne as a pillar of the Jacobean church, he might have been made a player in the tangled thicket of Victorian ecclesiastical controversies. Yet members of the Oxford Movement generally averted their eyes from him. Coleridge's question "why are not Donne's sermons published at Oxford?" points up his omission from the growing corpus of Anglo-Catholic reprints. Among those who thought of Donne as a writer, *Pseudo-Martyr* was widely considered his most important work, because it exposed Catholic duplicity and self-deception. Coleridge, who in his youth had annotated Wordsworth's copy of Donne's *LXXX Sermons*, posed his question after annotating another copy in his maturity. The two sets of annotations appeared together in his *Literary Remains* in the 1830s, when more editions of Walton's *Lives* were printed than in any other decade. This provided the decisive impetus for the first republication of Donne's sermons.

In 1839 the London publishing house of John W. Parker, which printed books for Cambridge University Press, brought out the only edition of Donne's writings ever called *The Works*. The collection was edited by Henry Alford, a young clergyman recently down from Cambridge, who aimed as the first scholarly endeavor of his career to offer Donne's sermons dressed in modern spelling and punctuation. Alford's six volumes also made available something under half the poems (many Divine Poems and all the verse letters), the *Devotions upon Emergent Occasions*, and the prose letters; as it turned out the letters were the most widely read section. Among those who scrutinized them closely was Augustus Jessopp, another young clergyman trained at Cambridge. In 1855 he published an edition of the *Essays in Divinity*, top-heavy with a sixty-page biographical introduction that opened questions about the nature and scope of Donne's ambitions. Jessopp never took much interest in Donne's poetry, but for half a century he studied his life. In the 1880s, when he was given the entry on Donne for *The Dictionary of National Biography*, he provided an account that filled in several gaps in Walton's narrative and brought the biography into line with developing canons of modern scientific inquiry. By this time a new edition of the poems had appeared (1872–73) in the privately published Fuller Worthies Library. Its editor, the indefatigable antiquarian A. B. Grosart, included Donne at first merely as one of many sixteenth- and seventeenth-century writers whose works he was republishing. In his long Memorial Introduction, however, Grosart put into sharp focus the eminently Victorian project of trying to reconcile the extraordinarily licentious character of much of the verse with the well-known story in which Doctor Donne had been an exemplary Jacobean clergyman. Emphasizing Donne's youthful Catholicism in far greater detail than any previous writer had, he developed a narrative that spoke to his contemporaries' principal interests in the life: developing Anna Jameson's perspective, Grosart made the idea that Donne experienced a "conversion" utterly central to the whole story, proposing that, once Donne gave up Catholicism, he fell into a state of moral turpitude from which he was delivered by the love of a good woman. This romance fed a diffuse but intensifying regard for some of the *Songs and Sonets*. The Victorians were after all more interested in love poetry than readers had been since the mid-seventeenth century. The edition was dedicated to Robert Browning. Ironically, Browning's dramatic monologues offered a model for reading Donne's lyrics that readers searching for details of Donne's "Augustinian" youth resisted.

Meanwhile, almost unbeknownst to anyone in Britain, Donne's poetry was gaining a significant readership in the United States, where there was little anxiety about the author's place in the history of his nation's established church. Emerson, who had acquired a copy of the 1719 edition, fostered an interest in Donne around greater Boston. Henry David Thoreau, Margaret Fuller, Henry Wadsworth Longfellow, and James Russell Lowell were among those who made it their own. In New York *The Literary World*, edited by Lowell's friend, Evert Duyckinck, published Coleridge's marginalia on the poems in 1853. Two years later, Lowell, who was editing Dryden for a British Poets series, persuaded the publishers to include Donne as well. Uniquely, the so-called Boston edition opened with the verse letters; this showed that Donne was a writer whose work was deeply embedded in a circle where literary production served as a mode of social interaction. By printing more variants than ever before, this edition offered a glimpse of the instability of Donne's text. In fact, Lowell continued to revise the text over the course of many years. When, in the 1880s, having been his country's minister to the Court of St. James, he returned to the United States and agreed to serve as president of the newly founded Modern Language Association, Lowell went back to editing Donne. His work was eventually brought to the press by his daughter, Mabel Burnett, who collated the early editions, and by his literary executor, Charles Eliot Norton, North America's foremost Dante scholar, whose knowledge of editorial principles led to the influential decision to give normative status to the text of 1633. After the Grolier Club edition appeared in 1895, in an essay called "The Text of Donne's Poems," Norton showed in detail not only the bungle that Grosart had made by employing inferior manuscripts, but how a better text might be established. His work was ignored in England, where the publishers of the Muses' Library series kept reprinting E. K. Chambers's 1896 edition of Donne's *Poems*. When Herbert Grierson was preparing a new edition, he chanced on Norton's work, and it showed him that he would need to study the manuscripts.[8] His great edition of 1912 was based on a far more extensive textual collation than was ever attempted until the *Variorum* project began in the early 1980s.

Grierson was the first editor of Donne who acquired his interest in the poet in an academic setting. This foreshadowed and helped to determine, for good and for ill, much of Donne's fate in the twentieth century. In his early years at Aberdeen, Grierson had been an assistant to William Minto, who, while he did not lecture on Donne, had published in 1880 an unusually perceptive essay on the effects of Donne's having written within a coterie. Explaining that Donne's poetry is at once more jesting and more serious than readers have appreciated, and that the lines between these extremes are barely to be discerned, Minto had concluded, provocatively, that while Donne had been highly esteemed among his contemporaries, he was likely to remain among the great failures in literature whose work will at best be appreciated by a studious few.[9]

The man who introduced Minto to Donne's poetry, his protégé, Edmund Gosse, eventually sought to prove that his mentor was wrong about this. From the 1870s, interest in Donne had been growing in Britain; and the monument of Donne that now stands in St. Paul's Cathedral, after two centuries of "languishing in the crypt," was restored.[10] By the 1890s, Donne's poems were being far more widely discussed than at any time since the mid-seventeenth century. Because Walton's *Life* had for so long defined "Donne," the editing of his letters to integrate them into a coherent account of his life was regarded as the most important project yet to be carried out in the study of late Elizabethan and Jacobean literature. Gosse undertook the work in what seemed ideal circumstances: Jessopp, unable to abide Donne's poetry, turned over to him the fruits of fifty years of research. The two-volume *Life and Letters* (1899) that emerged from this uneasy collaboration offered the most sustained study of Donne ever published. Gosse read Donne's poems as transparent windows onto the poet's own experience and used them to weave together a titillating plot about a young man's sexual awakening and long-delayed religious conversion. The results so disturbed the foremost biographer of the era, Leslie Stephen, that he wrote an extended biographical essay himself. He disdainfully compared Walton's *Life* to *The Vicar of Wakefield* and sought to empty its narrative of all religious feeling. Expressing his puzzlement that Donne had boldly liberated himself from the shackles of religion only to submit to serving the established church, Stephen emphasized the venal motivations that governed Donne's behavior as a priest. He presented Donne's personal history as an anticipation of the great – and dismaying – national story that had since worked itself out: despite a period of enlightenment that enabled many to reject traditional religious faith, religion kept refusing to go away. To Stephen's mind, Donne was especially culpable for the persistence of religion, because as a churchman, instead of insisting on differences, he had been conciliatory and accommodating, stirring up hopes for reconciliation among traditionally opposed parties who might otherwise have eradicated one another. A generation later, Stephen's daughter was no more sympathetic to the religion in Donne; yet Virginia Woolf gave many characters in her novels a knowledge of the poet, and she herself counted reading the poetry among her joys.[11]

Stephen's good friend Norton contributed to bringing Donne into the realm of academic study across the Atlantic. By collecting seventeenth-century editions and manuscripts and by editing Donne's poems, Norton made an investment that helped to turn Donne into a more significant figure in the Harvard English curriculum than he was in any other university in the world. Even before Norton completed the Grolier Club edition, Donne was the anchor of the course on seventeenth-century English literature. First taught by Le Baron Russell Briggs in 1888, the course gave considerable scope to the verse letters, to "Satyre III," and to a handful of *Songs and Sonets*. It was in a lecture by Briggs in January, 1906, that a young student from St. Louis named Tom Eliot first encountered John Donne.

In his essay of 1931, "Donne in Our Time" Eliot paid tribute to Briggs and claimed that he was unable to trace with certainty his subsequent history with Donne, although he acknowledged that by the time he went to London in 1911 the poet was well known. Indeed, as Eliot was aware, since the 1890s many poets (including Arthur Symons, W. B. Yeats, and especially Rupert Brooke) were avidly reading Donne's poetry. By the thirties, Donne was thought of as a poet who had taken an active, and disillusioning, interest in the new science; and the phrase "new Philosophy calls all in doubt" was frequently quoted. Donne spoke to readers and writers from diverse stances: as love poet, dandy, rebel, satirist, melancholic, priest. Poets as different as Wilfred Owen, William Empson, Hart Crane, Edna St. Vincent Millay, and Stephen Spender engaged variously with Donne in poems of their own. In Djuna Barnes's *Nightwood* (1936), Dr. O'Connor enlisted one of the sermons to explicate the night. Hemingway took the title of *For Whom the Bell Tolls* (1940) from the *Devotions*, and thereafter the passage beginning "no man is an island" gained unprecedented currency; today it is among the most widely quoted bits of non-biblical prose in the English language. In the 1950s, the ubiquity of the quotation prompted the Hallmark Hall of Fame series to broadcast on American television a screenplay dramatizing Donne's elopement with "the boss's daughter."[12]

Nonetheless, it was the author of *The Waste Land* who generally received credit for Donne's new prominence. When Grierson brought out *Metaphysical Lyrics and Poems of the Seventeenth Century* (1921), Eliot had been commissioned by the *Times Literary Supplement* to review it. Having long since been interested in Donne, he seized the moment to propose a revisionary account of literary history according to which "the metaphysicals" constituted "the direct current of English poetry," in relation to which line his own poetry would be seen to best advantage.[13] Republications of the review as "The Metaphysical Poets" disseminated Eliot's claim that a "dissociation of sensibility" had taken place in the later seventeenth century. This fed a virtual cult of admirers of these earlier writers, whose "unified sensibility" was said to have fused thought and emotion. Donne was proclaimed a greater poet than Spenser and Milton and was treated as a great intellectual, curious, skeptical, and penetrating. He was the decisive precursor of modernism, and it was the special glory of the moderns to have understood him at last.

While Eliot rather lost interest in Donne, his theory of the "impersonality of the artist" helped to move the center of gravity away from biographical concerns and to stimulate a range of contextual studies. Historians of ideas sought to place Donne's writings in relation to medievalism, Neoplatonism, Petrarchism, the new science, alchemy, and other movements. By the late forties, Louis Martz was encouraging readers to consider the poetry in wider European contexts. *The Poetry of Meditation* (1954) brought the two long *Anniversary* poems to unprecedented prominence within the Donne canon. Later Barbara Lewalski's *Donne's "Anniversaries" and the Poetry of Praise* (1973) made these poems intelligible to the widest audience that they have ever had. It also refocused the reading of Donne in narrower contexts by launching the project to define a distinctively English brand of "Protestant poetics."

At mid-century the sheer amount of historical scholarship on Donne seemed to justify the University of California Press's lavish ten-volume edition of the *Sermons* (1953–62). Meanwhile, Oxford set itself up as the center of Donne studies, publishing a series of handsome editions of the poems. Presided over by Helen Gardner, these volumes were assumed to embody the most fastidious of scholarly standards. It was from Oxford as well that the standard biography by R. C. Bald came forth in 1970. A decade later it was followed by John Carey's more entertaining *John Donne: Life, Mind, and Art* (1981), likely the most widely read book on Donne during the last quarter of the century. Carey made Donne's "apostasy" from Catholicism the key to understanding his personality and his poetry; and he made an outsider's rank ambition the central explanation for the course of Donne's career. Historical studies of Donne have continued right down to our own time. The work of various hands in *John Donne's Professional Lives* (ed. David Colclough, 2003) reinflects biographical concerns: an unprecedented intensity of interest in Donne's training in the law and in his work as a minister in the national church suggests the power of the assumption that, more than psychology, sociopolitical contexts now provide the fundamental explanatory framework within which literature is to be understood.

As an innovative poet Donne has also been the focus for stylistic and formal analysis. Such an approach has long since ceased to be wedded to the neoclassical criteria by which his poetry was once demoted and, like his monument in the crypt, virtually buried. Yet, as John Roberts influentially observed in 1982, the striking thing about the massive industry that since 1912 turned out hundreds of books and articles on Donne is that it narrowly confined its attention to a mere handful of the *Songs and Sonets*, a few elegies, the *Holy Sonnets*, "Goodfriday, 1613" and the hymns, and the *Anniversaries*; in short, to much less than half the canon.[14] These are the works that typically appear in the anthologies used by university students; and the focus on them bespeaks the degree to which pedagogical consider-ations have yielded a "synecdochal understanding" of Donne that reduces him to a quintessentially "canonical" author.

The curtailed understanding of Donne that circulated in the Academy in the third-quarter of the twentieth century was not inevitable. It owed a good deal to pedagogical imperatives of the sort that came into the universities as early as the 1920s, when at Cambridge, for instance, I. A. Richards made "At the round earths imagin'd corners" an object of "practical criticism." As teachers began to encourage their students to discover how the various parts of poetic artifacts worked in concert with one another, certain poems of Donne (already the object of a cult among practicing poets) came increas-ingly to be cultivated by teachers. The results were often productive, as Coleridge, a champion of "organic unity," had envisaged. Donne's lyrics were valued, moreover, insofar as they could be shown to entail the ambi-guity, paradox, and tension that were said to characterize good modernist poems. Readings of individual Donne poems proliferated, both in class-rooms and in professional journals. By the 1980s, however, amidst a ferment of attempts to "apply" new theories, those seeking to open up the canon often made Donne a special object of attack.

The assault required a new, still more narrow synecdoche. "The Canonization," which had never been the object of much attention until the 1940s, was made to epitomize Donne's verse. Deconstructionist, new historicist, and feminist criticism increasingly made the poem a focus for exposing the pretensions of those responsible for "the canon." The case was powerfully articulated by John Guillory in a narrative constructed to explain how the regnant canon of English literature had been made the special provenance of an *"incognito* clergy," the university professors who inducted willing neophytes into the mysterious knowledge of an "aristocracy" of quasi-sacred texts.[15] The organizing conceit of Donne's poem, whereby the speaker establishes himself and his lover as a marginal elite who transcend the petty concerns of "Countries, Townes, [and] Courts," served Guillory's purposes admirably. With a whiff of a conspiracy theory, Guillory figured the previously "new" criticism as a covert attempt to shore up an outdated liberal pluralist consensus and to smuggle religious orthodoxy back into literary education. The *bête noire* in this narrative (along with Eliot, who had canonized Donne in order to edge out dissenters like Milton and Shelley) was Cleanth Brooks, who in *The Well-Wrought Urn* had teased out of "The Canonization" a naïve and disingenuous "theory of poetry." The wide influence of Guillory's analysis is attested by Robert Scholes's wholesale incorporation of it into his account of the "fall" of English studies.[16]

Not everyone has subscribed to this picture of Donne, of course. Outside the English departments Bob Dylan and Van Morrison have invoked Donne in their music. Joseph Brodsky and Yehuda Amichai have drawn inspiration from him in writing their verse. Among writers of fiction Borges became a serious reader of Donne after finding in *Biathanatos* a remarkable ground on which to contemplate the Crucifixion. Updike gave his fictional Henry Bech an ironic passage from "Death be not proud" to read while he attempts to keep to himself his success in having murdered a rival. Meanwhile, real-life scholars now peruse the *John Donne Journal*, which published Roberts's critique of the old "synecdoche" and has since been printing essays on a broader range of materials, many of the essays disseminating work first presented at the annual conference of the John Donne Society.[17] Many undergraduates continue to respond enthusiastically to the *Songs and Sonets*; and Edward Docx's novel of 2003, *The Calligrapher*, makes those poems integral to the plot of a failed romance.

The jury is still out on what impact the most important work now being carried out on Donne, *The Variorum Edition of the Poetry*, will ultimately have. When Gary Stringer conceived the project, it seemed a rather old-fashioned enterprise. Yet the making of this variorum has depended upon an unprecedented constellation of possibilities, including the publication of Peter Beal's listing of early manuscripts, the dramatic growth of new computer technologies, and greater ease of intercontinental travel. The first-fruits are already abundant enough to have established *The Donne Variorum* as a norm for future editions of early modern non-dramatic literature. It offers a model for editing manuscript poetry, and it has begun to show that Donne carefully revised many of his poems. So far its most intriguing contribution to Donne's afterlife may be its demonstration, poem by poem, of what has been vaguely troubling and largely unexplored: that the original holographs have been "lost." Speed Hill, in the essay in which he has described the grounds on which the *Variorum* constitutes a "landmark," proposed that the editors' recurring need to invoke the hypothesis of a lost holograph suggests that Donne himself succeeded in destroying many originals.[18] This surmise, which squares with what Jonson reported and with Walton's remarks about the poems' "funerals," is not incompatible with the notion that previously Donne had put his poems into manuscript circulation. In any event, the absence of fully authorial documents to work with in a project so resolutely built upon the importance of a particular author is wonderfully anomalous. It opens up a range of interpretative possibilities and complicates our questions about the author's putative intentions for his writings at different times in his life.

Beyond the questions that the textual sections of the *Variorum* help to raise, its history of commentary documents a continuing uncertainty about "meaning" that is unlikely to be cleared up even when we have the best, most complete edition that scholarship can create. Whatever theoretical grounds one invokes to account for the indeterminacy of language in general, the particular case of Donne seems to exceed the theoretical explanation. The notes and glosses in the *Variorum* show that occasionally progress is made in identifying one or other reference in a poem. The mass of commentary suggests, however, that in any given poem "meanings" are, if not potentially infinite, extraordinarily difficult to limit. For all the supposed authority of editors such as Gardner, who looms large in the imagination of the fictional heroine of Margaret Edson's recent Pulitzer-prize-winning drama, *W;t* [sic] (1999), Donne repeatedly exceeds the best attempts to nail him down. This is what makes the presence of the poet in another recent play, Wallace Shawn's *The Designated Mourner* (1996), more profound: it is just the Donne of excess, even of bad taste, that proves especially challenging to those who would obliterate poetry from the face of the earth. Shawn's foreboding fantasy of a world in which there is no longer anyone who is able to read "John Donne" reminds us that the project of integrating the two sets of data that are commonly considered to constitute Donne's "life" and Donne's "works," which Gosse undertook and failed satisfactorily to execute, still remains unaccomplished. So various are the results of the industrious scholarship of the last century, and so weighed down with them has the reading of Donne become, that the challenge now is to try to construct a larger, more inviting picture that, while it can never deliver a full understanding of this complex figure and his works, will help future readers to long for one.

NOTES

1 A. S. Byatt, *Possession: A Romance* (New York: Random House, 1990), p. 483.
2 See Achsah Guibbory, "A Sense of the Future: Projected Audiences of Donne and Jonson," *JDJ* 2.2 (1983), 11–21.
3 For ease of reference many quotations from older writing on Donne are taken from A. J. Smith (ed.), *John Donne: The Critical Heritage* [hereafter, *CH*] (London: Routledge, 1975); Jonson is quoted from pp. 69–70.

4 See Richard B. Wollman, "The 'Press and the Fire': Print and Manuscript Culture in Donne's Circle," *SEL* 33 (1993), 85–97.

5 Through a whole series of publications over the past quarter century, Arthur F. Marotti has been the preeminent explorer of the implications of Donne's having been made into an "author."

6 See David Norbrook, "'This blushinge tribute of a borrowed muse': Robert Overton and his Overturning of the Poetic Canon," *English Manuscript Studies 1100–1700* 4 (1993), 220–66.

7 See Philip Bliss (ed.), *Athenæ Oxonienses*, by Anthony à Wood, 3rd edn., 4 vols. (London: F. C. and J. Rivington, et al., 1813–20), vol. 2 (1815), pp. 504, 505. On the popularity of Walton's *Lives*, see Raoul Granqvist, "Izaak Walton's *Lives* in the Nineteenth and Early Twentieth Century: A Study of a Cult Object," *Studia Neophilologica* 54 (1982), 247–61.

8 On the relations among the Boston, the Grolier, and the Grierson editions, see Dayton Haskin, "No Edition Is an Island: The Place of the Nineteenth-Century American Editions within the History of Editing Donne's Poems," *TEXT* 14 (2002), 169–207.

9 William Minto, "John Donne," *The Nineteenth Century* 7 (1880), 845–63.

10 Richard S. Peterson, "New Evidence on Donne's Monument: I," *JDJ* 20 (2001), 1–51, at 4.

11 Leslie Stephen, "John Donne," *Studies of a Biographer*, 2nd Series (London: Duckworth, 1902), pp. 36–82; on Virginia Woolf, see Judith Scherer Herz, "Under the Sign of Donne," *Criticism* 43 (2001), 48–49.

12 See Helene Hanff, *84, Charing Cross Road* (New York: Avon, 1970), p. 58. On Donne's importance to the poets, see Joseph Duncan, *The Revival of Metaphysical Poetry* (Minneapolis: University of Minnesota Press, 1959). Cf. Herz, 29–58; this fine essay treats Donne's place in the work of numerous twentieth-century artists and provides many bibliographical details.

13 See Anne Ferry, *Tradition and the Individual Poem: An Inquiry into Anthologies* (Stanford: Stanford University Press, 2001), pp. 245–55.

14 John R. Roberts, "John Donne's Poetry: An Assessment of Modern Criticism," *JDJ* 1 (1982), 55–67, at 62.

15 John Guillory, "The Ideology of Canon-Formation: T. S. Eliot and Cleanth Brooks," *Critical Inquiry* 10 (1983), 173–98, at 186, 175.

16 Robert Scholes, *The Rise and Fall of English: Reconstructing English as a Discipline* (New Haven: Yale University Press, 1998), pp. 24–28. Cf. Dayton Haskin, "A History of Donne's 'Canonization' from Izaak Walton to Cleanth Brooks," *JEGP* 92 (1993), 17–36.

17 See Gary A. Stringer, "An Introduction to the Donne Variorum and the John Donne Society," *Anglistik* 10 (1999), 85–95.

18 W. Speed Hill, "*The Donne Variorum*: Variations on the Lives of the Author," *Huntington Library Quarterly* 62 (2001), 445–54.

16

A. S. BYATT

Feeling thought: Donne and the embodied mind

Ever since I discovered Donne, as a schoolgirl in the 1950s, I have been trying to puzzle out why he is so very exciting. The short-story writer, Frances Towers, remarked that women reading his love-poems feel seduced, which was true of the girl I was, though odd, since he wrote "Hope not for minde in women" and described them as, at their best "*Mummy*, possest." He also speculated that women might not have souls, since there is no record of God having breathed one into Eve.[1] Nevertheless, his great love-poems stir both body and mind in an electric way that resembles nothing else. As a student, I puzzled over T. S. Eliot's dictum about the dissociation of sensibility since the metaphysical poets. "Tennyson and Browning are poets and they think; but they do not feel their thought as immediately as the odour of a rose."[2] What precisely does it mean, to "feel your thought"?

It seemed to me that Tennyson, who was despised when I was a student, felt his thoughts much more immediately than the Metaphysicals. Christopher Ricks indeed claimed that Tennyson thought precisely *with* sensuous images, fusing sensation and thought. The imagery of trees, for instance, in *In Memoriam*, contained in the musical chain of closed balladic verses, is a thought process made up of imagining the objects. Each tree changes all the other trees. Two examples:

> And if that eye which watches guilt
>   And goodness, and hath power to see
>   Within the green the mouldered tree
>   And towers fallen as soon as built –   (XXVI)

And

> Old Yew, which graspest at the stones
>   That name the underlying dead,
>   Thy fibres net the dreamless head,
>   Thy roots are wrapped about the bones ...

> And gazing on thee, sullen tree
> > Sick for thy stubborn hardihood,
> > I seem to fail from out my blood
> And grow incorporate into thee. (II)[3]

These are part of a painful meditation on death and dissolution and the permanence of death. The conceit of the eternal eye which simultaneously sees the green tree and the mouldered one is metaphysical in its startling intensity. But I feel it works – in conjunction with all the other living and dying trees in the poem – by making the reader imagine the tree in his/her body – the tree is grasping the dead man, the poet is failing "from out my blood" and is becoming the old (mouldering) tree. This is thinking with the senses in the mind. The trees are as immediate as the odour of roses. I don't think this is almost ever true of the way Donne's poetry works – on my mind at least.

Nevertheless, I have recently come to see that Eliot may have meant something quite different – he confused the issue with the example of the rose odor for reasons I shall come to. Donne does feel his thought. But what he feels – and makes us his readers feel – is the peculiar excitement and pleasure of mental activity itself. It isn't smelling roses. It's being aware of, and delighting in, the electrical and chemical impulses that connect and reconnect the neurones in our brains. Thought is material, according to neuroscience. I think of it in terms of Sir Charles Sherrington's description of the waking brain, the "head-mass" as "an enchanted loom where millions of flashing shuttles weave a dissolving pattern, always a meaningful pattern, though never an abiding one . . . ."[4] The pleasure Donne offers our bodies is the pleasure of extreme activity of the brain. He is characteristically concerned with the schemas we have constructed to map our mental activities – geometry, complex grammatical constructions, physiology, definitions. He is thinking about thinking. (And about smelling roses, but he is not immediately inducing us to smell any in our imaginations.)

Reading Jean-Pierre Dupuy's extraordinary account of the 1950s meetings of the cybernetics group,[5] which discussed minds and machines and what it was to be human, I came across a remark by a neural network designer about puns. I think it was Von Neumann but can't be sure. Maybe, this scientist said, we delight in puns because the neurone connections become very excited by the double input associated with all the stored information for two arbitrarily connected things or ideas. Maybe we enjoy this excitement. It occurred to me reading this that complex metaphors produced infinitely more subtle versions of this excitement and pleasure. I started to think – to use a *double entendre* that is very pertinent – about the play on words, the play of light on a landscape, the mind at play. I know that this excitement is the primitive thing at the source of why I want to spend my life writing and thinking. I do not have a message to give to the world, I do not wish to seduce or persuade, I want to think as fast as possible, in as complex a way as possible, and put the thinking into verbal forms. I think I knew even as a schoolgirl that Donne excited me because he was a pattern-maker – with light and language. The other poet who has the same qualities of excitement is Wallace Stevens. The geometry of the lights that portion out and give form to the meaningless dark water in "The Idea of Order at Key West," the sections of "Notes Towards a Supreme Fiction" – *It Must be Abstract, It Must Change, It Must Give Pleasure* – are part of the mental mapping I am reaching for. I think both Donne and Stevens describe not images, but image-making, not sensations but the process of sensing, not concepts but the idea of the relations of concepts. I like glass because, as Herbert said, you can look at it and through it simultaneously. I always think of both Donne and Stevens as "glassy" poets, as Herbert himself is not, because he is too much of a perfectionist, his poems are made objects, their form is what they are and contains them: more like porcelain. Donne and Stevens make skeletons of poems.

It has been much easier to think about this aspect of poetry since there have been books to read about neuroscience, and increasing quantities of information about the myriads of neurones in different areas which fire when things are perceived, are reinforced by connections with previous perceptions and previous connections, and make up the constantly changing matter of mind which Jean-Pierre Changeux calls "'L'Espace de travail' neuronal."[6] Changeux's 'neural work-space' is itself part schema, part description of what goes on in our brains when our minds are at work. In it there are millions of cells with connecting dendrites and long questing axons, some of which can cross into the opposite hemisphere of the brain. In *L'Homme Neuronal* he describes the construction of a *mental object*, which is a physical state created by the activation (*correlated* and *transitory*) of a large number of neurones from different layers and areas of the brain. This mental object can be represented by a graph. He then describes an increasingly complex sequence of mental objects.

(a) The *primary percept* is a mental object whose graph and activity are constructed by direct contact with the external world.
(b) The *image* is an object of the memory, "autonome et fugace" [autonomous and fleeting] whose evocation requires no contact with the environment. It can only exist autonomously if there exists a "*couplage*" [a linking together] of neurones in the graph which is stable in time and already exists before it is evoked. (Called up?)
(c) The *concept*, like the image, is a memory object, but has only a weak or even no sensory content. It is the result of the recruitment of neurones present in

areas of association with multiple sensory or motor specificities. The passage from image to concept follows two distinct and complementary paths – the "élagage" [pruning, or excising] of the sensory component, and the enrichment due to the *combinations* resulting from the way the mental objects are linked.

(d) The associative properties of mental objects allow them to link themselves spontaneously and autonomously. They are constrained by the wiring structures of the mental machine, which in fact imposes its own "grammar" on the linking of mental objects.[7]

Elsewhere Changeux refers to the combination of neurones in concepts as an "algebra," derived from the isomorphs of perceptive acts. He describes language itself as a system of arbitrary signs, constructed as a vehicle for the communication of concepts *in a society*. Language has to be learned (laid down as stable neural linkages) in a "long apprenticeship." Changeux distinguishes this social language from the "langage de la pensée" [language of thought]– concepts derived from images derived from percepts – which is "permanently connected to (branchée sur) the real." Changeux sees mental activity as a kind of musical rhythm of firing cells, and has a very specific and beautiful image, both a description and a metaphor – which Donne would have loved – for its combination of the precise and the random. The cerebral cortex is organized in cellular crystals which establish local connections over millimetres, which are superposed on contacts at distances of centimetres or decimetres. The long axons reach out as far as the opposite hemisphere. This organization is at the same time precisely localized and delocalized. The mental object is, he says "entre le crystal et la fumée" – between crystal and smoke. Quite different parts of the system fire when the thinking subject is simply perceiving, and when he/she is struggling with understanding or forming concepts.

I do not imagine we are yet in reach of a neuroscientific approach to poetic intricacy, although Semir Zeki has made interesting observations on the relations between certain abstract works of visual art and neurones in the brain that detect movement, direction, and colour.[8] What I felt on reading Changeux was that the neurones Donne excites are largely those of the reinforced linkages of memory, formed concepts, and learned formal structures like geometry, algebra, and language. There is poetry that is mimetic of primary perception, and that is not – except in very special senses – what Donne is doing. I thought I might get help from cognitive psychologists about why we take such pleasure in complex metaphors. But the work they do on metaphor appears to be largely directed to understanding how metaphor fits into "normal" cognition and social construction of communication. They like to work on hidden dead metaphors, and construe from these metaphors rules about why we like to link things. In terms of Donne's fantastic webs of language it is not greatly helpful to have it made clear how automatically we use military imagery for normal argument. The fact that the direction "up" in language describing human emotions represents a positive, whilst "down" is usually bad, is of great interest in terms of the human body firing perceptual neurones and making language from images and concepts.[9] But the psycho-linguists are not much interested in complex play of words.

On the other hand, I was very excited by Elaine Scarry's dizzily ambitious *Dreaming by the Book*.[10] Scarry's brilliantly original project is to describe a kind of grammar or algebra of the instructions by which a writer causes a mental image to be reconstructed in the mind of a reader. She is mostly interested in novelists and epic poets setting scenes – from Homer to Tolstoy to Hardy. She analyzes phenomena like mental solidity or mental spaces, the description and evocation in the mind of movement and color and flesh. She has various names for the constructive instructions – "Radiant Ignition" "Rarity" "Addition and Subtraction," "Stretching, Folding and Tilting," and "Floral Supposition" – she has complex explanations for our human preference for describing flowers in detail. When I read her chapter on "Radiant Ignition" I immediately thought of Donne and Stevens. Radiant Ignition for Scarry is the verbal calling up of sharp bright lights in the mind – which she says is a way of focusing the imagination which will then see a scene. The interesting thing about brilliant lights in both Stevens and Donne is that mostly the excitement is simply in the brief radiant ignition. There is no following expansive imagined scene. The poetry is perhaps *about* this mental tool and its excitement, not about particular lit faces or fields.

Take, for instance, "Aire and Angels." It has a crescendo of radiant igni-tion. "So in a voice, so in a shapeless flame" we are told, angels affect us. The mistress is first perceived as "Some lovely glorious nothing." Love, in the second stanza can inhere "nor in nothing, nor in things / Extreme, and scatt'ring bright" – a phrase unforgettable for its combination of an abstract adjective "extreme" and the concrete visual stimulus of "scatt'ring bright" which is ambiguously linked to the mistress's every hair. We readers see neither angel nor woman, though the woman is present, as often in Donne, in a string of nouns – "thy lip, eye, and brow." We see mental flashings.

There is a kind of *intellectual-bodily* imagination of the embodied soul. Donne's soul "takes limbs of flesh, and else could nothing doe." At the end of the poem we imagine the embodiment of the angel which takes "face, and wings / Of air, not pure as it, yet pure." In the first part of the poem the bright light and the angelic presence were the woman. Now it turns out that her body is the sphere in which Donne's love may be enabled to "do." At this point the difficulty of the syntax at first hides the barb (if you are a woman).

Just such disparitie
As is 'twixt Aire and Angells puritie,
'Twixt womens love, and mens will ever bee.

Donne began by a complimentary comparison of a beloved to an angel. He ends by claiming that she is the airy sphere which clothes his purer spirit. The syntax imposes the reading which the sense is not quite expecting. The pleasure is in untangling it. It is a poem haunted by the brightness of the unseen, the embodying of the bodiless. And the embodiment is, as also often in Donne, the embodiment of a central consciousness in a circle or sphere. If you are thinking in terms of mapping the concepts arising from the images arising from the percepts of bodily space, it is arguable that you are reading the ghostly – or angelic – image of a male body inside a female one.

There are other poems in which the abstract forms of geometry are used both for the argument of the ideas, and for immediate bodily images. Take the famous compasses of "A Valediction: forbidding mourning." These too appear after one of the most beautiful images of radiant ignition in literature. The two souls of the lovers are really one, and endure "not yet/ A breach, but an expansion, / Like gold to ayery thinnesse beate." We see and don't see the beaten gold – which is impossible as a solid because its thinness, like the shapeless flame of "Aire and Angells," is *aery*. As in that poem Donne follows the arresting brightness with the geometry of the stiff twin compasses – in which again, the male and female elements oddly appear to change places. (The solidly sensual adjective "stiff" is one of those ambiguous fleeting evocations of the senses.)

It is the male soul which runs obliquely in a circle. It is the female soul which sits in the center and "growes erect, as that comes home." Again in this poem the disembodying of the body has been carried out by a list of nouns – the lovers "inter-assured of the mind / Care less, eyes, lips, and hands to misse." The mention of eyes, lips, and hands of course evokes some sort of imaginative response to these things, even as they are dismissed. They are the surfaces. In the center is an erect twin compass, in a just circle, made of two lovers "inter-assured of the mind." It is hard to say how – to go back to Eliot's feeling thought – those compasses represent human love and human certainty of reciprocal love. But they do, and they do it by evoking mental processes of conceptualization and mapping that are somewhat remotely to do with sex and affection.

I could add more examples of this kind of geometric intensity of abstraction. "Loves growth" works by using a string of disparate conceits to make what looks like a rhetorical *jeu d'esprit*. It contains one of Donne's rare references to the natural as opposed to the human or metaphysical world.

(Though this, it is worth remarking, follows a ghostly radiant ignition, in the idea that stars in the firmament are not enlarged, but shown, by sunlight.)

> Gentle love deeds, as blossomes on a bough,
> From loves awakened root do bud out now.

This comparison depends on a simple identification of the root of a plant in spring and the male body awakened. It has more in common with Tennyson's trees than most of Donne's arguing metaphors, and is at home in a poem which argues

> Love's not so pure, and abstract, as they use
> To say, which have no Mistresse but their Muse.

But Donne follows this rare comparison with flowers and boughs immediately with another conceptual image of the containing circle.

> If, as in water stir'd more circles bee
> Produc'd by one, love such additions take,
> Those, like so many spheares but one heaven make
> For, they are all concentrique unto thee.

A remembered observed physical image of water. A linking with the concept of the cosmos. A ghostly graph of female pleasure, or joint sexual pleasure. Followed immediately by a joky reference to taxation. The mind has to fire in every direction it can.

A concentrated example of Donne at play with our capacity to make mental links and reinforce them wildly is "The Crosse." Historically this poem is about a dispute in the Church as to whether to abolish the sign of the cross in baptism and other things. Theologically it is about the omnipresence of the Crucified God in the macrocosm and the microcosm. Poetically it uses perceptual frames and bodily imaginings, as well as linguistic patterning and punning, to make a graph of the world which demonstrates the pervasive presence of crosses. It begins with an image of Christ's body as the Cross, or the cross as the image of that body.

> Since Christ embrac'd the Crosse it selfe, dare I
> His image, th'image of his Crosse deny?

The Cross is the instrument of torture and death in the abstract form of the human body – here Christ is seen "embracing" the abstract shape of his death, so that the poet cannot afford to deny the power of "the image." Later in the poem Donne uses the bodily experience of the Cross as concept, very simply.

> Who can deny mee power, and liberty
> To stretch mine armes, and mine own Crosse to be?

What he is saying here – in terms of the theological controversy – is that the idea of body as cross is so automatic that it cannot be proscribed. In terms of the mental imagery he is demonstrating that we abstract our sense of vertical and horizontal from our own bodies (as he says also in "Goodfriday, 1613. Riding Westward" when he extends the crucified body to the spanning of the Poles.) But in "The Crosse" he moves from his own body echoing Christ's to a mad bravura demonstration of the brain's power to detect – or confer – abstract forms as it pleases.

> Swimme, and at every stroake, thou art thy Crosse
> The Mast and yard make one, where seas do tosse;
> Looke downe, thou spiest out Crosses in small things;
> Looke up, thou seest birds rais'd on crossed wings;
> All the Globes frame, and spheares, is nothing else
> But the Meridians crossing Parallels.

Later still he remarks that the brain in the skull is itself contained in a bony structure crossed by a cross

> And as the braine through bony walls doth vent
> By sutures, which a Crosses form present ...

Suggesting that the brain, looking upwards through the skull has to pass through a cross to make contact with the outside world.

It has to be said that this is nonsense at any level of logic except the brain's pleasure in noticing, or making, analogies. The birds' wings are crossed at one particular moment of human perceiving attention. The meridians are geometers' patterns imposed on the globe to make a map of it. Only at some very primitive neurological level of finding horizontals and verticals is all this coherent – at the point where some primitive and deep perceptual order gives rise to the connections and reinforced connections which make concepts, and lead to this kind of mental pleasure in the process of connection itself. In the second half of the poem (which is not one of Donne's best or most successful) Donne superposes grammatical and linguistic graphing on his visual patterns.

> ... therefore Crosse
> Your joy in crosses, else, 'tis double losse.
> And crosse thy senses, else, both they, and thou
> Must perish soone, and to destruction bowe.

He instructs his reader to "cross" his/her inclinations and then triples the pun:

> And crosse thy heart: for that in man alone
> Points downewards, and hath palpitation.

The heart is a downward-pointing shape, and is also the seat of human desires, pulling man down to Hell, whereas the head Donne described in a sermon "erected to heaven."[11] This is an extreme version of the metaphor noticed by the psycholinguists, the badness of "down" and the goodness of "up" – originating in the idea of the body as a cross perhaps. Donne has also played with the superstitious idea of "crossing the heart" and maybe the religious gesture of doing so. What he has certainly done is make an elaborate graph, in Changeux's terms, of images and connections with which to construct a world of ideas – derived oddly and distantly from percepts.

Both geometry and grammar are wild in "The Crosse." I'd like to add that some of Donne's most beautiful effects are derived from the foregrounding of the difficulty and complexity – and density – of grammatical constructions. I am thinking not only of his long verse paragraphs, as in "Lovers infinitenesse," but of difficult structures like the whole of "The Dreame," where the meaning (which is not difficult to understand) has to be waited for, and puzzled out, through the syntax. I have the impression that Donne rhymes more than most poets on a delayed/hanging part of the verb "to be."

> I must confesse, it could not choose but bee
> Prophane, to thinke thee any thing but thee.

The poem is about the real and the dreamed or imagined, so the verb to be is important. The beginning of the following verse is syntactically awkward, and once understood, powerful in its assertion of the reality of the "being" of the woman.

> Comming and staying show'd thee, thee
> But rising makes me doubt that now,
> Thou art not thou.

The double thee and the double thou offer a verbal image of the simultaneous possibility that she is identical to herself, and real, or that there are two, one only dreamed – thee or thee, thou or thou. It isn't a poetry of soft flesh – it's a poetry of the puzzling head – but it is powerful and erotic.

I think Donne's poetry is paradoxically easy to learn by heart and to retain over long periods partly because of this syntactical play. I have noticed that if I try to remember verse – or even prose – I have known by heart – what comes back first into the mind is the rhythm, the beat of iamb or trochee, or the break of regularity. Then I seem to remember the connecting words – participles, prepositions, conjunctions – followed by the verbs. The nouns come last, and proper names, which should be the most particular, are curiously elusive. It seems to me possible that this searching for the remembered piece of language (concept, image, idea) finds first the deepest and strongest neuronal reinforced links, where the firing of the cells is surest, most frequent and steadiest. And if this is so, it is a possible reason why Donne's games with grammar (and complicated rhythms) are primitive as well as difficult. They are the feeling of thought.

Donne himself was interested in physiology, in the sinewy string his brain let fall, in the propagation of lovers by the reciprocal pictures in their eye-balls. I'd like to make a final speculation about mirror neurones. Mirror neurones are neurones recently discovered in the frontal lobes of monkeys which have the curious capacity to fire not only when the monkey performs an action, but when it observes the same action performed by another monkey. V. S. Ramachandran, and others, have speculated that human culture may have derived from the communicative possibilities of this ability to internalize the bodily – and mental?- states of other humans. We have neurones that feel in the mind what we see others feel with their fingers or tongues. I want to look briefly at one of Donne's most evocative erotic poems in terms of language and mirror neurones. It is the elegy "Going to Bed." I am thinking particularly of the two lines

> Licence my roving hands and let them go,
> Before, behind, between, above, below.

Elaine Scarry discusses these lines in terms of her aesthetic instructing category "Addition and Subtraction." She is writing about

> the general phenomenon – a verb that appears to describe motion within the text that instead prompts and describes the arrival of a picture in the imaginer's mind – can be recognized in many ... places. Half in the imperative and half in the voice of petition John Donne addresses his mistress for permission to let him move his hands across her undressed body –

> Licence my roving hands and let them go but it is also the imaginer who is being solicited to make the picture of Donne's hand move across the picture of the woman's body, a sense of movement achieved by a sequence of five stills, five locations on the woman's body:

> Before, behind, between, above, below.

Scarry remarks in a footnote that Donne "immediately follows the five stills with a line of awed exclamation that tells us the pictures, whether or not we quite realized it, did indeed successfully get made: 'O my America, my new found land ...' It is as though he had said to the reader, Please do this, and a moment later, Thank you for doing that, and in the momentum of being thanked we had the impression of the pictures having been successfully made."[12]

Scarry has noticed what is important about this very sensuous image – it is, like Donne's uses of her other imaginative marker, bright ignition, stopped off. He starts an imaginative process, and leaves the reader to carry it through, or to respond to the marker. I do not see the succession of adverbs as "stills" at all, partly because I do not expect Donne to make a picture, and partly because they are like Donne's other erotic lists – "eyes, lips, hands" "thy lip, eye, and brow" – parts of speech evoking a sensuous graph. I think – though this can't be proved, and is merely a hypothetical folly – that Donne's adverbs of a flow of movement, like his enumeration of parts of an imagined face – are an appeal to mirror neurones. And the mirror neurones that respond to "Before, behind, between, above, below" are not picture-making neurones, but locations on the body of both writer and reader, the more powerful because the more purely *brief* firings in the mind of a deep habit of imagining motion in the body, and linking these images to other emotions to form concepts and map them with grammar.

NOTES

1 "Loves Alchemie" and verse letter "To the Countesse of Huntingdon."
2 In A. J. Smith and Catherine Phillips (eds.), *John Donne: The Critical Heritage*, vol. 2 (London: Routledge, 1996), p. 444.
3 Christopher Ricks (ed.), *The Poems of Tennyson*, 3 vols., 2nd edn. (Berkeley: University of California Press, 1987), vol. 2.
4 Sir Charles Sherrington, *Man on His Nature*, 2nd edn. (Cambridge: Cambridge University Press, 1953), p. 178.
5 Jean-Pierre Dupuy, *Aux Origines des Sciences Cognitives* (Paris, 1994); trans. M. B. De Bevoise as *The Mechanization of the Mind: On the Origins of Cognitive Science* (Princeton: Princeton University Press, 2000).
6 Jean-Pierre Changeux, *L'Homme de Verité* ([Paris]: Odile Jacob Poches, 2002), pp. 123 *et seq.*, for instance; trans. M. B. DeBevoise as *The Physiology of Truth: Neuroscience and Human Knowledge* (Cambridge, MA: Harvard University Press, 2004).
7 Jean-Pierre Changeux, *L'Homme Neuronal* ([Paris]: Hachette Pluriel Poche, 1983), pp. 174 *et seq.*; trans. Lawrence Garey, *Neuronal Man: The Biology of Mind* (New York: Pantheon, 1985).
8 Semir Zeki, *Inner Vision: An Exploration of Art and the Brain* (Oxford: Oxford University Press, 1999).
9 See, for instance, George Lakoff and Mark Johnson, *Metaphors we Live By* (Chicago: University of Chicago Press, 1980).
10 Elaine Scarry, *Dreaming by the Book* (New York: Farrar, Strauss and Giroux, 1999).
11 See A. J. Smith's footnote on these lines in *John Donne: The Complete English Poems* (Harmondsworth: Penguin, 1971), p. 648.
12 Scarry, pp. 106 and 271 n. 7.

L. E. SEMLER

Select bibliography

Editions and texts

Alford, Henry (ed.), *The Works of John Donne, D.D., Dean of Saint Pauls 1621–31, With a Memoir of his Life*, 6 vols., London, John W. Parker, 1839.

Carey, John (ed.), *John Donne: The Major Works*, Oxford, Oxford University Press, 1990, [rev. edn.] 2000.

(ed.), *Selected Poetry*, Oxford, Oxford University Press, 1996.

Chambers, E. K. (ed.), *The Poems of John Donne*, 2 vols., London, Lawrence and Bullen, 1896.

Clements, Arthur L. (ed.), *John Donne's Poetry: Authoritative Texts, Criticism*, New York, Norton, 1966, [rev. edn.] 1992.

Coffin, Charles M. (ed.), *The Complete Poetry and Selected Prose of John Donne*, New York, Modern Library, 1952.

Donne, John, *Deaths Duel*, 1632, facsimile rpt., Menston, Scolar, 1969.

Poems by J. D. with Elegies on the Authors Death, 1633, facsimile rpt., Menston, Scolar, 1969.

Poems on Several Occasions, London, Jacob Tonson, 1719.

The Variorum Edition of the Poetry of John Donne, Volume 2: The Elegies. Gen. ed. Gary A. Stringer; text eds. Ted-Larry Pebworth, Gary A. Stringer, Ernest W. Sullivan II, Dennis Flynn, and Theodore J. Sherman; comm. ed. John R. Roberts; contrib. ed. Diana Treviño Benet. Bloomington, Indiana University Press, 2000.

The Variorum Edition of the Poetry of John Donne, Volume 6: The Anniversaries and the Epicedes and Obsequies. Gen. ed. Gary A. Stringer; text eds. Ted-Larry Pebworth, John T. Shawcross, Gary A. Stringer, and Ernest W. Sullivan II; comm. ed. Paul A. Parrish; contrib. eds. Donald R. Dickson and Dennis Flynn. Bloomington, Indiana University Press, 1995.

The Variorum Edition of the Poetry of John Donne, Volume 8: The Epigrams, Epithalamions, Epitaphs, Inscriptions, and Miscellaneous Poems. Gen. ed. Gary A. Stringer; text eds. Ted-Larry Pebworth, Gary A. Stringer, and Ernest W. Sullivan II; comm. ed. William A. McClung; contrib. ed. Jeffrey Johnson. Bloomington, Indiana University Press, 1996.

Enright, D. J. (ed.), *John Donne*, London, Dent, 1997.

Gardner, Helen (ed.), *The Divine Poems*, Oxford, Clarendon, 1952, [2nd edn.] 1978.

(ed.), *The Elegies and the Songs and Sonnets*, Oxford, Clarendon, 1965.

(ed.), *The Metaphysical Poets*, Harmondsworth, Penguin, 1957, [rev. edn.] 1966, [2nd rev. edn.] 1972, 1981, 1985.

and Timothy Healy (eds.), *John Donne: Selected Prose*, Oxford, Oxford University Press, 1967.

Gill, Richard (ed.), *John Donne: Selected Poems*, Oxford, Oxford University Press, 1990.

Grierson, Herbert J. C. (ed.), *The Poems of John Donne*, 2 vols., Oxford, Oxford University Press, 1912.

(ed.), *Poems of John Donne*, Oxford, Oxford University Press, 1929.

Grosart, Alexander B. (ed.), *The Complete Poems of John Donne, D.D., Dean of St. Paul's*, 2 vols., London, Robson and Sons, 1872.

Hayward, John (ed.), *John Donne, Dean of St. Paul's: Complete Poetry and Selected Prose*, London, Nonesuch, 1929, [rev.] 1967, 1990.

Healy, T. S., SJ (ed.), *Ignatius His Conclave*, Oxford, Clarendon, 1969.

Hester, M. Thomas (ed.), *Letters to Severall Persons of Honour*, 1651, facsimile rpt., New York, Scholars' Facsimiles and Reprints, 1977.

Jessopp, Augustus (ed.), *Essays in Divinity*, London, John Tupling, 1855.

Lowell, James Russell, and Charles Eliot Norton (eds.), *The Poems of John Donne from the Text of 1633*, 2 vols., New York, The Grolier Club, 1895. [This is a rev. edn. of James Russell Lowell (ed.), *The Poetical Works of Dr. John Donne, with a Memoir*, 1855.]

Manley, Frank (ed.), *John Donne: The Anniversaries*, Baltimore, Johns Hopkins, 1963.

Merrill, Charles Edmund (ed.), *Letters to Severall Persons of Honour*, New York, Sturgis and Walton, 1910.

Milgate, Wesley (ed.), *The Epithalamions, Anniversaries and Epicedes*, Oxford, Clarendon, 1978.

(ed.), *The Satires, Epigrams and Verse Letters*, Oxford, Clarendon, 1967.

Moses, John, Dean of St Paul's (ed.), *One Equall Light: An Anthology of the Writings of John Donne*, Norwich, Canterbury Press, 2003.

Motion, Andrew (ed.), *Devotions Upon Emergent Occasions and Death's Duel: With the Life of Dr. John Donne by Izaak Walton*, New York, Vintage, 1999.

Mueller, Janel M. (ed.), *Donne's Prebend Sermons*, Cambridge, MA, Harvard University Press, 1971.

Oliver, P. M. (ed.), *John Donne: Selected Letters*, New York: Routledge, 2002.

Patrides, C. A. (ed.), *The Complete English Poems of John Donne*, London, Dent, 1985, [rptd.] 1990, [rev. edn. with Robin Hamilton] 1994, [rptd.] 1996.

Peters, Helen (ed.), *Paradoxes and Problems*, Oxford, Clarendon, 1980.

Potter, George R., and Evelyn M. Simpson (eds.), *Sermons*, 10 vols., Berkeley, University of California Press, 1953–62.

Raspa, Anthony (ed.), *Devotions Upon Emergent Occasions*, Montreal, 1975; rptd. Oxford, Oxford University Press, 1987.

(ed.), *Pseudo-Martyr*, Montreal, McGill-Queen's University Press, 1993.

Redpath, Theodore (ed.), *The Songs and Sonets of John Donne*, London, Methuen, 1956, [2nd edn.] 1983.

Rhodes, Neil (ed.), *John Donne: Selected Prose*, Harmondsworth, Penguin, 1987.

Shawcross, John T. (ed.), *The Complete Poetry of John Donne*, New York, Doubleday, 1967.

Shami, Jeanne (ed.), *John Donne's 1622 Gunpowder Plot Sermon: A Parallel Text Edition*, Duquesne, Duquesne University Press, 1996.

Simpson, Evelyn M. (ed.), *Essays in Divinity*, Oxford, Clarendon, 1952.
— (ed.), *Sermons on the Psalms and Gospels, with a Selection of Prayers and Meditations*, Berkeley, University of California Press, 1963.
Smith, A. J. (ed.), *John Donne: The Complete English Poems*, Harmondsworth, Penguin, 1971, [rev. edn.] 1976, [rptd.] 1996.
Sparrow, John (ed.), with bibliographical note by Geoffrey Keynes, *Devotions upon Emergent Occasions*, Cambridge, Cambridge University Press, 1923.
Sullivan, Ernest W., II (ed.), *Biathanatos*, Newark: University of Delaware Press, 1984.
— (ed.), *The First and Second Dalhousie Manuscripts: Poems and Prose by John Donne and Others: A Facsimile Edition*, Columbia, University of Missouri Press, 1988.

Bibliographies and concordance

Bush, Douglas, *English Literature in the Earlier Seventeenth Century, 1600–1660*, Oxford, Clarendon, 1945, [rev. edn.] 1962, [crtd edn.] 1966.
Combs, Homer Carroll, and Zay Rusk Sullens, *A Concordance to the English Poems of John Donne*, Chicago, 1940, rptd. New York, Haskell House, 1969.
Keynes, Geoffrey, *A Bibliography of Dr. John Donne, Dean of St. Paul's*, London, 1914, [2nd edn.] 1932, [3rd edn.] Cambridge, 1958, [4th edn. rev.] Oxford, Clarendon, 1973.
Partrides, C. A., and Robin Hamilton, "Bibliography" and "Supplementary Bibliography," 419–72, in C. A. Partrides and Robin Hamilton (eds.), *The Complete English Poems of John Donne*, London, Dent, 1994.
Roberts, John R., *John Donne: An Annotated Bibliography of Modern Criticism (1912–1967)*, Columbia, University of Missouri Press, 1973.
— *John Donne: An Annotated Bibliography of Modern Criticism (1968–1978)*, Columbia, University of Missouri Press, 1982.

Biographies

Bald, R. C., *John Donne: A Life*, Oxford, Oxford University Press, 1970.
— *Donne and the Drurys*, Cambridge, Cambridge University Press, 1959.
Edwards, David, *John Donne: Man of Flesh and Spirit*, London, Continuum, 2001.
Evans, Robert C., "John Donne, Governor of Charterhouse," *John Donne Journal* 8 (1989), 133–50.
Flynn, Dennis, *John Donne and the Ancient Catholic Nobility*, Bloomington, Indiana University Press, 1995.
Gosse, Edmund (ed.), *The Life and Letters of John Donne, Dean of St Paul's*, 2 vols., London, 1899, rptd. Gloucester, MA, Peter Smith, 1959.
Hughes, Richard E., *The Progress of the Soul: The Interior Career of John Donne*, New York, William Morrow, 1968.
Le Comte, Edward, *Grace to a Witty Sinner: A Life of Donne*, New York, Walker, 1965.
Parfitt, George, *John Donne: a Literary Life*, Houndmills, Macmillan, 1989.
Parker, Derek, *John Donne and His World*, London, Thames and Hudson, 1975.
Sellin, Paul R., *So Doth, So is Religion: John Donne and Diplomatic Contexts in the Reformed Netherlands, 1619–1920*, Columbia, University of Missouri Press, 1988.

Smith, A. J., "John Donne" 77–96, in *Dictionary of Literary Biography 121: Seventeenth-Century British Nondramatic Poets, First Series*, ed. M. Thomas Hester, Detroit, Gale Research, 1992.

Walton, Izaak, "The Life of Dr. John Donne" in *Izaak Walton: Selected Writings*, ed. Jessica Martin, Manchester, Carcanet, 1997.

   The Lives of John Donne, Sir Henry Wotton, Richard Hooker, George Herbert and Robert Sanderson, ed. George Saintsbury, London, Oxford University Press, 1927, [rptd.] 1950.

Monographs on Donne

Andreasen, N. J. C., *John Donne: Conservative Revolutionary*, Princeton, Princeton University Press, 1967.

Baumlin, James S., *John Donne and the Rhetorics of Renaissance Discourse*, Columbia, University of Missouri Press, 1991.

Carey, John, *John Donne: Life, Mind and Art*, London, Faber and Faber, and New York, Oxford University Press, 1981, [rev. edn.] 1990.

Davies, Stevie, *John Donne*, Plymouth, Northcote House and British Council, 1994.

Docherty, Thomas, *John Donne, Undone*, London, Methuen, 1986.

Everett, Barbara, *Donne: A London Poet*, London, Oxford University Press, 1972.

Hunt, Clay, *Donne's Poetry: Essays in Literary Analysis*, New Haven, Yale University Press, 1954, [rptd.] 1969.

Kermode, Frank, *John Donne*, London, Longmans, Green and Co., 1957, [rev. edn.] 1961.

Leishman, J. B., *The Monarch of Wit: An Analytical and Comparative Study of the Poetry of John Donne*, London, Hutchinson University Library, 1951, [rev. edn.] 1962.

Novarr, David, *The Disinterred Muse: Donne's Texts and Contexts*, Ithaca, Cornell University Press, 1980.

Nutt, Joe, *John Donne: The Poems*, New York, Palgrave Macmillan, 1999.

Ray, Robert H., *A John Donne Companion*, New York, Garland, 1990.

Roston, Murray, *The Soul of Wit: A Study of John Donne*, Oxford, Oxford University Press, 1974.

Sanders, Wilbur, *John Donne's Poetry*, London, Cambridge University Press, 1971.

Stein, Arnold, *John Donne's Lyrics: The Eloquence of Action*, Minneapolis, University of Minnesota Press, 1962.

Unger, Leonard, *Donne's Poetry and Modern Criticism*, Chicago, Henry Regnery, 1950, [rptd.] 1962.

Warnke, Frank J., *John Donne*, Boston, Twayne, 1978.

Wiggins, Peter DeSa, *Donne, Castiglione and the Poetry of Courtliness*, Bloomington, Indiana University Press, 2000.

Winny, James, *A Preface to Donne*, New York, Longman, 1970, [rev. edn.] 1981.

Zunder, William, *The Poetry of John Donne: Literature and Culture in the Elizabethan and Jacobean Period*, Sussex, Harvester, 1982.

Collections of critical essays on Donne

Bloom, Harold (ed.), *John Donne: Comprehensive Research and Study Guide*, Broomall, PA, Chelsea House, 1999.

Fiore, Peter Amadeus (ed.), *Just So Much Honor: Essays Commemorating the Four-Hundredth Anniversary of the Birth of John Donne*, University Park, Pennsylvania State University Press, 1972.

Gardner, Helen (ed.), *John Donne: A Collection of Critical Essays*, Englewood Cliffs, Prentice-Hall, 1962.

Hester, M. Thomas (ed.), *John Donne's "Desire of More": The Subject of Anne More Donne in His Poetry*, Newark, University of Delaware Press, 1996.

Kermode, Frank (ed.), *Discussions of John Donne*, Boston, Heath, 1962.

Marotti, Arthur F. (ed.), *Critical Essays on John Donne*, New York, G. K. Hall, 1994.

Mousley, Andrew (ed.), *The New Casebooks: John Donne*, Houndmills, Macmillan, 1999.

Pepperdene, Margaret W. (ed.), *That Subtle Wreath: Lectures Presented at the Quatercentenary Celebration of the Birth of John Donne*, Atlanta, Agnes Scott College, 1974.

Roberts, John R. (ed.), *Essential Articles for the Study of John Donne's Poetry*, Hamden, CT, Shoestring, 1975.

and Gary A. Stringer (eds.), "A Special Issue: John Donne," *South Central Review* 4 (1987).

Smith, A. J. (ed.), *John Donne: Essays in Celebration*, London, Methuen, 1972.

Spencer, Theodore (ed.), *A Garland for John Donne, 1631–1931*, Cambridge, Harvard University Press, 1931, rptd. Gloucester, MA, 1958.

Stringer, Gary A. (ed.), *New Essays on Donne*, Salzburg, University of Salzburg, 1977.

Summers, Claude J., and Ted-Larry Pebworth (eds.), *The Eagle and the Dove: Reassessing John Donne*, Columbia, University of Missouri Press, 1986.

Other monographs and collections featuring Donne

Berley, Marc (ed.), *Reading the Renaissance: Ideas and Idioms from Shakespeare to Milton*, Pittsburgh, Duquesne University Press, 2003.

Bush, Douglas, *English Literature in the Earlier Seventeenth Century, 1600–1660*, Oxford, Clarendon, 1945, [rev. edn.] 1962, [crtd edn.] 1966.

Colie, Rosalie L., *Paradoxia Epidemica: The Renaissance Tradition of Paradox*, Princeton, 1966; [rptd.] Princeton, Princeton University Press, 1976.

Corns, Thomas N. (ed.), *The Cambridge Companion to English Poetry, Donne to Marvell*, Cambridge, Cambridge University Press, 1993.

Doebler, Bettie Anne, *"Rooted Sorrow": Dying in Early Modern England*, Rutherford, NJ, Fairleigh Dickinson University Press, 1994.

Felperin, Howard, *The Uses of the Canon: Elizabethan Literature and Contemporary Theory*, Oxford, Oxford University Press, 1990.

Ford, Boris (ed.), *From Donne to Marvell*, Baltimore, 1956, [rev. edn.] Harmondsworth, Penguin, 1982.

Goldberg, Jonathan, *James I and the Politics of Literature: Jonson, Shakespeare, Donne, and their Contemporaries*, Baltimore, Johns Hopkins University Press, 1983.

Guibbory, Achsah, *The Map of Time: Seventeenth-Century English Literature and Ideas of Pattern in History*, Urbana, University of Illinois Press, 1986.

Hollander, John, *Vision and Resonance: Two Senses of Poetic Form*, New Haven, Yale University Press, 1985.

Kermode, Frank, *Shakespeare, Spenser, Donne: Renaissance Essays*, London, Fontana, 1971.

Low, Anthony, *Love's Architecture: Devotional Modes in Seventeenth-Century English Poetry*, New York, New York University Press, 1978.

The Reinvention of Love: Poetry, Politics and Culture from Sidney to Milton, Cambridge, Cambridge University Press, 1993.

Loewenstein, David, and Janel Mueller (eds.), *The Cambridge History of Early Modern Literature*, Cambridge, Cambridge University Press, 2002.

Martz, Louis L., *The Wit of Love: Donne, Carew, Crashaw, Marvell*, Notre Dame, University of Notre Dame Press, 1969.

Nardo, Anna K., *The Ludic Self in Seventeenth-Century English Literature*, Albany, State University of New York Press, 1991.

Parfitt, George, *English Poetry of the Seventeenth Century*, London, Longman, 1985, [rev. edn.] 1992.

Praz, Mario, *The Flaming Heart: Essays on Crashaw, Machiavelli, and Other Studies in the Relations between Italian and English Literature from Chaucer to T. S. Eliot*, New York, Doubleday Anchor, 1958.

Post, Jonathan F. S., *English Lyric Poetry: The Early Seventeenth Century*, New York, Routledge, 1999.

Ricks, Christopher (ed.), *English Poetry and Prose 1540–1674*, London, Sphere, 1970, [rev. edn.] 1986.

Roberts, John R. (ed.), *New Perspectives on the Seventeenth-Century English Religious Lyric*, Columbia, University of Missouri Press, 1994.

Shuger, Debora K., *Habits of Thought in the English Renaissance: Religion, Politics and the Dominant Culture*, Berkeley, University of California Press, 1990.

Smith, A. J., *The Metaphysics of Love: Studies in Renaissance Love Poetry from Dante to Milton*, Cambridge, Cambridge University Press, 1985.

Stein, Arnold, *The House of Death: Messages from the English Renaissance*, Baltimore, Johns Hopkins University Press, 1986.

Strier, Richard, *Resistant Structures: Particularity, Radicalism and Renaissance Texts*, Berkeley, University of California Press, 1995.

Summers, Claude J., and Ted-Larry Pebworth (eds.), *Fault Lines and Controversies in the Study of Seventeenth-Century English Literature*, Columbia, University of Missouri Press, 2002.

Donne and metaphysical poetry

Austin, Frances, *The Language of the Metaphysical Poets*, New York, St. Martin's Press, 1992.

Bennet, Joan, *Four Metaphysical Poets: Donne, Herbert, Vaughan, Crashaw*, Cambridge, Cambridge University Press, 1934, [rev. as *Five Metaphysical Poets: Donne, Herbert, Vaughan, Crashaw, Marvell*] 1964.

Bloom, Harold (ed.), *John Donne and the Seventeenth-Century Metaphysical Poets*, New York, Chelsea House, 1986.

Bradbury, Malcolm, and David Palmer (eds.), *Metaphysical Poetry*, Bloomington, Indiana University Press, 1970.

Dime, Gregory T., "The Difference between 'Strong Lines' and 'Metaphysical Poetry,'" *Studies in English Literature* 26 (1986), 47–57.

Eliot, T. S., *Selected Essays*, London, Faber and Faber, 1932, [rev. edn.] 1934, [enlgd. edn.] 1951.

The Varieties of Metaphysical Poetry: The Clark Lectures at Trinity College, Cambridge, 1926, and the Turnbull Lectures at the Johns Hopkins University, 1933, by T. S. Eliot, ed. Ronald Schuchard, New York, Harcourt Brace, 1993.

Ellrodt, Robert, *Inspiration personelle et l'esprit du temps chez les poetes métaphysiques Anglais*, 1960, [2nd edn.] Paris, Corti, 1973.

Holmes, Michael Morgan, *Early Modern Metaphysical Literature: Nature, Custom and Strange Desires*, Basingstoke, Palgrave, 2001.

Hunter, Jim, *The Metaphysical Poets*, London, Evans Bros, 1965.

Keast, William R. (ed.), *Seventeenth-Century English Poetry: Modern Essays in Criticism*, New York, Oxford University Press, 1961, [rev. edn.] 1971.

Leishman, J. B., *The Metaphysical Poets: Donne, Herbert, Vaughan, Traherne*, Oxford, Clarendon, 1934, [rptd.] New York, Russell and Russell, 1963.

Miner, Earl, *The Metaphysical Mode from Donne to Cowley*, Princeton, Princeton University Press, 1969.

Mourgues, Odette de, *Metaphysical, Baroque and Précieux Poetry*, Oxford, Oxford University Press, 1953.

Raynaud, Claudine (ed.), *La Poésie Métaphysique de John Donne*, Tours, GRAAT, 2002.

Sloane, Mary C., *The Visual in Metaphysical Poetry*, Atlantic Highlands, Humanities Press, 1980.

Smith, A. J., *Metaphysical Wit*, Cambridge, Cambridge University Press, 1991.

Stampfer, Judah, *John Donne and the Metaphysical Gesture*, New York, Funk and Wagnalls, 1970.

Tuve, Rosemond, *Elizabethan and Metaphysical Imagery: Renaissance Poetic and Twentieth-Century Critics*, Chicago, University of Chicago Press, 1947, [rptd.] 1961.

Wanamaker, Melissa C., *Discordia Concors: The Wit of Metaphysical Poetry*, Port Washington, NY, Kennikat Press, 1975.

White, Helen C., *The Metaphysical Poets: A Study in Religious Experience*, New York, Macmillan, 1936.

Williamson, George, "Strong Lines," *English Studies* 18 (1936), 152–59.

Religion and politics

Bossy, John, *The English Catholic Community, 1570–1850*, London, Darton, Longman and Todd, 1975.

Bredvold, Louis I., "The Religious Thought of Donne in Relation to Medieval and Later Traditions" 193–232 in *Studies in Shakespeare, Milton and Donne by Members of the English Department of the University of Michigan*, New York, Macmillan, 1925, [rptd.] 1964.

Brown, Meg Lota, *Donne and the Politics of Conscience in Early Modern England*, Leiden, E. J. Brill, 1995.

Cain, Tom, "John Donne and the Ideology of Colonization," *English Literary Renaissance* 31 (2001), 440–76.

Cefalu, Paul, "Godly Fear, Sanctification, and Calvinist Theology in the Sermons and 'Holy Sonnets' of John Donne," *Studies in Philology* 100 (2003), 71–86.

Colclough, David (ed.), *John Donne's Professional Lives*, Suffolk, D. S. Brewer, 2003.

DiPasquale, Theresa M., *Literature and Sacrament: The Sacred and the Secular in John Donne*, Pittsburgh, Duquesne University Press, 1999.

Doerksen, Daniel W., *Conforming to the Word: Herbert, Donne, and the English Church before Laud*, Lewisburg and London, Associated University Presses, 1997.

and Christopher Hodgkins (eds.), *Centered on the Word: Literature, Scripture, and the Tudor-Stuart Middle Way*, Newark, University of Delaware Press, 2004.

Evans, Gillian R., "John Donne and the Augustinian Paradox of Sin," *Review of English Studies* 33 (1982), 1–22.

Ferrell, Lori Anne, and Peter McCullough (eds.), *The English Sermon Revised: Religion, Literature and History 1600–1750*, Manchester: Manchester University Press, 2000, pp. 2–21.

Fincham, Kenneth (ed.), *The Early Stuart Church, 1603–1642*, Basingstoke, Macmillan, 1993.

Flynn, Dennis, "Donne's Politics, 'Desperate Ambition,' and Meeting Paolo Sarpi in Venice," *Journal of English and Germanic Philology* 99 (2000), 334–55.

Frontain, Raymond-Jean, and Frances M. Malpezzi (eds.), *John Donne's Religious Imagination: Essays in Honor of John T. Shawcross*, Conway, UCA Press, 1995.

Grant, Patrick, *The Transformation of Sin: Studies in Donne, Herbert, Vaughan, and Traherne*, Montreal, McGill-Queen's University Press, 1974.

Guibbory, Achsah, "Donne's Religion: Montagu, Arminianism, and Donne's Sermons, 1624–1630," *English Literary Renaissance* 31 (2001), 412–439.

Harland, Paul W., "Donne and Virginia: The Ideology of Conquest," *John Donne Journal* 18 (1999), 127–52.

"Donne's Political Intervention in the Parliament of 1629," *John Donne Journal* 11 (1992), 21–37.

Henley, Mary Ellen, W. Speed Hill, and R. G. Siemens (eds.), *Wrestling with God: Literature and Theology in the English Renaissance. Essays to Honour Paul Grant Stanwood*, Vancouver, M. E. Henley, 2001.

Hughes, Richard E., *The Progress of the Soul: The Interior Career of John Donne*, New York, 1968, rptd. London, Bodley Head, 1969.

Jackson, Robert S., *John Donne's Christian Vocation*, Evanston, Northwestern University Press, 1970.

Johnson, Jeffrey, *The Theology of John Donne*, Cambridge, D. S. Brewer, 1999.

Lewalski, Barbara Kiefer, *Protestant Poetics and the Seventeenth-Century Religious Lyric*, Princeton, Princeton University Press, 1979.

Manley, Lawrence, *Literature and Culture in Early Modern London*, Cambridge, Cambridge University Press, 1995.

Martz, Louis L., *The Poetry of Meditation: A Study in English Religious Literature of the Seventeenth Century*, New Haven, Yale University Press, 1954, [rev. edn.] 1962.

McCullough, Peter, *Sermons at Court: Politics and Religion in Elizabethan and Jacobean Preaching*, Cambridge, Cambridge University Press, 1998.

Milton, Anthony, *Catholic and Reformed: The Roman and Protestant Churches in English Protestant Thought, 1600–1640*, Cambridge, Cambridge University Press, 1995.

Morrissey, Mary, "Interdisciplinarity and the Study of Early Modern Sermons," *Historical Journal* 42:4 (1999), 11–24.

Norbrook, David, "The Monarchy of Wit and the Republic of Letters: Donne's Politics," 3–36 in Elizabeth D. Harvey and Katherine Eisaman Maus (eds.),

Soliciting Interpretation: Literary Theory and Seventeenth-Century English Poetry, Chicago, University of Chicago Press, 1990.

Oliver, P. M., *Donne's Religious Writing: A Discourse of Feigned Devotion*, London, Longman, 1997.

Papazian, Mary Arshagouni (ed.), *John Donne and the Protestant Reformation: New Perspectives*, Detroit, Wayne State University Press, 2003.

Parry, Graham, *The Golden Age Restor'd: The Culture of the Stuart Court, 1603–42*, Manchester, Manchester University Press, 1981.

Patterson, Annabel, *Reading Between the Lines*, Madison, University of Wisconsin Press, 1993.

Sellin, Paul R., *John Donne and "Calvinist" Views of Grace*, Amsterdam, VU Boekhandel, 1983.

Shami, Jeanne, *John Donne and Conformity in Crisis in the Late Jacobean Pulpit*, Suffolk, D. S. Brewer, 2003.

Shaw, Robert B., *The Call of God: The Theme of Vocation in the Poetry of Donne and Herbert*, Cambridge, MA, Cowley Publications, 1981.

Slights, Camille Wells, *The Casuistical Tradition in Shakespeare, Donne, Herbert, and Milton*, Princeton, Princeton University Press, 1981.

Stevens, Paul, "Donne's Catholicism and the Innovation of the Modern Nation State," *John Donne Journal* 20 (2001), 53–70.

Strier, Richard, "Donne and the Politics of Devotion," 93–114 in Donna B. Hamilton and Richard Strier (eds), *Religion, Literature and Politics in Post-Reformation England*, Cambridge, Cambridge University Press, 1996.

Valbuena, Olga L., "'Bind Your Selves by Oath': Political Allegiance and Infidelity in Donne's Thought," 38–78, in *Subjects to the King's Divorce: Equivocation, Infidelity, and Resistance in Early Modern England*, Bloomington, Indiana University Press, 2003.

Wabuda, Susan, and Caroline Litzenberger (eds), *Belief and Practice in Reformation England*, Aldershot, Ashgate, 1998.

Wilcox, Helen, Richard Todd, and Alasdair MacDonald (eds.), *Sacred and Profane: Secular and Devotional Interplay in Early Modern British Literature*, Amsterdam, Free University Press, 1996.

Young, R. V., *Doctrine and Devotion in Seventeenth-Century Poetry: Studies in Donne, Herbert, Crashaw and Vaughan*, Cambridge, D. S. Brewer, 2000.

Philosophy and the new science

Bredvold, Louis I., "The Naturalism of Donne in Relation to Some Renaissance Traditions," *Journal of English and Germanic Philology* 22 (1923), 471–502.

Cathcart, Dwight, *Doubting Conscience: Donne and the Poetry of Moral Argument*, Ann Arbor, University of Michigan Press, 1975.

Coffin, Charles M., *John Donne and the New Philosophy*, New York, Columbia University Press, 1937, [rptd.] 1958.

Empson, William, *Essays on Renaissance Literature: Volume 1, Donne and the New Philosophy*, Cambridge, Cambridge University Press, 1993, [rptd.] 2002.

Harris, Victor, *All Coherence Gone: A Study of the Seventeenth-Century Controversy over Disorder and Decay in the Universe*, Chicago, 1949, rptd. London, Cass, 1966.

Linden, Stanton J., "'A True Religious Alchimy': The Poetry of Donne and Herbert," 154–92, in *Darke Hierogliphicks: Alchemy in English Literature from Chaucer to the Restoration*, Lexington, University Press of Kentucky, 1996.

Mazzeo, Joseph Anthony, "Notes on John Donne's Alchemical Imagery," 60–89 in *Renaissance and Seventeenth-Century Studies*, New York, Columbia University Press, 1964.

Moloney, Michael F., *John Donne: His Flight from Mediaevalism*, Urbana, University of Illinois Press, 1944, [rptd.] 1965.

Nicolson, Marjorie Hope, *The Breaking of the Circle: Studies in the Effect of the "New Science" upon Seventeenth-Century Poetry*, Evanston, Northwestern University Press, 1950, rev. edn., New York, 1960.

Scodel, Joshua, *Excess and the Mean in Early Modern English Literature*, Princeton, Princeton University Press, 2002.

Sherwood, Terry G., *Fulfilling the Circle: A Study of John Donne's Thought*, Toronto, University of Toronto Press, 1984.

Language, logic, rhetoric, genre (and Petrarchism)

Aers, David, Bob Hodge, and Gunther Kress, *Literature, Language and Society in England, 1580–1680*, Dublin, Gill and Macmillan, 1981.

Bradshaw, Graham, "Donne's Challenge to the Prosodists," *Essays in Criticism* 32 (1982), 338–60.

Brodsky, Claudia, "The Imaging of the Logical Conceit," *ELH* 49 (1982), 829–48.

Cousins, A. D., and Damian Grace (eds.), *Donne and the Resources of Kind*, Madison, Fairleigh Dickinson University Press, 2002.

Dubrow, Heather, *Echoes of Desire: English Petrarchism and Its Counterdiscourses*, Ithaca and London, Cornell University Press, 1995.

Fish, Stanley, "Masculine Persuasive Force: Donne and Verbal Power," 223–52 in Elizabeth D. Harvey and Katherine Eisaman Maus (eds.), *Soliciting Interpretation: Literary Theory and Seventeenth-Century English Poetry*, Chicago, University of Chicago Press, 1990.

Guss, Donald L., *John Donne, Petrarchist: Italianate Conceits and Love Theory in the "Songs and Sonets,"* Detroit, Wayne State University Press, 1966.

Herz, Judith Scherer, "'An Excellent Exercise of Wit that Speaks So Well of Ill': Donne and the Poetics of Concealment," 3–14 in Claude J. Summers and Ted-Larry Pebworth (eds.), *The Eagle and the Dove: Reassessing John Donne*, Columbia, University of Missouri Press, 1986.

McCanles, Michael, "Paradox in Donne," *Studies in the Renaissance* 13 (1966), 266–87.

Miner, Earl (ed.), *Seventeenth-Century Imagery: Essays on Uses of Figurative Language from Donne to Farquhar*, Berkeley, University of California Press, 1971.

Nelly, Una, *The Poet Donne: a Study in his Dialectic Method*, Cork, Cork University Press, 1969.

Partridge, A. C., *John Donne: Language and Style*, London, André Deutsch, 1978.

Ruffo-Fiore, Silvia, *Donne's Petrarchism: A Comparative View*, Florence, Grafica Toscana, 1976.

Rugoff, Milton Allan, *Donne's Imagery: A Study in Creative Sources*, New York, Corporate, 1939, [rptd.] 1962.

Sloane, Thomas O., *Donne, Milton, and the End of Humanist Rhetoric*, Berkeley, University of California Press, 1985.

Visual arts

Cousins, A. D., "The Coming of Mannerism: The Later Ralegh and the Early Donne," *English Literary Renaissance* 9 (1979), 86–107.

Evett, David, "Donne's Poems and the Five Styles of Renascence Art," *John Donne Journal* 5 (1986), 101–31.

Farmer, Norman K., Jr., *Poets and the Visual Arts in Renaissance England*, Austin, University of Texas Press, 1984.

Frost, Kate Gartner, "The Lothian Portrait: A Prolegomenon," *John Donne Journal* 15 (1996), 95–125.

Gilman, Ernest B., *Iconoclasm and Poetry in the English Reformation: Down Went Dagon*, Chicago, University of Chicago Press, 1986.

Hurley, Ann, "More Foolery from More?: John Donne's Lothian Portrait as a Clue to his Politics," in Ann Hurley and Kate Greenspan (eds.), *So Rich a Tapestry: The Sister Arts and Cultural Studies*, Lewisburg, Bucknell University Press, 1995.

Martz, Louis L., *From Renaissance to Baroque: Essays on Literature and Art*, Columbia, University of Missouri Press, 1991.

MacKenzie, Clayton G., *Emblem and Icon in John Donne's Poetry and Prose*, New York, Peter Lang, 2001.

Milgate, W., "Dr. Donne's Art Gallery," *Notes and Queries* 194.15 (23 July 1949), 318–19.

Peterson, Richard S., "New Evidence on Donne's Monument: I," *John Donne Journal* 20 (2001), 1–51.

Roebuck, Graham, "Donne's Visual Imagination and Compasses," *John Donne Journal* 8 (1989), 37–56.

Semler, L. E., *The English Mannerist Poets and the Visual Arts*, Madison, Fairleigh Dickinson University Press, 1998.

Gender, sexuality, and subjectivity

Bell, Ilona, "Courting Anne More," *John Donne Journal* 19 (2000), 59–86.
   Elizabethan Women and the Poetry of Courtship, Cambridge, Cambridge University Press, 1998.

Belsey, Catherine, "John Donne's Worlds of Desire," 130–49 in *Desire: Love Stories in Western Culture*, Oxford, Oxford University Press, 1994. [Rptd., 63–80, in Andrew Mousley (ed.) *The New Casebooks: John Donne*, Houndmills, Macmillan, 1999.]

Corthell, Ronald, *Ideology and Desire in Renaissance Poetry: The Subject of Donne*, Detroit, Wayne State University Press, 1997.

Ellrodt, Robert, *Seven Metaphysical Poets: A Structural Study of the Unchanging Self*, Oxford, Oxford University Press, 2000.

Estrin, Barbara L., *Laura: Uncovering Gender and Genre in Wyatt, Donne, and Marvell*, Durham and London, Duke University Press, 1994.

Ferry, Anne, *The "Inward" Language: Sonnets of Wyatt, Sidney, Shakespeare, Donne*, Chicago, University of Chicago Press, 1983.

Halley, Janet E., "Textual Intercourse: Anne Donne, John Donne, and the Sexual Poetics of Textual Exchange," 187–206 in Sheila Fisher and Janet Halley (eds.), *Seeking the Woman in Late Medieval and Renaissance Writings: Essays in Feminist Contextual Criticism*, Knoxville, University of Tennessee Press, 1989.

Hodgson, Elizabeth M. A., *Gender and the Sacred Self in John Donne*, Newark, University of Delaware Press, 1999.

Holstun, James, "Will You Rent our Ancient Love Asunder?: Lesbian Elegy in Donne, Marvell, and Milton," *ELH* (1987), 835–68.

Klawitter, George, *The Enigmatic Narrator: The Voicing of Same-Sex Love in the Poetry of John Donne*, New York, P. Lang, 1994.

Meakin, H. L., *John Donne's Articulations of the Feminine*, Oxford, Oxford University Press, 1998.

Mintz, Susannah B., "'Forget the Hee and Shee': Gender and Play in John Donne," *Modern Philology* 98 (2001), 577–603.

Sabine, Maureen, *Feminine Engendered Faith: The Poetry of John Donne and Richard Crashaw*, London, Macmillan, 1992.

Scarry, Elaine, "Donne: 'But yet the Body is his Booke,'" 70–105 in Elaine Scarry (ed.), *Literature and the Body: Essays on Populations and Persons*, Baltimore, Johns Hopkins University Press, 1988.

Summers, Claude J., and Ted-Larry Pebworth (eds.), *Renaissance Discourses of Desire*, Columbia, University of Missouri Press, 1993.

Coterie, audience, and manuscript studies

Beal, Peter, "'It shall not therefore kill itself; that is, not bury itself': Donne's *Biathanatos* and its Text," 31–57 in *In Praise of Scribes: Manuscripts and Their Makers in Seventeenth-Century England*, Oxford, Oxford University Press, 1998.

"John Donne, 1572–1631," 243–564 and 566–68 in *Index of English Literary Manuscripts: Volume 1: 1450–1625, Part I: Andrewes–Donne*, London, Mansell, 1980.

Bell, Ilona, "'Under Ye rage of a hott sonn and Yr eyes': John Donne's Love Letters to Ann More," 25–52 in Claude J. Summers and Ted-Larry Pebworth (eds.), *The Eagle and the Dove: Reassessing John Donne*, Columbia, University of Missouri Press, 1986.

Flynn, Dennis, "Donne and a Female Coterie," *Lit: Literature Interpretation Theory* 1 (1989), 127–36.

Hobbes, Mary, "Early Seventeenth-Century Verse Miscellanies and Their Value for Textual Editors," *English Manuscript Studies 1100–1700* 1 (1989), 189–210.

Early Seventeenth-Century Verse Miscellany Manuscripts, Aldershot, Scholar Press, 1992.

Love, Harold, *Scribal Publication in Seventeenth-Century England*, Oxford, Oxford University Press, 1993.

MacColl, Alan, "The Circulation of Donne's Poems in Manuscript," 28–46 in A. J. Smith (ed.), *John Donne: Essays in Celebration*, London, Methuen, 1972.

Marotti, Arthur F., *John Donne, Coterie Poet*, Madison, University of Wisconsin Press, 1986.

Manuscript, Print, and the English Renaissance Lyric, Ithaca, Cornell University Press, 1995.

"Manuscript, Print, and the Social History of the Lyric," 52–79 in Thomas N. Corns (ed.), *The Cambridge Companion to English Poetry, Donne to Marvell*, Cambridge, Cambridge University Press, 1993.

Pebworth, Ted-Larry, "John Donne, Coterie Poetry, and the Text as Performance," *Studies in English Literature* 29 (1989), 61–75.

"Manuscript Poems and Print Assumptions: Donne and His Modern Editors," *John Donne Journal* 3 (1984), 1–21.

"The Early Audiences of Donne's Poetic Performances," *John Donne Journal* 15 (1996), 127–39.

"The Editor, the Critic, and the Multiple Texts of Donne's 'Hymne to God the Father,'" *South Central Review* 4.2 (Summer 1987), 16–34.

Saunders, J. W., "The Stigma of Print: A Note on the Social Bases of Tudor Poetry," *Essays in Criticism* 1 (1951), 139–64.

Shapiro, I. A., "The 'Mermaid Club,'" *Modern Language Review* 45 (1950), 6–17, 58–63.

Sullivan, Ernest, II, and David J. Murrah (eds.), *The Donne Dalhousie Discovery: Proceedings of a Symposium on the Acquisition and Study of the John Donne and Joseph Conrad Collections at Texas Tech University*, Lubbock, TX, Friends of the University Library/Southwest Collection, 1987.

Wollman, Richard B., "The 'Press' and the 'Fire': Print and Manuscript Culture in Donne's Circle," *Studies in English Literature* 33 (1993), 85–97.

Donne's influence, afterlife, and comparative author studies

Altizer, Alma B., *Self and Symbolism in the Poetry of Michelangelo, John Donne, and Agrippa d'Aubigné*, The Hague, Nijhoff, 1973.

Alvarez, A., *The School of Donne*, New York, Chatto and Windus, 1961.

Bald, R. C., *Donne's Influence in English Literature*, Morpeth, St John's College Press, 1932.

Clements, Arthur L., *Poetry of Contemplation: John Donne, George Herbert, Henry Vaughan, and the Modern Period*, Albany, State University of New York Press, 1990.

Duncan, Joseph E., *The Revival of Metaphysical Poetry: The History of a Style, 1800 to the Present*, Minneapolis, University of Minnesota Press, 1959.

Ferry, Anne, *All in War with Time: Love Poetry of Shakespeare, Donne, Jonson, Marvell*, Cambridge, MA, Harvard University Press, 1975.

Granqvist, Raoul, *The Reputation of John Donne 1779–1873*, Uppsala, Almqvist and Wiksell International, 1975.

Guibbory, Achsah, "A Sense of the Future: Projected Audiences of Donne and Jonson," *John Donne Journal* 2.2 (1983), 11–21.

Guillory, John, "The Ideology of Canon-Formation: T. S. Eliot and Cleanth Brooks," *Critical Inquiry* 10.1 (1983), 173–98.

Haskin, Dayton, "No Edition is an Island: The Place of the Nineteenth-Century American Editions within the History of Editing Donne's Poems," *TEXT* 14 (2002), 169–207.

"A History of Donne's 'Canonization' from Izaak Walton to Cleanth Brooks," *Journal of English and Germanic Philology* 92 (1993), 17–36.

Herz, Judith Scherer, "Under the Sign of Donne," *Criticism* 43.1 (2001), 48–49.

Hoover, L. Elaine, *John Donne and Francisco de Quevedo: Poets of Love and Death*, Chapel Hill, University of North Carolina Press, 1978.

Larson, Deborah Aldrich, *John Donne and Twentieth-Century Criticism*, Madison, Fairleigh Dickinson University Press, 1989.

Minto, William, "John Donne," *The Nineteenth Century* 7 (1880), 845–63.

Norton, C. E., "The Text of Donne's Poems," *Studies and Notes in Philology and Literature* 5 (1896; Child Memorial Volume), 1–19.

Perry, T. Anthony, *Erotic Spirituality: The Integrative Tradition from Leone Ebreo to John Donne*, Alabama, University of Alabama Press, 1980.

Smith, A. J. (ed.), *John Donne: The Critical Heritage*, London, Routledge and Kegan Paul, 1975.

and Catherine Phillips (eds.), *John Donne: The Critical Heritage Volume 2*, London, Routledge, 1996.

Sullivan, Ernest W., II, *The Influence of John Donne: His Uncollected Seventeenth-Century Printed Verse*, Columbia, University of Missouri Press, 1993.

Summers, Joseph H., *The Heirs of Donne and Jonson*, Oxford, Oxford University Press, 1970.

Williamson, George, *The Donne Tradition: A Study in English Poetry from Donne to the Death of Cowley*, New York, Peter Smith, 1930, [rptd.] 1958, 1961, 1973.

Donne's works addressed individually

The Anniversaries

Festa, Thomas A., "Donne's *Anniversaries* and his Anatomy of the Book," *John Donne Journal* 17 (1998), 29–60.

Grossman, Marshall, *The Story of all Things: Writing the Self in English Renaissance Narrative Poetry*, Durham, Duke University Press, 1998.

Lewalski, Barbara Kiefer, *Donne's "Anniversaries" and the Poetry of Praise: The Creation of a Symbolic Mode*, Princeton, Princeton University Press, 1973, [rev. edn.] 1979.

Martin, Catherine Gimelli, "*The Advancement of Learning* and the Decay of the World: A New Reading of Donne's *First Anniversary*," *John Donne Journal* 19 (2000), 163–203.

Martz, Louis L., *John Donne in Meditation: The Anniversaries*, New York, Haskell House, 1947, [rptd.] 1970.

Tayler, Edward W., *Donne's Idea of a Woman: Structure and Meaning in "The Anniversaries,"* New York, Columbia University Press, 1991.

Divine poems

Bellette, Anthony F., "'Little Worlds Made Cunningly': Significant Form in Donne's *Holy Sonnets* and 'Goodfriday, 1613,'" *Studies in Philology* 72 (1975), 322–47.

Cummings, Brian, *The Literary Culture of the Reformation: Grammar and Grace*, Oxford, Oxford University Press, 2002.

Maurer, Margaret, "The Circular Argument of Donne's *La Corona*," *Studies in English Literature* 22 (1982), 41–68.

Milward, Peter, *A Commentary on the Holy Sonnets of John Donne*, Tokyo, Renaissance Institute, Sophia University, 1988.

Roebuck, Graham, "Donne's 'Lamentations of Jeremy' Reconsidered," *John Donne Journal* 10 (1991), 37–44.

Ruf, Frederick J., "'Intoxicated with Intimacy': The Lyric Voice in John Donne's *Holy Sonnets*," 37–49 in *Entangled Voices: Genre and the Religious Construction of the Self*, New York, Oxford University Press, 1997.

Spurr, Barry, "The Theology of *La Corona*," *John Donne Journal* 20 (2001), 121–39.

Stachniewski, John, "John Donne: The Despair of the 'Holy Sonnets,'" 254–91 in *The Persecutory Imagination: English Puritanism and the Literature of Religious Despair*, Oxford, Oxford University Press, 1991.

Strier, Richard, "John Donne Awry and Squint: The 'Holy Sonnets,' 1608–1610," *Modern Philology* 86 (1989), 357–84.

Young, R. V., "Donne's Holy Sonnets and the Theology of Grace," 20–39 in Claude J. Summers and Ted-Larry Pebworth (eds.), *"Bright Shootes of Everlastingnesse": The Seventeenth-Century Religious Lyric*, Columbia, University of Missouri Press, 1987.

Elegies

Armstrong, Alan, "The Apprenticeship of John Donne: Ovid and the Elegies," *ELH* 44 (1977), 419–42.

Guibbory, Achsah, "'Oh, Let Mee Not Serve So': The Politics of Love in Donne's *Elegies*," *ELH* 57 (1990), 811–33.

Hester, M. Thomas, "'Over reconing' the 'Undertones': A Preface to 'Some Elegies' by John Donne," *Renaissance Papers* (2000), 137–53.

"Donne's (Re)Annunciation of the Virgin(ia Colony) in 'Elegy XIX,'" *South Central Review* 4 (1987), 49–64.

Mueller, Janel, "Lesbian Erotics: The Utopian Trope of Donne's 'Sapho to Philaenis,'" *Journal of Homosexuality* 23 (1992), 103–34.

Young, R. V., "'O my America, my new-found-land': Pornography and Imperial Politics in Donne's *Elegies*," *South Central Review* 4 (1987), 35–48.

Epigrams, Epithalamions, Epicedes and Obsequies

Dubrow, Heather, "'The Sun in Water': Donne's Somerset Epithalamium and the Poetics of Patronage," 197–219 in Heather Dubrow and Richard Strier (eds.), *The Historical Renaissance: New Essays on Tudor and Stuart Literature and Culture*, Chicago, University of Chicago Press, 1988.

"Tradition and the Individualistic Talent: Donne's 'An Epithalamion, Or Marriage Song on Lady Elizabeth ...,'" 106–16 in Claude J. Summers and Ted-Larry Pebworth (eds.), *The Eagle and the Dove: Reassessing John Donne*, Columbia, University of Missouri Press, 1986.

Hester, M. Thomas, "Donne's Epigrams: A Little World Made Cunningly," 80–91 in Claude J. Summers and Ted-Larry Pebworth (eds.), *The Eagle and the Dove: Reassessing John Donne*, Columbia, University of Missouri Press, 1986.

Lebans, W. M., "The Influence of the Classics in Donne's *Epicedes and Obsequies*," *Review of English Studies*, n. s. 23 (1972), 127–37.

McGowan, Margaret M., "'As Through a Looking-glass': Donne's Epithalamia and their Courtly Context," 175–218 in A. J. Smith (ed.), *John Donne: Essays in Celebration*, London, Methuen, 1972.

Prose works

Carrithers, Gale H., Jr., *Donne at Sermons: A Christian Existential World*, Albany, State University of New York, 1972.

Carey, John, "John Donne's Newsless Letters," *Essays and Studies* 34 (1981), 45–65.

Chamberlin, John S. *Increase and Multiply: Arts-of-Discourse Procedure in the Preaching of Donne*, Chapel Hill, University of North Carolina Press, 1976.

Davis, Walter R., "Meditation, Typology, and the Structure of John Donne's Sermons," 166–88 in Claude J. Summers and Ted-Larry Pebworth (eds.), *The Eagle and the Dove: Reassessing John Donne*, Columbia, University of Missouri Press, 1986.

Doebler, Bettie Ann, *The Quickening Seed: Death in the Sermons of John Donne*, Salzburg, Institut für Englische Sprache und Literatur, Universität Salzburg, 1974.

Fish, Stanley E., *Self-Consuming Artifacts: The Experience of Seventeenth-Century Literature*, Berkeley, University of California Press, 1972.

Hall, Michael L., "Searching and not Finding: The Experience of Donne's *Essays in Divinity*," *Genre* 14 (1981), 423–40.

Merchant, W. Moelwyn, "Donne's Sermon to the Virginia Company, 13 November 1622," 433–52 in A. J. Smith (ed.), *John Donne: Essays in Celebration*, London, Methuen, 1972.

Mueller, William R., *John Donne: Preacher*, Princeton, Princeton University Press, 1962.

Patterson, Annabel, "Misinterpretable Donne: The Testimony of the Letters," *John Donne Journal* 1 (1982), 39–53.

Price, Michael W., "'Jeasts which Cozen your Expectatyonn': Reassessing John Donne's Paradoxes and Problems," *John Donne Journal* 14 (1995), 149–84.

Quinn, Dennis B., "John Donne's Principles of Biblical Exegesis," *Journal of English and Germanic Philology*, 41 (1962), 313–29.

Salenius, Maria, *The Dean and His God: John Donne's Concept of the Divine*, Helsinki, Société néophilologique, 1998.

Sanchez, Reuben, "Menippean Satire and Competing Prose Styles in *Ignatius his Conclave*," *John Donne Journal* 18 (1999), 83–99.

Schleiner, Winfried, *The Imagery of John Donne's Sermons*, Providence, Brown University Press, 1970.

Shami, Jeanne, (ed.), Donne's Sermons [special issue of *John Donne Journal* 11 (1992)].

Simpson, Evelyn M., *A Study of the Prose Works of John Donne*, Oxford, Clarendon, 1924, [rev. edn.] 1948.

Stanwood, P. G., and Heather Ross Asals (eds.), *John Donne and the Theology of Language*, Columbia, University of Missouri Press, 1986.

Stein, Arnold, "Handling Death: John Donne in Public Meditation," *ELH* 48 (1981), 496–515.

Summers, Claude, and Ted-Larry Pebworth, "Donne's Correspondence with Wotton," *John Donne Journal* 10 (1991), 1–36.

Webber, Joan, *Contrary Music: The Prose Style of John Donne*, Madison, University of Wisconsin Press, 1963.

The Eloquent "I": Style and Self in Seventeenth-Century Prose, Madison, University of Wisconsin Press, 1968.

White, Helen, C., *English Devotional Literature (Prose) 1600–1640*, Madison, 1931, rptd. New York, Haskell House, 1961.

Satires (including "*Metempsychosis*")

Andreason, N. J. C., "Theme and Structure in Donne's Satyres," *Studies in English Literature* 3 (1963), 59–75.

Baumlin, James S., "From Recusancy to Apostasy: Donne's 'Satyre III' and 'Satyre V,'" *Explorations in Renaissance Culture* 16 (1990), 67–85.

Biester, James. *Lyric Wonder: Rhetoric and Wit in Renaissance English Poetry*, Ithaca, Cornell University Press, 1997.

Courthell, Ronald J., "Donne's *Metempsychosis*: An 'Alarum to Truth,'" *Studies in English Literature* 21 (1981), 97–110.

Dubrow, Heather, "Donne's Satires and Satiric Traditions," *Studies in English Literature* 19 (1979), 71–83.

Fulton, Thomas, "Hamlet's Inky Cloak and Donne's *Satyres*," *John Donne Journal* 20 (2001), 71–106.

Hester, M. Thomas, *Kinde Pitty and Brave Scorn: John Donne's Satyres*, Durham, NC, Duke University Press, 1982.

Kerins, Frank, "The 'Business' of Satire: John Donne and the Reformation of the Satirist," *Texas Studies in Literature and Language* 26 (1984), 34–60.

Kernan, Alvin, *The Cankered Muse: Satire of the English Renaissance*, New Haven, Yale University Press, 1959.

Klause, John, "The Montaigneity of Donne's Metempsychosis," 418–43 in Barbara Kiefer Lewalski (ed.), *Renaissance Genres: Essays on Theory, History, and Interpretation*, Cambridge, MA, Harvard University Press, 1986.

Lauritsen, John R., "Donne's *Satyres*: The Drama of Self-Discovery," *SEL* 16 (1976), 117–30.

Stein, Arnold, "Voices of the Satirist: John Donne," 72–92 in Claude Rawson (ed.), *English Satire and the Satiric Tradition*, Oxford, Oxford University Press, 1984.

Strier, Richard, "Radical Donne: 'Satire III,'" *ELH* 60 (1993), 283–322.

"Songs and Sonets"

Beliles, David Buck, *Theoretically-Informed Criticism of Donne's Love Poetry: Towards a Pluralist Hermenuetics of Faith*, New York, Peter Lang, 1999.

Bell, Ilona, "'If it be a shee': The Riddle of Donne's 'Curse,'" 106–39 in M. Thomas Hester (ed.), *John Donne's "Desire of More": The Subject of Anne More Donne in His Poetry*, Newark, University of Delaware Press, 1996.

"The Role of the Lady in Donne's *Songs and Sonnets*," *Studies in English Literature* 23 (1983), 113–29.

Gross, Kenneth, "John Donne's Lyric Skepticism: In Strange Way," *Modern Philology* 101 (2004), 371–99.

Guibbory, Achsah, "Donne, Milton, and Holy Sex," *Milton Studies* 32, ed. Albert Labriola, Pittsburgh, University of Pittsburgh Press, 1995, 3–21.

Interpreting "Aire and Angels" [special issue of *John Donne Journal* 9.1 (1990)].

"'The Relique,' *The Song of Songs*, and Donne's *Songs and Sonets*," *John Donne Journal* 15 (1996), 23–44.

Halpern, Richard, "The Lyric in the Field of Information: Autopoiesis and History in Donne's *Songs and Sonnets*," *The Yale Journal of Criticism* 6 (1993), 185–215.

Herz, Judith Scherer, "'An Excellent Exercise of Wit that Speaks So Well of Ill': Donne and the Poetics of Concealment," 3–14 in Claude J. Summers and Ted-Larry Pebworth (eds.), *The Eagle and the Dove: Reassessing John Donne*, Columbia MO, University of Missouri Press, 1986.

Hester, M. Thomas, "'This cannot be said': A Preface to the Reader of Donne's Lyrics," *Christianity and Literature* 39 (1990), 365–85.

Legouis, Pierre, *Donne the Craftsman: An Essay upon the Structure of the Songs and Sonnets*, London, 1928, [rptd. with errata list] New York, Russell and Russell, 1962.

Lovelock, Julian (ed.), *Donne, "Songs and Sonets": A Casebook*, London, Macmillan, 1973.

Low, Anthony, "Donne and the Reinvention of Love," *English Literary Renaissance* 20 (1990), 465–86.

Marotti, Arthur F., "'Love is not love': Elizabethan Sonnet Sequences and the Social Order," *ELH* 49 (1982), 396–428.

McKelvin, Dennis J., *A Lecture in Love's Philosophy: Donne's Vision of the World of Human Love in "Songs and Sonets,"* Lanham, University Press of America, 1984.

Pinka, Patricia Garland, *This Dialogue of One: The "Songs and Sonnets" of John Donne*, Alabama, University of Alabama Press, 1982.

Rajan, Tilottama, "'Nothing Sooner Broke': Donne's *Songs and Sonets* as Self-Consuming Artifact," *ELH* 49 (1982), 805–28.

Shullenberger, William, "Love as a Spectator Sport in John Donne's Poetry," 46–62 in Claude J. Summers and Ted-Larry Pebworth (eds.), *Renaissance Discourses of Desire*, Columbia, MO, University of Missouri Press, 1993.

Young, R. V., "Love, Poetry, and John Donne in the Love Poetry of John Donne," *Renascence* 52 (2000), 251–73.

Verse letters

Aers, David, and Gunther Kress, "'Darke Texts Need Notes': Versions of Self in Donne's Verse Epistles," *Literature and History* 8 (Autumn 1978), 138–58.

Cameron, Allen B., "Donne's Deliberative Verse Epistles," *English Literary Renaissance* 6 (1976), 369–403.

DeStefano, Barbara L., "Evolution of Extravagant Praise in Donne's Verse Epistles," *Studies in Philology* 81 (1984), 75–93.

Lein, Clayton D., "Donne's 'The Storme': The Poem and the Tradition," *English Literary Renaissance* 4 (1974), 137–63.

Maurer, Margaret, "The Real Presence of Lucy Russell, Countess of Bedford, and the Terms of John Donne's 'Honour is so Sublime Perfection,'" *ELH* 47 (1980), 205–34.

Mizejewski, Linda, "Darkness and Disproportion: A Study of Donne's 'Storme' and 'Calme,'" *Journal of English and Germanic Philology* 76 (1977), 217–30.

Nellist, B. F., "Donne's 'Storm' and 'Calm' and the Descriptive Tradition," *Modern Language Review* 59 (1964), 511–15.

Palmer, D. J., "The Verse Epistle," 73–99 in Malcom Bradbury and David Palmer (eds.), *Metaphysical Poetry*, Bloomington, University of Indiana Press, 1971.

Pebworth, Ted-Larry, and Claude J. Summers, "'Thus Friends Absent Speake': The Exchange of Verse Letters between John Donne and Henry Wotton," *Modern Philology* 81 (1984), 361–77.

Yoklavich, John, "Donne and the Countess of Huntingdon," *Philological Quarterly* 43 (1964), 283–88.

Journals and electronic resources

Chadwyck-Healy, Poetry Full-Text Database, 1992. *Poems by J. D.*, 1633, 1635; *The Complete Poems of John Donne*, ed. A. B. Grosart, 1872; *Poems of John Donne*, ed. E. K. Chambers, 1896; *The Life and Letters of John Donne*, ed. E. Gosse, 1899. <http://www.il.proquest.com/chadwyck/>

EEBO [Early English Books Online]. <http://eebo.chadwyck.com/home>

EMLS [*Early Modern Literary Studies*]. <http://www.shu.ac.uk/emls/emlshome.html>

John Donne, Luminarium, (ed.) Anniina Jokinen. <http://www.luminarium.org/sevenlit/donne/>

John Donne, The Literature Network. <http://www.online-literature.com/donne/>

John Donne Journal, 1982–, ed. M. Thomas Hester and R. V. Young. <http://www.ncsu.edu/johndonne/>

The John Donne Society. <http://johndonnesociety.tamu.edu/>

The John Donne Variorum. <http://www.donnevariorum.tamu.edu/>

Literature Online, Cambridge, 1998–. <http://lion.chadwyck.com/>

MLA: Modern Languages Association International Bibliography, New York, 1922–; rpt. <http://www.mla.org/howtouse_mlabiblio>

Renascence Editions, (ed.) Risa Bear. <http://darkwing.uoregon.edu/~rbear/ren.htm>

Selected Poetry of John Donne, Representative Poetry Online, gen. ed. Ian Lancashire. <http://eir.library.utoronto.ca/rpo/display/poet98.html>

INDEX

Cambridge companions to culture